Slum Travelers

The publisher gratefully acknowledges the generous support of Adele M. Hayutin as a member of the Literati Circle of University of California Press.

Slum Travelers

LADIES AND LONDON POVERTY,
1860 – 1920

*Edited with Introductions
by Ellen Ross*

UNIVERSITY OF CALIFORNIA PRESS

BERKELEY   LOS ANGELES   LONDON

University of California Press, one of the most
distinguished university presses in the United States,
enriches lives around the world by advancing scholarship
in the humanities, social sciences, and natural sciences. Its
activities are supported by the UC Press Foundation and
by philanthropic contributions from individuals and
institutions. For more information, visit
www.ucpress.edu.

University of California Press
Berkeley and Los Angeles, California

University of California Press, Ltd.
London, England

Library of Congress Cataloging-in-Publication Data
Slum travelers : ladies and London poverty 1860–1920 /
edited and with introductions by Ellen Ross.
     p.   cm.
  Includes bibliographical references and index.
  ISBN: 978-0-520-24905-9 (cloth : alk. paper)
  ISBN: 978-0-520-24906-6 (pbk. : alk. paper)
  1. Women social reformers—England—London—
History.   2. Women social reformers—England—
London—Biography.   3. Women in charitable work—
England—London—History.   4. Poor—Services for—
England—London—History.   5. Social problems—
England—London—History.   6. London (England)—
Social conditions—19th century.   7. London (England)—
Social conditions—20th century.   I. Ross, Ellen.
  HQ1600.L6 s58   2007
  362.5'5740922421 — dc22   2006036218

Manufactured in the United States of America

15   14   13   12   11   10   09   08   07
10   9   8   7   6   5   4   3   2   1

This book is printed on New Leaf EcoBook 50, a 100%
recycled fiber of which 50% is de-inked post-consumer
waste, processed chlorine-free. EcoBook 50 is acid-free
and meets the minimum requirements of ANSI/ASTM
D5634–01 (Permanence of Paper).

In memory of my mother, Jeanette C. Ross
1916–2005

In the faces of men and women I see God, and in my own
face in the glass,
I find letters from God dropt in the street, and every one is
sign'd by God's name . . .

Walt Whitman, "Song of Myself," stanza 48

CONTENTS

LIST OF ILLUSTRATIONS / *xii*

PREFACE / *xiii*

ACKNOWLEDGMENTS / *xvii*

ABBREVIATIONS / *xxi*

MAP OF LONDON IN 1888 / *xxiii*

INTRODUCTION: Adventures among the Poor / *1*

1. "Sketch of Life in Buildings," 1889
   "A LADY RESIDENT" / *40*

2. "White Slavery in London," 1888
   ANNIE (WOOD) BESANT / *45*

3. From *Makers of Our Clothes*, 1909
   CLEMENTINA BLACK AND ADELE (LADY CARL) MEYER / *52*

4. "Marriage in East London," 1895
   HELEN (DENDY) BOSANQUET / *64*

5. From *Munition Lasses,* 1917
   AGNES KATE FOXWELL / *72*

6. "A School Settlement," 1911
   CLARA ELLEN GRANT / *81*

7. "Barmaids," 1889
   MARGARET HARKNESS / *89*

8. "In a London Tramp Ward," 1906
   MARY (KINGSLAND) HIGGS / *97*

9.   "The Fur-Pullers of South London," 1897
     EDITH (MRS. F. G.) HOGG / *104*

10. From *A London Plane-Tree, and Other Verse*, 1889
     AMY LEVY / *117*

11. "A Slum Mother" (1908) and "Guy and the Stars" (1919)
     MARGARET MCMILLAN / *124*

12. "Gilding the Gutter," 1905
     OLIVE CHRISTIAN MALVERY / *136*

13. "The Irresponsibility of the Father," 1918
     ANNA MARTIN / *148*

14. "Eating the Apple," 1899
     HONNOR MORTEN / *161*

15. "The Evacuation of the Workhouse," 1918
     MARGARET WYNNE NEVINSON / *172*

16. Selections from *The Woman's Dreadnought*, 1916–1917
     SYLVIA PANKHURST / *178*

17. From *The Pudding Lady*, 1910
     FLORENCE PETTY / *192*

18. Selections from *The Missing Link Magazine*, 1878
     ELLEN HENRIETTA RANYARD / *198*

19. Selections from *Round about a Pound a Week*, 1913
     MAUD PEMBER REEVES / *208*

20. "Drunkenness," 1878
     MAUDE ALETHEA STANLEY / *226*

21. From *London Street Arabs*, 1890
     DOROTHY TENNANT (LADY STANLEY) / *239*

22. "Petticoat-Lane," 1895
     ETHEL BRILLIANA (MRS. ALEC) TWEEDIE / *249*

23. "An Epiphany Pilgrimage," 1906
     KATE WARBURTON / *256*

24. "Pages from a Work-Girl's Diary," 1888
     BEATRICE (POTTER) WEBB / *262*

APPENDIX 1: The Geography of London Wealth and Poverty / *281*
APPENDIX 2: The Texts Arranged Thematically / *287*
GLOSSARY OF TERMS, INSTITUTIONS, AND ORGANIZATIONS / *291*
INDEX / *305*

ILLUSTRATIONS

London in 1888, showing location of sites associated with authors in this anthology / *xxiii*

1. Poor children befriending a lady / *2*
2. A concert at the Jewish Working Girls' Club, Soho / *9*
3. The Sisters of the People in 1932 / *18*
4. Members of the Matchmakers' Union / *49*
5. Children waiting for a free school meal / *82*
6. Olive Christian Malvery / *137*
7. Maude Alethea Stanley / *227*
8. Ragged street boys / *240*
9. Children dancing to a hurdy-gurdy / *241*
10. Two homeless children taking shelter on the pavement / *242*
11. Encounter between a ragged and a well-dressed boy / *244*
12. Children playing blind man's bluff / *245*
13. Street seller with her children / *247*
14. Middlesex Street (Petticoat Lane), c. 1900 / *252*

PREFACE

EACH OF THE SELECTIONS that follow is introduced by a short biography of its author and, often, information about the text's immediate historical environment. I have made a point of adding very little of my own commentary on the texts themselves, which I know will be read in many different settings. The biographies are not uniform in length and style. I have actually given extra space to a few little-known women—such as Maude Stanley and Honnor Morten. For some authors, such as Agnes Foxwell and Florence Petty, I could find only a little information. The well-known figures, such as Beatrice Webb, are the subjects of many ample biographies and needed only brief overviews. In the "Further Reading" section following each biography and its notes, I have listed other works by the author as well as additional biographical sources. The bibliographic information is not meant to be exhaustive, but rather to give students a start in exploring an author whom they find interesting. I also have included brief explanations in brackets in some of the texts. My criteria for choosing these texts were so varied that no theme or issue will account for them: length of the piece, its readability for students, its genre, its date, and, in some cases, simply my fondness for a particular piece.

As this book's anthology format is unusual, some information on how it is structured might be useful to readers. There are two listings of the book's contents. The first is the table of contents, organized alphabetically by the author's last name. The second is appendix 2, a list of the texts arranged by theme and designed to be useful to students and faculty members, and possibly also to general readers. In this list many texts appear more than once, because most of them fit into more than one category.

Monetary amounts appear frequently in these accounts of poverty, and many of the selections include detailed family budgets. The ancient monetary system in use during the period in which the readings originated is no longer used, replaced by a decimal system in 1971. Before that, there were a dizzying number of coins of different denominations. A pound (£) was the largest note used by the London poor (it also existed in gold coin form and was called a sovereign), though notes of up to £1,000 did exist. A pound is sometimes designated by a lowercase letter *l.* placed after the monetary amount. Some other basic denominations:

£ = 20 silver shillings (abbreviated *s.*)
10*s.* = a half sovereign (this also came in a note form)
5*s.* = a crown
2½*s.* = a half crown

Each shilling contained 12 pence (abbreviated *d.*). Sixpence, threepence, and twopence coins were also minted. Those living hand to mouth had a great deal to do with parts of a penny, of which there were several, including a halfpenny and a farthing (¼ of a penny).

There is no reasonable way to translate these values into those of today in sterling or any other currency, so it may be useful to know the wages of some categories of workers. A male teacher's average pay per year was about £118 in 1890; it was only about £89 for women, according to Dina Copelman.[1] A pound a week was the estimated pay of male manual workers who were just making ends meet in the early twentieth century, and it was used as a title for Maud Pember Reeves's study of Lambeth families before World War I. More-skilled workers such as cabinetmakers, carpenters, or typesetters might earn up to £100 a year. The median pay of Anglican clergymen in the 1870s was a little under £300. To be part of the "comfortable classes" in the 1870s required an income of about £400 a year; later, in 1905, economist Chiozza Money labeled "comfortable" all incomes between £160 (the level at which income taxes had to be paid) and £700 a year.[2]

Here are some prices of a few ordinary purchases: a large loaf of bread (called a quartern loaf, weighing more than four pounds) cost 5*d.* in 1895. Cab fare for a mile ride was 6*d.* in London, the same as the fare on the underground.[3]

NOTES

1. These estimates are provided by Dina Copelman in *London's Women Teachers: Gender, Class and Feminism 1870–1930* (London: Routledge, 1996), 75.

2. K. Theodore Hoppen, *The Mid-Victorian Generation 1846–1886* (Oxford: Oxford University Press, 1998), 466; L. G. Chiozza Money, *Riches and Poverty* (London: Methuen, 1905), 41–42, from Harold Perkin, *The Rise of Professional Society: England since 1890* (London: Routledge, 1989), 78.

3. For these prices I am indebted to Sally Mitchell's useful *Daily Life in Victorian England* (Westport, CT: Greenwood Press, 1996), 32–37.

ACKNOWLEDGMENTS

HEARTFELT THANKS TO THE MANY FRIENDS, students, and colleagues who have helped bring this project to completion. Judith Walkowitz read and commented astutely on many versions of the introduction; the section on the wardrobes of the slummers, among others, was written at her suggestion. Barbara Caine and Martha Vicinus also did their very impressive best to advance this project. Leonore Davidoff has generously shared her deep knowledge of and new ideas about the lives of upper-class women in Britain. I also enjoyed and profited from comments on a version of the introduction by Sally Alexander, Catherine Hall, Cora Kaplan, Lynne Segal, and Barbara Taylor. Anna Davin's intense engagement with working-class London has been a constant inspiration. Conversations with the following colleagues have been enormously helpful: Caitlin Adams, George Behlmer, Dina Copelman, James Hinton, Angela John, Seth Koven, Peter Mandler, John Marriott, Clare Midgley, Frank Mort, Deborah Nord, George Robb, Anne Summers, Pat Thane, Pamela Walker, and Eileen Yeo. I have been cheered on by the lively interest of my Ramapo College social work colleagues Mitch Kahn, Peggy McLaughlin, and Sue Scher. My History 242 students at Ramapo in 2005 were forced to try out a few of the readings and, to my relief, declared them "not boring." I am grateful to Professor Vicinus for also "trying out" a group of texts from this collection with her Victorian literature class at the University of Michigan. I keep permanently at desk side four stimulating and informative studies of adventurous philanthropic women in London: Martha Vicinus's *Independent Women*, Judith Walkowitz's *City of Dreadful Delight*, Deborah Nord's *Walking the Victorian Streets*, and Seth Koven's *Slumming*.

For help and delightful conversations on Olive Christian Malvery, Ethel B. Tweedie, and Maude Stanley, my thanks to Judith Walkowitz; on Margaret

Nevinson, I am grateful to Angela John; on Maud Pember Reeves, to Sally Alexander. Pamela Walker advised me on nineteenth-century Nonconformity, Phyllis Mack on Methodism, and Dr. Aimée Price on Dorothy Tennant. I am much indebted to Caitlin Adams for her thoughtful and detailed research on women's settlements, and to Daniel Stedman Jones for skilled help with newspaper research. Thanks to Geoff Field of Purchase College, State University of New York; Pamela Walker, Carleton University; Leonore Davidoff, University of Essex; and Jim Chaffee, Ramapo history student, for their advice on many items in the glossary.

I received very welcome and much appreciated funding for this work from Ramapo College's Separately Budgeted Research Fund, The National Foundation for the Humanities Fellowships for College Teachers, and from the Leverhulme Foundation's Visiting Professorship program.

This volume's introduction, and my work on female slum philanthropy in general, has been enriched by the ideas of lecture and seminar audiences at Ramapo College and at Rutgers University; at York and Carleton Universities in Canada; at Monash University and the University of Melbourne in Australia; and, in England, at the University of Greenwich, the University of Essex, the Women's Library at London Metropolitan University, the Seminar on Women's History at the Institute of Historical Research, University of London, and at the University of Liverpool's Four Hundred Years of Charity conference in September of 2001. I also have been educated repeatedly over the years by audiences at the North American Conference on British Studies and at the Middle Atlantic Conference on British Studies. My semester in 2003 at the Women's Library, as a Leverhulme Visiting Professor attached to the London Metropolitan University, also enriched this project. My lecture series at the Library was a chance to hear from the many members of voluntary organizations who attended. This wonderful experience I owe to Clare Midgley, who sponsored the Leverhulme grant, and Antonia Byatt, director of the Women's Library. The daylong conference we organized there on Women's Voluntarism in April of 2003 was especially important for me, and I thank the day's speakers: Clare Midgley, Maria Luddy, James Hinton, Anne Summers, Pat Thane, and Eileen Yeo.

I am much indebted to the personnel of many libraries and archives at home and abroad. For this and all my other research I have relied on the Ramapo College Library, Columbia University Libraries, the New York Public Library Humanities Division, and the British Library. I also thank staff members at the following archives for their kindness and efficiency: the

Archives Department of Bedford Royal Holloway College; Archives Department of the British Library of Political and Economic Science; the Berg Collection at the New York Public Library; Chester and Cheshire Archives and Local Studies Library; Columbia University Library Rare Books Division; Essex County Record Office; Fern Street Settlement; Hackney Archives Department; Imperial War Museum Women and War Collection and Women's Work Inventory; the International Institute of Social History (Amsterdam); Kensington Local Studies, London Metropolitan Archives; Newham Local Studies Library; Southwark Local Studies Library; Tower Hamlets Local History Library and Archives; University of London Archives; University College, London, Special Collections; the West London Mission, and the Women's Library.

Many members of the University of California Press staff have generously offered this book, and me, their care and talent. I thank Sheila Levine, Niels Hooper, and Rachel Lockman for their faith and interest in this venture. In its later stages, this collection has been enormously enhanced by the attentive and analytical minds of production editor Jacqueline Volin and of copy editor Sue Carter.

Richard Glendon, my beloved partner and tireless computer support team, was ably assisted for *Slum Travelers* by our younger daughter, Hope Glendon-Ross, with general cheerleading by our elder daughter, Maude Glendon-Ross. That these girls would grow into thriving teens was our deepest wish when I was finishing my book *Love and Toil* in 1992.

ABBREVIATIONS

BDBF	*Biographical Dictionary of British Feminists*
DLB	*Dictionary of Labour Biography*
DNB	*Dictionary of National Biography*
LCC	London County Council
Oxford DNB	*Oxford Dictionary of National Biography*
THLHL	*Tower Hamlets Local History Library*

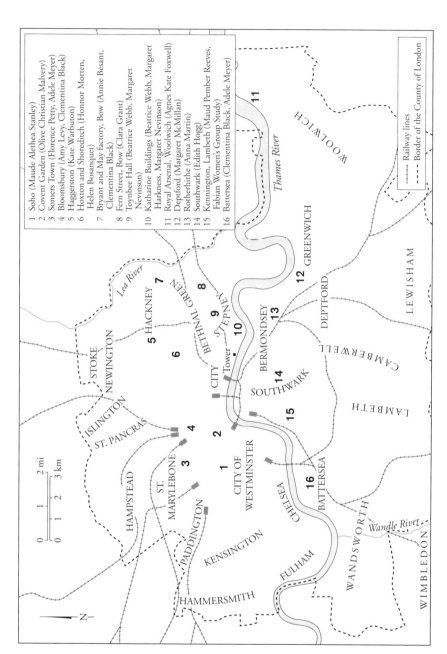

1 Soho (Maude Alethea Stanley)
2 Covent Garden (Olive Christian Malvery)
3 Somers Town (Florence Petty, Adele Meyer)
4 Bloomsbury (Amy Levy, Clementina Black)
5 Haggerston (Kate Warbuton)
6 Hoxton and Shoreditch (Honnor Morten, Helen Bosanquet)
7 Bryant and May factory, Bow (Annie Besant, Clementina Black)
8 Fern Street, Bow (Clara Grant)
9 Toynbee Hall (Beatrice Webb, Margaret Nevinson)
10 Katharine Buildings (Beatrice Webb, Margaret Harkness, Margaret Nevinson)
11 Royal Arsenal, Woolwich (Agnes Kate Foxwell)
12 Deptford (Margaret McMillan)
13 Rotherhithe (Anna Martin)
14 Southwark (Edith Hogg)
15 Kennington, Lambeth (Maud Pember Reeves, Fabian Women's Group Study)
16 Battersea (Clementina Black, Adele Meyer)

London in 1888, showing the approximate location of sites associated with the authors in this anthology.

Adventures among the Poor

THE POOREST URBAN DISTRICTS OF BRITAIN exerted a magnetic pull on the middle- and upper-class women of the two generations that preceded World War I. Thousands from "the best circles" forsook dinner parties, balls, and picnics, and headed instead for the slums. The term *slums* had been in existence since the 1820s; I will use it in implied quotation marks to denote districts of concentrated poverty.[1] Long before cities were routinely seen from the sky, these women journeyed at ground level, often as pedestrians, into the undiscovered "dark space" inhabited by the London poor.[2] Along with their male peers, the women "travelers" embodied a mass movement dedicated to improving the lives of a traditionally ignored and isolated population. According an estimate from the mid-1890s, about half a million women in England were involved in philanthropy "more or less continuously"—a figure that does not include paid professionals or religious sisterhoods.[3] Those in London, the world's largest city and the administrative heart of a gigantic empire, were especially visible nationally and internationally. Their efforts helped to create a complex inheritance for the twentieth century: vital local government, female public service, at least a degree of communication and collaboration across social classes—and a stereotype of clumsy and officious well-born females meddling in the lives of Britain's workers.

Women approached slums with a variety of purposes. Some were volunteers attached to charities or to parish churches; others were paid professionals such as teachers, nurses, or sanitary officers. Artists, journalists, and social investigators also tramped through streets and alleys, chronicling poverty.[4] These slum travelers included such diverse figures as Marie Hilton, a devout Quaker who founded a nursery for the children of the poorest working mothers; and Eleanor Marx, daughter of Karl, who

Figure 1. Poor children befriending a lady, from Dorothy Tennant, *London Street Arabs* (London: Cassell and Company [now a division of The Orion Publishing Group], 1890). This beautifully composed happy meeting of a lady (she resembles Tennant as a young woman) and four ragged children of different ages is an idealized slum encounter. Unlike some slumming ladies, this one is very approachable, unafraid of the children's imparting head lice or smudges; the children, in turn, feel no reserve and are eager to present their gifts. The small girl on the right is being supervised by her sister. This kind of pair, a "little mother" and younger child or children, was at hand wherever children were found. (The titles of Tennant's engravings are mine; the images are uncaptioned in *London Street Arabs*.)

worked tirelessly with striking laborers in East London and enjoyed "slumming" strolls there.[5] As reading their work and biographies will show, there is no single way to characterize these women or their aims; they were complex and full of contradictions, a mingling, as Seth Koven puts it, of "loving sympathy" and "petty tyranny," of "good intentions" along with prejudice and condescension.[6]

Missionaries and church lay workers, who increasingly were women, had led the way early in the nineteenth century.[7] Through about the 1860s, most of the slum workers were still Anglican or Nonconformist missionaries. Catholic laywomen, as well as those in orders, also intensified their philanthropy among London's large Irish population in the second half of the nineteenth century. The numbers of women to be found in slum districts expanded in the 1870s and 1880s, as better transportation and the founding of new philanthropic institutions made it easier for women to participate in relief efforts. District nursing associations were formed, and the Charity Organisation Society (COS), founded in 1869 and central in the history of social work in Britain, maintained offices and paid officials at several district branches. After the establishment of compulsory education in London in 1871, thousands of women volunteered to serve as "managers" in poor districts (later called Care Committees), doing school-based social work.[8] As Jewish refugees from eastern Europe poured into London in the 1880s and 1890s, well-off West End Anglo-Jewish women, with some ambivalence, organized philanthropies on their behalf. In the 1890s, the field of slum philanthropy was so heavily in women's hands that well-born slum clergyman James Adderley issued an earnest call to "the sons of the upper classes" to join them.[9]

Scholars have labeled nineteenth-century Britain a surveillance society, in which various social categories—criminals, paupers, the insane—came under the controlling gaze of authorities of all kinds. The enterprise of scrutinizing the poor looks less castigatory, however, when we foreground these women philanthropists, who, as women, lacked full authority over others. Moreover, their clients were, rather than inmates of institutions, families in their own dwellings and thus protected by a powerful national tradition of the "privacy" of the home. Probably more than their male philanthropic counterparts, women were involved in both the service and the regulation of the poor. Care Committee workers, for example, organized country holidays for children and secured funding for free dinners or eyeglasses. But committee members also badgered parents when, for example, their children were found by school officials to have head lice; the members were the ones who investigated the finances of parents of children who had applied for free meals. Many of the new institutions and jobs for women in infant-welfare work, which proliferated in the 1900s and 1910s, had the same double edge. A lady visitor might offer free meals to pregnant women, or milk for their children, but also, depending on borough procedures, insist on weekly monitoring of babies' feeding and sleeping arrangements. And we must remember that many slummers became committed defenders of their clients. By the 1890s, they had become active in local government bodies, from the London County Council down to vestries and poor law guardians, who were in charge of local poor relief. As such, they often found themselves challenging local elites on behalf of the poor in the perpetual class war that local government could represent.[10]

One common thread connecting many of these women is their experience as Anglican clergymen's daughters. There were over 24,000 Anglican clergymen in 1891 and about 9,000 of other denominations. In general, while the Anglicans were better off than the others, they were not wealthy; their median income of under £300 in the 1870s was below the amount a gentleman was thought to require (£400 per year). Nonetheless Anglican clergymen, especially those in charge of a parish—as opposed to assistant clergymen—belonged to the genteel classes. The majority had the education that marked them this way; in the 1860s two-thirds of the clergy had Oxbridge degrees and the others had gone to training colleges. In such families, girls would have been educated in the long-standing tradition of church philanthropy. Less widely known, perhaps, is that daughters in clerical families actually received a thorough grounding in what was beginning to be termed social work. The clergy and their families were important figures in rural and town life. The Victorian parsonage, as Midori Yamaguchi points out, was less a private residence than it was a public place where clerical wives and children played prominent roles. They worked with parish children's groups, organized musical and dramatic events, taught Sunday school, and visited ill parishioners. Many were excellent public speakers, and indeed several became prominent as stage actors.[11] Surely many of these young women would have trained for the ministry if they could have, and a significant number did become missionaries. Slum philanthropy was another available alternative. Daughters of the clergy were active in social reform movements, the amelioration of poverty, and a variety of feminist causes—including suffrage.[12]

Socialists and social reformers are also well represented among the slummers. The case of Beatrice Webb, who devoted her life to social reform but disliked face-to-face encounters with the poor, is a reminder that political activism to ameliorate poverty does not necessarily involve direct contact with poor individuals. As a young woman still working in East London, Webb was intrigued by her coworker Emma Cons, an effective and compassionate woman who relished daily contact with her clients but who took relatively little interest in the wider social picture that was coming to fascinate Webb.[13] Londoner Eleanor Marx demonstrates in another way the difference between political commitment on behalf of the people and actual "slum travel." Though she had fully embraced her father Karl's socialism, and the Marx family had been hard-up, it was not until Eleanor was in her thirties that she encounted slum districts. She was deeply moved by what she witnessed of the East London dockers' working and living conditions and became a passionate supporter of their strike in 1889. She also became involved with India rubber and gas workers in Silvertown, on the eastern edge of London, and she traveled daily to "that end-of-the-world place." As Marx's friend Friedrich Engels somewhat patronizingly commented, Eleanor had become "quite an East Ender."[14] But the grim elements of London workers' poverty had been as new to her as they were to women from far more conventionally genteel families.

Slum Travelers reprints some of these well-born women's narratives of their encounters with poverty and the poor in London. The pieces included here are weighted toward the domestic sphere and the lives of women and children. A number of them represent the process of observing or investigating poverty in itself: knocking on doors, alighting from a tram in a strange district, or even just looking out a window at the street life outdoors. The selections range over a fifty-year period and over several genres: journalism, policy-oriented social observation, fiction, art, and poetry.[15] These documents are not intended to offer a consistent or comprehensive portrait of London's poorest inhabitants, or of those who observed them. Except for Adele (Lady Carl) Meyer, who was Jewish, all the authors were Protestants, many of them Nonconformists. The collection omits many elements of working-class life, such as male workplaces, crime, sports, and electoral politics. Yet, because of the detail the writers here include, and the variety of voices they represent, these readings offer a crash course in social history covering charity, family life, childhood, health care, and women's work. We also see several versions of the encounter between this group of "ladies" and their clients, helping us to judge these encounters more finely— beyond sentimentalized images of female selflessness, satirical "lady bountiful" stereotypes, or social-control simplifications.

The biographies that begin each chapter reveal something about each author, but so do the texts themselves. Depicting others, the writer displays herself as subject: her own fear, disgust, affection, excitement, anger, and impatience.[16] Like their male contemporaries who painted working-class women on canvas, these social explorers also "painted" themselves into their pictures.[17]

Slum Travelers, finally, is a contribution to the recovery of "lost" or "hidden" women writers, the enterprise that in the 1970s inaugurated the newly revived subdiscipline of women's history. Many of these authors are known today, of course, but Jack London is much more often read as an explorer of workhouse casual wards than is Mary Higgs or her later counterpart, Ada Chesterton. The idealist social philosopher Bernard Bosanquet is mentioned in more social theory textbooks than his intellectually prolific, creative, and influential wife, Helen (Dendy) Bosanquet. To rediscover these women as writers and activists is to redraw the gender map of Victorian and Edwardian London.

An Imperial City in Ferment

Dispatches from the London slums addressed questions being discussed in the journals, parliamentary sessions, and the dinner parties of the educated classes in the late Victorian and Edwardian decades: how extensive was abject poverty? This was the question that motivated Charles Booth to undertake his massive social surveys in the 1880s and 1890s.[18] As the preoccupation with Britain's colonized peoples waxed and waned, the home-grown poor could be assigned some of their qualities. Were the urban poor really heathens desperately in need of missions? Were there "nomads" or "savages" among them? How did they manage to survive, given what economists knew was an average income that barely provided subsistence? What, if anything, did poor Britons have in common with the articulate and well off? Could they be fully incorporated into the nation? The social explorers, women and men alike, sought answers to these questions, whose significance was magnified in the 1870s and after by a distinct set of political and social circumstances.

The frightening increase in the populations of many cities was one factor that brought poverty into sharp relief. Overcrowded, chaotic, and seemingly impenetrable slums deepened longstanding elite fears of popular godlessness and social disorder generated by the French Revolution. Domestic missionaries became active early in the century among the threatening urban poor. The Church of England's district visiting societies began to form in the 1820s; the all-male London City Mission was founded in 1835; and a few hearty women established missions in London slums in the 1840s. The Chartist movement's decline by mid-century perhaps made the urban poor appear a little less menacing, but, on the other hand, the 1851 census offered the disquieting news that the majority of workers seldom attended church. The waning of antislavery energy in the 1860s and the dramatic decline of Christian proselytizing in India after the 1857 mutiny of Muslim and Hindu troops under British command both led evangelicals to intensify their missionary activities in London. The London Missionary Society, for one, accelerated its efforts to reach working-class men in the 1880s and 1890s, supporting five hundred agents at its peak in 1890.[19]

Beatrice Webb defined the development of middle-class social reform efforts in another way, as a secularized version of Christian guilt and atonement. From early in the Victorian era, as she saw it, "among men of intellect and men of property" there grew "a new consciousness of sin," a sense that their own comforts had come at the price of intolerable conditions "for a majority of the inhabitants of Great Britain."[20] The sense of crisis reached a crescendo in the late 1870s and 1880s, following a series of exposés of the horrors of London's overcrowded housing, and of massive and sometimes violent London demonstrations. The well off feared the crowd but also acknowledged their own culpability. Webb, who in the 1880s was both a churchgoer and a social investigator, began to identify her "special mission to society at large." It was at this point that she and her peers became conscious of "a new motive; the transference of the emotion of self-sacrificing service from God to man."[21] Now secularized, this awareness of sin would lead to Fabianism, to non-Christian forms of spirituality like secularism and Theosophy, to the settlement movement, and to an outpouring of charitable giving, social reform agitation, and social service.[22]

Another circumstance lending intensity to the enterprise of slum exploration was the enfranchisement, surrounded by intense agitation, of two successive groups of male voters in 1867 and in 1884. About two-thirds of British men had become full citizens. Both Liberals and Conservatives in Parliament had new motives for knowing about the working classes, especially in the 1890s, when the expanded electorate would enable the creation of a political party that represented organized labor. Working men were also rapidly joining labor unions (membership quadrupled from the 1870s to 1914) and benefit clubs and participating in the remarkable expansion of and democratization of urban local government going on in the 1880s and 1890s.[23]

Developments in education and public health also helped to generate a new awareness of poverty. The Education Act of 1870 mandated schooling for all children to age ten, and was gradually extended into the early teens. Compulsory education had the unintended effect of exposing to public scrutiny millions of ragged and hungry children. Their welfare now was, to some extent at least, a national obligation.[24] Statistical techniques being developed for charting birth, morbidity, and death rates also brought the misery of the poor into stark relief. The ability to trace the incidence of infectious diseases like typhoid and tuberculosis and to track infant and child mortality rates by district made it clear that poverty enormously diminished a person's life span. The spread of contagious diseases, it was now also understood, meant that neglecting the basic needs of the poor could jeopardize the lives of the wealthy. Finally, the nationalist rivalries, especially between Britain and the German Empire, which accelerated from the 1890s, made political leaders more conscious of their populations as potential soldiers. Nutrition, education, medical care, and sanitation for working people became matters of potential military significance.[25]

Feminism, Freedom, and Social Service

Female interest in efforts to ameliorate urban poverty was part of a wider development in the history of women. By the late 1870s and 1880s, adventurous women were visibly making new claims on urban spaces of all kinds. They began to use trains, buses, and the Underground to enjoy the shops, museums, restaurants, clubs, and theaters of the city. An 1882 article in *The Queen,* a sophisticated women's magazine, claimed, with some ambivalence, that all this was open to reputable young ladies if they had the "courage and cleverness" to deal with the "dangers and difficulties" they would encounter.[26] In the 1890s, first the women's press, then the general press, began defining the "New Woman." Her defenders classified her as educated, intelligent, possibly self-supporting, and civic-spirited, but also as a bold traveler in urban spaces.[27] The same forces that opened the West End to female shoppers, restaurant diners, and theatergoers—a weakening of the institution of chaperonage, changing conceptions of the public realm and women's place in it, and expanding urban transportation systems—also made slums and work in them more accessible to genteel women.

The fact that many middle-class suffragists and other feminist activists had been, or continued to be, what we would now call social workers is one indication of the relationship between the movement for women's rights and the outpouring of female concern with poverty. A number of women's

Figure 2. A concert at the Jewish Working Girls' Club, Soho, from George Sims, *Living London* (London: Cassell and Company, 1902), 1: 118. Lily Montagu (1873–1963) established this club in Soho in 1893 and later, in 1919, a settlement house. She and Maude Stanley, whose girls' club was also in Soho, cooperated on a number of projects, including the founding of a national organization of girls' clubs. Both women were committed to offering music and music education at their clubs.

suffrage organizations, such as the Women's Freedom League and Sylvia Pankhurst's East London Federation of Suffragettes, provided services to local working-class women. Well-off suffragists meeting or even just learning about the lives of their working-class "sisters" (as they were indeed sometimes called) were shocked by the vivid embodiments of oppression they encountered. One of these wealthy feminists was aristocrat and suffrage militant Constance Lytton, who had a sudden revelation as she marched in one of her first suffrage processions. In a group of conventionally dressed gentlemen wearing starched white shirts and collars, she pictured the "gnarled hands, the bent backs, [and] the tear-dimmed eyes" of the thousands of laundresses who had made this possible."[28] For some branches of the women's suffrage movement, the figure of the overburdened working-class woman was in fact an important icon; the membership card that Sylvia Pankhurst designed in about 1905 pictured a group of poor women with shawls, one with outstretched arms and others carrying a baby and a bucket. Suffrage posters depicted workingwomen at factory gates or at sewing machines, and their newspapers regularly chronicled injustices to working-class wives and mothers and sponsored campaigns in favor of victims of gender injustice. *The Vote,* a newspaper published by the Women's Freedom League, carried regular columns documenting the legal disabilities of working-class women with such titles as "Criminals All," "Justice," "The 'Protected' Sex," and "How Men Protect Women."[29]

History as Literature, Literature as History

Many texts of social observation can be read as both literary and historical documents. They are artful enough for literature students to sink their critical teeth into while also offering readers routes into the history of women in modern Britain. Changes in literature and history as disciplines have softened the boundaries between them. As scholarship in literature has expanded its register of "interesting" texts, a number of well-known literary scholars have demonstrated how much there is to say about minor authors like Maud Pember Reeves or Margaret Nevinson.[30] Historians, for their part, have also come to recognize the value of reading their own sources and pursuing their own subjects using concepts and methods from literary criticism and philosophy.[31] In writings of social exploration, in any case, it is impossible to mark out academic disciplinary turf by distinguishing fact (history) from fiction (literature). A study of eighteenth-century novels underscores the intermixing in its title, *Factual Fictions,* and a recent collection of slum nonfiction writings astutely labels them "semi-factual accounts."[32] Factual and fictional work was often produced by the same writers. Among those collected here, Margaret Harkness, Honnor Morten, Margaret Nevinson, and Clementina Black all wrote in several genres. Harkness and Black actually enjoyed some success as novelists.

The novel—the nineteenth century's classic fictional form—had developed around a hard core of fact; novels offered realistic portrayals of time, place, and environmental details.[33] Victorian and Edwardian novelists not only poured over slum journalism but also were often heavily indebted to briefings by slum investigators for the details they sought. Charles Dickens, of course, drew heavily on his years with the *Morning Chronicle,* and on his encounters with ragged schoolchildren and prostitutes during the years when he acted as unofficial almoner for philanthropist Angela Burdett-Coutts.[34] George Gissing called on his friend Clara Collet, an expert on women workers, for advice on social detail for his almost obsessively realist novels.[35] And for *Sir George Tressady* (1896), Mary Ward, hoping to write a book "which is not merely fanciful," but convincingly "real," combed through parliamentary blue books to craft a bill designed to protect the worst-paid ("sweated") workers that her heroine Marcella would champion in her second fictional appearance.[36] A philanthropic relative could fill in what the novelist may have lacked in personal experience. For *Marcella* (1894) Ward drew on her sister-in-law Gertrude Ward's district nursing patients, whom Gertrude brought her to meet.[37] In the case of Virginia Woolf, some of Eleanor Pargiter's housing scenes in *The Years* were based on the experiences of Stella Duckworth Hills, Virginia's half-sister, who for years served as a manager of some Southwark buildings run by housing reformer Octavia Hill.[38]

Fiction and nonfiction bring different strengths to the portrayal of poverty and suffering. Novels, notwithstanding their realistic presentation, mobilize individual and collective fantasies and, to quote Mary Poovey's *Uneven Developments,* "shared anxieties and tensions can surface as well as be symbolically addressed." Novelistic treatments of slum exploration such as *A Princess of the Gutter* (1896), by the highly successful and prolific novelist L. T. Meade, as Seth Koven argues, represent what for contemporaries could not be "fully understood," or articulated—such as same-sex love or intimacy between the "dirty" poor and the wealthy. A novel asks for a greater emotional investment than do most works of nonfiction. Elizabeth Gaskell's *Mary Barton* (1848) intervenes in contemporary discussions of urban poverty in the 1840s not with mortality statistics or family budgets, but through fleshed-out characters whose interiority is displayed.[39]

Nonfiction slum accounts are certainly capable of representing poverty in a detailed, realistic way. Family life is vividly portrayed, for example, by Maud Pember Reeves or Florence Petty, yet their writing is probably less apt than Gaskell's to fully engage a reader's emotions over a sustained time. This is perhaps because their subjects' interiority is only known through what they say to interviewers, and their lives can only be described over a fairly narrow temporal dimension. Perhaps just as important in this regard is the writer's need to sustain her authority as an investigator through the use of distancing techniques like the reporting of statistics to situate the subjects as "cases" that illustrate a broader social reality.

The advantages of fiction over nonfiction were recognized by several of the lady explorers; Honnor Morten, Margaret Nevinson, Margaret McMillan, and Margaret Harkness breathed life into their "cases" via fictional treatment. Social explorers' nonfiction writings were, however, better at some kinds of "work," to misuse Mary Poovey's term. They usually explain their subjects' needs concretely and seek to educate readers about the lives of the poor. Journalists could mobilize their readers to act quickly in support of very specific contemporary policies and causes. Annie Besant's readers, protesting the ill treatment of the company's young workers, would boycott the matches made by Bryant and May and donate money to the match girls' strike fund; Margaret Nevinson's readers would support poor law reform; Edith Hogg's would lobby for anti–sweated labor legislation; Maud Pember Reeves's would press for more services for infants and children.[40]

All writing on poverty and the poor, factual or fictional, shares a common set of literary forebears. Missionary societies' lectures and reports from the field, for one, had been reaching a huge swath of the population from early in the nineteenth century.[41] These documents set out the heroism of venturing among the distant heathen, the value of Christian sympathy for the benighted, and the expectation of their gratitude and submissiveness. Educated Victorians were also familiar with the language, urban characters, and disguises of Dickens, and of journalists like Henry Mayhew, James Greenwood, and, later, George Sims. And no urban adventurer could have avoided being affected by the sensational mass-circulation newspaper stories of starvation, crime, and vice that had become commonplace by the 1880s. What was labeled "the new journalism" in the later decades of the century was by no means "straight" reporting. It was an international form that incorporated pathos, melodrama, crime writing, interviewing, and extensive use of visual media; urban scandal and slum spectacle were the new journalists' stock-in-trade.[42]

Women's narrations of London poverty borrow, as well, from the flourishing female travel-writing genre. Female travelers abroad, like their male counterparts, used a great variety of distancing devices—such as reiterating known images, condescension, and racist stereotyping. But the female traveler was, in many cases, intent on representing foreigners "sympathetically, as individuals," as Shirley Foster has put it, more than "as symbols of an alien 'otherness'"; their work was also punctuated by attempts at connecting their own lives with those who were the objects of their observations. Female travel accounts, in addition, often dealt with "women's" topics. They directed their attention to other women—their clothing, manners, domestic arrangements, and child-care methods—an oblique critique of the kinds of subjects that dominated masculine travel literature.[43]

Women as Chroniclers of Poverty

Female slummers' narrations of their personal encounters with poverty and the poor often depart from their male counterparts' version of the urban slum, with its complex system of crafts and trades, its cruelty, crime, opium dens, prostitution, and its beguiling ragged boys. Women helped to write new and different "legends" (the word's etymology implies reading) about London and its people that now would include factory girls and worn mothers, domestic interiors rather than street scenes, schoolchildren rather than child beggars. They thus superimposed the stoic mother sitting up with a sick infant or the earnest twelve-year-old caring for younger siblings over more traditional slum figures like the wily pickpocket or the Ratcliff opium addict.[44] Some women were conscious of their different "place" in writing the city, and they were proud of it. Their view was closer to the truth, as they saw it. As Helen Dendy (later Bosanquet), a COS case-worker in Shoreditch for five years, wrote rather scornfully in the 1890s, only hackneyed images of poverty could emerge from "the impression of the outsider who confines his investigations to the main thoroughfares, or makes official visits during the business hours." Marie Hilton, the Quaker nursery founder, criticized most slum journalists as too ready to judge from a glance, which produced accounts obviously "written by people who do not look below the surface."[45]

Yet pervasive literary caricatures of Ladies Bountiful and *Punch* cartoons of buxom busybodies undermined the authorial confidence of many women. Self-doubt was reflected, for one thing, in the humorous self-deprecating language so many of them used. Like international explorers such as Mary Kingsley, they—at least those who were not missionaries—avoided taking themselves too seriously; they were ready to mock their illusions and pretensions, as Alice Hodson, a settler at Lady Margaret Hall in Lambeth, did when she confessed her clumsiness as a "nervous amateur" whose indelicate questions were "apt to make the people abusive," so that she would find "the door shut in her face."[46] A light, anecdotal style is another symptom of the women's liminal position as national interpreters of poverty—the "imagination, emotionalism, sensationalism" that author E. M. Delafield deplored in women's writing in the early twentieth century.[47] Even knowledgeable and serious-minded female social investigators were sparing with statistical material, social analysis, or the complexities of legislation, something Beatrice Potter disapproved of in her associates Margaret Harkness and Emma Cons.[48] Euphemisms also abound. The imperatives of ladylike writing, as well as the conventions of many of the periodicals in which they were published, obviated detailed, clinical descriptions of filth, squalor, or diseased bodies. There are several exceptions, however. Workhouse investigator Mary Higgs's graphic *Daily News* accounts of vomiting and hearing others doing so during a night at a female casual ward is representative of her workhouse reporting and of the whole genre (see chapter 8 of this volume). And to demonstrate their patients' suffering, Ellen Ranyard's nurses and Bible sellers give vivid clinical details of their home visits: a mother "covered with sores" and with "abscesses" on her left calf, remnants of a severe burn so badly infected that the "stench from her wounds and the horror of her appearance prevent assistance from her neighbours."[49]

Pathos was perhaps the most powerful of the specifically feminized styles of slum writing both factual and fictional. One of the most important books ever written in the English language, *Uncle Tom's Cabin,* published in 1852, demands social amelioration through its forceful use of the pathetic vein. The pathetic, "a queer ghoulish emotion," in Northrop Frye's terms, could be a powerful literary mode, moving readers to tears and to action.[50] It went hand in hand with women's social activism in the Victorian era: it was a tool of antislavery crusaders, of course, but also of opponents of harsh prison conditions, child labor, homelessness, sweated working conditions, and the internment of prostitutes rather than their clients under the Contagious Diseases Acts of the 1860s.[51] Among "our" authors, there were few so skilled at pathos as Ellen Ranyard in her accounts of the simple Christian faith and of deathbed sufferings and conversions in London's most poverty-stricken districts. Like many other evangelicals at work in the slums, Ranyard operated through a "feminized epistemology of sympathy," the antithesis of the statistician's attempt to capture the pattern rather than the feeling of a life.[52] Hunger, pain, the death of loved ones—all are offered up, often as the subjects' verbatim stories, and with evidence of their courage and resignation to God's will.

The slum as *visual* spectacle was certainly an established gentlemanly mode; male writers' frequent portrayal of blind men at loose ends in the city may have indirectly signaled recognition of this heavy reliance on the visual sense. Indeed Victorian Britain was a culture enthralled by the practice of looking. Opportunities for spectatorship were multiplying—theaters, shopping, and of course slum exploration—along with new technologies such as railroad trains offering a moving panorama, balloon rides, and photography. Urban life, as Georg Simmel put it in 1903, was both a festival of "visual impressions" and an onrush of unsettling visual stimuli.[53]

Women's accounts are striking, however, for their emphasis on the *aural.* In reporting conversations and quoting their subjects at length, writers were certainly drawing on the interview, one of the core techniques of the new journalism being developed by mass-market newspapers from the 1880s on. But accenting speaking and conversation also reflects the material realities of upper-class women's work in slum settings, where so many were in positions that required them to listen and to talk—district nurses, charity caseworkers, rent collectors, and later, school managers and health educators (called health visitors). Having circulated through the world of female philanthropy for a few years in the 1880s, Beatrice Potter characterized this new generation of articulate "governing and guiding women." They spoke with "the dignity of habitual authority," deploying a "peculiar combination of sympathy and authority."[54]

Listening was also central to women's work in the slums. Clementina Black and her wealthy colleague Adele Meyer, in their 1908 investigation of women sewing garments in their homes, discovered that even women working on piece rates and racing against the clock often welcomed the listening ears of the social investigator.[55] "Lady" rent collectors, or housing managers, as they were also called, needed to talk and listen to tenants on their weekly rounds, and those who enjoyed this sociability found the work congenial. Beatrice Potter quickly became bored and dispirited by this doorsill talk. On the other hand, Ellen Chase, an American blue blood, was an outgoing woman full of "human sympathy" and "joy in her work," according to her boss, Octavia Hill, whose helpers included a number of other sociable women. Chase's weekly rounds in a rundown group of cottages in Deptford in the 1880s drew out many stories of abandoned families, neighbors' quarrels, romance, and violence—hundreds of distilled conversations that she later retold in her *Tenant Friends in Old Deptford*.[56]

"The Woman Element"

The female middle-class presence in London's sprawling slum districts was unmistakable in both religious and secular affairs. As the nineteenth century progressed, it was women who sustained the Church of England's preindustrial tradition of personal contacts in the uncongenial environment of the large industrial cities. In the late 1890s, Charles Booth's researchers found parishes with more than two dozen women door-to-door visitors, a few of whom were paid.[57] As Mark Guy Pearse, an ebullient reforming Methodist minister, quipped, speaking of the many women associated with the Soho-based West London Mission, "*They practice* what *I preach.*" Samuel Barnett, the Anglican founder and warden of Toynbee Hall and an attentive student of slum dwellers and explorers, agreed that "the woman element" was "the most potent" in philanthropy. Another clergyman, in 1897, claimed that women district visitors were essential in populous urban parishes. Only a small group of households would be known by pastors were it not for these helpers: "These ladies report who are in the parish and what is going on."[58] Unlike many other male professionals whose work centered on the slums—such as missionaries, physicians and medical officers, and journalists, to name a few—these three clergymen acknowledged their dependence on women volunteers. Anne Summers acidly observes, however, that in using women to visit the sick in their homes and to pray with workhouse inmates, the clergy were asking them "to replicate the functions which they themselves had hitherto performed" and had abandoned.[59]

As their connections with clergymen suggest, the women who are the focus of this volume did not always operate in an all-female world, but mingled daily not only with clergymen but also with male philanthropists, politicians, and social researchers. The COS hired both women and men to work through its district offices. At Toynbee Hall, men were the residents, but the warden's dynamic wife, Henrietta Barnett, presided over a large group of women activists. Many settlements were, in any case, officially "coeducational," especially Nonconformist enterprises like the Bermondsey Settlement and Mansfield House (which had a women's branch), and the West London Mission—whose associated "sisters" lived nearby, as settlement workers would have. Charles Booth's enormous London research project employed at least five women as investigators, and the dinner table of Charles and Mary Booth was a setting where both men and women discussed the social issues of the day.[60] Marriages among poverty activists and investigators emerged from this socializing, beginning with the Barnetts' wedding and including that of Kate Potter and Leonard Courtney, her sister Beatrice Potter and Sidney Webb, Helen and Bernard Bosanquet, and Emmeline Pethick and Frederick Lawrence.[61]

As they moved about among their clients or parishioners, women, because of their dress, were far more conspicuous as classed bodies than were their male counterparts. Men clothed themselves effortlessly for slum expeditions in expensive but dark-hued tweeds. For women, dressing was more involved, for true female gentility was signaled by elaborate costumes, underclothing, and headgear. In the 1870s trains, ruffles, and pleats were in style; in the 1880s, heavy, showy fabrics such as brocades and velvets were in vogue; in the 1890s, padded hips, bosoms, and voluminous sleeves formed a contrast to tiny waists. Hats, often showy and heavily adorned, became increasingly popular from the 1890s until the First World War.[62]

Reflecting the movement of women into new spaces in the later Victorian decades, however, fashionable women were now offered a variety of specialized practical dress options: dresses for country life, for remaining at home, or for town wear. Tailored styles and heavier fabrics originated with ladies' riding gear in the 1860s. Some dresses were high waisted and did not require tightly laced corsets—which were going out of style among the fashion vanguard by the 1900s, according to Valerie Steele. Women doing serious social work wore their skirts on the short side and chose dark colors, washable fabrics, and simple styles. The skirt and (washable) blouse were a favored option from the 1890s on for seasoned slum workers. More casual visitors displayed their amateurishness by dressing in high-fashion clothing. As Alice Hodson wrote, possibly tongue in cheek, "West End ladies" attending the weekly visitors' meetings at a West Lambeth vestry, "come down to us in pretty frocks and feathered hats; they are very smart and gay, and are a great help because they look so nice."[63]

Yet the dark and washable outfits were not without their difficulties. They were certainly practical. They also denoted, say some fashion historians, virtue, self-discipline, respectability, and sexual propriety. Yet as Helen Norman, George Gissing's earnest and soberly dressed leader of an evening school for working girls in *Workers in the Dawn,* is acutely aware, the very things that render her genteel engender distrust in her charges: "My speech, my dress, perhaps, revolts them." She longs to be less conspicuous. While she cannot (and would not want to) speak "in their uncouth tongue," she has "made my dress as plain as it possibly can be, to be respectabler."[64] Such somber dress also created extra distance between philanthropists and factory girls, so often clad in vivid scarlets, blues, or greens thanks to cheap and effective new aniline dyes. The upper classes associated such colors with children, primitive peoples, and the lower classes.[65] Hodson, in a typical account, describes a factory girls' club member with a "strong will" and a temper like a "lunatic" whose favorite costume was "a bright red gown, with which she wears a large feather hat." District nurses and women in religious orders of one kind or another had an easy way out in their uniforms of sober colors with a simple collar and bonnet—fairly close to the prim outfits that caused their peers such difficulty. Ward's fictional Marcella, in her year as a district nurse in Central London, preferred wearing her nursing dress with its apron and plain black bonnet to even the simplest and darkest of her ordinary dresses.[66] The West London Mission's "Sisters of the People," volunteers rather than nuns, wore the same uniform—bonnet, col-

Figure 3. The Sisters of the People in 1932. By the 1930s, there were several generations of women involved in the Soho-based West London Mission's social work, which began in 1887. The founder of the Sisters, Katherine Price Hughes, is in the center. Three more of the other original Sisters are in the photograph, all of whom have retained their traditional bonnet and train rather than switching to the more modern uniform introduced after World War I. In profile is Sister Hope, who had been running the Mission's modern nursery since 1890. Reprinted with the permission of the West London Mission.

lar, dark gown—from their founding in 1887 until World War I; this uniform made them both more and less visible than other upper-class women would have been.

Public or Private?

The activist female cohorts of the 1860s and later may have had unprecedented access to new geographical and social arenas, yet many more remained closed to them. Respectable women in the mid-nineteenth century were formally excluded from voting and office holding, from most economic activity, and from the vast majority of professions and trades. When they ventured out, they needed a chaperone. Most were educated in their homes by parents or governesses. Even in the missionary and charitable organizations in which they abounded, females at mid-century were almost always excluded from policy-making positions.

The various kinds of women's education, charity, and parish work that intensified in the 1860s can all be seen as wedges with which women could pry their way into national life as they moved across the shifting divide between the public and private spheres. Separate "spheres" for men and women was a concept central to Victorian gender ideology, but vague and unstable from the very beginning.[67] From the 1850s on, in any case, some middle-class girls were being educated in large, professionally run "public" institutions, rather than privately at home or in tiny one-woman schools. The first colleges for women were founded in 1849 and 1850. Attending public schools, along with church work such as visiting parishioners and teaching Sunday school, occupies an ill-defined gray area between traditional and innovative female social locations. The creative prison reformer Elizabeth Fry (1780–1845) exemplifies the mutability of this gray area. She was convinced that her femininity bound her to the "private" or "civil" sphere. In her view, however, not only church work but also the prison reform efforts she began in the 1810s were entirely appropriate for women. On the other hand, working in a large, formal organization involving "matters of law or public policy" would have been stepping over the border into the "public," as Anne Summers has recently characterized Fry's attitude.[68] Fry's certainty that she was working within a traditional women's sphere gave her the courage to battle aggressively at the highest levels of government for more humane treatment of women in prison. Antisuffrage philanthropists like Octavia Hill and Mary Ward are later examples of this thinking. Both warmly embraced female activism in the realms of church, charity, and education. These were properly "women's sphere." Ward was a dynamic and hardworking founder, administrator, and supporter of Somerville College, one of the very earliest colleges for women, from the 1870s through the 1890s. Hill was a housing reformer and passionate champion of public parklands. Voting in parliamentary elections, in Ward's view, was outside of women's realm. And rather than voting, as Hill wrote in a letter to *The Times,* women should devote themselves to arenas she considered private, such as "the care of the sick, the old, the young, and the erring, as guardians of the poor, as nurses, as teachers, as visitors." Even signing an *anti*suffrage petition was too close to national politics for Hill's taste, and she refused![69]

Patterns of recruitment for slum philanthropy in the 1880s and 1890s reveal the degree to which the lives of young middle-class women were changing. Vibrant secondary and university school ties, as well as the friendship networks that brought many women into slum work, reveal young women's greater participation in worlds outside their families. Many secondary schools and colleges supported settlements in poor districts, including Cheltenham College, which sponsored the Ladies Settlement at Mayfield House in Bethnal Green and St. Paul's Girls' School, which ran a settlement (Dame Colet House) in Stepney. Many students spent vacations at their settlements, and a few spent longer periods as settlers. Octavia Hill's rent collectors included a number of old pupils from the school on Nottingham Place that Hill and her sisters ran.[70] Also, in her efforts to recruit the first Sisters of the People associated with the West London Mission, Katherine Price Hughes, the young wife of the mission's head clergyman, renewed her contacts with her own secondary school, Daleham.[71]

Tiddlywinks or "the Harlots of Piccadilly"

London's slum districts were known not for their glamour, but for their monotony, dreariness, bad odors, and lurking dangers. So what was it about poverty that gripped so many well-born women?

Religious conviction was one of these forces. The Evangelical movement in the established (Anglican) church, as much as the Nonconformist churches—Methodist, Quaker, Unitarian, Congregationalist, and Baptist—had long taught a more earnest and personal Christianity, informing daily family life as well as public service.[72] Two generations later, the dual impact of Darwinian evolutionary biology and German biblical criticism made literal belief in the Creation and in the historicity of the Bible more difficult. Some doctrines, such as eternal damnation and predestination—and even Christ's sacrifice on the cross—were deemphasized, while the life and teachings of Christ (the Incarnation) became more central elements of Christian belief. Christlike service to others was a better sign of religious conviction than personal austerities or private meditation. As the Methodist reformer Hugh Price Hughes put it, "Every kindness that you show to the drunkards of the Regent Street slums, to the harlots of Piccadilly, and to the starving poor everywhere, is a kindness shown to Jesus Christ."[73] Clergymen and church organizations were very active in political crusades on behalf of slum dwellers, and in slum social service. Samuel Barnett and J. Scott Lidgett, both wardens of settlement houses, were clergymen, Barnett in the Anglican and Lidgett in the Methodist church. The famous pamphlet *The Bitter Cry of Outcast London* (1883), a vivid picture of overcrowding and intense poverty in East London, was sponsored by the Congregational Union, and its probable author, Andrew Mearns, was a former pastor. Whitefield's Tabernacle in London was a leader in social welfare programs.[74] Several religious groups—the Forward Movement in Methodism, the movement that was sometimes called "muscular Christianity" within the Anglican church, and Christian Socialism—all preached a gospel of service to the needy.

Intense disgust with middle-class drawing rooms, a less exalted though very powerful emotion, motivated another large group of the women slummers. Society rituals establishing "campaigns of alliance, inclusion, and social placing," as Leonore Davidoff has put it, were extremely burdensome to young women. The endless round of social duties—to accompany their mothers everywhere, to answer piles of letters, to dress and undress several times a day, to entertain sickly relatives—generated excruciating boredom. Most daughters would be rescued from this frustrating life by marriage. In large genteel families, however, one daughter was what we might call the "designated spinster," whose lifetime job was to endure dull domestic routines while caring for siblings or aging parents. Until their marriages, other daughters were expected to carry out similar duties.[75]

The monotonous life of a young woman of good family is manifest in the early 1890s letters of Alice Mayor, who chose to stay at home when her sister went to university. Alice and her twin sister, Flora, were daughters of a very comfortably off religious scholar and lived in elegant suburban Kingston Hill. In letters to Flora, Alice reported, among other diversions, "a nice walk round the garden." She also reported: "I painted some mistletoe and holly," and "Most of our mornings have been filled with mending."[76] To my mind, Alice's low point was at age twenty-seven (September 1899) when an aunt came to lunch. She recounted to her sister: "Conversation languished so much we were thankful to untwist tangles of gimp [fancy cord used as trimming]. . . . We rather wondered how conversation on schools, foreign parts and the Congress could last us through the evening but luckily Tiddlywinks was thought of and we had a fine game over which everyone got excited."[77]

Many women strenuously questioned family and domestic imperatives. Advice writer Dinah Mulock Craik, for example, wrote in 1863, "The chief canker at the root of women's lives is the want of something to do." No one stated this grievance more sharply than Florence Nightingale. "Living from breakfast till dinner, from dinner till tea, with a little worsted work, and . . . looking forward to nothing but bed," was her description of this life, which she poured out in "Cassandra," her plea for women's freedom to work.[78] Similarly, Beatrice Potter, returning to her family's county estate in 1879 from a trip to Germany, wrote of her "perfectly lonely life and want of employment which makes life almost torture."[79]

Maude Stanley, who is still known today for organizing clubs and classes for working girls, was her wealthy and titled family's unhappy designated spinster after her four sisters all married. "What would they do without a sister at home?" her sister Kate reassured her, pointing out how much her parents and brothers needed her. But family conflict with her father's heir after his death in 1869 seems to have precipitated a crisis. Maude and her mother had to leave their palatial home, Alderley, in Cheshire, settling in their London house in Dover Street. Here Maude Stanley threw herself into parish visiting and an increasing number of services for her parishioners.[80] Ejected, and also freed, from designated spinsterhood, she began a productive career in slum philanthropy.

Beatrice Potter's elder sister Kate Potter's life as a single daughter unhappy at home epitomizes how volunteer poverty work could function as an escape hatch. After all of her "eligible" sisters were married, Kate Potter was next in line to serve as the family housekeeper. She resolved to leave home after a particularly "troubled year" when, as she put it circumspectly, "many mistakes had been made, much trouble endured and some lessons learnt." Her plan was to "to go to Miss Octavia Hill to be trained for her work in London [as a housing reformer]." Though her parents and her oldest sister strongly disapproved, Kate eventually received a small allowance from her father and established herself in rooms in Great College Street in Westminster. She became Hill's full-time assistant, collecting rents and running several children's clubs, working in this capacity from 1876 until her marriage in 1883. When working with Hill, Kate continued to attend some Potter family events, and her family were sometimes coerced into attending what they called "poor people's parties," from which they retreated as quickly as possible. A dour male coworker scathingly labeled Kate's housing management efforts as nothing but "fancy-work," likening it to a young lady's fine needlework. Yet it kept Potter so busy that she sometimes felt "like a bit of lifeless perpetually moving machinery."[81] As the Potter sisters' collective biographer, Barbara Caine, shrewdly points out, Kate Potter's extremely tight schedule served as natural protection from her family's demands.[82]

London's growing bus and train systems, as well as the close proximity between poor and wealthy areas, meant that slum service did not always require the rupture with home and family that Kate Potter welcomed. Stella Duckworth, Virginia Woolf's half-sister, older by thirteen years, served as a "designated spinster" in the Stephen family, especially after her mother's death in 1895. She managed the house and servants and looked after her younger siblings and half-siblings. Yet her diary shows that in

1896 she faithfully devoted Tuesday mornings to collecting rents and organizing repairs for poor tenants in Southwark, and Thursday afternoons to reading to workhouse inmates. This work is interspersed with shopping for gifts and clothing for her brothers, family visitors, and a courtship with Jack Hills, her future husband. Stella died young, in 1897, but Virginia gave her a long life—and a continued commitment to improving slum housing—as Eleanor Pargiter in *The Years*.[83] Dorothy Ward, who administered Passmore Edwards, the settlement in Bloomsbury serving poor children that her mother, Mary Ward, had founded, was another young woman who combined an upper-class young woman's social life with steady and efficient work at a settlement. On Tuesday, January 13, 1903, to give one example, Dorothy dashed out of her children's club rehearsal, sped home by cab at 7:20, dressed, and arrived at the theater on time. She shopped, went to dances, was fitted for dresses, had her hair waved, relaxed on weekends at her parents' country house—all while attending innumerable committee meetings, organizing the settlement's musical programs, and working with the girls in her clubs.[84]

Descending from the Castle

Taking risks, working hard, and growing in expertise still did not hold at bay the specter that haunted all women slum activists: the figure of the lady bountiful. The image encapsulated the continued implausibility of these female cross-class ventures and the ambivalence of their contemporaries about granting women power in public roles. The term *lady bountiful* was always pejorative. Fiction as well as nonfiction accounts, even by the charity-giving classes themselves, ridicule this figure for her ineptness, her gullibility, and her indiscriminate giving. *My District Visitors,* written by an anonymous clergyman in the 1890s, portrays the imperious Mistress Agatha Comfort and other visitor candidates as too frivolous, too nosy, or too fanatical. Mrs. Pardiggle from Dickens's *Bleak House* probably was and still is the best known characterization of the type.[85]

This negative image did not deter very many, and the wealthiest women were, in any case, probably immune from it. For them, London could serve as a hobby, a source of adoring and respectful clients, or as a platform for significant social reform. The activities of female benefactors remain stamped on many parts of London today. The money of women millionaires went to churches and other established institutions, to services for specific parts of the working class (factory girls, cab drivers, costermongers [street sellers]), and to efforts to improve the poor, and especially children, through education or religion. Lady Charlotte Guest, wife of a railroad magnate, to take one example, became well known in the 1880s for her heated shelters for London cab drivers, which offered a place to rest, hot meals, and even mittens and scarves knitted by Lady Guest's wealthy friends. There were forty-one shelters by the 1890s. Lady Guest was devoted to this project. As she passed through London she often stopped at a shelter or at the cabdrivers' office to find out if her knitted scarves were the right size, whether the shelters' opening hours were adequate, which newspapers they would prefer (her choice of *The Times* was not popular), and even, on one occasion, if the cabmen would like to try out a new device, the umbrella.[86]

Perhaps the best known, and certainly the richest, of the bountiful ladies was Angela Burdett-Coutts, sometimes called "the Queen of the Poor." She inherited her banker grandfather's fortune in 1837 when she was only twenty-three, and, not having been raised in great wealth, Burdett-Coutts was oppressed by this responsibility. A humble, even mousy, woman, she took courage from the belief that her fortune was God-given, meant to "feed my sheep." In taking to heart the biblical parable of the Good Shepherd, she set out to help both animals and humans. Burdett-Coutts dispensed her largesse in many forms. Charles Dickens, whom she met not long after becoming a millionaire, befriended her and recruited her into funding the ragged school movement (which promoted free education for poor children). During the 1867 cholera epidemic in London, her wealth and reputation gave her quasi-official status: she supplied food, clothing, and medicine to the sick; funded several health visitors; and even hired two sanitary inspectors. In the 1850s, Burdett-Coutts had funded a model dwelling project in Bethnal Green called Columbia Square, followed soon after by a magnificent covered market, intended as a gift to the costermongers whom she had befriended en masse ("Queen of the costermongers" was another of her epithets). The market, an attempt both to protect and to regulate the costers, was a failure; gathered together under a single roof they lost most of their customers. Apt symbol of the limitations of individual philanthropies and reminder that unwanted or inept regulation was often the other face of caring, the Columbia Market was closed for good in 1885, and the apartment project was eventually torn down too. Yet this bountiful lady left other, more enduring, material imprints of herself in the form of bathhouses, drinking troughs for animals, street names, and St. Stephen's Church in Westminster.[87]

"The Marcella Crop"

Fictional versions of the philanthropic experience highlight its potential for personal growth: its intense emotions and the chances it offered women to exercise leadership and display intelligence. Deborah Nord points out that work with the poor offered women new and specialized knowledge—of the details of working-class life—hitherto the domain of only a few male professions, such as medicine or the clergy.[88] In the plots of such mid-century novels as Dickens's *Bleak House* and Elizabeth Gaskell's *North and South,* a woman's visit to the interior of households is a personal turning point, bringing wisdom and a recognition of social responsibility.[89] By the 1880s and 1890s, in dozens of novels depicting the New Woman of this era, female slum explorers were incorporating their encounters with urban poverty and suffering into a refashioned subjectivity.[90]

Mary Ward's 1894 novel, *Marcella,* one of the many social exploration novels of its era, together with its sequel, *Sir George Tressady,* is an encomium to female slum service. The book's eponymous heroine uses an urban interlude to signal her determination to make amends for her earlier reckless and destructive acts as a newly installed daughter in an imposing country house, Mellor. Once in London, Marcella trains as a district nurse to serve the very poor and takes modest lodgings in a block of model dwellings for workers.[91] Slim, elegant, wealthy, and eventually married to a titled husband, Marcella is, as Ward intended her to be, a poster girl for slum social work, and she was indeed a beacon for women in the 1890s and 1900s, called "the Marcella crop" by H. G. Wells in 1911.[92] Before Ward began her work on the novel, she had founded her own settlement, Passmore Edwards, in Bloomsbury—though her daughters Janet and Dorothy were much more involved with its daily life than was Ward herself. Ward had also rented a large country estate (similar to Marcella's Mellor) in Hertfordshire. To write the novel's third section, in which Marcella undertakes her self-rehabilitation through district nursing, Ward moved back to London. Here she drew on the experiences of her sister-in-law Gertrude Ward, who, in 1891, after years of often reluctant assistance in the Humphry Ward household, had begun her own nursing training.[93]Marcella expands morally and intellectually through her slum work. She is first depicted as ladylike and soft-voiced among a group of "loud-tongued, large-eyed Jewesses," the neighbors of one of her patients. Despite her long hours of work, with its pain and tragedy, Marcella thrives as never before. Her life is "freer, more elastic; allowed room at last to self-consciousness."[94] An acquaintance from her Mellor days, meeting her again in London, finds her ennobled by her new vocation: "How richly human the face had grown! . . . It seemed to him absorbed in something new—something sad and yet benignant, informed with all the pathos and the pain of growth." She is also more intellectually confident and systematic, and she enters commandingly (albeit on the side of country landlords) into a discussion of socialism and the importance of a Labour party with a group of knowledgeable, trade-union-oriented men. In *Sir George Tressady,* Marcella, now the wife of a wealthy but self-effacing Conservative M.P., is a competent lobbyist for legislation to restrict sweated home work. She also impresses her husband's major parliamentary opponent with her intelligence and competence—skills signaled initially by her quiet nurse's competence.[95]

Canning Town to Calcutta

These generations of women at work in London were full participants in the global wanderings of the British middle classes of their time. The texts collected here would have been read by contemporaries as less "local" than they seem today. For one thing, the slums of London were exotic and unknown enough to the reading public before 1918 to enable these women to be thought of as real "travelers," to cite the distinction made by James Buzard, rather than the derogatory "excursionists," "tourists," or even "commuters." Their close contact with "the natives"—a word that really was in the vocabularies of many—solidified this image.[96] Martha Vicinus, in her pathbreaking *Independent Women,* likens the movement of well-off women into slum districts to a kind of "emigration," analogous to the imperial travel and employment easily available to their brothers.[97] Vida Scudder, Oxford-educated American founder of a settlement house in Boston, vigorously advanced this analogy when she wrote in a 1938 memoir: "The spirit of adventure drives some men to explore the Gobi desert, or to seek the Pole; others to research in the buried past, or to travel among alien races. Me, it filled with a biting curiosity about the way the Other Half lived, and a strange hunger for fellowship with them."[98]

Metropolitan and imperial destinations were closely linked for these late Victorians and Edwardians. Educator Clara Grant was planning to join her missionary fiancé in Central Africa, but his sudden death led her to undertake another kind of "missionary" work (as one newspaper inaccurately put it), among London's poor.[99] At its annual meeting, the National Union of Women Workers, a large and varied mainstream gathering of British women philanthropists, routinely included lectures on philanthropies and government policies in India. Settlement houses and district nursing programs in London and other "home" cities trained thousands of empire-bound women. To take one example among hundreds, the small hospital that the Canning Town Women's Settlement established in the 1890s to serve its local community soon became a way station for medical missionaries en route to other continents.[100]

Conversely, foreign missions adopted approaches which had been developed in the metropole. This had been so from early in the nineteenth century, when both charitable domestic "visiting" and foreign mission fund-raising were undertaken by the same organizations. And women eventually became as central in foreign missions as they were in the metropolitan branches.[101] The Protestant missions in the Punjab saw a large influx of unmarried women missionaries in the 1880s and 1890s. By 1900, two-thirds of all British missionaries worldwide were women. Since they could not preach, women abroad did work very similar to that of their sisters and friends in the slums at home. They educated the young, did administrative tasks, and provided medical care as trained nurses and doctors.[102] Ideas from the field and from the metropolis were constantly being exchanged. The Bible women attached to many Protestant missions in India in the late nineteenth century, women who visited in homes and villages telling Bible stories and talking about the gospel, were closely modeled on domestic church visitors.[103] Ellen Ranyard's enlistment of local women to serve as the foot soldiers of her London mission was based in part on the older missionary principle of "native agency." Ranyard, in turn, influenced Hudson Taylor, who used her approach in his Chinese Inland Mission, and she financed several of the ten women recruits sailing with Taylor in 1866.[104]

Flora Shaw's life illustrates this intermingling of local and global ambitions with a vengeance. A general's daughter raised in Woolwich, she sought spiritual purpose in her teen years by organizing bulk shopping for working-class women in Greenwich. As a young woman in the 1880s, she, along with Mary Steer, rescued young prostitutes in the waterside district of Ratcliff. As she later put it, the sight of hundreds of docked ships in that riverside district diverted her attention to the empire—not surprising for a child of generals and imperial officials. She became a leading colonial journalist, an ardent imperialist who had a role in precipitating the Boer War,[105] and in 1902 married top imperial official Frederick J. D. Lugard.

As Shaw's case suggests, any number of the London explorers were closely attached to major imperial ventures by family or marriage ties. Another, equally famous, case in point is Dorothy Tennant, an accomplished and highly successful artist whose work included many sympathetic studies of London street children. At age forty, after a courtship that enthralled the nation, she married celebrity journalist Henry Morton Stanley. Stanley is, of course, famous for having met up with missionary Dr. David Livingstone in Zanzibar and for carrying out the exploratory legwork—inflicting immense hardship and loss of life among his own African crews—that was the basis of the notoriously brutal Congo Free State. Despite Dorothy's sympathy with the poor in her own country, there is no evidence that she found fault with her husband's actions.[106]

New Questions

The encounter between rich and poor, between women especially, in the 1860–1920 generations highlights a specific group of historical questions. Did the kind of detailed knowledge of poverty and the poor to which women and men slummers alike had access generate particular kinds of stances in political debates? Did pathetic narratives "block" (in Edward Said's sense) or at least inhibit more politically radical versions of the meaning of poverty from forming among those receiving charity?[107] Which kinds of clients benefited most from contact with the middle-class visitors? Could friendship and real conversation actually develop between the outsiders and their clients, or did this contact always follow well-established scripts?

To pose an even broader and also more awkward question, is it possible to chart lasting social effects of this era of tremendous volunteer enthusiasm on national life in Britain? A large and sophisticated body of writing has authoritatively demonstrated the importance of voluntary programs in the shaping of welfare institutions in the interwar period and during the 1940s. A more speculative query concerns the volunteers, their organizations, and their personal contacts in slum districts, in heightening a national identity that could override other identities. Were the genteel slummers an element in Britain's relative stability in 1917 and 1918, when most of the other World War I belligerents fell apart or nearly did so in revolution and mutiny?

One final question: did the seemingly tame institutions through which these women encountered the slums—settlement houses, children's charities—serve to prepare a generation of women for leadership?

This is a question I can begin to answer. Outside of the women's suffrage movement, in which many of these philanthropic women participated, the accomplishments of this generation are not very well known. Considering the sheer volume of the female slum explorers and of their efforts, they ought to be, because they shaped life in the twentieth century. A few of the most ambitious women established lasting institutions such as hospitals, convalescent homes, and holiday homes for children; several of the women's settlements they established still exist today, having been headed by women of their founding generations for decades. Philanthropists Susan Lawrence, whose work was in London, and Eleanor Rathbone, in Liverpool, were elected to Parliament—among its first women. Thousands more were active in the Labour party, unions, local government, health care, League of Nations support, or feminist politics for decades. In a period of world crisis, the 1930s and 1940s, many of the women slum philanthropists exercised leadership in new ways. They campaigned on behalf of the struggling Spanish Republic, rescued refugees from Hitler, organized the massive evacuation of schoolchildren from London in 1939, located Jewish survivors in 1945, even served in the Resistance. In the mid-Victorian decades resolute women eager to enlarge their world and accomplish something had had few opportunities beyond "slumming." But for many of them it was a very good choice.

NOTES

1. Some of the material in the introduction is based on my earlier essay, "Slum Journeys: Ladies and London Poverty 1860–1940," in *The Archeology of Urban Landscapes,* ed. Alan Mayne and Tim Murray (Cambridge: Cambridge University Press, 2001). On the social life of the wealthy: Leonore Davidoff, *The Best Circles: Women and Society in Victorian England* (Totowa, NJ: Rowman and Littlefield, 1973); Hilary Evans and Mary Evans, *The Party That Lasted 100 Days: The Late Victorian Season, a Social Study* (London: Macdonald and Jane's, 1976). Nearly all of the women discussed in this book were "ladies," but I have generally avoided using the term because it is now so trivializing. See the glossary. A brief economic, social, and political sketch of London before 1914 is given in appendix 1 of this book.

2. This formulation is adapted this from de Certeau's image of New York as seen from the World Trade Center and is meant to suggest how rare it was that urban travelers saw the city from afar—a trip in a hot-air balloon being one exception. Many Victorians did imagine themselves above the city looking down at it, and thousands read journalist Henry Mayhew's 1852 account of viewing London from the Nassau, a famous balloon on its last flight, which was published in the *Illustrated London News.* Aerial viewing is discussed in Kate Flint, *The Victorians and the Visual Imagination* (Cambridge: Cambridge University Press, 2000), 9–10. See Michel de Certeau, *The Practice of Everyday Life,* trans. Steven Rendall (Berkeley: University of California Press, 1984), 92.

3. Louisa M. Hubbard, "Statistics of Women's Work," in *Woman's Mission: A Series of Congress Papers on the Philanthropic Work of Women,* ed. Baroness Angela Georgina Burdett-Coutts (London: Sampson Low, 1894), 364. See also Ellen Ross, "Housewives and London Charity, 1870–1918," in *The Uses of Charity: The Poor on Relief in the Nineteenth-Century*

Metropolis, ed. Peter Mandler (Philadelphia: University of Pennsylvania Press, 1990), and Brian Harrison, "Philanthropy and the Victorians," *Victorian Studies* 9, no. 4 (June 1966): 353–74.

4. Scholars have assessed the importance of philanthropy as an aspect of women's history in Britain, in developing local and national welfare institutions, and as an effort to regulate the metropolitan poor. Some of the most important studies are Harrison, "Philanthropy and the Victorians"; Anne Summers, "A Home from Home—Women's Philanthropic Work in the Nineteenth Century," in *Fit Work for Women,* ed. Sandra Burman (London: Croom Helm, 1979); F. K. Prochaska, *Women and Philanthropy in Nineteenth-Century England* (Oxford: Clarendon Press, 1980); Martha Vicinus, *Independent Women: Work and Community for Single Women 1850–1920* (Chicago: University of Chicago Press, 1985); Dorothy Thompson, "Women, Work, and Politics in Nineteenth-Century England: The Problem of Authority," in *Equal or Different: Women's Politics 1800–1914* (London: Blackwell, 1987); Mandler, *The Uses of Charity;* Maria Luddy, *Women and Philanthropy in Nineteenth-Century Ireland* (Cambridge: Cambridge University Press, 1995); Anne Summers, *Female Lives, Moral States: Women, Religion and Public Life in Britain 1800–1930* (Newbury, England: Threshold Books, 2000); Kathleen D. McCarthy, ed., *Women, Philanthropy, and Civil Society* (Bloomington: Indiana University Press, 2001); Ross, "Slum Journeys"; and Seth Koven, *Slumming: Sexual and Social Politics in Victorian London* (Princeton, NJ: Princeton University Press, 2004). An illuminating contemporary sociological study is Rebecca Anne Allahyari, *Visions of Charity: Volunteer Workers and Moral Community* (Berkeley: University of California Press, 2000).

5. Yvonne Kapp, *Eleanor Marx* (New York: Pantheon Books, 1976), 2: 261; Liselotte Glage, *Clementina Black: A Study in Social History and Literature* (Heidelberg: Carl Winter, 1981), 23.

6. Koven, *Slumming,* 3, 226.

7. Donald M. Lewis, *Lighten Their Darkness: The Evangelical Mission to Working-Class London, 1828–1860* (New York: Greenwood Press, 1986); Kathleen Heasman, *Evangelicals in Action: An Appraisal of Their Social Work in the Victorian Era* (London: Geoffrey Bles, 1962).

8. For an introduction to Catholic urban philanthropy, see Prochaska, *Women and Philanthropy.* Margaret McMillan, who journeyed to Deptford as a school manager in the early 1900s, is an example of a Care Committee member among the authors included in this volume.

9. On wealthy Jewish women and London poverty, see Susan L. Tananbaum, "Philanthropy and Identity: Gender and Ethnicity in London," *Journal of Social History* 97, no. 4 (summer 1997): 937–62, and Lara Marks, *Model Mothers: Jewish Mothers and Maternity Provision in East London, 1870–1933* (Columbia: Ohio University Press); the Adderley quotation is from Koven, *Slumming,* 6–7.

10. George Behlmer, in making a convincing case for the ineffectiveness of most state and private efforts to regulate poor families before 1940, points to the English tradition of protection for "the home." Those who wanted to change the behavior of parents or children would succeed only by making their case convincingly. See his excellent against-the-grain study: *Friends of the Family: The English Home and Its Guardians, 1850–1940* (Stanford, CA: Stanford University Press, 1998), introduction. On the London County Council, see

appendix 1 and the glossary. Many thanks to Sally Alexander for her reminder about local government bodies as central sites of unmediated class warfare, something well appreciated by the Fabians. Personal communication, May 2003.

11. K. Theodore Hoppen, *The Mid-Victorian Generation 1846–1886* (Oxford: Oxford University Press, 1998), 466, 468. Sybil Thorndike, Irene Vanbrugh, Winifred Beech, and Noelle Sonning, among others, had successful careers as stage actors. See Midori Yamaguchi, "'Unselfish' Desires: Daughters of the Anglican Clergy, 1830–1914," Ph.D. diss., Department of Sociology, University of Essex, 2001, 14, 94. Thanks to Leonore Davidoff for introducing me to this enlightening dissertation by her student.

12. Daughters of Anglican clergymen were also disproportionately represented among early Oxbridge students, according to Yamaguchi's research.

13. Beatrice Webb, *My Apprenticeship* (London: Longmans, n.d.), 239.

14. On Eleanor Marx in East London and her friendship with Margaret Harkness (whose "Barmaids" appears in chapter 7 of this volume), see Lynne Hapgood, "'Is this Friendship?' Eleanor Marx, Margaret Harkness and the Idea of Socialist Community," in *Eleanor Marx (1855–1898): Life, Work, Contacts,* ed. John Stokes (Aldershot, England: Ashgate, 2000), 131–34. On Marx's involvement with striking workers in 1889 and 1890, see Chushichi Tsuzuki, *The Life of Eleanor Marx 1855–1898: A Socialist Tragedy* (Oxford: Clarendon Press, 1967), 196–203. The Engels quote is on p. 198; her use of "end-of-the-world place," also p. 198, was in a letter to her sister Laura in late December 1889.

15. I did not include memoirs or autobiographies, most of which were written many decades after the authors' slum efforts had concluded. Mainly written well after 1920, such texts were intended for different readers in a changed cultural context.

16. *The subject* is a central term in social and literary theory; it implies individuals' constructed and situated nature, through ideology, language, discourse, or culture. For an introduction to this concept, see the section "Locating the Subject" in *Feminist Literary Theory: A Reader,* 2nd ed., ed. Mary Eagleton (Oxford: Blackwell, 1986), 339–420; Catherine Belsey's "Constructing the Subject," in *Feminisms: An Anthology of Literary Theory and Criticism,* ed. Robyn R. Warhol and Diana Price Herndl (New Brunswick, NJ: Rutgers University Press, 1991), 593–609; and Reginia Gagnier, *Subjectivities: A History of Self-Representation in Britain, 1832–1920* (New York: Oxford University Press, 1991), 8–14. On psychoanalysis, Marxism, Foucault, and the subject, see the thoughtful discussion in Michele Barrett's *Politics of Truth* (Palo Alto, CA: Stanford University Press, 1991).

17. Kristina Huneault, *Difficult Subjects: Working Women and Visual Culture, Britain 1880–1914* (London: Ashgate, 2002), 17.

18. Charles Booth, *Life and Labour of the People in London, First Series: Poverty,* 5 vols., reprint of the 1902 ed. (London: Macmillan and Company, 1902). On Booth as a student of poverty, see E. P. Hennock, "Concepts of Poverty in the British Social Surveys from Charles Booth to Arthur Bowley," in *The Social Survey in Historical Perspective 1880–1940,* ed. Martin Bulmer, Kevin Bales, and Kathryn Kish Sklar (Cambridge: Cambridge University Press, 1991). For another discussion of Booth, see Gertrude Himmelfarb, *Poverty and Compassion: The Social Ethic of the Late Victorians* (New York: Knopf, 1991), bk. 2.

19. My sketch of the issues that agitated the educated classes is based on Summers, *Female Lives,* 29–39; Jeffrey Cox, *Imperial Fault Lines: Christianity and Colonial Power in India, 1818–1940* (Stanford, CA: Stanford University Press, 2002); Susan Thorne, *Congregational*

Missions and the Making of an Imperial Culture in Nineteenth-Century England (Stanford: Stanford University Press, 1999), 92–93, 108–10; Catherine Hall, *Civilising Subjects: Metropole and Colony in the English Imagination 1830–1867* (London: Polity Press, 2002), chap. 7; and John Marriott, introduction to John Marriott and Masaie Matsumura, eds., *The Metropolitan Poor: Semi-Factual Accounts, 1795–1910,* (London: Pickering and Chatto, 1999), 1: xxii–xlii.

20. Webb, *My Apprenticeship,* 179–80.

21. Deborah Epstein Nord, *Walking the Victorian Streets: Women, Representation, and the City* (Ithaca, NY: Cornell University Press, 1995), 47; Webb, *My Apprenticeship,* 130.

22. This "special mission" did not have to be secularized to generate a commitment to social service and social change. Believing Christians were an important part of this movement to reach the urban poor; Christian Socialists, "muscular" high church adherents, Forward Movement Methodists, and the Salvation Army are just a few of the church-based social movements. Many social reformers and politicians were nurtured in these settings.

23. Harold Perkin, *The Rise of Professional Society: England since 1880* (London: Routledge, 1989), 41–42.

24. The best discussion of the impact of compulsory education is David Rubinstein, *School Attendance in London, 1870–1914* (Hull: University of Hull Publications, 1969).

25. See Anna Davin, "Imperialism and Motherhood," *History Workshop* 5 (spring 1978): 9–65; and Deborah Dwork, *War Is Good for Babies and Other Young Children: A History of the Infant and Child Welfare Movement in England 1898–1918* (London: Tavistock, 1987); Ellen Ross, "Mothers and the State in Britain, 1904–1914," in *The European Experience of Declining Fertility: A Quiet Revolution, 1850–1970,* ed. John Gillis, Louise Tilly, and David Levine (Oxford: Blackwell, 1992); and Anna Davin, *Growing Up Poor: Home, School and Street in London 1870–1914* (London: Rivers Oram, 1996), chap. 11.

26. Erika Diane Rappaport, *Shopping for Pleasure: Women in the Making of London's West End* (Princeton, NJ: Princeton University Press, 2000), 138; Judith Walkowitz, "Going Public: Shopping, Street Harassment, and Streetwalking in Late Victorian London," *Representations* 62 (spring 1998): 1–30. On fashion: Sharon Marcus, "Reflections on Victorian Fashion Plates," *differences: A Journal of Feminist Cultural Studies* 14, no. 3 (fall 2003): 4–33.

27. For a discussion of this mid-1890s debate, see Michelle Elizabeth Tusan, "Inventing the New Woman: Print Culture and Identity Politics during the Fin-de-Siècle," *Victorian Periodicals Review* 31, no. 2 (summer 1998): 169–82.

28. Constance Lytton, *Prisons and Prisoners. Some Personal Experiences by Constance Lytton and Jane Wharton, Spinster* (1914), reprint ed. (London: Virago, 1988), 43–44.

29. Lisa Tickner, *The Spectacle of Women: Imagery of the Suffrage Campaign 1907–1914* (Chicago: University of Chicago Press, 1988), 28. Pankhurst had devoted a lot of time to drawing working women, but this interest was to be thwarted by the Women's Social and Political Union's (WSPU) effort to dissociate itself from its earlier labor and socialist ties.

30. Vicinus, *Independent Women;* Deborah Epstein Nord, *The Apprenticeship of Beatrice Webb* (Amherst: University of Massachusetts Press, 1985), and *Walking the Victorian Streets,* as well as numerous articles. Mary Poovey is also a literary scholar who has specialized in the reading of "historians'" texts. Especially relevant to female philanthropy is her *Making a Social Body: British Cultural Formation, 1830–1864* (Chicago: University of Chicago Press, 1995). Also of interest: Reginia Gagnier's tart criticisms of some new historicist writ-

ing in "Methodology and the New Historicism," *Journal of Victorian Culture* 4, no.1 (spring 1999): 166–22.

31. On the history side, see Judith Walkowitz, *City of Dreadful Delight: Narratives of Sexual Danger in Late-Victorian London* (Chicago: University of Chicago Press, 1992). For other comments by historians on the impact of literary and linguistic theory on their discipline, see James Vernon, "Who's Afraid of the 'Linguistic Turn'? The Politics of Social History and Its Discontents," *Social History* 19, no. 1 (1994): 81–97; and Raphael Samuel, "Reading the Signs," *History Workshop Journal* 32 (autumn 1991): 988–1009; and "Reading the Signs: Part II," *History Workshop Journal* 33 (spring 1992): 220–51. Mark Freeman, however, makes the point that the connections between fiction and slum reportage can be overestimated. He reminds us that many authors situated themselves in the social-survey tradition and took considerable risks and trouble in their search for sociological accuracy. See his "'Journeys into Poverty Kingdom': Complete Participation and the British Vagrant, 1866–1914," *History Workshop Journal* 52 (autumn 2001): 99–121.

32. The eighteenth-century novels' blending of fact and fiction is explored in Lennard J. Davis, *Factual Fictions: The Origin of the English Novel* (New York: Columbia University Press, 1983); Marriott and Matsumura, *The Metropolitan Poor: Semi-Factual Accounts.*

33. Davis, *Factual Fictions,* chaps. 1–3, and 9 (which it titled "Daniel Defoe: Lies as Truth").

34. Edna Healey, *Lady Unknown: The Life of Angela Burdett-Coutts* (London: Sidgwick and Jackson, 1978). See 64–69, 80–82, 97–99, and chap. 4.

35. Dina Copelman, "From Philanthropy to Economics: Gender and the Construction of a Discipline," paper given at the Middle Atlantic Conference on British Studies, April 8, 2000. Many thanks to Dr. Copelman for sharing her texts and ideas on Collet.

36. *Sir George Tressady,* in *The Writings of Mrs. Humphry Ward,* 16 vols. (London: John Murray, 1911), vols. 7 and 8.

37. Janet P. Trevelyan (Mary Ward's daughter), *The Life of Mrs. Humphry Ward* (London: Constable, 1923), 115, 126–27.

38. On Stella Duckworth Hills, see Hermoine Lee, *Virginia Woolf* (New York: Alfred Knopf, 1997), 120–22; and Gillian Darley, *Octavia Hill* (London: Constable, 1990), 153–54. In working for Hill, Stella was following in the footsteps of her mother, Julia Duckworth, and of her aunt-by-marriage, Caroline Stephen, a friend of Octavia who herself had built a model dwelling in Chelsea in 1877. Lace curtains and geranium care were required of all the tenants in Caroline Stephen's building!

39. Mary Poovey, *Uneven Developments: The Ideological Work of Gender in Mid-Victorian England* (Chicago: University of Chicago Press, 1988), 123–24. See also Koven's thoughtful explanation of his use of two novels (Vernon Lee's *Miss Brown* and Mrs. L. T. Meade's *A Princess of the Gutter*) as a way of finding the unconscious association many made between "dirt" in the slums and "nasty" forms of love (*Slumming,* 204–27).

40. Arlene Young, *Culture, Class and Gender in the Victorian Novel: Gentlemen Gents and Working Women* (London: Macmillan, 1995), 3–5; Poovey, *Making a Social Body,* chap. 7. The term *ideological work,* which I am only alluding to here, comes from her *Uneven Developments.* The campaigns discussed in this paragraph are explained in the texts that follow or in their introductions.

41. Alison Twells, "'Happy English Children': Class, Ethnicity, and the Making of Missionary Women in the Early Nineteenth Century," *Women's Studies International Forum* 21, no.

3 (1998): 235–45, and "'A Christian and Civilised Land': The British Middle Class and the Civilising Mission, 1820–42," in *Gender, Civil Culture and Consumerism: Middle-Class Identity in Britain 1800–1940*, ed. Alan Kidd and David Nicholls (Manchester: Manchester University Press, 1999); see also her "Philanthropy, Domestic Reform and Hierarchies of Civilisation in Early Nineteenth Century Missionary Practice," paper delivered at Conference on the History of Voluntary Action, University of Liverpool, September 12, 2001.

42. Alan Mayne, *The Imagined Slum: Newspaper Representation in Three Cities 1870–1914* (Leicester: Leicester University Press, 1993), 2.

43. Shirley Foster, *Across New Worlds: Nineteenth-Century Women Travelers and Their Writings* (Hemel Hempstead, England: Harvester, 1990), 24. See also contemporary commentator William H. Davenport Adams's comments on female travel writers, *Celebrated Women Travelers of the Nineteenth Century* (London: W. Swan Sonnenschein, 1883).

44. On "legends," see De Certeau, *Practice of Everyday Life*, 106. The importance of male urban missionaries in formulating this slum image is demonstrated both in the texts Marriott has collected and in his pathbreaking introduction to *The Metropolitan Poor*.

45. Helen Bosanquet, "Children of Working London," in *Aspects of the Social Problem* (London: Macmillan, 1895), 29; John Deane Hilton, *Marie Hilton: Her Life and Work 1821–1896* (London: Isbister and Company, 1897), 90, 95.

46. Alice Hodson, *Letters from a Settlement* (London: Edward Arnold, 1929), 28.

47. Quoted in Alison Light, "Forever England: Femininity, Literature and Conservatism between the Wars," in *Feminist Literary Theory*, 2nd ed., ed. Mary Eagleton (Oxford: Blackwell, 1986), 207.

48. On Harkness, see Norman MacKenzie and Jeanne MacKenzie, eds., *The Diaries of Beatrice Webb*, vol. 1: *"Glitter Around and Darkness Within," 1873–1892* (Cambridge, MA: Harvard University Press, 1982), 79–80; on Webb's meeting with Cons, see *My Apprenticeship*, 266–27. Emma Cons, a girlhood friend of Octavia Hill and founder of the Old Vic Theatre, was an immensely creative social worker and organizer. Webb's disapproval of Cons's approach demonstrates her lack of interest in and respect for this branch of slum involvement. See Cecily Hamilton and Lilian Baylis, *The Old Vic* (New York: George H. Doran, n.d.), 248–85.

49. Ellen Ranyard, *Nurses for the Needy, or Bible Women Nurses in the Homes of the London Poor* (London: James Nisbet, 1875), 23–24.

50. Northrop Frye, *Anatomy of Criticism* (Princeton, NJ: Princeton University Press, 1957), 38–39.

51. On pathos and American antislavery literature, see Jane Tompkins, *Sensational Designs: The Cultural Work of American Fiction 1780–1860* (New York: Oxford University Press, 1985), chap. 5.

52. Poovey, *Making a Social Body*, 43. For an astute, but I think overly harsh, reading of Ranyard and her mission see Frank Mort, *Dangerous Sexualities: Medico-Moral Politics in England since 1830*, 2nd ed. (London: Routledge, 2000), 44–46.

53. On the visual and the blind man trope see Lynda Nead's *Victorian Babylon: People, Streets and Images in Nineteenth-Century London* (New Haven, CT: Yale University Press, 2000), 57–62; Daniel Pick, "Stories of the Eye," in *Rewriting the Self: Histories from the Renaissance to the Present*, ed. Roy Porter (London: Routledge, 1997); and Flint, *Victori-*

ans and the Visual Imagination, chap. 3. On the multiplication of technologies of spectatorship, ibid., 3–13.

54. August 12, 1885, entry, MacKenzie and MacKenzie, *Diaries of Beatrice Webb,* 1: 136–37. I discuss middle-class women's "talking" in slum settings in "Slum Journeys: Ladies and London Poverty, 1860–1940," in *The Archaeology of Urban Landscapes: Explorations in Slumland,* ed. Alan Mayne and Tim Murray (Cambridge: Cambridge University Press, 2001), 11–21.

55. Clementina Black and Adele (Lady Carl) Meyer, *Makers of Our Clothes* (London: Macmillan, 1913), 508. See chapter 3 of this volume.

56. C. Edmund Maurice, ed., *Life of Octavia Hill, as Told in Her Letters* (London: Macmillan, 1913), 508; Ellen Chase, *Tenant Friends in Old Deptford* (London: Williams and Norgate, 1929), 172–73 and 186–90.

57. Summers, *Female Lives,* 130–31; Rosemary O'Day, "Women in Victorian Religion," in *Retrieved Riches: Social Investigation in Britain 1840–1914,* ed. David Englander and Rosemary O'Day (Aldershot, England: Ashgate, 1998), 351–58.

58. Mrs. George Unwin and John Telford, *Mark Guy Pearse: Preacher, Author, Artist* (London: Epworth, 1930), 159; Henrietta Barnett, *Matters That Matter* (London: John Murray, 1930), 2; Anon., "Practical Articles on District Visiting. I. A General View of the Work," *Supplement to the Churchwoman,* April 2, 1897, 34.

59. Summers, *Female Lives,* 130–31.

60. On Booth's research project, see Seth Koven, "Henrietta Barnett: The (Auto)biography of a Late-Victorian Marriage," in *After the Victorians,* ed. Susan Pedersen and Peter Mandler (New York: Routledge, 1993); and Rosemary O'Day, "Women and Social Investigation: Clara Collet and Beatrice Potter," in Englander and O'Day, *Retrieved Riches,* 165.

61. On Kate Potter's independent life and new associations in East London, see introduction text, below, and note 82.

62. This bird's-eye summary of fashion history is based on Christopher Breward, *The Culture of Fashion: A New History of Fashionable Dress* (Manchester: Manchester University Press, 1995); and C. Willett Cunnington, *English Women's Clothing in the Nineteenth Century* (New York: Dover Books, 1990.

63. Lou Taylor, "Wool Cloth and Gender: The Use of Woolen Cloth in Women's Dress in Britain, 1865–85," in *Defining Dress: Dress as Object, Meaning and Identity,* ed. Amy de la Haye and Elizabeth Wilson (Manchester: Manchester University Press, 1999); Valerie Steele, *The Corset: A Cultural History* (New Haven, CT: Yale University Press, 2001), 47–49; Stella Mary Newton, *Health, Art and Reason: Dress Reformers of the 19th Century* (London: John Murray, 1974), 153–54; Hodson, *Letters from a Settlement,* 140.

64. George Gissing, *Workers in the Dawn* (1880) Reprint ed. (New York: AMS Press, 1968), 2: 224.

65. Breward, *Culture of Fashion,* 161; Suzanne Keen, "Quaker Dress, Sexuality, and the Domestication of Reform in the Victorian Novel," *Victorian Literature and Culture* 30, no. 1 (2002): 211–36; also Alison V. Matthews, "Aestheticism's True Colors: The Politics of Pigment in Victorian Art, Criticism, and Fashion," in *Women and British Aestheticism,* ed. Talia Schaffer and Kathy A. Psomiades (Charlottesville: University of Virginia Press, 1999): 172–91.

66. Hodson, *Letters from a Settlement,* 191; Iris Dove, "Sisterhood or Surveillance? The Development of Working Girls' Clubs in London, 1880–1939," Ph.D. diss., Greenwich University, 1996, 35–38; Mrs. Humphry Ward, *Marcella* (1894; reprint, New York: Viking Penguin, 1985), 346–47.

67. Among many studies of the ideology of women's sphere, those I have found most useful are Ellen Jordan, *The Women's Movement and Women's Employment in Nineteenth Century Britain* (London: Routledge, 1999), especially chap. 6; and Summers, *Female Lives,* particularly chap. 1, "Common Sense about Separate Spheres." For a discussion of recent debates on this issue, see Leonore Davidoff, "Gender and the Great Divide: Public and Private in British Gender History," *Journal of Women's History* 15, no. 1 (spring 2003): 11–27. Also enlightening is Seth Koven's recent study of Ruskin's *Sesame and Lilies.* Long thought of as a manual on women's sphere, *Sesame and Lilies* explores what Koven calls "fundamental instabilities in the theory and practice of separate spheres." See Seth Koven, "How the Victorians Read *Sesame and Lilies,*" in *Sesame and Lilies: John Ruskin,* ed. Deborah Nord (New Haven, CT: Yale University Press, 2002). See also Davidoff's illuminating pioneering study of women's work in maintaining upper-class status, *The Best Circles.*

68. Summers, *Female Lives,* 16.

69. Quoted in Nord, *Apprenticeship of Beatrice Webb,* 150–51.

70. E. Moberly Bell, *Octavia Hill: A Biography* (London: Constable, 1942), 102.

71. Philip S. Bagwell, *Outcast London: A Christian Response* (London: Epworth Press, 1987), 26.

72. The classic statement on religion and domestic life is Leonore Davidoff and Catherine Hall's *Family Fortunes,* rev. ed. (London: Routledge, 2002), esp. part 1. On the domestic religious responsibilities of middle-class fathers between about 1830 and 1880, see John Tosh, *A Man's Place: Masculinity and the Middle-Class Home in Victorian England* (New Haven, CT: Yale University Press, 1999), 34–39, 146–50.

73. Richard J. Helmstadter, "The Nonconformist Conscience," in *Religion in Victorian Britain,* vol. 4: *Interpretations,* ed. Gerald Parsons (Manchester: Manchester University Press, 1988), 85. An excellent study of Price Hughes's theology and of the West London Mission he headed is Christopher Oldstone-Moore, *Hugh Price Hughes: Founder of a New Methodism, Conscience of a New Nonconformity* (Cardiff: University of Wales Press, 1988).

74. Helmstadter, "Nonconformist Conscience," 89–91.

75. The quotation is from Leonore Davidoff, "The Origin of the Species," *Avenue Magazine,* September 1989, 72–75; see also *The Best Circles.* Dorice Williams Elliott, in *The Angel Out of the House: Philanthropy and Gender in Nineteenth-Century England* (Charlottesville: University Press of Virginia, 2002, 7–10), argues that novels in particular did a great deal of the "cultural work" of constructing imaginary worlds in which women functioned in the public as well as the domestic realm. Such novels date from as early as the middle of the eighteenth century. "The Revolt of the Daughters" was the title of an 1894 article in *The Nineteenth Century,* a major periodical. The author, Blanche Alethea Crackanthorpe, defended the rights of unmarried daughters to professional training and unchaperoned movement outside the home. See the discussion of this "revolt" in David Rubinstein, *Before the Suffragettes: Women's Emancipation in the 1890s* (New York: St. Martin's Press, 1986), chap. 2.

76. Sybil Oldfield, *Spinsters of the Parish: The Life and Times of F. M. Mayor and Mary Sheepshanks* (London: Virago, 1984), 43.

77. Ibid., 53–54. Alice attended lectures and painting classes at the Slade until the sarcasm of a teacher drove her away. In 1896 she tried volunteering at the Women's University Settlement but did not like it at all: "The children are rather revolting I think on the whole," she wrote to her sister (53).

78. See Janet Oppenheim, "A Mother's Role, a Daughter's Duty: Lady Blanche Balfour, Eleanor Sidgwick, and Feminist Perspectives," *Journal of British Studies* 34 (April 1995): 196–232; Craik is quoted in Elliott, *Angel Out of the House,* 162. Nightingale wrote the book of which "Cassandra" was a part in 1852 when she was thirty-two, and had it printed privately in 1859. "Cassandra" is published as an appendix to Ray Strachey's *"The Cause": A Short History of the Women's Movement in Great Britain* (1928; reprint, Port Washington, NY: Kennikat Press, n.d.), 403.

79. Quoted in Jane Lewis, *Women and Social Action in Victorian and Edwardian England* (Stanford, CA: Stanford University Press, 1991), 86.

80. Letter from Kate Amberley (ten years younger than Maude) to Maude Stanley, November 24, 1864, in Cheshire and Chester Archives and Local Studies Library, DSA 175/1 (1860–65). The nature of the family crisis is partially revealed in a group of letters written to Maude Stanley by her mother in 1869–1870 (DSA 173).

81. Darley, *Octavia Hill,* 215.

82. Barbara Caine, *Destined to Be Wives: The Sisters of Beatrice Webb* (Oxford: Clarendon Press, 1986), 59–60.

83. Based on my reading of Stella Hills (Duckworth), Holograph Diary, 1896, Berg Collection, New York Public Library; also Lee, *Virginia Woolf,* 119–23. Lee's point about *The Years* is on 119. Jane Marcus presents Virginia's aunt Caroline Stephen rather than Stella Duckworth as a model for Eleanor Pargiter in her "The Niece of a Nun: Virginia Woolf, Caroline Stephen, and the Cloistered Imagination," in *Virginia Woolf: A Feminist Slant,* ed. Jane Marcus (Lincoln: University of Nebraska Press, 1983), 14.

84. Diary of Dorothy Ward for 1903, Ward Family Papers, As. Add.202, University College London Special Collections.

85. A Parson, *My District Visitors* (London: Skeffington, 1891), chap. 3.

86. Revel Guest and Angela V. John, *Lady Charlotte: A Biography of the Nineteenth Century* (London: Weidenfeld and Nicolson, 1989), 242, 246. Lady Charlotte's children were recruited into philanthropic causes; most of them continued their work in adulthood. On her attentiveness toward the cabmen, see the Earl of Bessborough, *Lady Charlotte Schrieber: Extracts from Her Journal 1853–1891* (London: John Murray, 1952), 189–90, 193–94, 198, 200.

87. Edna Healy, *Lady Unknown: The Life of Angela Burdett-Coutts* (London: Sidgwick and Jackson, 1975), 17, 55, 77, 164–65.

88. Nord, *Walking the Victorian Streets,* 210–11.

89. Ibid.

90. In a thought-provoking formulation I would nonetheless challenge, Carolyn Steedman shows how London's slum "cellars, attics and greasy lodging houses" helped New Women—in fiction and in reality—to formulate "a new story of themselves." Steedman contrasts what she defines as the "bourgeois" (sentimental and self-oriented) meaning of slum exploration for most of them with Eleanor Marx's focused political agenda. But significant numbers of Marx's peers had political agendas similar to hers; there were many

socialists and labor activists among them. And as you will see in the materials that follow, many were as vigorous and efficient as Marx, devoting years of their lives to this work. Eleanor Marx's truncated life, of course, makes it impossible for us to chart her future course as a political activist. Marx was, moreover, part of a female community that included some with "bourgeois" orientations. See Steedman, "Fictions of Engagement: Eleanor Marx, Biographical Space," in *Eleanor Marx (1855–1898): Life, Work, Contacts,* ed. John Stokes (Aldershot, England: Ashgate, 2000), esp. 34–35.

91. Ward, *Marcella,* 336.

92. Cited in David Rubinstein, *Before the Suffragettes: Women's Emancipation in the 1890s* (New York: St. Martin's Press, 1986), 37, n. 47. Another woman referred in her later memoir to her own "Marcella period" in the 1890s when she ran a London club for working girls (33).

93. On the writing of *Marcella* see John Sutherland's *Mrs. Humphry Ward: Eminent Victorian, Pre-eminent Edwardian* (Oxford: Clarendon Press, 1990), 140–49.

94. Ward, *Marcella,* 336–38, 351, 365.

95. *Sir George Tressady,* 7, 86–93.

96. James Buzard, *The Beaten Track: European Tourism, Literature, and the Ways to "Culture" 1800–1918* (Oxford: Clarendon Press, 1993), 1–11.

97. Vicinus, *Independent Women,* 220.

98. Vida Scudder, *On Journey* (New York: E. P. Dutton, 1938), 139–40, quoted in Ruth Crocker, "Unsettling Perspectives: The Settlement Movement, the Rhetoric of Social History, and the Search for Synthesis," in *Contesting the Master Narrative,* ed. Jeffrey Cox and Shelton Stromquist (Iowa City: University of Iowa Press, 1998), 175–209; 178.

99. "Miss Clara Grant," *Somerset Standard,* 1927, clipping in THLHL, Clara Grant file; also "Clara Grant Memorial Number," *All Hallows' Bromley-by-Bow, Church Monthly,* November 1949.

100. *Mansfield House Magazine* 14 (October 1907): 193; Canning Town Women's Settlement, *Executive Committee Minutes,* June 1904–February 1906; June 22, 1904, and April 12, 1905, Newham Record Office, London.

101. See, especially, Twells, "'Happy English Children.'" On women's efforts to define themselves as missionaries see Clare Midgley, "Can Women Be Missionaries? Envisioning Female Agency in the Early Nineteenth-Century British Empire," *Journal of British Studies* 45 (April 2006): 335–58.

102. Thorne, *Congregational Missions,* 17–22; Cox, *Imperial Fault Lines,* 153.

103. Cox, *Imperial Fault Lines,* 105.

104. See Ranyard entry in the DNB, 47; also Donald Lewis, *Lighten Their Darkness,* 221–22. As evidence of the influence of native agency on Ranyard, Lewis cites Ranyard herself (*True Institution of Sisterhood* [1862], 8). Also Peter Williams, "'The Missing Link': The Recruitment of Women Missionaries in Some English Evangelical Missionaries Societies in the Nineteenth Century," in *Women and Missions: Past and Present,* ed. Fiona Bowie, Deborah Kirkwood, and Shirley Ardener (Oxford: Berg Publishers, 1993), 47–48.

105. Jonathan Schneer, *London 1900: An Imperial Metropolis* (New Haven, CT: Yale University Press, 1999), 140–41.

106. Hird, *H. M. Stanley: The Authorized Life* (London: Stanley Paul, 1935), and John Bierman, *Dark Safari: The Life behind the Legend of Henry Morton Stanley* (London: Hodder and

Stoughton, 1990). Stanley also figures prominently, and looks very different, in Adam Hochschild's *King Leopold's Ghost* (Boston: Houghton Mifflin, 1999). His bride must have known nothing of his ruthlessness and cruelty as an employer of African labor, nor of the routinized genocide that was the hallmark of the colony he was instrumental in creating for the Belgian king.

107. Edward Said, *Culture and Imperialism* (New York: Vintage Books, 1993), xiii.

"A Lady Resident"

THIS APPEALING ACCOUNT APPEARED in the first edition, titled *East London*, of Charles Booth's *Life and Labour* in 1889. By "buildings" the author is referring to what Americans would call apartment buildings—a new form of housing in London where few dwellings were over four stories high.[1] The "T. Buildings" is not the block of buildings that Beatrice Potter mentioned in her *Pall Mall Gazette* article of February 18, 1886, "A Lady's View on the Unemployed in the East," and I have been unable to go beyond the Booth piece's pseudonym.[2] Some possible candidates, all of whom lived for at least a time in model dwellings in East London, are Margaret and Henry Nevinson, Margaret Harkness, Constance Black (Clementina's sister), and Ella Pycroft. The historian Rosemary O'Day, an expert on the Katharine Buildings—a set of model dwellings in East Smithfield—has tentatively nominated Margaret Harkness, who lived in the Katharine Buildings for a time and had a tendency to disguise her identity.[3] My guess is Margaret Nevinson, who, with a small baby to care for, was probably at home more than the others (see chapter 15).

NOTES

1. Charles Booth, *Labour and Life of the People in London,* vol. 1, *East London* (London: Williams and Norgate, 1889). The first volume in what would eventually be a seventeen-volume series, it was published separately in 1889.
2. Beatrice Potter, "A Lady's View on the Unemployed in the East," *Pall Mall Gazette,* February 18, 1886, 11.
3. Personal communication, August 4, 1999; see also Rosemary O'Day, "How Families

---

"Sketch of Life in Buildings," in Charles Booth, Life and Labour of the People in London, *First Series:* Poverty, *revised ed., vol. 3 (London: Macmillan and Company, 1902), 37–44. "A Lady Resident" was listed as the author.

Lived Then: Katharine Buildings, E. Smithfield, 1885–1890," in *Sources and Methods for Family and Community Historians: A Handbook,* vol.1, *From Family Tree to Family History,* ed. Michael Drake and Ruth Finnegan (Milton Keynes, England: Open University Press, 1994), 129–66. David Garnett, whose mother was Constance Black, points out that his parents lived in the College Buildings, East London, before their first child was born. See *The Golden Echo* (London: Chatto and Windus, 1954), 10.

Sketch of Life in Buildings

Life in "Buildings," we may say, depends more on the class of inhabitants than on structural arrangements. It is curious, on the principle of "like to like," how quickly a Building forms for itself a certain character—Jews' Buildings, rowdy Buildings, genteel Buildings, &c., all being estimated as such by public opinion. And public criticism, it may be added, resting on strong prejudices, may be trusted to define sharply and to perpetuate the distinctions between the tenants of different Buildings. Racial prejudices keep the Christians apart from the Jews, and a taste for cleanliness or for quietness determines folk who can afford to indulge it to spend a little more on rent for the sake of mixing with those who are "particular," and who "keep themselves to themselves."

T. Buildings, where I lived for a year, is a pretty red brick building, with five storeys of tenements, two sides of a square, and enclosing a good-sized asphalted court. My dwelling consisted of two tiny rooms, about 9 ft. square, opening into one another. The front door, with its separate number and knocker, opens out of the front room into a common open balcony; and the back door out of the back room into a tiny private balcony, about a yard or so square, leading to the sink, *&c.* These little balconies are often turned to good account with flower boxes and hanging baskets, and one woman had rigged up a pigeon-house, and kept pigeons very successfully there. Each tenement is complete in itself, except for the want of a tap; to fetch water the tenants have to take their buckets to a common tap on each balcony. Though so small, the rooms are fresh and very clean, brightly coloured and painted once every year. The asphalted court provides a large and safe playground for the children, and the flat roof is utilized for wash-houses and a drying ground. Each tenant is bound in turn to clean and whiten a part of the balcony and stairs, and each in turn on her fixed day enjoys the use of a wash-house and the roof to dry her clothes. These common rights and duties lead, of course, to endless contention. (I may quote the remark of a neighbour on the ferocity of the combatants in a washing-day dispute: "Why, they'd tear you to pieces; bull-dogs I call 'em.") In the summer, T. Buildings was very pretty, with its red bricks and white stairs and balconies and flowers in most of the windows.

S. Buildings, in which I also lived for nearly a year, was on a much larger scale, and the rents were higher. The tenants were of the most varied description. The Buildings were in the form of a quadrangle, enclosing a very large asphalted square; a few miserable shrubs flourished, or rather decayed, in the centre. The various tenements opened on steep ill-lighted staircases and dark narrow corridors; the rooms inside were a great improvement on those in T. Buildings, large and well-fitted with every convenience; but in spite of advantages in this respect, S. Buildings could not compare with my former quarters. I am convinced that nothing is of more importance to the inhabitants of towns than light and colour; T. Buildings is built to admit as much air and sunshine as possible; S. Buildings to exclude them; and I think the great difference I noticed in the cheerfulness and temper of the children must have been largely due to this cause.

The very large number of tenements (200 to 300) destroyed the feeling of neighbourly responsibility and interest which was strong in T. Buildings; and the narrow resounding passages and stairs made domestic disputes and crying children more disagreeably prominent.

The character of a Building is also largely influenced by the character of the caretaker in charge, and in this respect S. Buildings was unlucky. If indifferent order is kept, and the few regulations are not enforced, the convenience of the majority has to give way to the small element in every community who are entitled to the name of public nuisances.

A short sketch of an average day in T. Buildings will give some idea of the way of life.

At 5 o'clock in the morning I hear the tenant overhead. Mr. A., getting up for his day's work. His wife, who does a little dressmaking when she can get it from her neighbours, was up late last night (I heard her sewing-machine going till 1 o'clock), so he does not disturb her. He is a carman at the Goods Depôt of a Railway Company, and has to be there at 6 o'clock, so he is not long getting his breakfast of tea and bread and butter. But before he has done, I hear a child cry; then the sound of a sleepy voice, Mrs. A., recommending a sip of tea and a crust for the baby. The man, I suppose, carries out the order, for the crying ceases, and I hear his steps as he goes downstairs. At eight o'clock there is a good deal of scraping and raking on the other side of the wall. This means that my neighbour, Mrs. B., an old woman partly supported by her dead husband's savings, partly by the earnings of two grown-up daughters, is raking out and cleaning her stove. Then the door is opened, the dust is thrown down the dust-shoot, and a conversation is very audibly carried on by two female voices. Among other topics, is the favourite one of Mrs. A.'s laziness in the morning—though Mrs. B. knows perfectly well that Mrs. A. has been up late at work, having indeed repeatedly complained of the noise of the sewing-machine at night, and though Mrs. C. openly avows that she will not say anything against Mrs. A., as she has always been very nice to her.

At half-past eight I hear the eldest child of the A. family lighting the fire and dressing her two little brothers for school. With the departure of the children there is a lull. At ten Mrs. A. gets up, and at eleven she sallies out to make sundry purchases. Before she goes, however, Mrs. A. has a brisk gossip on her threshold with Mrs. C., the tram-conductor's wife, who has looked in to return the head of a loaf borrowed on the previous Sunday night. In the dialogue, which lasts more than five minutes, I hear Mrs. B's name repeated a good many times, and catch also the phrase "spiteful old cat," and I believe that Mrs. B.'s remarks at 8 o'clock are being now repeated with Mrs. C.'s artistic variations.

Soon after twelve there is a great hubbub of children's laughter and shrieking in the courtyard under my window. The children have returned from school and they seem to have a good deal of fun together till we begin to hear the mothers calling them in to dinner.

In the afternoon a certain torpor falls upon the Buildings, only broken by the jingling cans and cat-calls of the afternoon milk-boys. But this is the favourite time for the women to call upon one another, and I can catch various fragments of conversation relating to the bad turn Mrs. D.'s illness is taking, to the uncalled-for visit of the curate to a lady who dislikes curates, to the shocking temper of little Maggie (Mrs. C.'s child), who is reported to be the tease and torment of all the children in the place. Looking out of window I do not see the unhappy Maggie, but find myself watching instead a spirited game of cricket between four girls on one side and three boys on the other. The wickets are chalked up against the wall and a soft ball is used. The game, however, collapses, for the boys, who are smaller than their opponents, refuse to go on, saying "it isn't fair," and the girls retire triumphant, but disgusted.

At 6 o'clock a row in the street calls a crowd of the inhabitants out on to the balconies, where we can look down exactly as from boxes in a theatre on to the stage. The parties to the quarrel are a man and his wife in a distinctly lower walk of life (like all the inhabitants of houses in the street) than any of the tenants of the Buildings. They are eventually separated after much "old English" on both sides.

The general impression among the spectators is in favour of the man, but the incident is soon forgotten.

Very soon after, various savoury smells begin to float out on to the landings. The favourite meal of the day, the "tea," is being prepared against the husband's return. All is comparative peace and harmony, the children's hands are washed, the room is tidied, and the cloth laid. The A.'s have sprats, as I have good reason to know. Mrs. A. is aware of my partiality for this fish, and in a neighbourly spirit sends me in a plateful by her most careful child, from whom I learn that Mrs. D. is much worse and wandering in her head, and that "mother is going to sit up with her." Mrs. D.'s husband is a night watchman, so he is at hand by day to look after her, and the neighbours are taking turns to nurse her at night.

In the evening some of the men go out to the neighbouring "Club" and sing songs or talk politics, one or two drop into the bar of the favourite "pub," but the majority simply stay at home with the wife and children. Mr. A., the carman, is essentially a family man, and he makes a point of going through some gymnastic tricks with his boys and putting them to bed. Occasionally he receives a visit from a mate, but this is rare; and generally he retires not later than 9.30. Mr. C., the tram-conductor, has a liking for the *Star,* and reads aloud striking passages after tea.

A not unfrequent incident in S. Buildings about midnight or later would not have been tolerated in T. Buildings. A man there on several occasions went to bed and locked out his wife, who returned home doubtfully sober. To her repeated knocks and entreaties, he maintained a sullen silence; then exasperated she thumped and kicked at the door, screaming, and rejoiced when a sarcasm at last evoked a reply. The whole side of the Building must have been awakened, but nobody made the least sign; it was not etiquette. In T. Buildings the quarrelling was more decent; such disturbances would lead to general complaints of the offenders, and they would soon be expelled.

The advantages of living in Buildings in my opinion far outweigh the drawbacks. Cheapness, a higher standard of cleanliness, healthy sanitary arrangements, neighbourly intercourse both between children and between the grownup people, and, perhaps above all, the impossibility of being overlooked altogether, or flagrantly neglected by relatives in illness or old age, seem to be the great gains; and the chief disadvantage, the absence of privacy and the increased facility for gossip and quarrelling, though it may sometimes be disagreeably felt, introduces a constant variety of petty interest and personal feeling into the monotony of daily life.

Annie (Wood) Besant

BEFORE HER FINAL CONVERSION TO THEOSOPHY in 1891, Annie (Wood) Besant (1847–1933) went through a series of dramatic political and philosophical transformations. Later in her life, she explained this succession of passions as different aspects of a "longing for sacrifice to something felt as greater than the self," "a tendency," she said, "brought over from a previous life."[1]

She was born Annie Wood in Clapham, London. (The first full paragraph of her autobiography is a horoscope showing the position of the planets at the moment of her birth, 5:30 P.M.) Annie Wood was the daughter of a brilliant, scholarly, and apparently comfortably off doctor who died of consumption when she was only five. A skeptic, he angrily refused a priest at his deathbed. Annie's affectionate mother, left with little income, supported her two children by running a boarding house for boys at Harrow, the public school Annie's brother attended. Annie herself was educated by a family friend, well-off Evangelical Christian Ellen Marryat, whose brother was the noted adventure writer. Ellen Marryat was a gifted teacher who ensured that her young charge got a thorough education and learned to think for herself.[2]

As a child, Besant was religiously earnest and intellectually precocious. *Pilgrim's Progress, Paradise Lost,* and tales of early Christian martyrs were her favorite childhood reading. When she was nineteen she met the Rev. Frank Besant (brother of Walter, the novelist) and married him the next year, ending her "girlish freedom" for good.[3] This marriage, an immediate disaster, was Annie Besant's awakening to the legal and social disabilities of women:

Originally published as "White Slavery in London," in The Link, *June 23, 1888, 2.*

Frank Besant was rigid, authoritarian, and, it appears, violent. Annie Besant's next ordeal, in 1871, was the weeks-long, nearly fatal illness of her second child, a daughter, after which the young mother had a breakdown and, on her recovery, rejected a God who had brought so much pain to her and those around her. She eventually separated from her husband, who had won custody of their daughter in 1879 by citing his wife's heterodox views in court. (Their son had already gone to live with Frank Besant; both children were reconciled with their mother when they were teenagers and remained close to her.) So began Besant's search for a way to help others. "Robbed of my own [children], I would be a mother to all helpless children I could aid, and cure the pain at my own heart by soothing the pain of others."[4]

Besant was a natural public speaker whose voice expressed "a beautiful soul," as Beatrice Webb put it; she was "the greatest orator in England, and possibly in Europe," wrote George Bernard Shaw.[5] British political life in the 1870s and 1880s would have been much poorer without her eloquence and her exceptional energy. The first of the movements with which she became involved was secularism, a humanistic philosophy that self-consciously and in careful detail rejected Christian doctrine. She met and formed a close friendship with Charles Bradlaugh, president of the National Secular Society. By the mid-1870s, Annie had begun working with him on his journal, *The National Reformer,* while also serving as a tireless speaker for the cause of secularism. In their now famous 1876 test case, she and Bradlaugh reprinted an old American book advocating birth control, a secularist cause, and were prosecuted for publishing an "obscene" book. Ironically, the heavy publicity surrounding the trial enormously advanced the cause of birth control. Besant published her own book on birth control in 1877, which sold phenomenally well. She worked with Bradlaugh on the *National Reformer* until 1887.

By the mid-1880s, through friendships—or possibly romances—with philandering socialist activist and author Edward Aveling (who dropped her to move in with Eleanor Marx in 1883) and George Bernard Shaw, Besant became a socialist. She and another male associate, the crusading journalist William T. Stead, formed the Law and Liberty League after the November 13, 1887, "Bloody Sunday" police charge on a workers' demonstration in and around Trafalgar Square. Three hundred people were arrested; the league provided bail money. Annie also staged a dramatic and celebrity-studded funeral for Alfred Linnell, a demonstrator who died as a result of injuries at another Trafalgar Square demonstration the following Sunday.[6]

Annie Besant found her next cause in June 1888, at a Fabian Society lecture by Clementina Black that generated a discussion of the labor practices of Bryant and May, a major match manufacturer, which had a sprawling factory in Bow, East London. The firm was already controversial because of a local clergyman's public exposure of the low wages and dangerous working conditions it offered to its mainly young and female workers. Besant quickly published the article included here. When the girls, well over a thousand of them, went on strike in July, Besant burst into action, organizing a boycott of Bryant and May and raising funds to sustain the strikers. The women formed a union, which eventually settled with Bryant and May.[7] The next year Besant ran for and won a position on the School Board for London, where she served energetically from 1889 to 1891. Though dominated by political conservatives, the SBL agreed to pay union wages in all its contracts, supported a resolution to abolish school fees, and carried out an investigation into the need for more meals for schoolchildren.

Besant had been active for fifteen years in different branches of British radicalism, yet within a few weeks of meeting the leading Theosophist Madame Helena P. Blavatsky, she announced her conversion and began to dissolve her formal political ties. Blavatsky died in 1891, and Besant herself became a leader in Theosophy and was president of the Theosophical Society from 1907 until her death. She moved to India in the early 1890s and there set out to strengthen Theosophy's Hindu elements. On her many return trips to England, though, she gave speeches supporting women's suffrage and demonstrated her sympathy for the Labour Party. She led the Theosophist contingent at the June 1911 Women's Coronation Procession, and Theosophy in England was, as Joy Dixon points out, long associated with "progressive politics broadly defined."[8]

Not surprisingly, decades of life in India made Besant an avid supporter of Indian independence and, as one of her biographers, David Rubinstein, puts it, she was "the dominant figure in Indian nationalism during the First World War." She was interned by the British in 1917 along with many other Indian nationalists, and elected President of the Indian National Congress in 1918. Through her English friends, she agitated for Dominion status for India throughout the 1920s. Gandhi and Nehru both acknowledged their debt to her.

Besant's article is the first of many in this book to talk about money: prices, wages, rent, and so on. The complicated nondecimal monetary system in use at the time of these writings is explained in the preface.

NOTES

1. Besant, *Annie Besant,* 43.
2. Ibid., 2, 14–15, 24, 29–34.
3. Ibid., 49.
4. Ibid., 195.
5. Quoted in Taylor, *Annie Besant,* 55; Rubinstein in the DLB, 22.
6. Both incidents are recounted in detail by Taylor in *Annie Besant,* 192–96 and 206.
7. The monument to which the employees were required to contribute is probably the ornate thirty-foot fountain erected by Bryant and May in 1872 when a proposed tax on matches was defeated in Parliament.
8. Dixon, *Divine Feminine,* 5.

White Slavery in London

At a meeting of the Fabian Society held on June 5th, the following resolution was moved by H. H. Champion, seconded by Herbert Barrows, and carried *nem. con.* after a brief discussion:

"That this meeting, being aware that the shareholders of Bryant and May are receiving a dividend of over 20 per cent., and at the same time are paying their workers only 2½ d. per gross for making match-boxes, pledges itself not to use or purchase any matches made by this firm."

In consequence of some statements made in course of the discussion, I resolved to personally investigate their accuracy, and accordingly betook myself to Bromley to interview some of Bryant and May's employees, and thus obtain information at first hand. The following is the outcome of my enquiries:

Bryant and May, now a limited liability company, paid last year a dividend of 23 per cent. to its shareholders; two years ago it paid a dividend of 25 per cent., and the original £5 shares were then quoted for sale at £18 7s. 6d. The highest dividend paid has been 38 per cent.

Let us see how the money is made with which these monstrous dividends are paid. [The figures quoted were all taken down by myself, in the presence of three witnesses, from persons who had themselves been in the prison-house whose secrets they disclosed.]

Figure 4. Members of the Matchmakers' Union, from *Annie Besant: An Autobiography* (London: T. Fisher Unwin, 1893). The young women, on strike, are not trying to please the photographer but to demonstrate their resolve.

The hour for commencing work is 6.30 in summer and 8 in winter; work concludes at 6 p.m. Half-an-hour is allowed for breakfast and an hour for dinner. This long day of work is performed by young girls, who have to stand the whole of the time. A typical case is that of a girl of 16, a piece-worker; she earns 4s. a week, and lives with a sister, employed by the same firm, who "earns good money, as much as 8s. or 9s. per week". Out of the earnings 2s. is paid for the rent of one room; the child lives on only bread-and-butter and tea, alike for breakfast and dinner, but related with danc-ing eyes that once a month she went to a meal where "you get coffee, and bread and butter, and jam, and marmalade, and lots of it"; now and then she goes to the Paragon, someone "stands treat, you know", and that appeared to be the solitary bit of color in her life. The splendid salary of 4s. is subject to deductions in the shape of fines; if the feet are dirty, or the ground under the bench is left untidy, a fine of 3d. is inflicted; for putting "burnts"—matches that have caught fire during the work—on the bench 1s. has been forfeited, and one unhappy girl was once fined 2s. 6d. for some unknown crime. If a girl leaves four or five matches on her bench when she goes for a fresh "frame" she is fined 3d., and in some departments a fine of 3d. is inflicted for talking. If a girl is late she is shut out for "half the day", that is for the morning six hours, and 4d. is deducted from her day's 8d. One girl was fined 1s. for letting the web twist round a machine in the endeavor to save her fingers from being cut, and was sharply told to take care of the machine, "never mind your fingers". Another, who carried out the instructions and lost a finger thereby, was left unsupported while she was helpless. The wage covers the duty of submitting to an occasional blow from a foreman; one, who appears to be a gentleman of variable temper, "clouts" them "when he is mad".

One department of the work consists in taking matches out of a frame and putting them into boxes; about three frames can be done in a hour, and ½d. is paid for each frame emptied; only one frame is given out at a time, and the girls have to run downstairs and upstairs each time to fetch the frame, thus much increasing their fatigue. One of the delights of the frame work is the accidental firing of the matches: when this happens the worker loses the work, and if the frame is injured she is fined or "sacked". 5s. a week has been earned at this by one girl I talked to.

The "fillers" get ¾d. a gross for filling boxes; at "boxing," *i.e.* wrapping papers around the boxes, they can earn from 6d. to 5s. a week. A very rapid "filler" has been known to earn once "as much as 9s." in a week, and 6s. a week "sometimes". The making of boxes is not done in the factory; for these 2¼d. a gross is paid to people who work in their own homes, and "find your own paste". Daywork is a little better paid than piecework, and is done chiefly by married women, who earn as much sometimes as 10s. a week, the piecework falling to the girls. Four women, dayworkers, spoken of with reverent awe, earn—13s. week.

A very bitter memory survives in the factory. Mr. Theodore Bryant, to show his admiration of Mr. Gladstone and the greatness of his own public spirit, bethought him to erect a statue to that eminent statesman. In order that his workgirls might have the privilege of contributing, he stopped 1s. each out of their wages, and further deprived them of half-a-day's work by closing the factory, "giving them a holiday". ("We don't want no holidays", said one of the girls pathetically, for—needless to say—the poorer employees of such a firm lose their wages when a holiday is "given".) So furious were the girls at this cruel plundering, that many went to the unveiling of the statue with stones and bricks in their pockets, and I was conscious of a wish that some of those bricks had made an impression on Mr. Bryant's—conscience. Later on they surrounded the statue—"we paid for it" they cried savagely—shouting and yelling, and a gruesome story is told that some cut their arms and let their blood trickle on the marble paid for, in very truth, by their blood. There seems to be a curious feeling that the nominal wages are 1s. higher than the money paid, but that 1s. a week is still kept back to pay for the statue and for a fountain erected by the same Mr. Bryant. This, however, appears to me to be only the nature of opinion.

Such is a bald account of one form of white slavery as it exists in London. With chattel slaves Mr. Bryant could not have made his huge fortune, for he could not have fed, clothed, and housed them for 4s. a week each, and they would have had a definite money value which would have served as a protection. But who cares for the fate of these white wage slaves? Born in slums, driven to work while still children, undersized because underfed, oppressed because helpless, flung aside as soon as worked out, who cares if they die or go on the streets, provided only that the Bryant and May shareholders get their 23 per cent., and Mr. Theodore Bryant can erect statues and buy parks? Oh if we had but a people's Dante, to make a special circle in the Inferno for those who live on this misery, and suck wealth out of the starvation of helpless girls.

Failing a poet to hold up their conduct to the execration of posterity, enshrined in deathless verse, let us strive to touch their consciences, *i.e.* their pockets, and let us at least avoid being "partakers of their sins", by abstaining from using their commodities.

Clementina Black and
Adele (Lady Carl) Meyer

CLEMENTINA BLACK (1854–1922) began her writing career as a novelist. At the age of twenty-three, still at home in Brighton caring for her sick father and two of her eight siblings, she wrote *A Sussex Idyll.* She went on to write at least half a dozen more novels of middle-class manners, the most successful of which, *The Linleys of Bath* (1911), was published in three different editions. Only one of her novels (*The Agitator* [1894], apparently now lost) dealt with the themes of her extensive social investigation into industrial workers' homes, wages, and working conditions.

Clementina Black was the daughter of David Black, a Brighton solicitor and town clerk. He was English but had been born in Russia. David Black had traveled extensively in Europe and North America before returning to England and marrying the sophisticated daughter of a court portrait painter. Clementina was the eldest girl in a group of remarkably brilliant and talented siblings. Possibly through a local school, and definitely with the help of her mother and brothers, Clementina was well educated in languages, geography, literature, and probably mathematics.

In the early 1880s Black moved to London and eventually lived with two younger sisters, Emma and Grace. Constance, another sister, was at Newnham College, Cambridge, and joined them in London in 1884. Constance is probably the best known of the Black sisters; under her married name, Garnett, she became a world-famous translator of Russian novels. Clementina

---

Originally published in Makers of Our Clothes: a case for trade boards. Being the results of a year's investigation into the work of women in London in the tailoring, dressmaking, and underclothing trades *(London: Duckworth and Co., 1909), selections from the introduction, 2–7, 10–14, and 16–18.*

supported herself in London by doing translations and research and by writing fiction. In the early eighties she found new contacts among women social explorers. The poet Amy Levy became a close friend, and so did Eleanor Marx, with whom she spent time exploring East London.[1] Black's "deceptively fragile and refined appearance belied her dedication and untiring industry," as a recent biographer has put it. She joined many organizations concerned with the welfare of working-class women, including the Women's Trade Union Association, and later, in 1907, the Women's Labour League (WLL). When the Women's Trade Union Association foundered and merged with the recently established Women's Industrial Council (WIC) in 1897, she became president of that organization. In this capacity she helped to orchestrate and sustain a campaign to regulate wages in "sweated" (very low-wage) industries.[2] She was on the executive board of the Anti-Sweating League, founded in 1906, as was Adele Meyer—which is probably where they met.

From 1906 on, Black was also a suffragist; she was a member of the executive committee of the National Union of Women's Suffrage Societies (NUWSS), serving as its vice president and editor of its journal, *The Common Cause*. She also wrote, in 1918, *A New Way of Housekeeping*, a plea for cooperative housekeeping, an issue that continued to interest her until her death.

Born in Belsize Park, London, philanthropist Adele (Lady Carl) Meyer (1855–1930),[3] née Levis, was described by Henry Adams as "a sprightly Jewess."[4] She was a society hostess, opera patron, and art collector. Meyer referred to herself in 1910, however, as "a humble social worker" with a lot of experience visiting "homes of the slum-dwellers in our large and small towns."[5] In 1883 she married wealthy international banker Carl Meyer, a German-born naturalized British subject who received a title of nobility in 1910.[6] The society painter John Singer Sargent did a portrait of Adele and her children in 1896 that was selected as the most notable work in the Royal Academy exhibit the next year. Sargent's canvas emphasizes the opulence of the Meyers' surroundings as well as Adele's liveliness and intelligence. Several prominent male viewers, Henry James for one, repellently placed the work within the genre of "portrait-painting of Jewesses and their children."[7]

But Lady Meyer was also a suffragist and leader in social work. Until 1928 she served as a benefactor as well as vice chairman[8] of the St. Pancras School for Mothers, an innovative baby clinic and community center. Meyer founded a similar health center near her estate in Newport, Essex. She was also, with Black, a member and officer of the Anti-Sweating

League, and it was Meyer who offered to subsidize the study of women's home manufacturing that would lead to *Makers of Our Clothes.*[9] In addition, Meyer served at least one term as president of the Care Committee Guild, an umbrella group representing the thousands of volunteers who worked with schoolchildren in London's poorest districts. Later in her life she was active in founding Queen Mary's Hostel for Women, now Queen Mary College.[10]

Adele Meyer was a constitutional suffragist and popular speaker at suffrage events and fund-raisers. She was also, along with Margaret Nevinson, an early and active member of a more militant suffrage organization, the Women's Tax Resistance League (WTRL). Such leagues appeared all over the country and were loosely federated. Members publicly protested their disenfranchisement by refusing to pay minor taxes—such as the "inhabited house duty"—and daring officials to impound some of their property by force.[11] The public auctions of their belongings were theatrical occasions on which the members demonstrated their contempt for the government.

Since the late 1890s, the WIC had focused on married women who did manufacturing in their homes—usually for employers who supplied them with materials and specifications. Their investigations convinced the WIC that the real problem with married women's work was not, as the dominant view would have it, neglected children, but rather rates of pay so low that women were forced to work practically around the clock. There had been several investigations and graphic public displays, like the *Daily News* exhibition of the sufferings of sweated workers, since the 1890s. The national investigation whose mechanics and researchers are described in this selection was begun in 1908, sponsored jointly by the WIC and the Central Branch of the WLL, with Meyer's funding (mentioned just above). The investigators were WIC members and associates as well as helpful vicars' wives, women settlers, and church workers. The industries studied would be regulated by the Trade Boards Act of 1909, which outlined procedures for setting minimum wages in some industries.

Clementina Black's steadfast support for minimum-wage laws appears to have drawn opposition from some of the WIC's most important members, including Margaret and Ramsay MacDonald, Lily Montagu, and Margaret Bondfield. These opponents feared that such laws would institutionalize low pay in the industries where they were applied; they resigned from the organization, as did Adele Meyer. Black, however, remained with the WIC and became its president in 1911.[12]

NOTES

1. Yvonne Kapp, *Eleanor Marx* (New York: Pantheon Books, 1976), 1: 219–36; Glage, *Clementina Black,* 21–25.

2. Black's entry in the Oxford DNB, by Janet Grener. For more on the Women's Industrial Council, see note 1 in the biography of Edith Hogg, in this volume.

3. The dates for Lady Meyer were traced through the Jewish Historical Society of England's Web site (www.hsjc.org/Geneology.htm) to a site maintained by Alan Ehrlich, a descendent of Meyer's husband, Carl Meyer. There is an Oxford DNB entry for Lady Meyer as well, by Serena Kelly. My thanks to Henry Roche of the Royal Opera House for his help.

4. Quoted in Trevor Fairbrother, *John Singer Sargent* (New York: Abrams, 1994), 94.

5. Miss Bibby, Mills Colles, Miss Petty, and Dr. Sykes, *The Pudding Lady* (London: Stead's Publishing House, for the St. Pancras School for Mothers [1910]), 100–101.

6. He was director of the National Bank of Egypt and chairman of the London Committee of De Beers (*Who Was Who 1916–1928* [London: A. and C. Black, 1930]). He had connections with the Rothschilds as well (DNB).

7. Fairbrother, *John Singer Sargent,* 51. Sargent later commented that he enjoyed painting Jews, "as they have more life and movement than our English women." Quoted in Kathleen Adler, "John Singer Sargent's Portraits of the Wertheimer Family," in *John Singer Sargent: Portraits of the Wertheimer Family,* ed. Norman L. Kleeblatt (New York: The Jewish Museum, 1999), 32, n. 21.

8. "Schools for Mothers," *Women's Industrial News* 54 (April 1911): 70.

9. Black and Meyer, *Makers of Our Clothes,* 2.

10. *The School Child* 2, no. 3 (February 1912); Serena Kelly, Oxford DNB entry on Lady Meyer.

11. Examples of Lady Meyer's suffrage speaking: *The Suffragette,* February 14, 1913, 278; and *Votes for Women,* June 6, 1913, 530. Women's Tax Resistance League, Minute Book 1 (1909–1913), Women's Library, London. Meyer began attending meetings as of October 14, 1910. See also Laura E. N. Mayhall, *The Militant Suffrage Movement: Citizenship and Resistance in Britain, 1860–1930* (New York: Oxford University Press, 2003).

12. On the split and the issues that divided the members, see Ellen Mappen's introduction to *Married Women's Work,* esp. iv. On Lady Meyer's resignation: *Women's Industrial News,* October 1910, 54. See also Christine Collette, *For Labour and for Women: The Women's Labour League, 1906–1918* (Manchester: Manchester University Press, 1989), 46, 116–19; and Glage, *Clementina Black,* 51–52, 55, and 63–65.

FURTHER READING

Other than Kelly's Oxford DNB article and Sargent's portrait, there is frustratingly little information about Adele Meyer. The materials cited in the notes give us only glimpses into her interests and commitments. As for her writings beyond the book that is excerpted here: there is a colleague's report on a lecture Meyer gave on the St. Pancras School for Mothers and reported in the *Women's Industrial News,* no. 54, April 1911, 70–72; also "An Appreciation by Lady Meyer" at the conclusion of *The Pudding Lady,* 100–103. In it she remarks that those who blame poor wives for lack of energy or skill "should ask ourselves whether, given these physical, mental, and material disabilities, we should any of us do

better?" (102).The list of Clementina Black's publications is lengthy. A useful chrono-
logical list may be found in the only biography of Black, Liselotte Glage's *Clementina
Black: A Study in Social History and Literature* (Heidelberg: Carl Winter, 1981), 189–92.

Black's novels include *Orlando* (1887), *The Princess Desiree* (1896), *The Pursuit of Camilla*
(1899), and *Caroline* (1908). Her nonfiction writings include *Sweated Industry and the
Minimum Wage* (London: Duckworth, 1907), and *Married Women's Work,* edited and
introduced by Black, who also wrote the London section of the volume (1915; reprint,
London: Virago, 1983); the reprint contains an informative introduction by Ellen
Mappen.

Information about Black is included in the BDBF, vol. 2, and the Oxford DNB, but
not in the DLB. As a sister of Constance Garnett, Clementina Black gets some billing
in Carolyn Heilbrun, *The Garnett Family* (London: Allen and Unwin, 1961), and in her
nephew David Garnett's autobiography, *The Golden Echo* (London: Chatto and Windus,
1954–1962), esp. vol. 2.

FROM *Makers of Our Clothes*

This volume contains the results of an investigation made during the year
1908, into the conditions of women's work, in London, in the tailoring,
dressmaking and underclothing trades. Though collected primarily for a
special purpose, the facts are, it is believed, of some general interest.

During the years 1906, 1907 and 1908 the project of a legal minimum
wage, long advocated by some economists of the newer school, advanced
rapidly into the sphere of practical politics. The *Daily News* exhibition of
"sweated" goods and of underpaid workers, held in the summer of 1906,
was followed by the formation of the National Anti-Sweating League, an
association of which the sole aim is the establishment by law of a minimum
wage. In 1907 and again in 1908 a Bill for the creation in this country of
Wages Boards on the Australian model was discussed in the House of
Commons, and on the latter occasion was read a second time without a
division. A Special Commissioner was sent out by government to report
upon the effects of Colonial legislation and a Select Committee of the
House of Commons was appointed to inquire into the conditions of Home
Work.

By many persons of experience, and especially by the executive of the
Anti-Sweating League, it was felt to be eminently desirable that detailed
information should be collected about the trades in which Wages Boards
seemed likely to be first instituted, *i.e.,* tailoring, dressmaking and the

making of underclothing. Early in 1908 one of the authors of this book offered to pay the expenses of such an inquiry; the work of investigation was begun on January 20, under the guidance of a small subcommittee, and the results are here presented.

Before proceeding to accounts of the trades and of their various departments, it may be as well to give some notion of the manner in which an inquiry of this kind is carried out. We began by drafting two sets of questions, together with a few hints to investigators. . . . Our method, we had decided, should be mainly that of personal interviews with both employers and workers, and our visits to workers should come earliest. The first step, therefore, was to obtain the addresses of a number of women working in the three trades, a task in which no directory affords assistance. Such addresses can be procured only from the small group of devoted people who live or work in industrial districts: local clergy, of all denominations, organisers of girls' clubs, Settlements, branches of the Women's Co-operative Guild, officials of women's trade unions, &c. These busy and widely scattered persons it was advisable to see, experience teaching very clearly how comparatively feeble is the appeal of pen and ink. Perhaps the history of one hot day when four of us descended upon a certain district of South London may serve as a sample of the sort of work that is needed as a basis for industrial investigation.

We alighted from a municipal tram in a busy but not wide thoroughfare, hot and full of mingled odours from the fruit, meat, fish, cheese, onions and other comestibles displayed freely in open shop windows. Sweet shops glowed with wares of vivid and alarming hues; vendors shouted; trams went grinding by, and busy pedestrians hustled each other on the narrow pavements. We divided into two parties, one pair going to one church, the second to another. These visits over, we were to meet again at a midway point and decide upon our further course.

The church to which the first pair were directing their steps appeared near on the map, but proved rather difficult to find. The door of the Rectory, when at last it was discovered, was opened by a woman of the care-taker description. The rector was away for his holiday. Who, they asked, was taking his duty? Mr. S. of St. Anne's. And where did Mr. S. live? In Victoria Terrace, out of Hanbury Road, on the other side of the High Street—third turning on the left. Having retraced their course, and taken the prescribed third turning, the investigators presently met their companions. These had been more fortunate; the clergyman upon whom they had called was at home and sympathetic, said his parish was full of underpaid people, would look up and send some addresses; hoped that a minimum wage would be established, and spoke indignantly of Messrs. E. and D., manufacturers of the neighbourhood, whose rates of payment were scandalously low. Of one of these sinners he gave the address; the other lived in a certain street, but he could not recollect the number. He had also furnished the name and address of a lady who helped in the work of the church and who would be able and willing to supply names. This lady lived on the farther shore of that main river of traffic which we had already crossed.

Emerging from the little green enclosure in which we had stood to look out the various streets in our maps, we once more divided into pairs. To one couple fell the duty of seeking that especially ill-paying employer the number of whose workshop we did not know. The street proved to consist of small dwelling-houses, each with steps to its front door, a basement window and other three windows above. None bore any sign of being a work-place; no door stood open, no hand-cart waited before any house, nor was any person either approaching or leaving with a bundle. Twice was the hot street perambulated in the hope that some indication might present itself, but none did; and our effrontery was not equal to knocking at door after door, and so arousing the observation of the whole thoroughfare. We turned away, therefore, towards the other factory, which lay on the way to Victoria Terrace. This time there was no difficulty in finding the place; a woman with a bundle of work, walking ahead of us, served unconsciously as a guide. We followed her in at the open door and addressed ourselves to a forewoman in a little office. In vain we explained to her that our inquiry was not inimical to employers and that no names would be published; she would not allow us to see the workrooms, and her answers were of the briefest and least informing.* We went on to Victoria Terrace, where the wife of Mr. S. of St. Anne's told us that her husband had gone over to administer a local charity at the church which we had previously

---

*At a later date an American lady, who happened to be with one of us in this same neighbourhood, had a long conversation with this woman, who gave her many particulars of hours, &c. Although her representations were, we believe, a little rose-coloured, we have evidence to show that the rates of payment in this factory are not on the very lowest scale. Of the other local employer, however, we eventually saw and copied a pay-sheet, the figures of which surprised even the experienced investigator to whom it was given. This man was paying 5 ½d. apiece for the machining, in the worker's home, of girls' coats measuring 49 inches in length. Each had two capes, the upper one being scalloped, piped with velvet and faced inside with ribbon, besides having two rows of stitching. The worker seen—a capable person—said that she could make only one in a day.

visited, and that if we hurried, we should probably find him there. We did hurry, accordingly, crossed the high road again, and again approached the first church. Near to it we met a tired looking gentleman in clerical attire and ventured to stop him. Yes, this was Mr. S., and he was ready to listen to us, and to agree as to the desirability of a minimum wage. But he could give us no addresses. The population of the district, he told us, was migratory in the highest degree; many families moved every few months. Miss H., who presided over a girls' club, would certainly be able to tell us the addresses of some workers. She lived in Castle Street, a turning out of Middle Street, on the model estate in the rear of the church. After quite a prolonged conversation with Mr. S., who had incidentally told us much about the problems of housing and of Sunday trading, and given a glimpse of the beneficent activities that were being carried on in this rather depressing neighbourhood, we went on our way, reflecting, as we often found ourselves doing, during the course of the investigation, upon the value of the social work that is being done by religious bodies of all sorts in the poorer parts of London. If these bodies did no more—and of course they do vastly more—than provide for the presence in each poor district of a few educated persons ready to give time and knowledge to the service of their neighbours, the public importance of them would be very great. In some parishes, whatever there is of mental opportunity, of sociability or of enlightened recreation, emanates directly from the church or chapel, and if these influences were to disappear the whole level of the district would drop.

The lady who lived in Castle Street, out of Middle Street, was not at home; and since it was already close upon the hour at which the two parties were to meet for lunch, we permitted ourselves the very rare extravagance of a cab, and were bowled away through the hot streets. Our lunch, almost as a matter of course, was inferior. It is one of the drawbacks of an investigator's work that decent meals are seldom procurable in the regions where that work is carried on. Indeed, at a later time we often carried food with us and sought some sequestered spot to eat it. We entertain pleasant memories of the old burying-ground around a Friends' Meeting House in a certain suburb, where the kind caretaker encouraged us to spend our luncheon interval, and where in the midst of a hot and fatiguing day we sat for three-quarters of an hour in the shade, with greenness and quietness around us. Another day two of us took our meal sitting on a pile of wood beside a countrified road in Upper Clapton, a green pasture on our right, and a half-built row of pretentious new houses before us. On this earlier occasion, however, we sat in a rather dark shop and tried to shut our eyes to the doubtful cleanliness of knives and forks. . . .

When found, the workers are often, and very naturally, at first inclined to be suspicious. It is necessary to explain to them the purpose of the inquiry and to assure them that no name will be made public; it is also necessary to let them tell their story in their own way. One has to hear far more than merely the industrial facts that one sets out to learn. The additional information is often very interesting—as a glimpse into any human life can hardly fail to be—but listening to it is apt to take a long time. Few persons who have not tried would guess how small is the number of "cases" that a competent investigator can collect in a day. Perhaps also few persons would guess how extremely rare it is to be received otherwise than courteously and communicatively. Home workers, especially, often seem really glad to see somebody whose visit breaks the monotony of their toil, and who shows genuine interest in their concerns. And if one has occasion to make a second call, the friendly smile of recognition and welcome sets one reflecting upon the dullness of a life in which the intrusion of an inquisitive stranger forms an agreeable landmark. On a retrospect of our twelve months' work, the essential virtues of the woman worker—her patience, her industry, her marked sense of fair play—stand out very clearly. Emphatically, the large majority of the women whom we have visited are good citizens who deserve well of their country, and who mostly receive, in return for prolonged and patient labour, a very small share in the joys, the comforts or the beauties of life. To go among them is to be at the same time gratified by a deepening sense of human worth and oppressed by the intolerable weight of human burdens.

Some horribly sad facts remain impressed upon the memories of those who have been active in this investigation. Two of us were busy for several days in a small district situated between what were once two pleasant residential suburbs. Fine historical houses lie on both sides, but in the little intermediate patch there is not one. Nothing is old but everything is shabby. Grey streets of mean dwelling-houses are punctuated by struggling shops that display tinned foods and galvanised pails; even the few public-houses show no sign of prosperity, and the church looks like the surrounding streets—at once new, poor and shabby. One or two of the streets are still unfinished; beyond them lies rough open land; fifteen years ago, perhaps ten years ago, this must have been a "building estate." To-day it is a pool of poverty, deep in the middle, shallower on the borders. Its inhabitants are not (as is the case in some outlying districts) vicious and foul of speech. They are quiet and peaceable, they seem, comparatively speaking, sober. Passing through these mournful thoroughfares one is not haunted by the thought that often besets the experienced visitor: "What a pandemonium this place must be at night!" And indeed it is nothing of the kind. The two ladies, who, thanks to a local Church worker, were able to survey this district pretty thoroughly, spent several evenings here, calling upon factory workers. At just after ten o'clock one night they made their last call and inquired for Miss X. "who works, I believe, in the under-linen." A woman came rushing out in her nightdress from some back room, she had caught a word or two, had hoped that she might be the person inquired for, and had sprung from her bed in fear that a chance of work might pass her by. She was a deserted wife with two small children and she made pompons for babies' shoes, "the best silk work," but did not get enough work to keep the children properly.

A street or two away live Mr. and Mrs. W. She is a tailoress and is paid about 1d. per hour. He is paralysed, but in order to save her time he carries her work to and fro. An hour each way does this poor crippled elderly man spend going with his bundle to the factory and back, and all that he and his wife ask of the world is sufficient work at sufficient pay to enable them to live on in their present way. But they are nearly starved, and the Poor Law authorities will not give them out-relief. Their rooms, it is true, are far from clean, and so are their persons. Their friends at the church advise their going into "the house." But Mrs. W. resists. "I should never get out again," she says. "They want me to come in because they know I am a good worker. They would keep me there if once I went. But I won't go. I'll die sooner." Probably the workhouse will win the battle. Her health will give way under long continued anxiety and privation; ill, she will be taken, whether she will or no, to the infirmary, and there, having lost the last stimulus remaining to her, will not have hope enough left to recover.

Not a hundred yards from Mr. and Mrs. W. on the outer edge of this depressing district, lives Miss P., also a home worker and also a tailoress. The conditions of her life, however, differ in every way from those of theirs. Her home, which she shares with a brother and sister, is clean and comfortable; her person and dress are neat and immaculate, she speaks carefully and with a good choice of words; she is, to the most superficial observation, a self-respecting, superior woman. The two sisters work together at waistcoat-making, and when visited, were engaged upon garments of a sort of corrugated stuff that simulated knitting. They put in the front pieces, bind these and the armholes, and make the three pockets. For this they are paid

9*s*. per dozen, they providing machine and cotton. Her machine was purchased long ago and has never needed repairing; cotton costs slightly less than fourpence for a dozen waistcoats. Work is fetched and returned twice a week, the sisters undertaking the journey alternately and paying fourpence each time for fares. On the previous day, working together from 9.30 to 7.30 the sisters had earned 7*s*. 6*d*., or 3*s*. 9*d*. each. Allowing an hour out of their day for meals, they would be earning 5*d*. an hour, less cost of cotton (not 3½*d*. a day) and less also a penny and ⅓ of a penny as a proportion of weekly travelling expenses. Their work is performed in a clean, comfortable and quiet room, the rent of the whole house, of six rooms, is 9*s*., the share of each tenant being thus 3*s*. a week. If the two sisters, instead of working at home were obliged to go into their employer's factory, the fares of each would amount to 2*s*. a week. Thus to these two worthy women it would be a real injury if home work were to be abolished. . . .

At best, the life of the woman earning a wage by some form of needlework is no easy one; and if, being dependent upon herself, she earns—as most women do—anything much short of £1 a week, she must go short of everything beyond the very barest necessaries. Girls partly supported by their relatives may enjoy a temporary and factitious prosperity, but, unless they marry, time by depriving them of these relatives, or by rendering elders no longer capable of supporting even themselves, eventually demands heavy repayment for the short period of comfort. In middle age many a woman who has never received a wage large enough to support her is faced by the need of supporting upon it an aged parent as well as herself. The unmarried woman, however indigent, never, in our experience, allows her old mother to go to the workhouse. As long as there is an unmarried daughter the mother lives with her. Marriage which, looked at in anticipation, presents itself as a way out, proves often but a second underpaid employment added on to the first. The wages of men in many branches of industry are not sufficient for the support of a growing family. The mother, who has to cook, clean, and wash for all, is driven to take some work that will add to the exiguous store of shillings available for household needs. The larger her family the more she finds herself compelled to neglect the children in order to earn clothing and food for them. Underpayment, borne gaily enough in girlhood, when she defrayed but a part of her real expenses, grows an intolerable burden upon the wife and mother. She hastens to send out her own girls that their earning may lighten the pressure, and the story begins over again for them. A small minority of the unusually quick, clever or fortunate rise to the higher positions, in which princely incomes of as much as 30*s.* a week may be gained, but for the great majority of indoor as of outdoor workers life is a steady round of work at high pressure combined with a ceaseless effort to make a weekly ten shillings equal to a pound. The spectre of slack time and the more dreadful spectre of unemployment are always lurking in the background. Life is one long drawn out uncertainty, in which the sole sure point is that age will be even less employed and even worse paid. That, in such circumstances, so many women go on quietly persisting in their toil, not often complaining aloud, although bitterly conscious that somehow they are not getting fair play, is, for those who have eyes to see, one of the strongest possible indictments of that social muddle which we are pleased to call a system. They are such good human material and for the most part so wasted. In a world of clamour the silent and long-suffering are exceedingly apt to be overlooked, although their patience forms an additional claim. If there is any immediate means by which legislation might diminish the evil of underpayment, it is the highest time that legislation should intervene in aid of a law-abiding, industrious and greatly oppressed class of citizens.

Helen (Dendy) Bosanquet

HELEN (DENDY) BOSANQUET (1860–1925) was a prolific and well-informed commentator on family and neighborhood poverty, on social work methods, and on social policy more generally. Social historians often cite her observations of life in Shoreditch, where she lived as a Charity Organisation Society (COS) district secretary for five years, until her marriage in 1895. She was also an influence on her husband, idealist social philosopher Bernard Bosanquet. Unlike Beatrice Webb, her contemporary, Bosanquet has not been the frequent subject of admiring biography; there are only a few studies of her work.[1] Webb's intense dislike of Bosanquet has been immortalized in Webb's widely read diaries.

Bosanquet's sometimes acid and ungenerous portrayals of working-class life can be off-putting, yet her work is admired by Ross McKibbin as "cultural sociology"; and both he and Jane Lewis have written appreciatively about her as a social observer.[2] Her political thought was considerably more complicated, and more liberal-minded, than she is usually given credit for. She was a lifelong Liberal and supporter of Irish Home Rule, and a staunch, though not militant, supporter of votes for women. She became increasingly outspoken, basing her argument on the special burdens that disenfranchisement places on working-class women. In a 1911 letter to *The Times,* she wrote, "The more I see and know of our working sisters the more I am amazed at the sheer waste of practical wisdom in our country due to the exclusion of women from politics."[3] Bosanquet tended to view poverty as a reflection of a worker's moral weaknesses, yet she conceded that

---

Originally published as "Marriage in East London," in Aspects of the Social Problem, *ed. Bernard Bosanquet (London: Macmillan, 1895), 75–81.*

the appalling pay rates of women workers were products of "custom" and not of the failings of the women.[4]

Helen Dendy was the fifth of the nine children in a Nonconformist family that resided mainly in Manchester. Her mother was the daughter of a Unitarian minister. Her father, also a minister, rotated among a number of different Nonconformist churches and a Manchester business that failed in 1883.

Helen and three of her siblings, including her sister Mary (who became an educator of disabled children), remained behind in the family home, supporting themselves, with Helen serving as the housekeeper. Finally, at age twenty-six, Helen was able to enroll at the recently established Newnham College, Cambridge, where she got the nicknames "Aunt Dendy" and "T. R." (for "tone-raiser").[5] She specialized in Political Economy and graduated with a "first" (conferring high honors) in Moral Sciences in 1889. Helen Dendy was an excellent college debater and exercised this talent and taste many times in later life as a lively and trenchant anti-Fabian propagandist.

Her membership in the London Ethical Society brought her into contact with Bernard Bosanquet, Balliol graduate and follower of T. H. Green, the social philosopher who championed civic effort on behalf of the poor. After their marriage the Bosanquets moved to Surrey. Helen Bosanquet continued, however, to write extensively on working-class life and class politics, drawing on her Shoreditch experience and on the COS work she continued to do as a volunteer. She was also active in founding social work training programs at Bedford College and the Women's University Settlement. The latter was eventually amalgamated with the London School of Economics. She served on the Royal Commission on the Poor Laws from 1905 to 1909 and was a leader of the majority faction, which supported the continuation of some aspects the country's harsh Poor Law and in general favored private charity over public welfare programs. She and Beatrice Webb, another commissioner (as was Octavia Hill), constantly sparred, because Webb wanted to abolish the Poor Law entirely and offer modern and efficient state-run services for children, the elderly, the unemployed, the ill, and the disabled.

NOTES

1. Lewis, *Women and Social Action;* McKibbin, *Ideologies of Class.*
2. McKibbin, *Ideologies of Class,* esp. 169; Lewis, *Women and Social Action.*
3. Lewis, *Women and Social Action,* 169, quoting Bosanquet's letter to *The Times,* December 21, 1911. José Harris's short entry in the Oxford DNB also asks for a reassessment of this interesting figure.

4. *The Economics of Women's Work and Wages,* vol. 5 of Transactions of the National Liberal Club Political and Economic Circle (London: P. S. King, [1907]).

5. McBriar, *An Edwardian Mixed Doubles,* 11.

FURTHER READING

For more writing by Helen Bosanquet, see "The Industrial Residuum," *The Economic Journal* 8 (December 1893), reprinted in *Aspects of the Social Problem* (London: Macmillan, 1895), 82–102; this is a very influential essay denouncing the casual poor and the poor relief on which they drew. Bosanquet based *Rich and Poor* (London: Macmillan, 1896) on her knowledge of life in Shoreditch. *The Family* (London: Macmillan, 1906) is a textbook that has been reprinted several times, as were several of her books, and *Social Work in London 1869–1912* (London: John Murray, 1914) is Bosanquet's history of the COS.

For information about Bosanquet, see the informative entry in the Oxford DNB by José Harris. In Jane Lewis's *Women and Social Action in Victorian and Edwardian England* (Palo Alto, CA: Stanford University Press, 1991), pages 146–92 are devoted to Bosanquet. Ross McKibbin includes a chapter on Bosanquet in *The Ideologies of Class: Social Relations in Britain 1880–1950* (Oxford: Clarendon Press, 1990). A. M. McBriar, in *An Edwardian Mixed Doubles. The Bosanquets versus the Webbs: A Study in British Social Policy, 1890–1929* (Oxford: Clarendon Press, 1987), does not always distinguish between the husbands' and the wives' ideas and activities.

<hr />

Marriage in East London

Opposite my study window stands the parish church, and the shady path leading from the gates up to the church door is strewn as white as if snow had fallen with rice, which will lie there until a shower of rain has softened it sufficiently to make an acceptable meal for the sparrows. It is Bank Holiday, the fashionable wedding-day in our part of the world, and large numbers of lads and lasses have celebrated it in the most approved way by getting married. All the morning there has been a noisy crowd round the church gates, and a row of the shabbiest vehicles and most broken-down horses in London has stood waiting to carry off the wedding parties to the railway station or to the nearest public-house. The path down from the church doors is a fairly long one, and affords ample opportunity for the boisterous merrymaking which is universal on these occasions, and which often degenerates into something very like a free fight—though generally of a good-humoured nature. Some twenty or thirty couples have chosen this way of spending their holiday, and it is interesting, if somewhat sad, to see their first start into the new life which awaits them. The majority have chartered an old cab; sometimes they rise to two or three, while sometimes two or three couples crowd into one. Five shillings a cab, to hold any number, is the standard charge for wedding; and a "walking wedding" is the exception. Into these vehicles they ascend with what dignity they can preserve amongst the mingled chaff and admiration of the ragged spectators, and it is significant of future relations that the brides generally sit with their backs to the horses, while the bridegrooms light their pipes as they drive away. If it is a walking wedding, the party separates into two groups: the men, including the bridegroom, lounge off smoking and shouting, followed by the group of excited, chattering women. In this way they will spend the day, "sampling" the public-houses and making merry among their friends, until any lingering traces of the sobering effects of the morning ceremony have been well washed away. One such party I have watched followed up and down the streets by a practical joker with a hand-bell, who was greatly appreciated by the corner-men and street arabs. The toilets are wonderful to behold. They range through all varieties, from the orthodox white veil and flowing train to the glowing greens and purples of the coster-girl, whose wedding dress and hat will make patches of dirty brightness up and down the slums for years to come. The men are hardly less wonderful in the varieties of their ready-made or second-hand suits; and figures which are passable enough as they stand behind their barrows, collarless and in shirt-sleeves, become deplorable spectacles of self-conscious awkwardness when attired for the first time in a complete suit, and adorned with a floral button-hole.

One wonders, watching them, at the light-hearted way in which they take this step. For the girls especially it means burdens which seem almost too heavy to be borne—of care and sickness and poverty, of hopeless squalor or unceasing toil, leading to premature old age or death. By the time they are twenty-five all the elasticity and vigour of youth are crushed out of them, and those who maintain their self-respect have nothing to look forward to but drudgery. These early marriages are the curse of the poor, yet the causes which lead to them are often almost inconceivably slight—a fit of pique, a taunt from some companion, the desire for a lark, or a bet; frequently there is no more substantial foundation than this in their choice of a life-companion, and the consequences cannot fail.

Among the more thoughtful, and more carefully brought up, there is, of course, a sort of courtship; but it is quaintly different from that which takes place in the higher ranks of society. From the first glimmerings of inclination there is no secret about it; Jack and Jane are "going together"; and when this going together passes into a formal engagement it is difficult to say—generally, I think, not until the day is fixed. It is a preliminary probation, rather than an engagement, and the experiment can be given up without much blame attaching to either side. "You wouldn't have us take the first that comes?" a girl will say; "and how can we know whether we like them unless we go with them?" How, indeed! in the crowded homes of the poor there is little room for quiet social intercourse, and parents have no time, if they had the inclination, to superintend the matrimonial ventures of their daughters. So acquaintance begins in the course of work or at some festivity, and ripens on trips to Kew Gardens and Hampstead Heath, is fostered by treatings to the theatre or music hall, and culminates when Jack gets a rise in wages and Jane has saved up enough for a wedding dress and her share of the furniture.

Such a pair will, perhaps, have as good a chance of happiness as any; they have learned to know each other under the ordinary routine of workaday life, and it is not left to marriage to divulge the failings of temper and character on either side. From a worldly point of view their position will not seem much to boast of to young people who regard money in the bank and a fixed income as indispensable conditions of life. Capital they have none, beyond what they may possess of skill and strength. Any little savings will be invested in the home, which—like Traddles—they mostly pick up bit by bit; beginning even before they have turned their attention towards any particular mate. The girl, if she is of the better sort, will probably have managed to get a sewing-machine on the hire system, and this will go a long way towards furnishing the single room in which they start life together. During the first year, while the wife is still earning, many little articles of luxury will be added, which will gradually disappear as the family increases and troubles accumulate. Have you never wondered, on looking in at the pawnbroker's windows, where all the gaudy little overmantels, and elaborate tea-services, and numberless plated spoons and forks come from? They are the harvest of the first "bad times" after marriage. It is not quite such a tragedy as it appears, though sad enough; "selling the home" is with East Londoners a recognised method of raising money, and many articles are avowedly bought with a view to being handy for the pawnbroker. It is a part of their principle of life, the subordination of future needs to present fancies, and they argue that it is better to enjoy luxuries while they can than to have money lying idle in the savings-bank.

Were it not for this false economy of borrowing from the future which vitiates all poorer London (and makes co-operative stores an impossibility) young people of this class might find it no bad venture to throw in their lots together, and trust to their own right hands to pull them through life. But at a little lower level we find courage degenerating into foolhardiness, and self-confidence into a childish inability to foresee even the inevitable claims of the future. What is to be said for instances like the following, which are to be numbered, not by tens or hundreds, but by thousands?

A. B. is aged twenty-one, and has a wife and three children to support; he does it by turning a piano-organ to the accompaniment of a tin whistle. His story is that he was put to work at fourteen, got tired of it, ran away to sea and got tired of that; he came home, and at sixteen married a girl of fifteen, and was obliged to do whatever he could to keep her. He is a well-made, active, rather intelligent young fellow, capable of doing better things by nature, but hopelessly dragged down by the responsibilities he has so recklessly assumed.

C. D. is of another sort; dull mentally and feeble physically, he has never supported even himself for a whole year, but has always been kept by his widowed mother through the winter. Last year he married a girl of eighteen, rather pretty and as helpless as a baby. He explains that he thought that two could get along as well as one, and "perhaps something might turn up." Something has turned up, and there are now three to keep; the mother declines the addition to her already heavy burden, and the Workhouse looms large before them.

Couples such as these will not even wait to get a decent home together. An old bedstead and bedding, two rickety chairs and a table to match, a strip of greasy carpet and two or three cracked cups and saucers—these will be collected from sympathising neighbours, or picked up for a few halfpence from the costermongers' stalls, and will satisfy the highest expectations of the young people. There are thousands of such homes which have not cost 10s. to get together, and would not realise 5s. if sold, and these afford all of decency and comfort at which their owners aim.

Another, and no less fatal, kind of recklessness is illustrated by the following case:—E. F., a young man already advanced in consumption, marries a crippled girl, incapable of doing anything beyond a little needlework. He had a little business, and was doing fairly well, but shortly after marriage was told that his only chance of life depended upon his passing the next winter in a milder climate. He sold the business, and handed over the greater part of the proceeds to his wife for the support of herself and the child during his absence; but she, resenting the thought of being left, invested the whole amount next day in a "melodeon" (from what I can gather, a large and expensive kind of musical box), and defied him to go and leave her destitute. He did not go, and from that time forward they sank lower and lower, picking up a living in the streets, buying old clothes and selling them again, and supported largely by charity, until he died and left her with two children to bring up as best she may.

What can be expected of lives in which the responsibilities are met in this spirit? You will find the results most manifest in the lower class Board Schools. The troops of ragged, dirty, stunted little urchins, neglected, and crippled in mind and body, that you will see there, are the offspring of these reckless marriages. Follow them home, and you will see the ruined lives of their parents; the mothers are either worn-out drudges before they have reached middle-age, or have developed into the careless slatterns who live on the doorstep gossiping with like-minded neighbours; the fathers, with all self-respect crushed out of them, are reduced to picking up odd jobs at the street-corner, and live more in the public-house than in their wretched homes. When we think, further, what the children brought up in such sur-roundings must become, this question of improvident marriage shows itself as one of the most serious of modern social life.

One root of the mischief lies in the overcrowding in our large towns. Too often marriage is accepted as the only way of escape from conditions which have become unbearable. Family life, which is carried on in one or two rooms, is bad enough when the family still consists of children; as they grow up to be young men and women it becomes intolerable. Nor is it a simple matter for the young people to be independent, even when they are earn-ing sufficient to support themselves. There are very few amongst the less educated classes who can endure the solitude of living quite alone, even if it were an easier matter than it is to break away from the home-life with-out some obvious excuse. For girls, moreover, it is hardly desirable; while to young men the prospect of preparing their own meals and doing their own household work is not an attractive one. The same overcrowding which makes family life difficult makes boarding in most cases impossible, and the one solution they have found to the problem is to look round for a more or less suitable companion. How far well-conducted boarding-houses for young men and women may meet the difficulty is an experiment yet to be tried; the great point will be to ensure their being well conducted without making them too oppressive for natures little wont to discipline and much given to self-indulgence.

Much of the evil is due also to false ideas about life which are not pecu-liar to the people of whom we are speaking. It is not only in the lower classes that girls are allowed to think, and even made to feel, that a woman's life has no legitimate interests outside those of marriage, and that, therefore, to lose an opportunity of getting married may be to miss all of good which life has to offer. Nor are those who should be the teachers of the young on such important matters wholly without blame; their doctrine that to discourage early marriage is to encourage immorality is a gross injustice to the great majority of the poor—perhaps, if they did but know it, the greatest of which they have as a class to complain at the present day. Evil enough there is, as all know who have much to do with the poor; but those amongst whom these marriages take place are just those who still have a respect for such obligations as they have been taught to recognise, and they are far more likely to sink to a lower level in consequence of their imprudence than they would be in consequence of judicious teaching and warning. As it is, they are acting up to the highest standard which has been set before them, and we have no right to assume that if they are shown one still higher they will not aim at that also. To realise that the people have a capacity for rising as well as falling is the next step towards the Social Utopia in which no one will enter upon the responsibilities of marriage without a fair prospect of being able to bring up a family in decency and comfort.

5

Agnes Kate Foxwell

DURING WORLD WAR I, up to a thousand educated women worked in munitions factories as forewomen, supervisors, or social workers in charge of the mainly young working-class women who flocked to the factories for their good pay and chance to advance the war effort. The Woolwich Arsenal staff included about twenty of such supervisors.[1] Agnes Kate Foxwell (1871– 1957)[2] worked in one of the more dangerous departments as a welfare supervisor at Woolwich Arsenal on the south side of the Thames in 1916 and 1917 (possibly through 1918).

Foxwell began her university education at age thirty-two, completing her studies at Bedford College in 1907. She received an M.A. in literature from the University of London in 1910 and published two books on the sixteenth-century poet Sir Thomas Wyatt. Foxwell was a suffrage organizer in her home London district of Harrow, working with the London Graduates' Union for women's suffrage. She got the Woolwich job through the University Women's War Service, which helped to place college graduates in these supervisory positions. She was assigned to the high-ranking management position of Principal Overlooker (above her was the Lady Superintendent for the entire arsenal, Lilian Barker) in sections of the factory that worked with especially dangerous chemicals, mercury in particular. She describes these workshops in the chapter reproduced here. Her pay was about four pounds a week, while ordinary workers received an average of about thirty shillings.[3] Foxwell's upbeat book, published in 1917, is a good example of how social exploration genres could be used as propaganda.

Originally published in Munition Lasses: Six Months as Principal Overlooker in Danger Buildings *(London: Hodder and Stoughton, 1917), chap. 4, "The Workshops: Morning."*

Foxwell's Bedford College file suggests that after the war she was involved in Missions to Seamen and "other church work," for which she tried at least once to solicit donations at the college.

Foxwell's descriptions of the manufacturing processes are cryptic. It is possible that, in a book published during wartime, she or the government's censors did not want to reveal too much about Britain's weaponry. Or she could unwittingly be revealing her acculturation to a "total" environment like the Woolwich Arsenal. Here are a few definitions:

The *shifting house* was a large cloakroom where the workers in "danger buildings" took off their street clothes, taking extra care to remove anything metal that could serve as a conductor and create an explosion. They then donned fireproof gowns and caps. Fitting the explosive cap or projectile into the hollow brass casing of the artillery shells was an important part of munitions manufacture. Possibly the women in the *filling room* were stuffing the assembled caps into the shells, but they may have been filling the shells themselves with chemicals, such as cordite, to propel the explosive caps—or carrying out both operations. In *cap shops* the actual projectiles were made, to be used in bullets or in larger shells. One of the substances used in making the caps was what Foxwell calls "compo," probably a mixture of TNT and another explosive.[4]

In addition to the fire hazards, the munitions workers were exposed to a number of toxic chemicals, as Foxwell acknowledges. TNT caused the best-known occupational illness. One of its symptoms was jaundice, which is why its victims were nicknamed "canary girls." Their skin turned bright yellow and their hair orange or green. The illness could subside, but there were also many deaths due to TNT or other toxic chemicals.

NOTES

1. See Angela Woollacott, *On Her Their Lives Depend: Munitions Workers in the Great War* (Berkeley: University of California Press, 1994), esp. 72–79; Deborah Thom, "Women and Work in Wartime Britain," in *The Upheaval of War: Family, Work, and Welfare in Europe, 1914–18,* ed. Richard Wall and Jay Winter (Cambridge: Cambridge University Press, 1988); and Gail Braybon and Penny Summerfield, *Out of the Cage: Women's Experiences in Two World Wars* (London: Pandora Books, 1987).

2. These dates are from her student file in the Archives of Bedford and Royal Holloway College, University of London, which includes a newspaper obituary, BC AR/203/1/74. Information about Foxwell is sparse. She is listed in the 1913 *Suffrage Annual and Women's Who's Who,* and I found her listed as an employee at the Arsenal in the Cap and Detonator Factory, serving from July 1, 1916, to June 27, 1918. These are not the months of service she gives in the dedication to the book. In the factory record she is called "Mrs. A. Foxwell." As previous employment she listed "Research work. Dr. of Literature." Impe-

rial War Museum, Women at Work Collection, Reel 73. Munitions IV, File 19/11; also Woman's Work Inventory, ED. 3/14 (Federation of University Women's list of appointees at Woolwich).

3. The salary estimate for ordinary workers is Angela Woollacott's in *On Her Their Lives Depend*, 167. For information on women welfare workers in munitions factories, see Woollacott, 166–70. The fact that the senior women's positions had two alternative names—Welfare Supervisor and Lady Superintendent—suggests the shift taking place in the meaning of middle-class women's authority. Foxwell's Lady Superintendent, Lilian Barker, was apparently widely popular, even with those who deeply resented having "ladies bountiful" meddling on the shop floor. For more on Barker, see Elizabeth Gore, *The Better Fight: The Story of Dame Lilian Barker* (London: Geoffrey Bles, 1965).

4. My thanks to James Chaffee of Ramapo College for his help with Fox's armaments terminology.

FURTHER READING

Agnes Kate Foxwell wrote *A Study of Sir Thomas Wyatt's Poems* (London: London University Press, 1911)—the subject of her M.A. thesis—and edited a collection of Wyatt's poems *(The Poems of Sir Thomas Wyatt,* edited from the MSS. and Early Editions. London: London University Press, 1914).

—————— ↞↠ ——————

FROM *Munition Lasses*

Man goeth forth unto his work and to his labour.
—PSALTER

From 7.15 to 7.30 daily and nightly the D.P.O.'s [Deputy Principal Overlookers] exert all their energy, all their force of will, all their patience, and not a little of their wit in getting the girls to their workshop. The phrase, "Come along, girls," is incessantly on their lips, the reiteration varied only by the stress. The command of the D.P.O. is (literally) enforced by the driving power of the attendants. Auntie Ellis's voice is heard: "Come along, you gals; this way for the up train," with a further admonishment: "Now, then, what yer doin' up there all of a heap?—out you go." So by dint of continually calling and propelling, the house is cleared by 7.30, and the door closed.

Once in the workshop, away from the temptation to gossip, or snatch a forbidden hasty meal on the dirty side of the Shifting-house, or to rest after the journey there, our women start work with energy. The outgoing shift must leave the shops clean and tidy. It is the business of the incoming shift to set up and burnish all machinery and tools. On cleanliness depends our safety. The three commandments of the Danger Buildings are Cleanliness, Gentleness, Punctuality, and on these principles depend all the regulations. The first two ensure safety, the last speeds munitions to the front, and will shorten the war. These three words might be written large in every Shifting-house in Great Britain, to impress it on all workers, as we endeavoured to impress it on our lasses.

The most acutely busy time of the shift for the D.P.O. is from 7.30 to 8 o'clock. She goes swiftly from shop to shop, noting absentees and arranging the gangs of workers for the operations. The filling shops must be kept to their full strength. Vacancies in these shops entail drawing from minor operations, or appointing new hands. Discernment must be made between what is vital and what is expedient. One operation leads to another, and if we are held up in one direction, the work as a whole is affected. Moreover, the work of the previous shift must be balanced by the following shift.

The foremen and D.P.O.'s are therefore engaged, as it were, in a game of chess, the factory being the board, the workers the pawns, and the other shift the "friendly foe." At the end of the week, when the exacting work necessitates a rest for some of our women, the volunteer workers are a great boon, in keeping gangs up to strength and preventing any lowering of the output.

It should be understood that workers are safe, as long as they follow out instructions and work to rule. Directions are printed in every shop. It is the overlooker's duty to see that the workers are following these directions, and the D.P.O. must see that every shop is working exactly in accordance with such regulations. She must be constantly on the alert to note any deviation whatever from the directions, and to watch for danger signals. She must be satisfied that the machinery is running smoothly and correctly, and if in doubt go to the experts. The men D.P.O.'s supervise, correct, and adjust machinery, and make constant tours of inspection. Still the woman D.P.O is responsible for the women, and she cannot relax a moment in watchful guard.

By 8 o'clock the filling machines must be up and running, the mould trays and plates must be thoroughly clean, the shop must have its complement of hands, the absentee lists must have been collected and signed by the D.P.O. and sent up to the office, and the programme of the day in working order.

On the night-shift work continues without a break until 11 P.M., the dinner-hour. On the morning shift dinner is at midday; and light refreshments are served in the canteen between 8 A.M. and 9 A.M. Every worker is allowed ten minutes: five minutes for refreshment. At 9 A.M. all stragglers are called in, the canteen is closed to workers, and inspection of workshops begins. The D.P.O. visits every shop, in more leisurely fashion than the first round. She watches the work, points out errors, notes the progress of new hands, inspects the supply of hypo and eye lotion and towels in the filling shops. The inspection is followed by a visit to the wash-houses and adjacent buildings, and to the Shifting-houses to see that everything is in a clean and sanitary condition. Lastly, reports are made, requisitions drawn up, and the ambulance baskets overhauled and depletions made good before the "turnout" hootah sounds at midday.

Starting on our morning's rounds, we enter the Cap shop. This is the largest shop in the factory; hence it appears to be the most busy. There is constant movement here, as the girl carriers go backwards and forwards with the plates for the different processes and operations, all of which are begun and completed in this shop.

The Cap Shop is always full of life. The girls sings [sic] their special Cap Shop songs and ragtime ditties. The row of merry faces round the star-turning table is one of the bright corners of our factory, while the bounces of bright-coloured shell add a touch of picturesqueness to the scene. It recalled to the memory a little fairy tale called the "Pot of Gold," describing the quest of a boy and girl for the golden treasure that was hidden at the foot of the sunset, and after many adventures they climb a mountain below which the sun is setting, and they fall asleep and dream they are laving their hands in streams of gold. But the fairy tale is more of an allegory; for every boy and girl, every man and woman sets forth to find that treasure, though some lose themselves by the way. But those who search are so taken up with the attractions on the road, and find such glories on the mountain top when they have scaled it, that almost before they are aware they near the sunset, and go down with it to learn the glowing mystery of what shall be revealed beyond. And sometimes, at different crossroads, there are partings from friends; but at every parting there is a trail of light, and a bright spirit remains with them, more real than the bodily presence they parted with, because the body is merely the semblance of the spirit and the soul.

The majority of the filling shops are staffed with women. The mercury shops have men overlookers, with women as second-in-charge. The shops, divided in three portions, are not large, owing to the nature of the operations, but each worker in the shop has an important process to carry out. These shops are remarkable for the happiness and general appearance of good health among the workers. Singing is the usual accompaniment to their work. The latest songs are introduced, but some songs which are rich in harmony remain favourites and are sung week in and week out with tireless energy. Carols were introduced for the Christmas season. "Noël" and "King Wenceslaus" were favourites, and were sung with a spirit and tunefulness hard to beat while the machinery made an undercurrent of rhythmic sound.

Many a time I have desired to sketch these workshops, but the limitations of perspective would only permit a portion to be seen, whereas it is the whole effect, the "tout ensemble" (as our friends across the water say) of rhythmic work and tuneful song that appeals to eye and ear. Though every filling shop is similar, each has its distinct characteristics to the initiated. The energetic overlooker of the —— shop was always wrapped up in his work, planning out the best possible arrangements of his workers, in order to add to the output, putting a machine in order at one moment, taking up a filling machine at another, giving a woman-pupil a lesson, making out attendance lists, talking over the work with the D.P.O.—never wasting a moment, and always engrossed in some plan ahead of the work. Foremost amongst those who help their comrades, he aided the Red Cross fund with much zeal, and at the Christmas season subscriptions were given from his shop sufficient to buy an adjusting-table for the St John's Relief Hospital. The woman second-in-charge ably supported him, and the whole shop following the tone of their leader, were known for their good work.

The next shop to them worked in close unison and friendly rivalry. Where one was in advance, the other essayed to lead. The overlooker was formerly a sailor and kept his shop as taut and clean as a ship's deck. The shop was noted, too, for its enthusiastic women-in-charge. Little Miss C——, beloved by all the workers, was sunny, sweet-tempered, and absolutely loyal to work, but eye-trouble necessitated transfer to another factory, to our mutual regret. Her place was ably filled by another loyal worker, who inspired the girls under her to good work. She is now overlooker in another shop.

Another shop was conspicuous for the number of fillers it turned out. There was always a prospective pupil here, willing to learn, and it had the honour of supplying fillers for other shops. The overlooker was a woman, supported by the man-filler of large experience. The other fillers were women with a long record of steady work. There was always in this shop a steady cheerfulness in the face of obstacles. The overlooker was ready to throw herself in the breach when emergency arose. Hence she inspired her workers, so that one saw a hand quietly going from one operation to another if there was any need, with no grumbling and no assertion that "it wasn't their place" to help in the operation required.

It was the aim of the D.P.O. to see that the hands in filling shops should be capable of turning from one operation to another. In this way much time is saved, and the shop is generally in a higher state of efficiency.

Another shop was distinguished for its women-fillers, who had a very long record at their work; and they were respected by all the workers of the shop. One of these has since become overlooker of the shop, and she has the good wishes and support of all, because we feel that she will make a loyal and good leader.

On the first day of the New Year, we opened the half of a new filling shop with much eager interest. Thither we brought picked hands from the old shop, and some promising new hands. The shop famous for its fillers supplied a hand for the filling machine. But one thing was lacking, and the D.P.O. was asked with some diffidence if H—— were not coming down. Now H—— was a bonny lassie who had worked in the old shop for *eleven* months—ever since the shop had been open to women, in fact. For this reason she was an integral part of the shop, and we were dubious of removing her. But when the D.P.O. went to see, she was confronted with a wistful face, and a sorrowful voice begged to be allowed to go to the new shop. "Let me go as a worker," she said; "I do not wish to be second-in-charge, but just to be allowed to work there. My friends X, and Y, and Z are all there, and I shall feel more at home with them in the new shop." We sympathised, and felt that she deserved a reward. Twice during the eleven months her eyes had shown signs of trouble, and we wanted to remove her, but she had begged hard to remain, so we carefully watched her until the eyes became normal again.

We considered that her long service merited the reward she asked, so, having received the master's assent, we took H—— down to the new shop, triumphantly presenting her to the workers there, to the great contentment of all.

We paid a flying visit to this shop the other day, and found proudly happy faces. The work was well pursued with great vigour to show us how well the shop was running. And the overlooker said in quiet tones: "All is well here; and next time you come to see us we hope to have the other half of the shop working."

The D.P.O. must keep a vigilant eye on the appearance of the workers during her daily rounds, noting especially the eyes and the skin, and inquiring into the state of teeth and gums. Experience has proved that careful watching and taking care of contact cases in the early stages has a most beneficial result. Some workers are better if left in the shop under surgery treatment; others, again, are better removed on the slightest symptoms. Some are immune, having remained for months without becoming contact. The preventative measures have greatly decreased the number of cases. Hypo for the hands and face, and eye lotion are placed in every mercury and compo shop, and workers can stop their work to use these preventatives at any moment during the day. Increased accommodation for washing and hot and cold water laid on in the shops, together with the free distribution of milk at every shift, has done much to raise the general health of our workers.

From filling we pass to finishing. The operation needs delicate handling and skilled labour: deftness of touch and a trained eye are essential. The work is particularly adapted to women, and overlookers and hands are women and girls who have reached a very high standard of efficiency and dexterity. The overlookers of both the filling and the finishing shops must be thoroughly experienced. They need to be observant and resourceful, with a taste for machinery, and must, moreover, be swift and dexterous in manipulation.

There is always something new to learn, some fresh difficulty to cope with, some slight amendment to try; hence the work is absorbingly interesting. The discs, their measurements, weight, thickness, and the variety of metal used, is a science in itself, as applied to the particular branch of work in these shops. The D.P.O. must watch closely, satisfying herself that the work is performed strictly to the printed rules of the shop. The total amount in a shop must never exceed a certain limit, and it must be constantly carried away.

The work of the Carriers is most important in relation to both the filling and the finishing shops. They carry away the finished work and supply the finishing shops with fresh work. All work must be removed as soon as it is finished, and it is often necessary to put an extra carrier on at busy times, when there is an increased amount to carry away. Detonator carrier duty is popular amongst the women and, now the carriers wear a rational uniform, they are prepared for all weather. They like the out-door life. A worker who has been suffering from contact with mercury often becomes quite well again under the out-door life; others again are so sensitive to mercury that the duties of a carrier immediately set up dermatitis, and they must be removed.

We finish our brief survey with the Examining Shops. The workers here are either permanent examiners as a reward for good service in mercury, and their subsequent contact with it, or they are mercury workers who are taking their weekly rest in the examining shop; the following week they will return to mercury, and other mercury hands will take their place for a week. It is hoped thereby to lessen the cases of contact, and the plan is working well. The examining shops are the quietest in the factory. Much responsibility devolves upon each worker; it is their duty to separate any imperfect or faulty specimen in the finished work brought to them. To pass a defective cap or detonator means the spoiling of a cartridge or a shell; the women know their obligation, and carry out the work with a gravity and quietude befitting their responsibility and the trust reposed in them.

At another examining shop the overlooker, Mr H——, cheerily greets us, and is ready to show us all flaws that it is possible to detect. This work is the most highly trained in the factory. All defects are put aside to be rectified if possible. The examined work is sent on to the official examining department, where it is again minutely examined and tested.

Morning inspection is not complete until Shifting-house and the various offices have been visited. Bright rows of taps and well-scrubbed boards meet the eye in the wash-houses. At the door of the Shifting-house a strong smell of disinfectant is noticeable. At the call of "Mrs Ellis," an answering voice replies, "Here I am, miss, on my knees agin," and a cheerful figure emerges from a dark corner whence a moment before sounds of scrubbing were heard. A hasty survey, and a talk about supplies of gowns and shoes, a glance into the medicine cupboard to see that it is well stocked, and it is time to return to the platform for the turn-out.

Standing at a point of vantage on the bridge where the shops can be surveyed, the foremen and D.P.O.'s watch the workers as they stream out, at the sound of the hootah, to their dinner and well-earned rest.

6

Clara Ellen Grant

SHE WAS ONE OF AT LEAST NINE CHILDREN of a fairly prosperous family in a quiet Wiltshire village; her musical and self-educated father owned an interior decoration business. But Clara Ellen Grant (1867–1949) had dreams of living in a wider world. As a young girl she aspired to be a teacher in London. Later, her plans shifted to working with the Universities' Mission to Central Africa, "but the East End gripped me, as it grips so many," she said later. Her missionary ambitions appear to have been linked to her marriage plans. She told a reporter for the *Somerset Standard* in 1927 that in her early twenties, just before coming to London, she had been in love with a missionary, who died abroad.[1] She kept the young man's photo, and close to her death she told reporters, "That is the only man I could have married," a version of her life story that several journalists found appealing.[2] After she finished her training as a teacher at Salisbury Training College, she served for a time as a head teacher of a church school in a small town in Wiltshire before arriving in London in 1891, at age twenty-three, along with her younger sister. Through 1900 she held teaching positions at two different East London schools.[3]

Grant's next position was in a small local Board (publicly funded) school on Bow Common, which was rebuilt and enlarged in 1905.[4] She remained in that district living and working for the next half century, and the school is now named after her. In making her home near her work she was quite unusual, as most teachers in poor districts left them for nicer neighborhoods at the end of the day. When asked about her choice in 1906, Grant

Originally published as "A School Settlement," a letter to The School Child *1, no. 14 (April 1911): 9–11.*

Figure 5. Children waiting for a free school meal, from George Sims, *Living London* (London: Cassell and Company, 1902), 1: 88. Soon after compulsory education began in London, in 1871, school managers and missions in poor districts began to organize meals for children who came to school hungry. Serving them—the quintessence of charity—was a popular task among the volunteers.

replied, "There was an immense economy of time and energy" in living on the spot, enabling her to pursue her "hobby" of organizing welfare for the families of her pupils.[5] She turned her little home into a settlement house in 1907, the Fern Street Settlement, designed to provide help and recreation to the school's children, but also to the neighborhood in general. As the settlement's work expanded, it absorbed adjacent houses, which were purchased for the settlement by a wealthy member of its governing council.[6] The staff was never larger than four, but neighbors who volunteered did much of the settlement's work, and in this it was also unique. Fern Street organized school meals, medical care, parties, cheap used-clothing sales, country outings, and the "farthing bundles" of toys for small children, which remained a neighborhood institution through the 1960s.[7]

Grant was involved in professional discussions about early childhood education at a time when elementary schools in Britain officially admitted children as young as three. She had earned a Froebel Certificate near the beginning of her career and become involved in the Child Study movement, one of whose leaders, Earl Barnes, became her good friend. She worked briefly, too, with Margaret McMillan (see chapter 11 of this volume) on a health clinic for her pupils. Many of her pedagogical views have since become common sense. For example, she supported children's free drawing rather than their copying of specific shapes. She thought the "thimble and knitting drill" for children as young as two was patently ridiculous.[8] She contributed frequently to education journals, especially *The School Child*, a journal directed at school social workers.

On Grant's retirement from teaching in 1927, journalists represented her as a sweet and saintly elderly woman, a portrait that effaces her early-twentieth-century years of political activism. Her own two published memoirs, however, also omit this phase of her life. In a settlement annual report for 1937 she declared herself no firebrand. She was "incurably a Liberal" and a onetime supporter of the National Government (the Conservative-dominated coalition government that included Liberals and the right wing of the Labour Party).[9] Yet in the fall of 1905 she was deeply involved in the agitation for government measures to combat unemployment, joining a campaign launched by a left-wing coalition that included the Women's Industrial Council.[10] She presided over and gave a rousing speech at one of a series of women's meetings organized by the Poplar Trades and Labour Representation Committee in October of that year. Grant was one of the speakers in a delegation of Poplar unemployed workers and their representatives to the prime minister, Arthur Balfour, in November. *Justice,* the Social Democratic Federation (Marxist) weekly, offered her the highest praise its jargon would allow, commending her in this period as "a school teacher, keen of perception, who has thrown in her lot with the workers."[11] A series of letters in 1911 to *The School Child* also shows her as a fiery champion of the poor against punitive charity workers. During World War I she tried to preach love and community in her district rather than "the gospel of hate." She was a well-informed observer of international events through the 1930s.[12]

At Grant's funeral in 1949, she was honored as an early childhood educator, a local elected official, and an important neighborhood figure. The funeral cortege was a long one; each street and each local institution had sent its own wreath. Clergymen of every denomination also attended, along with many London officeholders. Mothers with babies in arms and children carrying flowers stood and watched the procession.[13] Grant had been awarded an OBE in the year of her death.

NOTES

1. Entry by Elizabeth J. Morse in Oxford DNB. *Somerset Standard,* (1927), clipping in Clara Grant file, THLHL; the quotation is from Grant's *Farthing Bundles* (London: Fern Street Settlement [1930]), 72.

2. "St. Clara of Bow," *The Daily Mail,* January 1, 1949 (on the occasion of her being awarded the Order of the British Empire [OBE], clipping in THLHL.

3. Clipping from *The Daily Express,* "'Saint' of the East End," May 31, 1927, in THLHL. This was one of many articles written after she retired from her teaching position.

4. According to Grant's testimony before the Select Committee on Education (Provision of Meals) Bill, Parliamentary Papers 1906, Qq. 2504–09. ("Qq." refers to the numbered questions and their answers in reports of parliamentary hearings.)

5. Ibid., Q. 2517, Q. 2597.

6. Documents now at the settlement titled "Points from Trust Fund," which include a copy of the Settlement Council minutes from July 13, 1909, mention the Hon. Lady Johnstone as guaranteeing the eight hundred pounds needed to purchase three adjacent houses. Grant also gives a brief history of the settlement in its 1937 *Annual Report,* 35–37. Available at the settlement, still on Fern Street, Bow.

7. By the 1960s, the price had doubled, however, to a half-penny. *Tower Hamlets News,* January 1966, 11–12 (clipping in THLHL). Meals were also still being served at the settlement in 2004, though mostly for old-age pensioners.

8. Grant, *Farthing Bundles,* 49–53.

9. Fern Street Settlement, 1937 *Annual Report,* 10.

10. See the introductions to chapters 3 and 9 for a discussion of the Women's Industrial Council (also described in the glossary).

11. *The Star,* October 2, 1905, 8; *Daily News,* November 7, 1905, 7; *Justice,* November 11, 1905, 4.

12. "A Fire in the Grate," *The School Child* 1, no. 16 (June 1911): 15; Fern Street Settlement, *Annual Reports,* 1919, 13. Grant also submitted an anti-Fascist (and anti-pacifist) letter written by a Dr. Cullen to the *East End News,* January 5, 1936; clipping in the THLHL.

13. This account of the funeral is based on *All Hallows, Bromley-by-Bow, Church Monthly,* November 1949, and *East End News,* October 21, 1949; clippings in THLHL.

FURTHER READING

Clara Ellen Grant's two autobiographical books repeat each other at times: *Farthing Bundles* (London: Fern Street Settlement [1930]), and *From 'Me' to 'We': Forty Years on Bow Common* (London: Fern Street Settlement [1940]). The Oxford DNB has an entry on Grant by Elizabeth J. Morse. Also see R. Pickard and C. A. Pickard, *Eighty Years on Bow Common* (London: Fern Street Settlement, n.d.)

Grant's testimony before the Select Committee on Education (Provision of Meals) Bill, 1906, provides information on both her views and the range of her activities. See *Parliamentary Papers* 1906, Cmd. 288, vol. 8, Qq. 2430–2625.

A School Settlement

To the Editor of THE SCHOOL CHILD.

Dear Sir,

I have been asked to give some fuller particulars of our little School Settlement, following up your kindly appreciation in the February number of THE SCHOOL CHILD.

Briefly, the inception of our Settlement rested upon certain conclusions to which many years of social work in a poor school had led us.

That some form of systematic social effort must be made in poor schools, in the interests both of humanity and of educational efficiency, is a principle now generally accepted and exemplified by the thousand Children's Care Committees established in L.C.C. schools. Slowly also we are beginning to see that these efforts point to the school as the true and natural centre for social work. Well coordinated and well controlled, the Care Committees will become the true "Charity Organisation Society" of a district and of a city. These main principles were obvious to us years ago, but the establishment of our Settlement rested upon one or two further conclusions which forced themselves upon us in practice.

1. *Need for trained resident workers.* It was soon obvious to us that a large proportion of the best work can only be done by residents and by trained workers. To be a true "Social Homocea" [remedy] one must be "on the spot" to "touch the spot." A trained nurse is an absolute necessity in one, or between two, large poor schools. Our Settlement Nurse attends at school daily for our own children, and at the Settlement in the evenings, at which "outsiders" are also eligible. She also attends our voluntary School Clinic, held on Monday afternoons by Dr. Tribe. In order to catch our little hares young, Nurse also visits, under the auspices of the local Health Association, every new baby born in our school group of families. These are visited least monthly for a year, and a monthly "Consultation" and "Baby Weighing Day" is also held. At the age of three the infants come under the beneficent supervision of the school which is most necessary in poor districts. To provide the missing link in our little chain of effort we hope one day to have a small Day Nursery— not large enough to tempt mothers to go out to work, but one in which a few carefully selected children from 1–3 years of age could be cared for, mothers advised, and young girls trained in Infant Care.

For the many other duties devolving upon the Care Committee a second resident worker seems necessary, *e.g.,* for running various thrift clubs, visiting families of children fed at school, special personal and friendly visiting in cases of drink, dirt, depression, trouble, etc., arranging hospital visits, sending children to country or convalescent homes, employment and recreation for boys and girls leaving school. All these demand workers on the spot at the moment when wanted. In our own case we have also six weekly sales of clothes to parents, with a Work Fund for those unable to pay in money. For such work as this it is difficult to find reliable workers locally, and though, of course, it is right to attract all the local and distant workers possible, their efforts are best organised under a small nucleus of trained workers always on the spot. Local helpers, as a rule, lack leisure, money and experience, whilst distant workers, even possessing all these, are too far off to guarantee regular daily, nightly, or even weekly service, and so the work suffers in efficiency and in continuity.

In our own case, through the kindness of friends, resident workers are paid. In many cases volunteers may be forthcoming, but here again we venture to predict that the field of social service gathering round the school will have a growing proportion of professional trained workers paid either through the many charities whose funds are now so largely wasted or misapplied, or through the Education Authority, thus securing a band of Social Officers, nurses, visitors, economic investigators, all as well equipped and as carefully selected as the teachers in the schools.

2. *Settlements. Large v. Small.* A second principle to which we firmly adhere is that where Settlements are necessary they should be small and personal. In order to share, understand and interpret the life around one must live in a simple, homely way in the ordinary cottage or flat. It is the only way in which one can enter into the difficulties and needs of one's neighbours, show them the potentialities of their own homes, and really attract them to come in a homely way for little chats. Settlements at best rank, after all, amongst the things which, as Canon Barnett [former warden of Toynbee Hall] so wisely said, should aim at their own extinction, and, if large, they tend to become elaborate and institutional, too remote from the life around for the inmates to feel the life around. Nor are women constituted by temperament and instinct to live together in large communities under necessarily fixed rules; they crave for their own little home with perhaps one or two companions. Many small congenial groups living together in an ordinary independent, natural way, scattered

over various poor streets, will leaven a poor neighbourhood far more effectually than a large institution in which the vision is, as a thoughtful writer in the *Morning Post* said, "a mere peephole into the life of the poor, with the 'Peeping Tom' a little too much on the safe side." Poor neighbours coming in for a chat would naturally rather call at a little house akin to their own than at a large palatial abode where it is impossible for each worker to have her own cosy little sitting-room for visitors. Probably the ideal Settlement would have as residents two men and two women, but England is perhaps scarcely ripe for this form of "Co-education."

I have purposely dwelt at length upon this point of the size of Settlements because the moment seems to me opportune. Everything points to a growing development of the Care Committee as the coming controlling force in our city schools and life, combining, in all probability, some share of the administrative work now done by Local Managers and the vast network of social effort amongst children in and out of school. The social problem would be largely solved if every Care Committee could be trusted to perform all its functions thoroughly and well, but, among the thousand Care Committees entrusted with this vast social responsibility in London alone, there must be many who are looking for some simple, inexpensive method by which the continuity and efficiency of their work can be secured, and the efforts of voluntary and supplementary workers duly co-ordinated and strengthened. "Committee" work is one thing, "Care" work quite another, and the School Settlement seems to be the best executive for the "Care" side of the work.

3. We need scarcely say that School Settlements, whilst inspired by the deepest spiritual motives, should be absolutely undenominational in their activities, supplementing, on the social side, the spiritual efforts of the churches, and working, of course, sympathetically with them.

4. *The Place of the Teacher.* Although it would seem to be too late to press the beneficient ideal of personal residence of teachers amongst their children in a general way, we cordially agree with Professor Findlay, who strongly holds that the ideal School Settlement will have at least one teacher attached to it. In our own case a teacher is responsible for the control, and, given capable, reliable workers and a sympathetic Care Committee, there is much to be said for the plan. It simply amounts to the addition of a couple of social assistants to one's ordinary staff. To live near the school means an enormous economy of time, strength and nerves, and, given the suitable temperament, the life is far more interesting and inspiring than the popular alternative, Suburbia. It is impossible to exag-

gerate the effect of life amongst the children upon one's personal attitude towards them, and also upon one's ideals of education. For too long have our schools been standing, big and grim, in the midst of a community with which they had nothing in common, and, if a School Settlement does no more than help to bring the school into a truer relation with the life around, it will have justified its existence.

We should be happy to send our annual report and appeal to children, "The Service of Children and the Children for Service," to any who desire to know more. Quite apart from its link with our own school (Devons Road, Bow, E.) we venture to hope that our little Settlement embodies an ideal worthy of extension in modern social work.

I am, Dear Sir,
Faithfully yours,
Clara E. Grant.
Hon. Sec.

Margaret Harkness

MARGARET HARKNESS (1854–1923) WAS BORN into a family thick with clergy-men, which was also her father's profession. When she was eleven her family moved to the country parish of Wimborne St. Giles in Dorset. From an early age Harkness felt cramped and bored at home. Because of the need to "repress her extraordinary activity of mind," as her famous cousin Beatrice Potter (Webb) later wrote, she was "an hysterical egotistical girl with wretched health and still worse spirits."[1] Despite her intelligence, Harkness only received a few years of belated formal schooling. She attended Stirling House, in Bournemouth, a finishing school where she got to know her fellow pupil and second cousin Beatrice Potter. In 1877, having refused to marry, and with her family's support, she went to London to begin nurse's training at Westminster Hospital. For the next few years Harkness appreciated her freedom but continued to be unhappy as she labored in health-care jobs that she was unsuited for: she worked as an apprentice in a dispensary, cared for her sick mother in Dorset, and worked at Guy's Hospital.[2]

She found her vocation in the early 1880s; her first publication was in 1881, an article titled "Women as Civil Servants," published in the well-known monthly *The Nineteenth Century.* Harkness became an energetic and prolific writer, "working almost night and day" in 1883, turning out novels as well as articles.[3] She was sustained by friendship with Beatrice Potter and a number of other single women who worked or wrote in London: Amy Levy (see chapter 10), Annie Besant (also in this volume, chapter 2), Eleanor Marx, and Olive Schreiner. Eleanor Marx was Harkness's frequent

Originally published as "Barmaids," in Toilers in London; or, inquiries concerning female labour in the metropolis *(London: Hodder and Stoughton, 1889), 205–14.*

companion on journeys of exploration in East London in 1888.[4] By the late 1880s a much happier young woman lived in a "little room in Gower Street" in Bloomsbury, near the British Museum, according Beatrice Potter.[5] Harkness also lived in East London for a short time, sharing quarters in the Katharine Buildings, the workers' flats where Beatrice Potter, like Margaret Nevinson, was a "lady rent collector" for the philanthropic East London Dwellings Company (see chapters 1, 24, and 15, respectively).[6]

Harkness acquired her knowledge of working-class London life and labor in a variety of ways: through her journalistic research, her travels and residence in poor districts, and, finally, her involvement with the London Dock Strike of 1889—which she later depicted in her novel *George Eastmont: Wanderer* (1905). Her political sympathies were with labor and socialism and she was a member of the Social Democratic Federation for a short time in the mid-1880s, but because of her sympathy for what she called the "slummers"—"a class below the unskilled labourers"—she came to feel very sympathetic toward the Salvation Army without being an actual adherent of their brand of low church Protestantism. Professed socialists were quarrelling and denouncing each other, as she saw it, without offering any direct aid to these impoverished thousands.

In the early 1890s Harkness traveled to Australia, New Zealand, and the United States, and from then until her death, made only short visits to England. She was in India and Ceylon between 1906 and World War I, and in France and Italy following the war.

NOTES

Toilers is a collection of unsigned series on sweated trades published in the *British Weekly: A Journal of Social and Christian Progress,* from April 27 through December 28, 1888. Harkness was the editor of the *British Weekly* series "female labour in the metropolis." She is also known to have been one of the several "Commissioners" who gathered material for the series and to have written pieces for it. "Barmaids" is likely to have been written by Harkness, but this is not known for certain. It is certainly a telling description of one of the sexualized women's jobs in the nineteenth-century metropolis. On Harkness's participation in the *British Weekly* series, see Seth Koven, *Slumming: Sexual and Social Politics in Victorian London* (Princeton, NJ: Princeton University Press, 2004), 166–67 and 340, n. 91. My biography draws heavily from the joint work of Joyce Bellamy and Beate Kaspar in the DLB, as well as material from Koven, *Slumming.*

1. Norman MacKenzie and Jeanne MacKenzie, eds., *The Diaries of Beatrice Webb,* vol. 1, *"Glitter Around and Darkness Within," 1873–1892* (Cambridge, MA: Harvard University Press, 1982), 79.

2. This assessment of her state in these early years in London is based on the DLB, 104, and Nord, *Walking the Victorian Streets,* 186–87.

3. Letter to Beatrice Potter, February 29, 1884, quoted in the DLB, 105.

4. This friendship did not last out the 1880s, though, probably because Harkness disapproved of Eleanor's liaison with Edward Aveling. See Yvonne Kapp, *Eleanor Marx* (New York: Pantheon Books, 1976), 2: 199–202, 261n.

5. MacKenzie and MacKenzie, *Diaries of Beatrice Webb,* 1: 266. Potter's diary entry was in November 1888.

6. The most detailed discussion of the Katharine Buildings and their rent collectors is Rosemary O'Day, "How Families Lived Then: Katharine Buildings, East Smithfield, 1885–1890," in *Sources and Methods for Family History,* ed. Michael Drake and Ruth Finnegan (Cambridge: Cambridge University Press with the Open University, 1994), 1: 129–66.

FURTHER READING

Margaret Harkness is best known for her novels of London poverty (all published under the pseudonym John Law), especially *A City Girl* (London: Vizetelly, 1887); *Out of Work* (London: Swan Sonnenschein, 1888), centered on the famous "Bloody Sunday" Trafalgar Square demonstration of November 1887; and *Captain Lobe: A Story of the Salvation Army* (London: Hodder and Stoughton, 1889). The latter is a story of the Salvation Army and East London poverty that was revised and reissued several times.

Harkness also wrote several travel books on India, a novel set in India (*The Horoscope,* 1914 or 1915), and many articles in newspapers and periodicals, some anonymously, including "Women as Civil Servants," *The Nineteenth Century* 10 (September 1881): 369–81; "A Year of My Life" (under the name John Law), *New Review* 5 (October 1891): 375–84; and "A Week on a Labour Settlement," *Fortnightly Review,* new ser. 56 (August 1894): 206–13.

There are a number of excellent books and articles that deal with Margaret Harkness. Peter Bailey's "The Victorian Barmaid as Cultural Prototype," in *Popular Culture and Performance in the Victorian City* (Cambridge: Cambridge University Press, 1998), is a fine companion to the selection that follows. There are biographies of Harkness in the DLB, vol. 8, by Joyce Bellamy and Beate Kaspar, with John Savillewell; and the entry by John Lucas in the Oxford DNB.

Also see John Goode, "Margaret Harkness and the Socialist Novel," in *The Socialist Novel in Britain: Towards the Recovery of a Tradition,* ed. H. Gustav Klaus (New York: St. Martin's Press, 1982); Lynne Hapgood's study of Harkness in *Eleanor Marx (1855–1898): Life, Work, Contacts,* ed. John Stokes (Aldershot, England: Ashgate, 2000); Beate Kaspar, *Margaret Harkness: A City Girl* [in German] (Tübingen, Germany: N. Niemeyer, 1984); Deborah Epstein Nord, *Walking the Victorian Streets: Women, Representation, and the City* (Ithaca, NY: Cornell University Press, 1995), a study that includes extensive discussions of Harkness (see esp. 192–97); Eileen Sypher, "The Novels of Margaret Harkness," *Turn-of-the-Century Women* 1, no. 2 (winter 1984): 12–26; Martha Vicinus, *Independent Women: Work and Community for Single Women, 1850–1920* (Chicago: University of Chicago Press, 1985), chap. 3 (on hospital nursing); and Ingrid Von Rossenberg, "French Naturalism and the English Socialist Novel: Margaret Harkness and Edwards Tirebuck," in *The Rise of Socialist Fiction, 1880–1914,* ed. H. Gustav Klaus (New York: St. Martin's Press, 1987).

Barmaids

The girls who serve behind the bars of restaurants and buffets, also behind the bars of theatres, hotels, and railway stations, consider themselves a step above ordinary barmaids; namely, the girls who serve in public-houses.

They are all young ladies of course, but the former are designated "the young ladies at the bar," while the latter are "young ladies in the public line of business."

A very telling little pamphlet, under the title of "Called to the Bar," was published some time ago by Miss Beale. This deals with first-class barmaids, and especially with those engaged in the Metropolitan Railway bars, or the "subterranean hotels," as Miss Beale calls them. Of all barmaids these girls are most to be pitied. Draughts, bad atmosphere, and sulphurous smoke give them sore throats and heart complaints. Not a few of them stand from seventy-six to eighty-six hours in the week, or about eleven hours a day. They work in shifts, coming on early in the morning, and working with stated intervals until midnight. One Sunday in the month is considered ample time for recreation. Yet the girls prefer this life to domestic service. They think it more "genteel" to be a barmaid than a servant.

They are seldom allowed to sit down, and they say if they might only have sliding seats to draw back from the bar—rather high, so that they could rest without appearing to sit—they would be less often on the doctor's books. But their employers, with a few exceptions, will not hear of this.

Some of the Metropolitan Railway bars are upstairs; for instance, the one at High Street, Kensington; but not a few are on the underground platform—small, dark places, without ventilation, full of smoke, reeking with alcohol. Let readers think what it means to stand ten, eleven hours in such places day after day, with no rest except on Sunday; to sleep in rooms below the streets, which must be lighted all the twenty-four hours with gas, and which never get a ray of daylight. But the girls say they would rather sleep four or six in such rooms, and two in a bed, than take the last train to another station, for sometimes they miss the train, and then they must walk home—or run, for they are afraid to go slowly through the empty streets at midnight.

Things are not managed much better at some of the largest London stations. At one terminus twenty-two barmaids are employed, with salaries of 8s. a week. The manageress receives 17s. 6d., and the sub-manageress 10s. a week. Each girl is allowed to consume 10*d.* a day in spirits, or 5*s.* 10*d.* a week. This money must be spent in drink, not food; but if the girl is a tee-totaler she is allowed ginger-beer or lemonade. The manageress, or her assistant, serves the 10*d.* allowances, and the girls are not supposed to help themselves. Nevertheless, they do it.

It is impossible for any manageress, be she (as the girls say) "ever so much of a cat," to watch all that goes on at the bar of a large station. So the girls cheat the customers if they dare not cheat their employers; and many an innocent customer swallows "waste" while the barmaid drinks his order for spirits. "Waste" is whatever is left in the glasses. This is, by order of the employers, put into the glass measures behind the bar. Each measure has a colour: white for brandy, blue for gin, green for whisky, and red for rum. The "waste" is kept in the measures and served to the customers, for, as the girls say, "We wouldn't touch that muck." So the customers swallow "waste," and the girls drink their orders for spirits.

Barmaids have other ways of getting more than their legitimate ten-pennyworth; but they dare not water the spirits, for if they did, it would certainly be found out. One excuse for this conduct is that their food is very bad. The meat they receive is generally tough, and the butter rancid, to say nothing of stale vegetables and bread. Their work is exhausting, and their little close sitting-rooms behind the bar or beneath the station are not likely to increase their appetites.

Most of them spend half of their money on stout, which is sustaining, and not a few take stout for lunch and for dinner. Some prefer a glass of ale for lunch, a glass of wine in the afternoon, and a glass of spirits when they have done work. The manageress takes gin and bitters, and other "nips," to help her on through the long hours of business.

Board and lodging are provided by the employers. At the terminus we are now speaking about the girls live quite a mile away from their work, and as they must wash up before they go home, it is often midnight before they reach their beds. Some of them complain bitterly of the long walk in winter when the ground is covered with snow, and others say they would not mind so much if the "hangers-on" did not follow them.

These "hangers-on" are the men who use bars as their clubs, who remain in them two or three hours, drinking. Some of them are "horsey" individuals; not a few are flash mobsmen, who go there to discuss business. These girls could, if they would, tell many secrets; but the bar has its code of honour, and they seldom peach. There is only one sin men never condone in women, and that is peaching.

Board and lodging, 5s. 10d. a week for spirits, and 8s. for extras, may seem ample to those readers who forget how well barmaids are supposed to dress, and their heavy bills for washing and breakages. The average weekly bill for a first-class barmaid's breakages is from 1s. 6d. to 2s. She not only has to pay for her own breakages, but for those of customers. In some places there is a regular breakage fund, and a certain amount is deducted from each girl's wages to put into it. This is very hard on the girls, for late at night, when customers get intoxicated, many things are broken. They dare not complain of their customers.

Not long ago three or four young men watched the manageress out of a railway bar, and then went in to have "a lark." They upset the bottles of water, put the napkins in the claret cup, and did other mischief. One of the barmaids ventured to remonstrate. They then complained to her employer that they had not been treated with sufficient courtesy; and the following day all of the girls were discharged at a moment's notice. Barmaids are obliged to put up with a great deal, for if they call in a policeman they are generally bound to charge some one, and this brings disgrace on the business. So they wink at many things, and try to keep their customers in good humour, merely making a few slight objections when a man jumps across the bar to give them a kiss, or wishes to act as an amateur hairdresser. Among barmaids there are of course many fast girls, as there are everywhere else; but all who know them well are aware that a large number of them are quiet, modest women, who work hard, who neither flirt nor drink.

But they must make themselves agreeable, or they are dismissed, and sometimes at a moment's notice. Many managers will only have girls who flirt. Again and again we have heard of girls turned away because they are too steady; and of others who are dismissed because managers think it well to exhibit new faces. "Men get tired of always seeing the same women at the bar," and managers wish to please their customers.

Fifteen to sixteen years of service count in some places for nothing if custom begins to fall off. First, the sub-manageress is removed, then a hint is given to the young ladies. The girls try to look smart; they laugh and chaff, then become reckless. No character is given when they are turned away; and they say to themselves:

"Who will give employment to a discharged barmaid?"

It is not the same everywhere, but in the greater number of places fast girls are preferred, and no questions are asked about what they do when away from the bar—where they get their smart clothes and jewellery. Drinking is the fatal sin of barmaids. They are surrounded by temptations; their hours are long, and their food is bad. It is difficult for them to resist spirits.

"We are most of us half-seas over when we go to bed," said a barmaid who lives in a well-known restaurant. She and her companions have rooms at the top of the house, under the superintendence of an ex-barmaid. The managers sleep on the same landing. In most cases the girls return at night, from restaurants, buffets, and theatres to depôts; but in some cases they live on the premises. The age of admittance used to be eighteen, but now it is lower. The distinction made with regard to morality is that "kept" girls are shunned by their more respectable companions. The latter marry men of their own station, or start in the public line of business, while "kept" girls become common prostitutes.

The "kept" girls take tips; but the others rarely accept presents, unless they are Christmas-boxes given to all, not to one in particular. We cannot mention names here, but there are several employers we should like to recommend on account of the care they take about accommodation and food for their young ladies. Their name is not legion, and as yet they do not seem to realise that girls cannot work ten and twelve hours a day without breaking down. At several of the large London stations barmaids are allowed to sit when at leisure; they receive a month's notice if turned away, and live in the hotels; but as a rule, employers do not seem to have any conscience about barmaids. The public ignore them altogether, if we except the hangers-on, who pester them with inane compliments, and the fast men, who decoy them to their ruin.

An attempt has been made by the Young Women's Christian Association to help barmaids, and Miss Gough, the secretary of the Restaurant Branch, is in communication with many of them. Morley Rooms, 14, John Street, Bedford Row, W.C., has been opened as a centre for those barmaids who care to use it; and we give an account of a barmaids' "at home" there, witnessed by a Commissioner.

But the Young Women's Christian Association cannot attack the evils from which these girls are suffering—namely, long hours, bad accommodation, low wages, and an excessive allowance of spirits.

The Society is afraid to interfere between employées and employers, because they are dependent on the latter to a great extent, and feel, if the doors were closed upon them, they could not do the work they are doing at present. They are evangelists, not economists. However, they feel much sympathy for the workers—in fact, one of them actually said the other day: "The present state of things is *almost* enough to make one a Socialist."

The Young Women's Christian Association only touches the fringe of the class at the bar. Our Commissioner says that when she arrived at Morley Rooms she found about thirty neatly-dressed young women playing at "coach," and Miss Gough looking on with great satisfaction.

The drawing-rooms they were in had beautifully decorated doors, the work of Mrs. Watts, the wife of the artist. Other ladies had helped to decorate the place, and the rooms were full of pictures, books, and games. One young woman was playing a piano, and the rest were romping in a dignified fashion. The next game was unique. Some newspapers were fastened inside an open doorway, and two holes having been cut large enough to show a pair of eyes, one of the company went behind the newspapers, and the others tried to guess whose eyes were exhibited.

Then some little musicians arrived, and the girls listened to an amateur concert. Downstairs were tables covered with fruit and cakes, tea and coffee, ready for the girls who came pouring in from their work. Miss Gough was in request everywhere; every one wanted to have a word with the hostess.

Morley Rooms, 14, John Street, Bedford Row, W.C., are open to members and friends of the Restaurant Branch of the Young Women's Christian Association for conversation, reading, music, and rest; members and non-members can also be accommodated with lodging and board at moderate prices.

Mary (Kingsland) Higgs

MARY (KINGSLAND) HIGGS (1854–1937) was a prolific writer and social reformer whose range extended from the needs of the itinerant poor, to early childhood, the rejuvenation of Christianity, Depression-era unemployment, and urban beautification. The selection included here is from one of her several incognito investigations of the lives of homeless women, this one undertaken in 1903, when she was nearly fifty. In one of her London investigations, her adult son accompanied her dressed as a working man.[1]

Higgs first encountered homeless women when she served as Secretary of the Ladies Committee visiting the Oldham workhouse. By 1899 she had set up a small independent shelter for such women and later established three more lodging houses for women in Oldham.

With her charitable efforts and social exploration went social theorizing, all three of which she thought interconnected. The existence of a large population of permanently unemployed and often homeless men and women was a symptom of a society in danger of degeneration, she believed. Her own theories of social evolution, based on William James and Plato, among others, single out such "nomads" as people who have been able to reach only a primitive level of social development.[2] Economic arrangements in which "massive fortunes" bare down on "all strata beneath" are just as dangerous to societies, however. Higgs was convinced that firsthand knowledge was the key to putting "our national treatment" of social questions on a scientific footing. Eyewitness experience, for example, demolishes "the

Originally published as "In a London Tramp Ward," in Glimpses into the Abyss *(London: P. S. King, 1906), 259–68.*

impression that the vast majority of so-called 'vagrants' are 'loafers.'" In fact, "the inmates of the casual ward are mostly found to be seekers for work. Little short of a revolution may be made in preconceived opinion by actual experience."[3]

One of the many clergymen's daughters to become urban explorers, Mary Kingsland, born in Devizes, Wiltshire, was the first of the three children of Congregational minister William Kingsland and his wife Caroline. Mary got a good education, first at home with her two brothers, and then at a local private school; from 1871 she attended the College for Women in Hitchin, which became Girton College, Cambridge, two years later. She was the first woman to take the Cambridge natural science tripos (cumulative final exams for the degree) and gained second-class honors. She lectured at Girton and then taught at two different secondary schools.

Higgs married a Congregationalist minister when she was twenty-five and eventually had four children. In the early 1890s, the family settled in the northern industrial town of Oldham. This is where Higgs began her activist career, working to found gardens and parks, helping crippled children, and rescuing prostitutes. She is best known for her involvement with vagrants and the issue of homeless people, work that she continued through the 1930s. But she was also a suffragist and a founder of Oldham's Garden Suburb. During World War I she set up model workrooms for women needing employment; she opposed conscription and joined the Society of Friends. She was awarded the OBE in 1937, shortly before her death.

Casual wards of workhouses, often set apart from the main buildings, offered meals for the homeless and a bed for a few nights in exchange for several hours of work that was purposely designed to be pointless: for men, picking apart hemp rope or breaking up stones into gravel, and for women, washing and scrubbing.

NOTES

1. Higgs, *Glimpses into the Abyss,* 255.
2. Author's preface, *Glimpses into the Abyss,* v–vi; also see her article, "The Geology of Society," based on a prize-winning essay.
3. Higgs, *Glimpses into the Abyss,* 23–24.

FURTHER READING

For more writing by Mary (Kingsland) Higgs, see *Three Nights in Women's Lodging* (N.p.: Privately printed, n.d.), available in the British Library; *The Tramp Ward* (London: John Heywood, 1904); *How to Deal with the Unemployed* (London: S. C. Brown, Langham and Company, 1904); "The Geology of Society," *Contemporary Review* 87 (April 1905): 36–

41; *Evolution of the Child Mind* (London: The Froebel Society of Great Britain and Ireland, 1910); and *Down and Out: Studies in the Problem of Vagrancy* (London: Student Christian Movement, 1924).

For writing about Mary Higgs, see the entries in *Who Was Who among English and European Authors 1931–1949,* compiled and reprinted by Gale (Detroit, 1978), in *The Suffrage Annual and Women's Who's Who* (first published in 1913), and in Sybil Oldfield's *Women Humanitarians: A Biographical Dictionary of British Women Active between 1900 and 1950* (London: Continuum, 2001). There also is a biography of Higgs by Rosie Chadwick in the Oxford DNB; my thanks to Chadwick for sending me her entry before its publication. Deborah Epstein Nord's *Walking the Victorian Streets: Women, Representation, and the City* (Ithaca, NY: Cornell University Press, 1995) contains on pages 90–95 a valuable reading and contextualization of *Glimpses into the Abyss.*

———— ◊◊◊ ————

In a London Tramp Ward

Towards six o'clock on a pleasant evening in March, my companion and I found our way to the casual ward of a London workhouse, selected because, on the testimony of Guardians, it was supposed to be well-regulated and ideal. *Real* beds and *porcelain* baths, perfect cleanliness and good management would surely afford comfortable conditions. We did not go together, as I was announced to speak publicly and known to take a companion, and it might therefore be difficult to escape detection. But we were, as it happened, the only inmates, save a woman going out in the morning.

The ward was spotlessly clean. The brown bread and gruel, at first glance, not unappetising. Alas! the bread was sour. Food first, and hot bath to follow, wet hair, though more time than usual to dry. Clean nightgown, and actually a bed. So far good.

Locked in at about seven o'clock to solitary meditation, I rejoiced to have found better conditions. Alas! I had not reckoned on the physical effects of the unwholesome combination of the sour bread, followed by hot bath, and backed up by imperfectly dried hair. Before long I was violently sick, and every portion of my first meal returned. In the darkness it was impossible to see if there was any means of communication to beg a welcome drink of water. Presently my friend began coughing and groaning. It seems the effect of the bath and wet head on her was to produce a violent cold, headache, and sore throat. Then in another cell a woman began retching and coughing badly. In the morning we learned she also had been upset by the bath when she entered, but no complaints were noticed. Her cough sounded like asthma or bronchitis, and very bad. We asked her why she did not see a doctor. "No tramps were allowed a doctor," she said.* She intended when out to try to get into an infirmary. She had been in three days, and could not eat.

This information, received after we had got up at 5.30, was somewhat disheartening, for we were both ill. Breakfast none of us touched. Our fellow tramp played with hers, pointing at the thick scum on the unappetising gruel (very salt), served in a worn enamel mug, with no spoon. "God alone knows," she said. "They will have to answer for it." She told us she was detained a third night because she had been in another casual ward during the month, and the officer "spotted" her. She was evidently a regular casual. "They all have to do it" (*i.e.,* to go from ward to ward), she said, describing how other wards were better and how harsh this one was—and no one came in who could help it. We asked how it was she came in herself. She said she had had "business" in that part of the town, and could not reach another ward. She said she was quite clean, as she had "been down" the previous week-end. She said the treatment had made her ill; at the time we hardly believed her. Later we knew. Seven o'clock, and a summons to work. We began cheerfully under charge of an old woman. But already some conception that we were under a hard task-mistress was dawning upon us. "Be sure you only do what you are told," said the woman. The ward was apparently clean, but the whole must be scrubbed. My portion was to do four cells and a long, long passage leading past eighteen cells (nine on a side), and two bathrooms, and a lavatory with two w.c.'s. Cloths, bucket, and soda were provided, no aprons till later. I had a kneeling pad, my friend none. She was told off to the bathrooms.

It seems such a simple thing to tell that it is hard to convey the real conditions. Presently our task-mistress came round. She was not unkind, but one of those women to whom, in ordinary health, work is a joy in itself, and the utmost scrupulosity of finicking cleanliness a thing to be exacted as a matter of course. For every single detail a standard was to be attained, at whatever cost to flesh and blood. For instance, all blankets to be re-folded to an exact shape, and laid so—no otherwise. To work hard, all day and every day, would probably be to her no task, and the difference between working hard on a full and on a meagre diet had never dawned upon her.

*This is not true, but where a doctor is not in residence it appears as if officials often will not take the trouble to detain tramps to see him, and permission if asked for is often refused.

Sickness was to be discredited—probably a "dodge"—in any case, the fault of previous misdoings. Work was to be exacted to the very last farthing. Faithfully she did her duty—as she knew it. Nine hours' solid work (five in the morning, four in the afternoon)—that was what the law exacted—and she got it.

Now, to work as a charwoman on a comfortable breakfast, with a pause for lunch, and prospective dinner, and the opportunity to chat and "take your own time" is one thing. To work for a taskmistress with prison in prospect for the slightest shirking—with no pause and no food—is quite another. The matron knew I had been very sick—her assistant told her—and also that I had had no food. "That old tramp, whom she couldn't bear," as she told my friend, "had been eating stale fish; that was what made her sick. She could tell that sort, she always knew what people were like." This was so humorous that it decidedly relieved the situation! We compared notes as we refilled buckets, but did not dare to loiter or show knowledge of one another. Walls had ears, or, at any rate, keyholes were handy. So we worked steadily, my friend's fate being worse, as she worked under the taskmistress's eye. She won prime favour, but never, never, in all her working days, had she worked so hard.* She cleaned the bathrooms and a whole flight of stairs, and then was put on the private sitting-room, to be done most particularly, not even the old woman attendant could be trusted to do it, it was usually the matron's own work; but she had been ill, and it had "got neglected." How hard my friend laboured she alone can tell. Every inch was gone over many times under the vigilant eyes. Meanwhile, the "old tramp" laboured as diligently as possible—when the eyes were upon her! They detected some signs of "scamping," when her back was turned, so doubtless I was "an old hand!" The fact of the matter was, that without such careful "scamping" I positively could not have sustained the long, long hours of labour. Four bucketsful of water—one for each cell—seven for the long passage, two for lavatory and w.-c.'s, brasses to clean, paint to dust. It seemed a Sisyphean task, no sooner ended than a new one was exacted. I wondered if by carefully husbanding strength I could hold out. At dinner-time, twelve o'clock, we stopped for an hour. I could not touch food. My friend, though fresh from the tantalising smell of beef steak and onions, managed to eat a small portion of bread and cheese, washed down by cold water. Our tea and sugar had been confiscated.

Tired! That is no word for it! We had already done a charwoman's day's

---

*My friend was at one time accustomed to wash for a family of nine.

work. My friend could hardly speak, and I had no strength save to lay my head on the table and wonder how I should survive the afternoon.

One o'clock and hard labour. My friend, on finishing two bedrooms, was put to clean the storeroom. So weary was she, that towards the close even her taskmistress saw that she had overrated her strength, and gave a sign of grace by saying she would help her to finish. Meanwhile, the "old tramp" must do the dayroom—it only served her right for the way she "tickled the boards!"

Five long and very ornamental forms [benches] and two long tables, to be scrubbed on every inch of surface to immaculate whiteness with soap and water. The floor to be scrubbed and every place dusted. Kneeling had become such torture that the straining of the body up to scrub the under-surface of the forms almost produced faintness. It must be remembered that all this work was exacted without a particle of food. The matron had come in at dinner-time and seen my food untasted. I told her I could not touch it. She looked at it as if it was some rejected dainty. "What a pity," she said— not at all as if it was a pity I could not eat, but a pity to leave such good food!

Flesh and blood found it hard to bear the long four hours' labour; over and over again I failed quite to please my taskmistress and tried her patience. She confided to my friend that she should have to keep out of the room or lose her temper. She did not recognise the arm growing weary, the heart sick and faint. But she did recognise the work of my friend, and rewarded it by a cup of tea and two slices of bread and butter. To eat these she was shut up in the storeroom, and was by no means to tell "that tramp" how she had been favoured! She did, however, manage to run in and give me a drink of tea, but such was my internal state, that it made me imme-diately violently sick. This was when work was over, fortunately. For one blessed three-quarters of an hour before I finished the taskmistress was away. She was very suspicious as to how I had done the work in her absence. It passed muster. I did not dare to stop, but certainly "hurried." It was nec-essary to survive.

At last—five o'clock and respite. We both were more dead than alive. It must be felt to be realised.

Again we could not touch the food, but my friend had had a little. Again no notice was taken of any symptoms of illness on my part, but a lozenge was given my friend for her throat, as she was "prime favourite."

At last 5.30, and we might seek bed. My friend was allowed to wear some of her underlinen, as she had been very cold the previous night. The "old tramp" must do as best as she could. What happened was another night of long misery, desperate sickness on an empty stomach—no sounds save the London sounds without, and the groaning and sighing of my tortured friend within, close by in another cell.

Long, long hours; would God it were morning! The cross-bars of the window faintly seen against the sky spoke of the cross that is never absent, of the woes of men and of Him Who is crucified in the least of these, His brethren. When will the long torture of the ages end, and men care for the poor? At last the torment ended—6.30. It was possible to rinse the mouth with water. Oh, what it is to know thirst and sickness combined!

Every limb ached; my poor friend was no better; her knees were too sore to touch. But soon there would be freedom. We ate no food, of course,—but welcome liberty! To me the worst agony was the last half-hour of patient waiting. No words can tell the passionate longing that seized me to breathe free breaths. No such inward struggle may come to those inured to hard conditions. Yet for them, also, the summer life is free, and for freedom they sacrifice much. Who knows how a tramp feels, save God? At last we are free; our money, tea, and sugar are returned. Shelter and friends are near.

. . . . .

But for them? At this hour a procession of women issues from our casual wards—hundreds, perhaps thousands, all over our land. Their faces are set in the grey dawn—whither? Not to the tramp ward again—not at once—it cannot be borne immediately; later it may be again a necessity. Now anything is preferable. Prison? It has lost its terrors—it cannot be harder. It is only an incident in life to "go down." Sin? What's the odds? It may pay for a decent bed and food. The river? That is best of all, if one could manage to face it. Silence, oblivion, and the mercy of the God above Who knows. Yet life is sweet, and it is a pleasant thing to behold the sun. To be a beggar is best—spring stirs already—God opens hearts. Food and shelter may be begged as "charity." It is best to fall into the hands of God, not into the hands of man. The vagrant life is sweetest. This is how tramps are made.

Edith (Mrs. F. G.) Hogg

EDITH (MRS. F. G.) HOGG (1856–1900) was a vice president of the Women's Industrial Council (WIC) and one of its founders.[1] When her death at age forty-four was regretfully announced at a WIC business meeting in November of 1900, speakers referred to some of the qualities that may be visible in this account of a visit to the South London homes of rabbit fur workers: "personal charm," "true womanly qualities," and also "generous sympathy, unremitting labours, and brilliant intellect."[2] She must have been an effective public speaker as well, for an audience member who heard her lecture at a conference in 1898 vividly recalled it in 1932.[3]

In 1896, just after a government commission had recommended that manufacturing done in the home be exempt from national safety and hours legislation, WIC activists Edith Hogg and Margaret Gladstone organized a team of women to investigate this kind of employment. Hogg and her colleagues came to believe that legislation must protect home workers as well as those in factories. This article deals with just one of these home industries, the preparation of rabbit fur to be sewn into coats. "Fur pullers," a group of particular concern to Hogg, prepared skins for curing by removing their long coarse hairs. *The Nineteenth Century*, where the article was published, was a journal very widely read by educated people. The WIC expanded the investigation to cover thirty-five London home industries, presenting its findings at a conference in November of 1897.

Another of Edith Hogg's concerns was child labor. She was a tireless lecturer in the late 1890s on the subject as well as on "women as citizens." As

Originally published as "The Fur-Pullers of South London," in The Nineteenth Century 42 *(November 1897): 734–43.*

head of the WIC's Education Committee, she organized an extensive investigation into the paid labor of schoolchildren, covering fifty-five London schools; these findings were published in *The Nineteenth Century* in 1897. The WIC expanded the Education Committee to include national representatives of many organizations. The new committee's efforts gained support for the Employment of Children Act of 1903, legislation that strengthened the authority of local government to restrict child labor.[4]

Hogg departs somewhat from journalism and social investigation conventions by using a number of references to works of literature and art. The "famous and jocund company of pilgrims" Hogg refers to early in the article are the thirty travelers in Chaucer's *Canterbury Tales* who meet at an inn in Tabard Street, Southwark, for their journey. When Hogg describes the defiant young woman who resembles the figure from "The Vagrants," she is referring to a dramatic 1868 painting by Frederick Walker, inspired by his seeing some gypsies encamped, of a group of two women and some children at a roadside. Finally, her quotations "like plants in mines . . ." and "still sad music of humanity . . ." are from Robert Browning's *Paracelsus* (slightly misquoted) and Wordsworth's *Tintern Abbey.*

NOTES

1. The Women's Industrial Council (WIC), an outgrowth of the Women's Trade Union Association, was founded in 1894 as a part of the labor and socialist ferment of the last decade of the nineteenth century and existed for about twenty-five years. Both organizations defined themselves as groups of "women of leisure and ability" who would help working women, with the newer group's emphasis being investigation and the dissemination of information. WIC's membership included a number of male labor leaders and politicians, and women with a variety of political positions from socialist to liberal, including Margaret Gladstone, who later founded the Women's Labour League (the women's section of the Labour Party) and in 1896 married the future Labour prime minister Ramsey MacDonald; Lily Montagu, the Jewish religious reformer and leader of girls' clubs; Beatrice Webb; Lady Aberdeen, a Liberal leader very active in philanthropy; and Clementina Black.

The WIC campaigned for legislative solutions to low (sweated) wages, dangerous or unhealthy working conditions, and long hours. They urged that women be hired by government bodies as factory inspectors to enforce these laws. Several members did receive such appointments. WIC also helped to organize a thriving network of clubs for working-class teenage girls (at this time such girls were usually already at work full time) not only for the girls' recreation but as a place where they could learn what legal protections they had. On the WIC, see the selection by Black and Meyer in this volume; also Mappen, *Helping Women at Work;* Schmiechen, *Sweated Industries;* Sheila Lewenhak, *Women and Trade Unions* (London: Ernest Benn, 1977), 118–20; and Shelley Pennington and Belinda Westover, *A Hidden Workforce: Homeworkers in England, 1850–1985* (Basingstoke, England, 1989), chap. 7.

2. "Council News and Notes," *Women's Industrial News,* December 1900, 208–9.

3. Daphne Glick, *The National Council of Women of Great Britain: The First One Hundred Years* (London: The National Council of Women of Great Britain, 1995), 200.

4. Some of this information on Hogg's child labor investigations comes from the testimony of another committee member, Nettie Adler, at a parliamentary inquiry. See Minutes of Evidence taken before the Inter-Departmental Committee on the Employment of School Children, *Parliamentary Papers* 1902, vol. 25, Cmd. 895, pp. 368–71, Qq. 3314–19, and appendix 26, 671.

FURTHER READING

For more writing by Edith Hogg, see "School Children as Wage Earners," *The Nineteenth Century* 42 (August 1897): 235–44; *Home Industries of Women in London: Report of an Inquiry into Thirty-Five Trades, by the Investigation Committee of the Women's Industrial Council* (London: Women's Industrial Council, 1897), which includes anonymous case notes from Hogg's investigations of fur pullers; "Home Industry in Its Bearing on Child-Life," a lecture, with audience comments, published in the *Official Report of the Conference [of the National Union of Women Workers] Held at Norwich, October 25, 26, 27, and 28, 1898* (Norwich: Jarrold and Sons, 1898), 140–55; and "Brush-Making," in *Sweated Industries: Being a Handbook of the Daily News' Exhibition,* ed. Richard Mudie-Smith (London: Burt and Sons, 1906), 92–95.

What we know best about Edith Hogg is her work with the WIC. For writing about her, see Ellen Mappen, *Helping Women at Work: The Women's Industrial Council, 1889–1914* (London: Hutchinson, 1985). James A. Schmiechen mentions Hogg and her work on p. 159, n. 67, and p. 162 of *Sweated Industries and Sweated Labor: The London Clothing Trades, 1860–1914* (Urbana and Chicago: University of Illinois Press, 1984). Hogg's lecture topics and research activities are documented in issues of WIC's monthly newsletter, the *Women's Industrial News,* throughout the 1890s.

The Fur-Pullers of South London

Among the 'dangerous trades' dealt with in the recently issued report of the Royal Commission is included one, of the very nature of which the vast majority of the public are totally ignorant. The fur-pullers of South London are the subject of the following article. The facts here related were obtained by personal investigation—forming a part of a general inquiry into the conditions of women's 'home-work' in South London; and truly, if it is well that light should be thrown on the dark places of the earth, there is no spot to be found where such light is more needed.

The employment of fur-pulling finds its slaves—there is no other word—only among those whose conception of life is strictly limited to keeping body and soul together; to whom a wage of ten shillings a week is wealth unattainable; to whom an eight-hour day is unimaginable. They belong one and all to that most pitiful, most helpless, most hopeless class which is produced by modern industrial conditions—those who acquiesce in starvation of body and soul as the state of life in which they were born, out of which they can never rise, in which they are doomed to die. To them, want and filth and disease are the normal inevitable conditions of existence, against which they lack the will as well as the power to rebel. Mr. Booth has said that they are the despair of those who work among them, 'not so much because they are bad as because their standard is hopelessly low.' They are 'not to be roused to better things, or else the right way to rouse them has not yet been found.'

Of the fur-pullers working in factories we shall have something to say in the latter part of this paper; it is with the home workers, however, that we shall have chiefly to deal.

The area within which our investigation was carried on is a small one [part of Southwark]: from Union Street on the north to the New Kent Road on the south; from Blackfriars Road on the west to Long Lane on the east. This district is the last refuge of the casual worker. Among the inhabitants, the few who have regular employment find it chiefly in that mysterious El Dorado which is always spoken of as 'the other side of the water;' but for the vast mass of the people on that grey south side, the broad sweeping bend of the river forms a moral no less than a physical barrier, shutting them off from every hope and every aspiration beyond the unending struggle somehow to keep alive.

This perpetually shifting population is as perpetually recruited from the larger pitiful army of the helpless and inefficient. The flotsam and jetsam from other quarters and other classes who come to merge their individual failure in the general failure of the invertebrate mass where room seems somehow to be made for all who drift into it. Hopelessly excluded by their own incompetence from a secure position in the labour market, with a natural abhorrence and incapacity for the discipline of regular employment, the men, for the most part, pick up odds and ends of jobs at the riverside or in the streets; working two or three days a week and loafing for the remaining four or five. Under these circumstances it is the women who must, perforce, become the staple breadwinners, and accordingly we find them working with far greater regularity than the men, rising in the early dawn, toiling through the long weary day, and snatching a few brief hours of sleep as the exigencies of their trade allow.

A few find employment in factories and workshops; others—and it is with these that we are dealing—take work given out at the factories to be done in their own homes. This work is, to an exceptional extent, fluctuating and casual; it demands little specialised skill or intelligence, and offers the maximum of long hours with the minimum of pay. There are, among these women, isolated cases of flower makers, tailoresses, machinists, sack makers, paper-bag makers, &c.; but a close investigation shows the main industries to be three, *i.e.* fur-pulling, box-making, and brush-drawing. Whole streets are given up to these, and in almost every room of some of the wretched tenement dwellings are inert, exhausted women plying one or other of these trades, and using up life and strength in a hard, unavailing struggle to keep the wolf from the door.

The inquirer who turns aside out of that historic street from which one April day there started long ago a famous and jocund company of pilgrims—where to-day a sadder stream of humanity ceaselessly ebbs and flows—and who plunges under one of the narrow archways on its western side, will find himself at once face to face with the lowest depths to which the toil of women can be dragged. Here, in an endless network of pestilential courts and alleys, into which can penetrate no pure, purging breath of heaven, where the plants languish and die in the heavy air, and the very flies seem to lose the power of flight and creep and crawl in sickly, loathsome adhesion to mouldering walls and ceilings—here, without one glimpse of the beauty of God's fair world, or of the worth and dignity of that human nature made after the image of the Divine, we find the miserable poverty-stricken rooms of the fur-pullers.

To apply the word 'homes' to dens such as these is cruel mockery. There are no 'kindred points' between them and heaven.

Of all these home-workers the fur-pullers are the hardest to find. Whether it is from some strange sense of the degradation of their work, some faint glimmer of the divine spark of self-respect, which makes them seek to hide from prying eyes; or whether it is merely from a vague terror lest discovery by the mysterious higher powers should deprive them of their last means of buying a crust of bread, the fact remains that they hide themselves away with a curious persistence. If you want to find them, the surest and quickest method is to inquire of the swarms of neglected unwashed children who are always to be found playing on the greasy pavements 'where the lady lives who does fur-pulling.' A dozen names will be instantly shouted out, with graphic descriptions of the owners and their abodes. Changes of residence are too much an affair of every day for either parents or children in these parts to burden themselves with remembering the numbers even of the houses in which they themselves are lodged for the time being.

It is the business of the fur-puller, broadly speaking, to remove the long coarse hairs from rabbit skins; the skins and the collected hairs having each their further uses. Accordingly, as we approach the first of those tenement dwellings to which the inquiry is directed, the countless miscellaneous odours of the alley are absorbed in one which overpowers the rest—the sickly unmistakable smell of uncleaned skins. On entering the house the air becomes thick with the millions of almost impalpable hairs which float in it. They force their way through every chink and crevice, clinging to everything they touch, and lying piled in layers of horrible dust on the dilapidated and dirty staircase.

Groping your way upwards, avoiding as carefully as possible all contact with the walls and low ceilings, and guided by the ever-increasing density of the 'fluff,' you enter a back attic in which two of the fur-pullers are at work.

The room is barely eight feet square, even less, because of its accumulation of dirt; and it has to serve for day and night alike. Pushed into one corner is the bed, a dirty pallet tied together with string, upon which is piled a black heap of bedclothes. On one half of the table are the remains of breakfast—a crust of bread, a piece of butter, and a cracked cup, all thickly coated with the all-pervading hairs. The other half is covered with pulled skins, waiting to be taken into 'shop.' The window is tightly closed, because such air as can find its way in from the stifling court below would force the hairs into the noses and eyes and lungs of the workers, and make life more intolerable for them than it is already. To the visitor, indeed, the choking sensation caused by the passage of the hairs into the throat, and the nausea from the smell of the skins, is at first almost too overpowering for speech.

The two prematurely aged women—whose unkempt matted hair is almost hidden under a thick covering of fluff, and whose clothing is of the scantiest, seeming to consist of bits of sacking fashioned into some semblance of garments—are sitting on low stools before a roughly made deal trough, into which they throw the long upper hairs of the skin, reducing them to the fine, silky down growing next to the skin itself, which is afterwards to be manufactured into felt hats. The heaps of skins by their side are dried, but uncleaned, and still covered with congealed blood.

At first the women are suspicious. They imagine that you are an emissary of the London County Council—in their eyes, the embodiment of unlimited and tyrannical power. The County Council and the law are their standing dread; for, if these take it upon them to interfere and deprive the fur-puller of her employment, there is nothing left but starvation. The idea of interference for the fur puller's benefit has never presented itself. But once they are satisfied that you have nothing to do with the law or the County Council, they become friendly and communicative, ready to tell you all about themselves and their work.

'Yes, it stuffs your chest up,' they admit—they can hardly deny it while you stand choking before them, and a tearing cough is racking them as they talk—'but you gets used to it when you've been at it all your life.' Even so, according to the proverb, eels get used to skinning.

What do they get for it? They say each of them can pull 'a turn and a half,' working twelve hours. A 'turn' means sixty skins; and the rate of pay is 11*d.* per turn—1*s.* 4½*d.* for the twelve hours. That is when they are supplied with 'English' skins. 'Furriners'—*i.e.* Australian and New Zealand skins—take longer; but the rate per turn is 1*s.* 1*d.* or 1*s.* 2*d.* From the point of view of wages, the English skins are preferred; but 'furriners' have one great point of superiority, due to the necessities of packing. They are properly cleaned, and the skins as white as parchment, a marked contrast to the repulsive state in which the English skins are given out to the workers.

The women provide their own plucking knives and the shields for their hands. The knives cost 8*d.* and last some time; but the shields, which cost 3*d.,* wear out quickly. Another 2*d.* a week usually goes in knife-grinding. The pulled-out hair is carefully collected, and weighed at the shop, a turn being supposed to yield two pounds. If the return is deficient in quantity, the value is, at some factories, deducted from the price of the work. These arbitrary deductions are, in the hands of tyrannous foremen, often made a means of grievous oppression to the half-starved creatures, who are only too well aware that if they resist there are plenty of others ready enough to step into their shoes and to take the work at any price that is offered for it.

In another room of the same house was an elderly woman, almost breathless from asthma, but working doggedly on to finish her 'turn' before closing time at the factory. Her hand was strained and swollen from the perpetual grasping of the knife, and she said that her skins, which were 'furriners,' were tough and hard to pull. She was paid 1*s.* 1*d.* a turn, but could make more in a day at English skins at a lower rate of pay. Sometimes her daughter pulled too, and then they made 2*s.* 2*d.* between them, working till eight o'clock or thereabouts. She had been left an orphan at ten years old, and had done the pulling ever since. Her husband was a waterside labourer, never in regular work, and his earnings did no more than pay the rent. Out of a family of eight she had 'buried' five, but did not apparently see any connection between this and the pulling, though it was 'dreadful unhealthy work.' When her son lived at home, they were able to have another room for the pulling; but it spoilt his clothes, and when 'a suit of black he bought for his grandfather' got spoilt with the dust he moved to pleasanter quarters elsewhere, leaving the old folks to do the best they could. 'And that's bad enough,' she added; 'for now I can't hardly do a turn a day, and that's the truth.'

In a small landing-room of the next house, choked up with fluff, and intolerable from the smell, was one of the many deserted wives with whom the poorer quarters of London abound. Doubtless she was better off without the husband, who never did a good day's work in his life. At any rate, it did not occur to her to attempt to find him, though she had heard of him no farther off than the Minories.

She kept herself and her child, a stunted, half-starved girl of nine, making, as it appeared from her wage book, an average of 7s. 6d. a week, working all day. The foreman had often promised her a place 'inside,' and the realisation of this was the height to which her ambition was able to soar; 'for the shop was a beautiful place, more like the 'orspital than a shop.' The child went to and fro with the work, wrangled with the costermongers of every description who supply the scanty needs of the street, did such intermittent cleaning as seemed good in her eyes, prepared the poor food hastily snatched in the intervals of work, and evaded the School Board officer with all the ingenuity of the true slum child. The mother had not left the house for weeks. When the day's work was over, she threw herself on the bed, too tired even to get 'a bit of victuals.'

In a kitchen of this house were three women, one lying ill in the bed, and two others working at the trough in front of the tightly closed window. One of these was old and garrulous, the other still young, as age is reckoned by years, and with traces of what had once been great beauty. In marked contrast to the apathetic endurance of the other workers, her worn, defiant face was arresting, as the central figure in Walker's picture of 'The Vagrants,' in its expression of fierce, unavailing protest against the cruelty of fate. Not even the dusty coating of fur could wholly conceal the beauty of the dark hair lying softly on the low, wide forehead, nor the symmetry of the large bowed figure in its coarse repulsive rags. She scarcely even glanced round as the door opened, and the harsh voices of the other women did not seem to reach her ears; but there was no submission in her utter immobility; every feature of her face told its story of fierce rebellion, not yet crushed into despair. She pulled on in the same oppressive silence until farewells were being exchanged. Then, lifting her great sombre eyes for an instant from her work, she said, with a tragic simplicity, *'Miss, I wish I had your life.'*

Further down the court was a woman snipping the hair from the tails and ears and corners of the skins which cannot be passed through the shearing machines at the fitting factories. Her hands were cut in several places by the shears she was using, and she mentioned, as an incident of little or no importance, that the acid in the fur made the wounds sore. Compared with the pulling, her work made little dust, and she looked clean and tidy. She had two rooms, using the kitchen for her work. She was paid 1s. a pound for corners, and 6d. for tails, and made about 8s. a week. 'Some can do pretty well at it; but if you want to make 10s. a week you can't mind the house as well.'

Her next-door neighbour, a paper-bag maker, was working long hours to complete an order for bags for hot cross buns. It may be incidentally mentioned that the rate of pay for these bags is ¾d. per gross. The woman—a widow—and her four children, who all helped out of school hours—and in them too when there was pressure of work—earned an average of 2s. 4d. a day, 'much less than could be earned in the shop.' The guv'nor employed eighty inside hands. She was sure he didn't even know the addresses of his out-workers, much less keep a register.

Next came an attic belonging to a fur-puller, a woman with six children, whose work was done in the one indescribably dirty bedroom, the boards black with grease from the skins. The factory at which she was employed had no inside pulling-rooms. All the work was given out.

And so on, through one close little street after another. Everywhere the same dead level of squalor, of joyless days and months and years passed in ceaseless and repulsive toil, with the reward of starvation wages, almost invariably supplemented by Poor Law relief. Everywhere these 'homes' in which leisure is unknown, or if it comes as the rarest of visitors, it comes as a curse. In them, these mothers with no time to rejoice in their motherhood, to give or receive love and sympathy and care from those for whom they are responsible; and children, who, from the time they are first launched into their troubled sea of life, must be a law unto themselves, who are born and nurtured in life's darkest places, 'like plants in mines that never see the sun.' Everywhere the cry of the city going up to heaven, not in the 'still sad music of humanity,' but in a sadder discord of sorrow, in a babel of oaths and curses and foul jests, and in the horrible hoarse laughter more piteous far than tears.

This life of the 'home' workers is sufficiently ghastly, though no words can adequately present its utter sickening repulsiveness. It must be seen and breathed in to be realised. Yet any attempt at remedying it by direct means involves enormous difficulties. Within the factory, however, the Government inspector can make his presence felt. Nevertheless, here too there is a general reluctance to admit visitors, an apparent fear of 'revelations,' a defensive attitude in speaking of the women and the work, which points to a lively dread of the possible effects of publicity, and a lively consciousness that improvement may be demanded.

To show that in fact little, very little, has been done to remove even the worst elements of the work, we may take the case of one workshop, said to be the best of its kind in South London, and employing large numbers both of in- and out-workers.

The process of treatment commences in a room where the smell of the skins is peculiarly overpowering. Here stands a large tank in which they are steamed and softened before being 'opened.' This opening is considered by the women to be the lowest work they can take. Those engaged on it, many of whom are only girls, will not take it up unless driven to do so by desperate straits. After the opening comes the drying process, done in large racks heated by stoves on the floor beneath. When dried the skins are brushed on the hairy side, with a solution of nitric acid, by machinery, tied up in 'turns' for 'pulling,' and given out. After the pulling (*i.e.* the removal of the longer and coarser hairs) the skins are again dried, put through an hydraulic press, and packed in bales, to be despatched to the great felt-manufacturing centres of Stockport and Macclesfield, or to America, where the felting process is largely carried on. There the soft fur is converted into felt, the actual skin being boiled down for fine glue and size. Skins of tame rabbits which are less valuable for felt, are made up into cheap muffs and linings for cloaks, and into the article of wearing apparel known as 'electric sealskin.'

The 'fluff' plucked by the fur pullers is collected and sold for cheap bedding, largely used by miners in the north of England. It may here be remarked that the report above mentioned is emphatic in condemning the foul condition of rags and other materials used for a similar purpose. It is all bought by weight, and it is no unusual thing for 40 per cent. of the weight to be lost in the process of washing. 'It is therefore obvious,' says the report, 'that an upholsterer who is content to use the lowest sample of flock can purchase enough to stuff two beds for about the same money as another upholsterer, willing to use only the best flock, has to pay for sufficient to stuff one bed, even apart from the cost of washing.' Any one who has seen the conditions under which the fur-pullers' 'fluff' is collected will probably judge that the percentage of foul matter accompanying it is particularly high.

Within our workshop every available inch of space, from the large tunnelled cellars to the storage rooms of the roof, is filled with rabbit skins. They are stacked in racks reaching to the ceiling; lying in heaps about the rooms; tied up in 'turns' ready for the home workers, or in great bales of 5,000 for sending away. The stench arising from them is noisome; yet, except in the manager's rooms, where disinfectants are freely used, no attempt is made to minimise it. Moreover, though the atmosphere of the whole building is absolutely befogged with hair; yet, while the managers and foremen are careful to wear linen overalls, not only are the women unprovided with anything of the sort, but their outdoor garments are actually allowed to remain all day long hung up *in* one of the pulling-rooms. Of course the effect is that the women carry with them into their homes the sickly smell with which these clothes have become saturated, and the abominable fluff which sticks to them with the pertinacity of an Old Man of the Sea.

Worse still, in total disregard of all factory regulations, the women actually cook and eat food in the pulling-room *at the same time* as others are at work at a table not three yards distant.

Although fur-pulling is not yet included in the list of 'dangerous' trades, it is evident from the chronic bronchial catarrh from which so large a percentage of the workers suffer, the attacks of fever to which young unseasoned workers are liable, and the enormously high rate of infant mortality among the home-workers, that it is a trade which stands in urgent need of further regulation.

The report of the Royal Commission (to which allusion has already been made) in connection with those diseases to which workers in hair of every form are peculiarly liable, contains recommendations which, if they were strictly enforced, would do much to lessen the sufferings of this class of workers in the factories. It is suggested (1) that the ventilation should be so arranged as to carry the fluff away from the worker by means of powerful extracting fans with a down-draught, such as are already in use in rag mills and other factories where the material carried away is of value in manufacturing processes; (2) that the wearing of overalls and caps made to exclude dust should be compulsory; (3) that a prohibition to take meals in workrooms or other places to which noxious dust may penetrate should be strictly enforced.

Within the factories and workshops the strict application of these rules would have a beneficial effect. But hitherto the new factory regulations as to air and space have had one result which was by no means desired: they have tended to drive a large quantity of the work from the factories to the home-workers. Now if the condition of things in the factories is bad, in the rooms of the home-workers it is many degrees worse; and it is exceedingly difficult to see how legislation is to interfere effectively in such places.

The report, having remarked that 'any old dilapidated buildings are considered good enough for the accommodation of the fur-pullers,' proceeds with suggestions—viz. that the Secretary of State should license every building in which the trade is carried on, that health registers should be kept, and periodical visits be paid by the certifying surgeons. But this would apply only to the factories. With the host of isolated workers, constantly changing and moving, the difficulty of efficient registration seems almost insuperable. To extend the rule effectively to home-workers, power would have to be given to factory inspectors to enforce sanitary regulations of a similar character and standard to those required in the factory; a license being granted only after the house had been visited and certified as a place where the work could be done without injury to those working there. Whereas, as the law now stands, the factory inspector, though empowered to demand from the employer a list of his out-workers and to visit them in their homes, has no authority to remedy any of the evils he may find there; and the sanitary authorities, who alone have power to act, can only do so in cases where complaints are made of a public nuisance. Moreover, every home-worker who can plead irregularity of employment—and *all* home-work is irregular—can thereby claim exemption from all the provisions of the Act.

It does not, in short, seem practicable to make the worker responsible. To prohibit home-work altogether is equally impracticable. But what does seem practicable is to throw the responsibility on to the employer. It is not beyond his power to ensure that the 'homes' to which work is given out answer to the necessary conditions. Moreover, the adoption of this principle would have one very marked advantage. In order to avoid the trouble of attending to the condition of the home-workers, the employer would find a strong inducement to get as much work as possible done in the factory or workshop proper. A tendency would set in, working towards the gradual extinction of home-work; and the effect of that would be infinitely more satisfactory than any system of registration, inspection, or regulation of actual home-work that can be devised.

The evils of both subcontracting and home-work in all departments have become so thoroughly realised in the United States that a Bill was last year introduced by Mr. Sulzer which certainly had the effect of annihilating home-work entirely. It provides that, when a wholesaler gives out work to be done not by his own employés but by a contractor, the wholesaler must prepay a tax of 300 dollars. If the contractor in turn sublets a part of his contract, he also must pay the same tax for each subcontractor. And if the subcontractor divides his work among home-workers and others not in his own direct employment, he must pay the same tax for each one of those home-workers. It is tolerably obvious that if the employer has to pay a tax of 60l. per head for every home-worker, he will give up employing home-workers.

For the legislative extinction of home-work by such drastic measures, neither the public nor the workers are probably at present prepared. The public, unaware of the conditions under which home-work—at least in such trades as these—must be carried on; deluded also to some extent by a vague idea that family ties, parental influence, and family affection are preserved by it; are either indifferent or adverse to any such measures. The workers would see in them not the opportunity of work under healthier conditions, but the loss of employment. But a system which gradually and automatically turned home-work into factory work would excite no serious opposition; the end accomplished would have the approval of every competent observer who knows what such home-work means.

An important conference on the subject of home-work, called by the Women's Industrial Council, will meet in November in London, under the presidency of Mrs. Creighton [a leading philanthropist and wife of the Anglican bishop of London]. The condition of the fur-pullers will be under discussion. It is earnestly to be desired that the problems in connection with the subject will have received full and careful consideration, and that practical suggestions duly weighed and thought out may be laid before the conference, for giving effect to the recommendations of the report, and for appreciably ameliorating the lot of the fur-pullers. Heaven knows, they need it!

Amy Levy

AMY LEVY (1861 – 1889), THE GIFTED AND PRECOCIOUS daughter of middle-class Anglo-Jewish parents who eventually made their home in Bloomsbury, read fluently in several languages, including Greek and Latin. She began producing sophisticated work as a teenager. "Xantippe," her defense of Socrates' much ridiculed wife, was published in the *Dublin University Magazine* in 1880, when Levy was only nineteen. She attended Newnham College, Cambridge, the first Jewish woman to do so. Her literary output during her short life was prodigious and included three novels, three volumes of poetry, and many short stories and works of literary criticism. But she struggled with loneliness, depression, unrequited loves (many for women), and increasing deafness. After Levy's suicide at the age of twenty-seven, Oscar Wilde warmly appraised her talent and achievements, citing "Xantippe" for its "qualities of sincerity, directness, and melancholy," and her novel *Reuben Sachs* for its "directness, its uncompromising truths, its depth of feeling, and, above all, its absence of any single superfluous word."[1]

At least by the end of her life, Levy thought of herself as a child of the city, with an "urban Muse" whose "place is among the struggling crowd of dwellers in cities."[2] She moved about in the city among a unique but shifting group of pioneering literary or philanthropic women, many of them "slum travelers" in this volume: Margaret Harkness, Eleanor Marx, Olive

"A London Plane-Tree," "London in July," "Ballade of an Omnibus," "Ballade of a Special Edition," "Out of Town," "The Piano-Organ," and "London Poets (In Memoriam)" were originally published in A London Plane-Tree, and Other Verse *(London: T. Fisher Unwin, 1889).*

Schreiner, Clementina Black, and Beatrice Potter among them. Eleanor Marx translated *Reuben Sachs* into German. Clementina Black, seven years older than Levy, was a close friend; they traveled to Italy together in the winter of 1885, and Black helped her find a publisher for "Xantippe."[3]

Though Levy was a supporter and contributor to the Women's Protective and Provident League, which promoted organizing and self-help among working women, only a small part of her work deals with working-class London or its poverty. Her novels and stories include acerbic depictions of contemporary Jewish social life as it expanded into such respectable West London districts as Bayswater and Maida Vale. She was also gripped by efforts of middle-class women to make places for themselves in the city; her *Romance of the Shop,* a novel about four self-supporting sisters trying to run a photography studio, predates and prefigures George Gissing's *Odd Women.* Her poetry deals with lost love, sadness, and suicide—supporting contemporaries' belief that it was depression ("constitutional melancholy," as biographer Richard Garnett put it) that plagued her despite her remarkable success. In the poems here, all from the first section of her posthumously published *A London Plane-Tree,* the sounds and sights of the streets of London are not so much the subjects as backdrops—distraction or consolation—for the narrator's vivid psychic pain. Garnett, reading the whole collection, found himself exhausted by "their monotony of sadness," which I hope is less likely to set in for readers after the few I have reproduced here.[4]

NOTES

1. Wilde was writing in *Woman's World,* the magazine which he founded in 1888, and to which Levy was a contributor; the quotation is from New, *The Complete Novels,* 1–2.

2. *A London Plane-Tree,* her second collection of poems (published in 1889, after her death), includes as a frontispiece two illustrations evoking the writer in the city and an Austin Dobson quotation: "Mine is an urban Muse, and bound/By some strange law to paven ground." The other quotation is cited by New in *Complete Novels,* 35. As Deborah Epstein Nord has noted in *Walking the Victorian Streets* (197), the first poems in *A London Plane-Tree* do celebrate the writer's urban vantage point.

3. Olive Banks, BDBF, vol. 2, 20 (Clementina Black entry); also Liselotte Glage, *Clementina Black: A Study in Social History and Literature* (Heidelberg: Carl Winter, 1981), 21–23.

4. Richard Garnett, Keeper of Printed Books at the British Library in the mid-1880s, first met Levy's close friend Clementina Black there, and his son Edward eventually married Black's sister Constance (who became well known as a translator of Russian classics). See Ellen Mappen, introduction to Clementina Black, *Married Women's Work* (1915) (reprint; London: Virago 1983), xi–xii; and David Garnett, *The Golden Echo* (London: Chatto and Windus, 1954), 6–9. See Richard Garnett's entry for Levy in the DNB (vol. 11) for his diagnosis of "constitutional melancholy" and his assessment of *A London Plane-Tree.*

For more writing by Amy Levy, see *The Complete Novels and Selected Writings of Amy Levy 1861–1889,* ed. Melvyn New (Gainesville: University Press of Florida, 1993); included are her three novels: *Reuben Sachs* (1888; it was translated into German by Eleanor Marx), *The Romance of a Shop* (1889), and *"Miss Meredith"* (1889). See also *A London Plane-Tree, and Other Verse* (London: T. Fisher Unwin, 1889); and *A Minor Poet and Other Verse* (London: T. Fisher Unwin, 1884).

Amy Levy has attracted the interest of many admiring scholars. Linda Hunt Beckman's *Amy Levy: Her Life and Letters* (Athens: Ohio University Press, 2000) is a complete and thoughtful biography that also includes her extant letters. For more information about her, see Joseph Bristow, "'All Out of Tune in This World's Instrument: The 'Minor' Poetry of Amy Levy," *Journal of Victorian Culture* 4, no. 3 (spring 1999): 76–103; Bryan Cheyette, "From Apology to Revolt: Benjamin Farjeon, Amy Levy, and the Post-Emancipation Anglo-Jewish Novel, 1880–1900," *Jewish Historical Studies* 29 (1988): 253–65; Emma Francis, "Amy Levy: Contradictions? Feminism and Semitic Discourse," in *Women's Poetry, Late Romantic to Late Victorian: Gender and Genre, 1830–1900,* ed. Isobel Armstrong and Virginia Blain (New York: Macmillan/St. Martin's, 1999); Linda Hunt, "Amy Levy and the 'Jewish Novel': Representing Jewish Life in the Victorian Period," *Studies in the Novel* 26, no. 3 (fall 1994): 235–53. Melvyn New's introduction to *The Complete Novels* includes a biographical and literary study that encompasses the range of Levy's work. See also Deborah Epstein Nord, *Walking the Victorian Streets: Women, Representation, and the City* (Ithaca, NY: Cornell University Press, 1995), esp. chap. 6; and Cynthia Scheinberg, "Canonizing the Jew: Amy Levy's Challenge to Victorian Poetic Identity," *Victorian Studies* 39, no. 2 (winter 1996): 173–200. Some recent articles are Alex Goody, "'Murder in Mile End': Amy Levy, Jewishness, and the City," *Victorian Literature and Culture* 34, no. 2 (2006): 461–79; and Perez F. Moine, "Victorian Female Poetry, or How to Sexualize the Angel in the House?" *Cahiers Victoriens & Edwardiens* 59 (April 2004): 229–38.

———◦◦◦———

FROM *A London Plane-Tree, and Other Verse*

A LONDON PLANE-TREE

Green is the plane-tree in the square,
   The other trees are brown;
They droop and pine for country air;
   The plane-tree loves the town.

Here from my garret-pane, I mark
   The plane-tree bud and blow,
Shed her recuperative bark,
   And spread her shade below.

Among her branches, in and out,
    The city breezes play;
The dun fog wraps her round about;
    Above, the smoke curls grey.

Others the country take for choice,
    And hold the town in scorn;
But she has listened to the voice
    On city breezes borne.

LONDON IN JULY

What ails my senses thus to cheat?
    What is it ails the place,
That all the people in the street
    Should wear one woman's face?

The London trees are dusty-brown
    Beneath the summer sky;
My love, she dwells in London town,
    Nor leaves it in July.

O various and intricate maze,
    Wide waste of square and street;
Where, missing through unnumbered days,
    We twain at last may meet!

And who cries out on crowd and mart?
    Who prates of stream and sea?
The summer in the city's heart—
    · That is enough for me.

BALLADE OF AN OMNIBUS

> *To see my love suffices me.*
> —BALLADES IN BLUE CHINA

Some men to carriages aspire;
On some the costly hansoms wait;
Some seek a fly, on job or hire;
Some mount the trotting steed, elate.
I envy not the rich and great,
A wandering minstrel poor and free,

I am contented with my fate—
An omnibus suffices me.

In winter days of rain and mire
I find within a corner strait;
The 'busmen know me and my lyre
From Brompton to the Bull-and-Gate.
When summer comes, I mount in state
The topmost summit, whence I see
Crœsus look up, compassionate—
An omnibus suffices me.

I mark, untroubled by desire,
Lucullus' phaeton and its freight.
The scene whereof I cannot tire,
The human tale of love and hate,
The city pageant, early and late
Unfolds itself, rolls by, to be
A pleasure deep and delicate.
An omnibus suffices me.

Princess, your splendour you require,
I, my simplicity; agree
Neither to rate lower nor higher.
An omnibus suffices me.

BALLADE OF A SPECIAL EDITION

He comes; I hear him up the street—
    Bird of ill omen, flapping wide
The pinion of a printed sheet,
    His hoarse note scares the eventide.
Of slaughter, theft, and suicide
    He is the herald and the friend;
Now he vociferates with pride—
    A double murder in Mile End!

A hanging to his soul is sweet:
    His gloating fancy's fain to bide
Where human-freighted vessels meet.
    And misdirected trains collide.
With Shocking Accidents supplied,

He tramps the town from end to end.
How often have we heard it cried—
    A double murder in Mile End.

War loves he; victory or defeat,
    So there be loss on either side.
His tale of horrors incomplete,
    Imagination's aid is tried.
Since no distinguished man has died,
    And since the Fates, relenting, send
No great catastrophe, he's spied
    This double murder in Mile End.

Fiend, get thee gone! no more repeat
    Those sounds which do mine ears offend.
It is apocryphal, you cheat,
    Your double murder in Mile End.

OUT OF TOWN

Out of town the sky was bright and blue,
    Never fog-cloud, lowering, thick, was seen to frown;
Nature dons a garb of gayer hue,
        Out of town.

Spotless lay the snow on field and down,
    Pure and keen the air above it blew;
All wore peace and beauty for a crown.

London sky, marred by smoke, veiled from view,
    London snow, trodden dun, dingy brown,
Whence that strange unrest at thoughts of you
        Out of town?

THE PIANO-ORGAN

My student-lamp is lighted,
    The books and papers are spread;
A sound comes floating upwards,
    Chasing the thoughts from my head.
I open the garret window,
    Let the music in and the moon;

See the woman grin for coppers,
    While the man grinds out the tune.

Grind me a dirge or a requiem,
    Or a funeral-march sad and slow,
But not, O not, that waltz tune
    I heard so long ago.

I stand upright by the window,
    The moonlight streams in wan:—
O God! with its changeless rise and fall
    The tune twirls on and on.

LONDON POETS
(IN MEMORIAM)

They trod the streets and squares where now I tread,
With weary hearts, a little while ago;
When, thin and grey, the melancholy snow
Clung to the leafless branches overhead;
Or when the smoke-veiled sky grew stormy-red
In autumn; with a re-arisen woe
Wrestled, what time the passionate spring winds blow;
And paced scorched stones in summer:—they are dead.

The sorrow of their souls to them did seem
As real as mine to me, as permanent.
To-day, it is the shadow of a dream,
The half-forgotten breath of breezes spent.
So shall another soothe his woe supreme—
"No more he comes, who this way came and went."

11

Margaret McMillan

MARGARET MCMILLAN'S NAME IS ASSOCIATED not only with education, but also with 1890s socialist and labor politics. Her political orientation shifted, however, to the "Liberal reformism and welfare philanthropism"[1] that characterized her in the late 1910s and 1920s. By the 1920s, for instance, she was a close friend and admirer of the wealthy American-born Conservative M.P. Lady Astor, who shared McMillan's commitment to nursery education and helped to subsidize her work.

Despite the enormous body of writing she has left, Margaret McMillan (1860–1931) remains a somewhat mysterious figure. For one thing, her vague and flowery writing style, "altogether too feminine and sentimental," as one contemporary reader put it,[2] obscures many elements of her life. Moreover, the first biography of McMillan is the hagiographic work of a disciple and thus not entirely reliable. Finally, as Carolyn Steedman observes in her thoughtful study of McMillan, Margaret's own "autobiography" is officially presented as a biography of her sister Rachel, commingling the lives of the two sisters.

Certainly, many facts about McMillan are known. She was born in 1860 in Westchester County, New York, to Scottish parents who had emigrated soon after their marriage. Her father was an estate manager and landscape gardener. Margaret returned to Scotland with her young, newly widowed mother and older sister Rachel in 1865. The girls were raised in Inverness

---

"A Slum Mother" was originally published in The Woman Worker, *the newsletter of the National Federation of Women Workers, July 8, 1908, 131. (The federation was founded in 1906 as a general labor union open to all women workers.) "Guy and the Stars" was originally published in* The Nursery School *(New York: E. P. Dutton, 1919), 154–63.*

in the home of their maternal grandparents. The household was middle class, Gaelic-speaking, Presbyterian, and committed to a rigorous education for its young. It was clear that both of the McMillan girls would have to support themselves, but Margaret got the better education of the two, and was prepared to be a teacher or a well-qualified governess.

After finishing her education in Germany and Switzerland, McMillan was a governess among well-off families, changing positions frequently between 1883 and 1887; Rachel, meanwhile, remained in Inverness but in 1888 moved to London, where she eventually became superintendent of a hostel for working girls in Bloomsbury. Margaret joined her for a time. Then, in 1893, Margaret moved to the Yorkshire woolen town of Bradford, where she had a teaching job; Rachel remained in London and trained as a sanitary inspector, eventually working for the Kent County Council, which brought her to shabby industrial and dockside Deptford, south of the Thames.

In Bradford, Margaret joined the Independent Labour Party (ILP), and as an ILP candidate, served three terms on the (elected) School Board. There she worked for measures to improve children's health and discovered her talent as a charismatic speaker. Her prodigious writing and speaking during these years helped to make national concerns of such local Bradford issues as the half-time system (which allowed school-age children to hold part-time paid jobs), school medical care, and publicly funded school meals.

After Parliament's dismantling of the municipal school boards in 1902, McMillan returned to London. One of her more notable London jobs was as companion and secretary to the brewing heiress Lady Meux, who, horrified, immediately burned McMillan's frumpy hat and dragged her out on a West End shopping trip. Margaret was also, after 1903, a school manager connected with a group of Deptford schools, where she found children who were far more neglected than those she had encountered in Bradford. McMillan was soon promoting medical care for schoolchildren.

The cause of poor children brought McMillan some strange political bedfellows—in addition to Nancy Astor. One of the early ones was Sir Robert Morant at the national Board of Education, who became her friend and adviser. Morant's fierce hostility to democratic forms of education and ruthlessness in dismantling the popular School Boards had made him the enemy of the teachers and of the labor movement.[3] Morant and McMillan formulated legislation, passed in 1907, mandating the medical examination of schoolchildren, but not offering any treatment of the ailments diagnosed.

This was the parents' responsibility, and though McMillan campaigned for school-based clinics, this scheme was never passed into law.

With funding from the radical American soap millionaire Joseph Fels, another of her associates, McMillan organized a clinic for schoolchildren attached to headmistress Clara Grant's (see chapter 6) Devons Road school in Bow. The clinic, which opened in 1908, was managed by the London branch of the ILP rather than by the school system. This was one of only three known school clinics in England at the time.[4] Two enthusiastic volunteer physicians, Reginald Tribe and David Eder, staffed the clinic; they also helped at McMillan's Deptford clinic, which first opened in 1910. Soon the Deptford complex included a nursery school, an outdoor camp for older children, and a training program for nursery teachers. It became the center of McMillan's career as an educator and advocate for children, and the setting for the two stories that follow.

As Steedman sees it, McMillan is a crucial figure in the history of Labour and socialist thought. Through her experience with children in Bradford and Deptford, McMillan was vividly aware that the class advantages of the wealthy were etched into their bodies through years of childhood cleanliness, warmth, nourishing food, outdoor sports, and sound education. True social justice would mean extending such advantages to the children of the poorest classes. McMillan was focusing on issues which most Labour leaders had not seriously pondered: how could the labor movement use its power to improve not only wages and working conditions but also workers' daily lives, including food, housing, and health care? And what could give the majority of workers—unskilled, ununionized, and often politically conservative—a stake in the labor and socialist movements? The association of working-class and "welfare" politics, Steedman argues, was forged through McMillan's pioneering thought and sharp intelligence, especially in her Bradford years.[5]

NOTES

1. Steedman, *Childhood, Culture and Class,* 8.
2. Quoted in Mansbridge, *Margaret McMillan,* 108.
3. Brian Simon, *Education and the Labour Movement 1870–1920* (London: Lawrence and Wishart, 1965), 236–39. Morant had been in the Education Department only a total of seven years when he was made Permanent Secretary of the Board of Education in October of 1902. He was knighted in 1907.
4. Mansbridge, *Margaret McMillan,* 73.
5. Steedman, *Childhood, Culture and Class,* 110.

FURTHER READING

For a listing of Margaret McMillan's extensive writings, see Carolyn Steedman, *Childhood, Culture and Class in Britain: Margaret McMillan, 1860–1931* (London: Virago, 1990; reprint, New Brunswick, NJ: Rutgers University Press, 1990). Most of the entries are for short articles and columns in labor and socialist periodicals.

Samson (London: Clarion Press, 1895) was McMillan's only novel, though she did publish serialized fiction in periodicals. See also *Early Childhood* (London: Swan Sonnenschein, 1900); *The Child and the State* (London: Metropolitan District Council, ILP, 1911); *The Camp School* (London: Allen and Unwin, 1917); *Education through the Imagination,* (London: Swan Sonnenschein, 1904; 2nd ed., London: J. M. Dent, 1923); and *Life of Rachel McMillan* (London: J. M. Dent, 1927).

Albert Mansbridge wrote McMillan's official biography just after her death: *Margaret McMillan: Prophet and Pioneer* (London: J. M. Dent, 1933). See also Viv Moriarty, *Margaret McMillan: "I Learn to Succor the Helpless"* (Nottingham: University of Nottingham Press, 1998), and Steedman, *Childhood, Culture and Class in Britain.* Emma Stevinson, who served as superintendent of the nursery school in the 1920s, wrote *The Open-Air Nursery School* (London: J. M. Dent, 1923). Carolyn Steedman's Oxford DNB entry is very helpful.

─── ⟢⟢⟢ ───

A Slum Mother

She sits in a back room of a small house in one of the meanest side streets of the great city. Through the door—which does not close properly—comes the confused sound of many voices, broken now and again by a shrill laugh.

All the mothers and grandmothers of Slop Alley are out in the sunshine, standing for the most part in open doorways, and conversing so as to be audible at times to friends on the other side of the street.

Mary Ann (that is her name) does not want to join her neighbours today. She wants to be alone. And it is a very strange desire for a woman living in Slop Alley.

Something has happened to Mary Ann. Not a very great event—only the death of a very small, very wizened baby, who never looked as if it could live, anyhow. It was born when its father was "doing time" for his treatment of the mother, and it looked from the first as if all the woes of both parents had gathered on its little head.

Now it is gone, and—what seems quite as strange—twenty-eight bright shillings (the insurance money won by three months of penny-a-week installments) has been received for the burial. It didn't cost quite so much. Four shillings were left over when all was paid. And a neighbour gave Mary Ann a black skirt and bodice.

For Mary Ann, this succession of events appears so marvellous, that in the wake of them she feels an amazement and quickened interest that are like the beginning of a new life.

For years nothing had happened to Mary Ann—nothing but that dreadful thing for which *he* was now doing time, and the melting away of the furniture. There is hardly anything left now—only a rickety table, a couple of chairs, and a saucepan. For months, Mary Ann has been conscious only of one thing in the room: the rent-book. Marked all down two greasy pages are entries of five shillings totalling up to an awful sum that can never be paid.

Mary Ann does not know what to do with this book.

The landlord comes every week, and looks in it, and writes in it. Even to-day Mary Ann is conscious of it. She is conscious also of the four bright shillings left over after all is paid—and, only very dimly, of the little dirty shawl in which the baby was wrapped always.

The door opens, and a touzled head is pushed in.

"Marianner," says the owner of the head, "you're a frettin'!"

"I ain't," says Mary Ann, truthfully.

The visitor, who is no other than the kind neighbour who gave her the dress, stares at her for a few moments and then withdraws, looking very startled.

Through the dirty panes, and above them through the open window, streams the flaming June sunshine. Above shines the flower of the sky—stainless and radiant. And Mary Ann, who has eaten a good meal to-day, and has tidied her hair, and put on the new dress, feels the strangeness and awe of life stealing in on her. The two children that are left to her are playing in the street, and they have eaten. And there is a strange hush and pause in life.

It is as though a burden had been taken away from an overdriven creature, and the currents of a new life were loosened in the numbed veins.

"To-morrow I'll take Louiser to the 'orspital," she thinks. "I'll try to give her a chance. And Sidney shall go to school reg'lar. If I could get a bit o' charin' some ways, perhaps we'd do better in time."

The tinkle of a church-bell floats in at the window, and she folds her hands, listening, with a sort of wonder. So absorbed is she that she does not hear the sound of footsteps on the stair.

Presently the door is pushed open, and a thin, open-mouthed boy of ten, very ill-shod, makes his appearance, holding by hand a little girl of three.

"If you please, mother," says the boy, politely, "Louisa Emma would like to come in."

"You go along," says Mary Ann, abruptly. "Don't you tell me no stories."

Louisa, the subject of this conversation, makes no remark, but buries a small finger in her mouth and sucks contentedly.

"Aren't you ashamed?" inquires Mary Ann, indignantly. "You to want to get rid o' yer pore little sister and go orf kicking a ball."

Sidney plucks up courage to answer this pointed question.

"I ain't ashamed," he says. "Teacher nor you won't let us play nowheres. Where 'ave I to play at all? Nowheres," says Sidney, with a sudden impulse of revolt.

Mary Ann stares at him in amazement. Then her anger rises swift as a tropic storm.

"Orf you go! Don't you let me 'ear another word! Don't you let me see her agen till I calls ye. D'ye hear me?"

Yes; Sidney hears. His face grows black for a minute. Then he seizes the sticky little hand of Louisa, and that young lady makes a rapid descent which could not be described as either running or flying, but which has something in common with both.

"He's a bad 'un," says Mary Ann, aloud; and the strange new current of her thoughts is broken up.

Yet, as the evening wanes, she rises, takes some food from the long empty cupboard, and sets it on the table. Then, taking a small clean pinafore from a shelf, she unfolds it, shakes it out, gazes at it with pride, and puts it back again.

"To-morrow I'll take Louiser and Sidney to the 'orspital; and they'll go to school reg'lar."

It is Hope that is waking in her, and its re-birth is breaking up the torpor of months.

In the morning, however, the landlord came; but he did not write any more in the book. He stormed and claimed the four shillings. Mary Ann and her children went into the workhouse.

The children have bread now, and they go to school regularly. But Mary Ann does not dream any more—nor make new resolutions.

Guy and the Stars

In midsummer the little houses in our back streets become very hot. People do not always open the windows then, because many have long forgotten that windows can open at all. The front door is wide, however, and in the doorway and on the hot pavement children play, and women linger, till the light fades. Guy and his brothers usually range over the streets, but to-night Guy played near the door of his own home in Rosemary Lane, which is, perhaps, the hottest, the dirtiest, alley in the south-east end.

Why did he keep so near home? For an excellent reason. Jim, an old Camp-boy, who had slept out for four years, and who had enlisted in 1916, and who got a medal at the front for bravery; Jim, the hero of Rosemary Lane, had promised to sleep out with him to-night in the large Campground.

"We shall go there after sundown," he said. "There are trestle-beds. We will fit them up and go to bed in the open."

Guy was so glad that he did not even smile. He had not slept nor eaten any supper because of excitement and joy, and though he was now playing hopscotch on the dirty pavement, he was keeping one eye always on the alley—near where at any moment Jim might appear.

The sun went down last night in great splendour. It was a red sunset, and all the sky was stained up to the zenith. After sunset a little wind got up. "It will rain," said Guy's mother, standing on the doorsteps with her bare arms folded, her dark eyes lighted up with a gleam of mischief and—with furtive pleasure, too, in her son's happiness.

Guy trembled.

A large and very dirty woman at a neighbouring door screamed out suddenly.

"He ain't comin'," she cried. "Down't ye know he's gone on night work at the box factory?"

Guy frowned, but grew pale under the tan.

"Down't tease 'im," said a younger woman, tall and mild-eyed. "It's a shime."

Almost in the same moment a tall, shockheaded, young man with handsome features and very bright, twinkling eyes appeared at the Close head. He was in his shirt sleeves, and carried some grey old blankets slung over one shoulder. It was Jim. Guy rushed at him.

"Well, kid," said the young man, with indulgent pride, shifting his blankets a little higher, and looking round on the company of admiring women and children. "Hot! an't it?" he observed, nodding to a young mother who had a group of blue-eyed little ones round her, all blue-eyed, dark eyelashed and with very pale, anaemic and dirty faces, all pretty, and giving an impression of trampled flowers. The young mother looked approvingly at Jim, but made no answer.

"I've been hauling the beds right out into the open," said Jim cheerfully. "Are ye ready, Guy?"

"*He's* ready, I think," said Guy's mother, leaning the back of her hand on her hip, and looking down at her son with grim pleasure. "Can't eat nor sleep for thinking he'll go in Camp to-night. Mind ye behave yourself!" she added, shaking her head at her son, as if conscious that joy was a fearful stimulus to wrong-doing. "Else ye'll never go again, I'll promise ye."

"Well, come on, Guy! So long" said Jim, looking around him like a lord. The two passed down the alley, followed by the wondering gaze of the whole neighbourhood. Women came to the door, children surged up and followed from the streets and green, and lined up to see them pass royally through the Camp-gate and close the door behind them.

Guy spoke no word. He had often heard how, long ago, boys used to sleep out in the Campground, and now the wonderful thing was going to happen to him. No, a better thing was happening to him. He was in a larger camp now, with a garden full of flowers and a wall of trees in the distance and a dug-out, and new buildings, on every side and painted in white and blue. And into the wide open space that was the playground Jim had drawn two iron bedsteads, on which he was now arranging the coverlets. A breath of sweetness flowed over the garden. It came from the briar rose beds under the fence and the hillock over the dug-out with its dim flowers.

Guy slipped between coarse, clean sheets, and lay down under the stars. It was strange at first. He looked round uneasily as if for the narrow wall that had always penned him in at night. He drew the coverings up, but flung them loose again because the night was so warm. Jim came and sat by him on the bed, and looked at the troubled face and bewildered dark eyes.

"Like it?" said Jim, tentatively.

Guy drew closer to him.

"It's very big, isn't it?" he ventured.

"Big," said Jim, looking round with the air of one who has seen greater things than these. "Of course it looks big to *you*."

Guy raised himself a little as if taking courage, and he looked round the garden, and away at the line of solemn trees. Then he glanced upwards, but his eyes fell, and he looked again at the dark flower-beds, and the half-covered arches, where young rose trees had been hindered by a frost. Jim, dimly conscious of every movement and impulse in this long-swaddled, half-strangled child of the gutters, folded his strong young arms calmly, and looked up at the sky.

"If ye come to stars now," he said, "there ain't a finer sky going than Deptford's. Not if ye took a ship and went right round the world. I've been to India, ye see, and I've been to Egypt and France, so I ought to know."

Guy looked up timidly at the sky. The deep, dark vault was strewn with light clouds like broken fleece, and they moved as if someone were driving them, and through the broken fleece here and there a star sparkled. Southward and almost overhead the full moon rose. She was half-hidden now behind a larger bank of cloud, through which she looked forth, all dazzling like some glorious face, veiled, and distressed by the blowing wind. All round her the clouds shone like silver. And all this beauty was changing and moving, and even hurrying, and the poor little slum-dweller looked up at it as if in fear.

"Lie down now, Jim," he said, in a low voice, "and tell me about it."

"About what?" said Jim, wondering.

"About that," said Guy, pointing with one arm, or rather by one movement of his half-covered shoulder, to the sky. "I never seen it before."

"You look at it then," said Jim, trying to remember what he had been told about the stars. "Look at it a bit as there ye lie."

It was worth some looking at, the sky; the hurrying clouds were quiet as if they had reached a harbour. Great stretches of blue lay between their white still fleecy hills, and the moon shone clear in a blue expanse.

The boys lay down side by side. The street was very quiet, and the Camp very still. All the students had left in the morning.

"That star right over us is the Polar star," said Jim. "You see it wherever ye are, a-shining down on ye, and them two stars at his side point always to him so you can't miss him. That's the Plough," Jim went on, pointing to it. "Ye never saw a real plough, did ye, kid? It's a thing farmers turn the earth up with before they put seed into the ground. Well, anyway, it's shaped like that. That whiteness you see all along the sky is a mist o' worlds. Thousands and thousands of them. That's the Dog-star, blazing away there in the south. It's nearer us than most of the others, and them two yellow stars right over yer head, I've forgotten their names, but I think they're called the Twins."

Guy made no answer. He listened, awe-struck, but allowed himself now to send his wandering eyes over the vast dome that stretched above him. He looked out as one who sees for the first time, who moves his limbs for the first time, astonished not only by the new world but also by himself. Suddenly he fell back a little, trembling.

"What's up?" said Jim, anxiously.

"I saw one falling," said the child. "It fell, and some one caught it like a ball."

Jim looked down at him, smiling.

"Can they—can they tumble on us?" whispered the child.

"No," said Jim stoutly. "That they can't. They're kept well in their places. Some of them are big worlds as I tell ye, with suns and moons of their own, worlds so big ye couldn't sail round them in a year. You haven't a notion yet how big the worlds and suns are!"

Guy was silent. A little wind stirred the lime trees near him, and through the dancing leaves he saw more stars looking down in golden beauty.

"Ye haven't been to school long, ye see," said Jim, conscious that he had himself left the Camp-school before his fourteenth birthday. "Ye couldn't know very much about the worlds and the stars yet. Years ago I used to sleep out with the other boys, and we saw the sky every night just as well as if we'd been shepherds looking after sheep on the hills. We'd a teacher too, and he could tell us no end o' yarns about the stars. Mr. Norman his name was, and he come from the North. He used to go to Greenwich Observatory. It's quite close, ye see. There, where the trees are, is Greenwich."

"I don't care about Greenwich," said Guy. "I want to know why the stars don't fall."

"As I was saying, this is a place where ye could learn it all off, and see it all if we slept in the right places. I been to Egypt, and to France, and they don't know any more there than Mr. Norman did; only the people at the Observatory know more I suppose than he did. Anyhow there an't any better sky anywhere than this sky," said Jim firmly.

"Jim," said the child, dreamily, "I want to sleep out all my life. Never in a room no more. No, never more." His voice trailed off into a whisper, and his eyes closed, for sleep arrived now, very suddenly, very imperiously, after the long vigil. Jim settled himself down too, glad that his knowledge of the heavenly bodies was to be put to no further tests.

Around them as they slept the garden seemed to waken to a new, mysterious life. The flowers poured out their perfume in the darkness, and above in the vast arch of the sky great changes took place, moving on every hour, every moment in majestic silence. It changed, it showed a brighter dust of stars, its clouds flitted away and massed themselves in new flocks, and at length, but long before the coolness of dawn the stars faded away, one by one. All the fields of heaven lay empty and gray, awaiting a new guest. He came. The east crimsoned, and below the deepening flush a great jewel glittered, blazed, and rose higher. Jim sat up in bed.

"Waken up, kid," he said, laying his hand on Guy's shoulder. "Time to get up."

Guy stirred, opened his eyes, saw Jim, and was filled with a sudden rapture of joy. It was the "joy of the waking" of the Red Indian, the gladness that comes in childhood or early youth when one remembers a new happiness in the first moment of return. Guy had never felt it before; he would never perhaps know it again. He sat up and looked around him, smiling.

Starlings twittered and flew in the old wall above the sand pit. The nasturtiums over the dug-out wall, the blue lupins and the early helleniums shone out in the pure light.

"You go and have your bath now round the back there," cried Jim, "and then you'll help me with these beds."

Guy came back looking fresh and radiant. It seemed to him that a new life must begin now, a life worthy of the joys of the night in the open. He moved the beds under the awning, folded the blankets, and questioned Jim with bright eager glance. Wonderful to see, Jim was not overjoyed. He was somehow changed. He was anxious to get back to work.

"Where do the stars go to in the morning?" asked Guy.

"They hide themselves, o' course. They wait till dark, and then come out again."

"But tell me," said the child. But Jim cut him short. "No! No! Come now! Your mother will be calling for you soon if you don't hurry. Are ye ready?"

"Ready! Yes," said Guy, but his face fell.

They were going out then to the old world, to the old life. A group of men stood outside the gate, unshaven, dirty, their hands buried deep in their trousers pockets. They looked stupidly at the two boys as they went by. At the alley head Guy and Jim parted company. Guy went up the lane by himself. The doors were closed now, and the lane was quiet and empty, but Guy's mother was standing on her doorstep waiting for him. She was more untidy than usual, and her face was stained with dirt and tears.

"Your father came home drunk," she sobbed. "He struck Albert and me. He's sleeping now."

Guy stood looking at her, his cheeks fresh and rosy, his eyes shining and yet clouded with fear. He seemed longing to balance her dark tidings with something glad, but he could not. He felt the black inrush of the old life, and stood looking at her helplessly.

"Where *you* been," she whimpered, wiping her eyes with her apron, "looking so jolly? You ain't got no feeling for me," she sobbed, touched by something in her son's face, and giving way a little. "He struck me and said this place wasn't fit for pigs. I ain't had no sleep. . . . "

"Mother," said Guy suddenly, taking her by the skirt. "I seen the stars!"

12

Olive Christian Malvery

OLIVE CHRISTIAN MALVERY (1877 [1882]–1914), of mixed European and Indian ancestry, was born in Lahore in the Punjab.[1] Her parents having separated, she, along with her brother, was raised in India as an Anglican by her maternal grandparents. The siblings were well educated. Malvery arrived in London around the turn of the twentieth century to attend music school.[2] She earned her living, meanwhile, giving elocution lessons and drawing-room performances based on Indian legends, as well as writing fiction for periodicals. In 1904 she was hired to do a photojournalism series on London's poor for *Pearson's Magazine,* from which this article is reproduced. The following year, in a theatrical and much-publicized ceremony, Malvery married Archibald Mackirdy, a Scottish-born U.S. diplomat. The bridesmaids were Hoxton costermongers, and a thousand other working girls were also invited guests. Malvery and her husband had three children before his death in 1911. She did well in her various professions and donated enough money to build two shelters for homeless women in London. Ill with cancer, she died at age thirty-seven, apparently of an accidental overdose of sedatives.[3]

Pearson's Magazine was a joint British and American venture that took advantage of new technologies for reproducing photographs, and the arti-

Originally published as "Gilding the Gutter: An Account of the Lives of the Costermongers," in Pearson's Magazine *(London ed.), January–June 1905, 40–46 and 48–49. The Pearson's series from which this selection comes had six other installments; it began with volume 18 of the magazine (July–December 1904) and ran through volume 20 (July–December 1905). It was reprinted, in somewhat modified form, as* The Soul Market, with Which Is Included "The Heart of Things" *(London: Hutchinson, 1907).*

Figure 6. Olive Christian Malvery, from *The Soul Market,* 2nd ed. (London: Hutchinson, 1907). Courtesy of Judith Walkowitz. This is one of very few photos of Malvery without a disguise of some kind. Photographed in costume, she often jauntily looks directly at the camera, while here her demure glance is downward.

cle below was heavily illustrated, mainly with images of Malvery in her street seller disguises posing at different spots and accompanied by various associates, including a donkey. Malvery posed, for other installments, as a barmaid, a factory girl, a homeless woman, and so on. Some of the accompanying photographs were street scenes, while others were studio shots emphasizing the author's outfits or her somewhat exotic Indian appearance. All in all, she presented herself as a bold and industrious lady traveler in London's streets. *Pearson's Magazine,* like the *Strand Magazine,* on which it was modeled, included fiction, travel, sports, business, and health articles without being so explicit as to offend the sensibilities of the middle-class readers for whom it was intended. Photos, their captions, and the written texts do not always fit together and may not say the same thing.

Malvery's prototype for the *Pearson's* series on the London poor, including its very poorest and its homeless, is probably Jack London's *People of the Abyss*, published the year before the *Pearson's* articles began to run. This kind of journalism, pioneered by American newspaper magnates Hearst and Pulitzer, was already well established by the early twentieth century. It involved authors in disguises, the disclosing of harsh and shocking social realities as well as government and industrial scandals, and the cultivation of journalists as celebrities. Malvery wrote several other books of social observation—on child labor, on unemployment, and on white slavery (the kidnapping of young girls for brothels in England or abroad), as well as another *Pearson's* series, on the Jews of East London, notable for its lack of sympathy for its subjects.

NOTES

1. Judith Walkowitz, "The Indian Woman, the Flower Girl, and the Jew," found that the birth date listed on Malvery's death certificate, 1877, does not correspond to that on her marriage certificate (married in May 1905, at the age of twenty-three, which would give her a birth year of 1882). Also see Mark Pottle's entry in the Oxford DNB.

2. This account relies heavily on Walkowitz's abundant research on Malvery, which is published in "The Indian Woman, the Flower Girl, and the Jew." My thanks to the author for sharing her research and thoughts on this interesting figure.

3. This account of her death is based on Mark Pottle's entry in the Oxford DNB. The wedding information is from the Oxford DNB entry by Mark Pottle.

FURTHER READING

"The Alien Question," Olive Christian Malvery's series on London's Jewish immigrants, entered the national debates on legislation designed to restrict further Jewish immigration (the Aliens Act, 1905). It was published in two parts in *Pearson's* contemporaneously with the cockney series. Malvery's book on sweated labor in London's slums is *Baby Toilers* (London: Hutchinson, 1907). She also wrote three novels: *Thirteen Nights* (1908), *A Year and a Day* (1912), and *Love's Soldier* (1913).

For writing about Malvery, see Mark Pottle's informative entry in the Oxford DNB; Judith Walkowitz, "The Indian Woman, the Flower Girl, and the Jew: Photojournalism in Edwardian London," *Victorian Studies* 42, no. 1 (autumn 1998–99): 3–46; and James Winter, *London's Teeming Streets, 1830–1914* (London: Routledge, 1993).

Gilding the Gutter

Miss Olive Christian Malvery, the well-known lecturer, reciter, and social worker, some time ago set herself the task of investigating the conditions under which the lives of the poor and destitute in great cities are lived. To do this she has entered into the very lives of the poor, becoming one of themselves and learning the inmost secrets of their lives. What she has seen, heard, and experienced she has related in two articles published in the November and December issues of PEARSON'S MAGAZINE *last year: the first dealt with the lives of "The Children of the Night," as Miss Malvery aptly christens the homeless wanderers of the Thames Embankment and the London streets; the second with the street pedlars of London, who throughout the year make a precarious living by selling matches, boot-laces, and other knick-knacks to passers by.*

In the following article she deals with her adventures among the costers—a very different class of people in that they are hard-working, and possessed of the business instinct. She has much of interest to tell of what she saw whilst living among them, and of her experiences when she set up as a coster herself. Next month she will relate her adventures among the organ-grinders and street musicians.

To the uninitiated it may come as a surprise to hear that among the poor and labouring classes of our great cities there are as many differences in modes and manners, as many nice distinctions of class, as there are among the higher grades of society.

A coster girl would not associate on equal terms with a street pedlar any more than the squire's wife with the village post-mistress. Between the factory girl and domestic servant there is as much natural contempt as between a belle of New York and a Chicago heiress.

It took weeks of working and planning before I could translate myself from a street-hawker into a *bona fide* coster girl.

Fortunately my familiarity with the many girls' clubs in the poor districts of London gave me an insight into the minds and lives of the coster girls, and I was able to profess some knowledge of the life before I entered the ranks as a worker.

It is in no wise easy to slip into a new life. Among the "people," as we term the labouring and poorer classes, an outsider is very quickly recognised.

I found, however, that my foreign appearance really helped me, for as I dealt mostly with women and girls, they made their own stories about me.

By maintaining a discreet silence, I managed to get through. Being small and young looking, too, helped me.

I get tired very quickly, and show it, and I had to give poor Mr. C., the friend who nearly always accompanied me on my rambles, the reputation for ill-treating me: consequently he got on the rough side of several "gentle" tongues on more than one occasion.

It helped me wonderfully to have a man so big and burly and such a splendid cockney actor to assume command of me. Together we were able to do what one alone could never have accomplished.

I wished to get right in among the costers and be one of them, so we decided we would seek opportunities and insinuate ourselves into the select circle as plausibly as possible.

There were several aspects of the life I desired to see, and we set out to learn the best localities for our purpose. I dared not go to the neighbourhood where I was known at the girls' clubs as the "Little Princess." They would have thought it the most splendid joke ever conceived to see me impersonate a coster girl, and I should have been mobbed by a good-humoured but embarrassing crowd. It is one of the extraordinary sights of a crowded slum to see a great rabble collect as if by magic. I did not care to risk this action, so Mr. C. enlisted the aid of a woman in Covent Garden, and she introduced us to a likely spot where we could sell things.

It was a wet day when we started, and the potted plants and ferns we had bought were dreadfully damp and uncomfortable to hold. Mr. C. went off to lean against a wall and smoke, and I stood with two pots in my hand. It was so cold and miserable that I almost determined to give up for that day, when I heard a loud but cheery voice say:

"Now then, missus, 'igher up; you're right on my pitch."

The owner of the voice was a big, strong, red-faced girl, who was pushing unassisted a hand-barrow heavily laden with potatoes and cabbages.

I moved up the street a little way, and the girl wiped her face on her coarse white apron and gave a good-humoured nod.

"Lor lumme! that ain't 'arf 'eavy," she said in answer to my inquiry as to whether it was a bad load. She swiftly set herself to dressing her stall by the kerb, and when finished she turned to me with "'Ow's the gime—'ad any luck, missus?"

"None," I answered.

"Ah, wet days, same as this, is rough luck on the likes of us. I wouldn't 'ave come out at all to-day only my old man is down with lumbager or somethink, and the doctor said it might settle 'im to come out."

I drew near, and ventured to sympathise.

"It won't be much good trying to-day, but I wants to get enough for the roast and boiled to-morrow. I do thinks one ought to keep Sundays somehow Christian-like."

She was very friendly, and inquired where I came from.

I pointed over my shoulder to Mr. C., and said:

"'E brought me. I'm a stranger to these parts."

"Is yer foreign?" she asked.

"Not by half," I said, "one can't help one's birth, but one can help one's heart."

This sentiment pleased her extremely. Presently she asked me to mind her stall a minute, while she went and had a drink.

While she was gone I sold two cabbages, and she was so gratified at my smartness when she returned that I ventured to ask her to let me help her.

"Does he knock yer about?" she inquired, referring to Mr. C.

"Not much; but it would be a long way better for me to be earning a few coppers."

"Well, if yer ain't particular about leaving him for a bit, I'll let yer 'elp me while my old man's ill, and find yer a bed with the girl, a cousin of Bill's, who lives near by."

I ran across and told Mr. C. the joyful news of my apprenticeship, and he said he would look out a room in the same street, so as to be able to reach me at any moment if necessary.

So began my first real taste of the life of the coster girl.

Mrs. Bolter was my friend's name, but she was known as Bess. She took me home with her that night, and I helped her to get a "bite."

"You're a 'andy sort of gal," she said, when I joined her by the fire after washing up the plates we had used at our meal.

The room she lived in was of a fair size, and had a big window, which, however, was kept shut. They lived, cooked, and ate their meals and slept all in this one room; fortunately Bess had no children. Her husband was, I could see, far gone in consumption. I nearly gave myself away by advocating more air. The one thing the poor will not tolerate in their dwelling-rooms is fresh air. Poor Bill was a nice sort of fellow, and the two were devoted to each other.

"Your bloke ain't much class?" he asked me sympathetically.

Bess had evidently told him of Mr. C. I nearly laughed, but managed to nod my head disconsolately. "Never mind," said Bill; "you'll be all right along of Bess." About eleven that night Bill's cousin came in, and I was introduced to the girl with whom I was to make my home for some time. Sal was her name, and she was a wiry girl with an enormous fringe and nice eyes. She had a huge mouth, and laughed most of the time. I began nodding, and Bess packed us off with an injunction to be spry in the morning.

Sal grabbed my arm and dragged me down the steep stairs into the street. I saw Mr. C. hanging about, and felt quite happy.

Sal's room was up a narrow neighbouring alley, in a house let out to thirty-seven lodgers. Entering, the air felt thick and stuffy, and I was glad to find Sal's room was a tiny attic right at the top. She paid half-a-crown a week for it.

The bed was unmade, the window shut of course, and ashes filled the grate. From one corner Sal pulled out an iron chair-bed; it did not look inviting, but fortunately I found it clean, so I forgave the hardness.

I was awake practically all that night, and had the fire lighted before Sal woke.

I took care to shut the window which I had opened while she slept.

At four o'clock I woke my companion. She sprang up, and scrambled into her clothes, without troubling to wash, though there was a basin and a jug of water in the little stand in the room.

We breakfasted by the firelight on bread and coffee, without milk. I always kept some meat lozenges and Plasm on biscuits in my pocket, and so managed to escape with very small quantities of the food taken by the people with whom I lived. This was a mercy, for I have never met a coster girl or a factory girl who could cook decently. Their life does not foster housewifely instincts.

Sal and I were at Covent Garden Market by five in the morning. There we encountered Bess. We bought the necessary stock of fresh vegetables to add to those we already had—Bess had deposited her unsold stock under her bed the night before.

Bess and I then started back to our pitch. Sal, who was a flower girl, went off elsewhere on her own business.

Bess gave me a shilling a day for helping her. For this sum I helped to push her barrow, and took her place at the stall when she ran in to look after Bill.

I cooked the supper, and washed the plates, and seeing how ill Bill was I tried to do a little amateur nursing, and showed Bess how to make one or two simple things for him.

Once, having made a halfpenny worth of sago into a pudding, with a tiny stick of cinnamon in it, I prepared to offer it to Bill. Bess laughed, and said:

"Lor, what's the girl after? Why, bless y'r 'eart, Bill won't swallow that mess."

But Bill did, and asked for more.

It was a hard life enough. Up at four each morning, to bed never before eleven; the long walks to the market, and the endless standing by the barrow in rain and shine. Sometimes we took as much as eight and ten shillings a day, at other times not more than four or five. But I wished, after a week of this, to find a new field for investigation, so one day, by a preconcerted plan, Mr. C. arrived and made a sort of row and ordered me to come off. I was sorry to leave Bess, but I was getting worn out. Mr. C. and I went to look up a woman we had made friends with at Covent Garden. She was also a coster woman, but lived in quite another district. She was out when we went, but we found her at the nearest "pub.," and getting into friendly conversation there, Mr. C. told her "the missus 'ad a aunt who was a kind of heiress in her way, poor dear, what had gone and died and left her niece £5." With this he suggested that I should set up costering in "slap up style, so that a poor, 'ard-working man could get a bit of peace and rest." The woman quite sympathised with this laudable desire, and gave us advice very readily.

It was arranged that I should meet her on the following Monday, which is the slackest day in the week for costers, the woman promised to take me to a place where I could hire a barrow of my own. On the following Monday morning she was waiting for me in her own house, as she had promised. Her home was part of a small house in a narrow court off the Fulham Road. In front of the house, as in front of most of the others, were baskets, stall-boards, and barrows. The majority of people occupying the houses were of the costermonger class.

"This is the gal I was telling yer about, 'Enery." This was my introduction to my coster friend's husband. He, a thick-set, short-haired man, was sitting in his shirt-sleeves smoking by the fire.

The room in which the introduction took place was not much larger than a good-sized cupboard. It contained a bed, a deal table, a sack that served as a hearthrug and another as a door mat. Some crockery and pots and pans were also visible, but what was most in evidence in the room was the mingled odour of smoke and vegetables. In one corner were piled sacks of potatoes, in another half-a-dozen baskets of green stuff. Under the table, under the chairs, even under the bed, I noticed baskets containing fruit and vegetables. My friend's bed and living room was also her store room. This, unfortunately, is the case with most of the lower class of coster-mongers.

Sometimes, as I found out later, the stock was even kept in the dirty, ill-ventilated stables, in company with their donkeys.

"'Enery, I'm going to take my pal over to Mrs. Rummings to get her a room."

"All right, Liz, 'op it, and look slippy about getting back."

She turned to me with "Come on, Em." I had told her my Christian name was Emma.

The house we went to was situated in the same street as the one in which my new friend lived. It was a two-storeyed house with a basement below the pavement. Many of its windows were broken, as also were the railings in front of the house. The street door was open, and sitting on the doorstep were three or four poor little children without boots or stockings, and bare-headed. In one of the ground-floor windows was a card, informing passers-by that a room was to let. Pushing past the children, my companion gave a resounding knock at the door. This summons brought a very vicious-looking, dirty, untidy woman, about forty years of age, up from the underground regions.

"Well, Liz, what's up?" she asked.

"My pal here wants a room; you got one to let, 'aven't yer?"

"Yes, come up and look at it." This after a very searching look at me.

I followed her through the passage and up the stairs past several more groups of little children. The house was swarming with them.

The woman opened the door of a tiny stuffy back room, containing a small iron bedstead, on which was a dirty unmade bed, a small washstand, a common chest of drawers, and a chair.

Fastened on the wall were two gaudy cards about twelve inches square. One asked in crudely coloured letters the pertinent question, "What is home without a mother?" and the other bore the legend, "Home, sweet home."

"I ain't 'ad time to tidy up this morning," Mrs. Rummings said. "I put up my brother Ben here last night."

"What is 'e out?"

"Yus, come out yesterday."

"Lor, don't time fly. I thought he got two stretch."

"So 'e did," said Mrs. Rummings, "but they knocked six months orf, 'cos of 'is good behaviour."

By this conversation I understood that the bedroom offered to me had been lately occupied by a recently discharged criminal. However, I had made up my mind to go through with the adventure, so I asked what rent was required.

"'Arf-a-crown a week, and down on the knuckle."

This I interpreted to be a request for payment in advance. I paid at once.

"When do you want to come in?" said Mrs. Rummings.

"To-morrow, if possible," I said. I also asked her to have the windows opened, to scrub the floor, and as a special favour not to allow the bed to be occupied that night.

All this my new landlady promised to do.

And now followed a sad, but typical, experience. After I had paid my half-crown, Liz said:

"Let us all go and have a gargle on the strength of the deal, eh?"

"Don't mind if we do," said my landlady.

"Come along, Em," Liz called to me, and we left the house, went through the court out into the main road, and straight into the common bar of a public-house.

It was midday. The bar was full of women, some quite young, others grey-haired, but the majority middle-aged.

All were drinking and talking loudly. The two or three men present were of the usual public-house loafer type.

I found afterwards that this Monday drinking is quite a custom with women of the lower working class.

In some parts of London more drunken women can be seen on a Monday afternoon than at any other time during the week. A visit to the police-courts on a Tuesday morning will illustrate to what a shocking extent this Monday tippling has developed.

Leaving the bar, Liz suggested that we should go to a barrow yard in the neighbourhood and hire a barrow. I was taken to a yard where there were a number of barrows of all descriptions. The owner, a fat, middle-aged woman, wearing a coarse apron in which was a pocket containing money which she clinked with her hands as she talked to me, agreed to let me have a barrow for a shilling a week or three halfpence per hour.

This woman was also a money-lender to coster-mongers, lending them money to buy stock. She charged them as much as twopence for the loan of every shilling borrowed, the time of the loan lasting generally from Friday to Monday. But the money is sometimes repaid in a few hours.

If bad luck should follow the transaction, the debt is an awful and grow-ing burden to the borrower. The establishment of State banks, which would lend the respectable poor money at reasonable interest to start them in their small business, is much to be advocated. The system has been tried in Germany with good results.

The next day I moved into the room I had engaged, with a few belongings, and Mr. C. got a lodging a few doors further down.

That night I slept but little. The streets below echoed and re-echoed with passing feet, coarse laughter, and drunken songs.

In the middle of the night, dreadful shrieks arose from the next house, where a woman was being beaten, and although she screamed "Murder," and her cries filled the neighbourhood, no one seemed to interfere.

At last the place grew quiet, and I fell asleep again for a few minutes. A loud knock at my door woke me, and on opening it I found Liz waiting for me to go to market with her. We started off with my empty barrow.

This was the hardest work I think I have ever done. My arms ached, and my legs almost refused to move; but my sturdy comrade made no trouble whatever about hers.

On arriving at the market we left our barrows in charge of a woman, to whom we each gave twopence for minding them. These women are quite necessary to prevent petty peculations that would occur if the carts and barrows were not watched.

We made up our minds to buy several boxes of tomatoes. By a system of mental arithmetic my guide computed that the tomatoes which these boxes contained, and for which we paid two shillings per box, would, if retailed at twopence per pound, bring us in a profit of one shilling a box. We bought twenty boxes.

We also bought four bushels of plums at four shillings a bushel. These, if sold at two pence a pound, would bring in a gross profit of four shillings per bushel. We had to pay the porter who carried our purchases to our barrows a penny per bushel, and sixpence for the twenty tomato boxes.

I was unfortunate in loading my barrow, for when I tried to move it I found the weight was so ill planned that I could not push it. My friend showed her trained skill and experience at this point. She swiftly packed her own barrow, so that the weight was adjusted to a nicety, and then re-arranged my load. Notwithstanding this, I found it quite impossible to push the loaded barrow from Covent Garden to our pitch, and was obliged to engage a man to help me.

On arriving at our chosen street, I found the "pitches," or places that barrows occupy, are in many cases looked upon as freeholds. Only in rare instances is it necessary for the costermonger to worry about his regular place in the street where he always sells. A stranger arriving earlier, and taking up what the regular costermonger considers his own particular position, would be very roughly handled indeed, that is, of course, if the usurper happened to be a weaker man, or had fewer friends than the rightful owner. The police often assist the regular costermonger to hold his position against interlopers. . . .

So ends my experience of life as a coster; and I am bound to say that the costers as a class are among the happiest of mankind. Many of them are prosperous, and nearly all have the business instinct wonderfully developed.

Were it not for two things, many costers would undoubtedly manage to save sufficient to launch out in business in quite a large way; as it is, a fair number do, by means of thrift, acquire considerable property.

But against them, as a class, is the drinking habit, which is almost a part of their lives. In times of special sorrow or joy, in times of prosperity or when things are going badly, drink is the universal panacea to which the coster turns either to celebrate the occasion or to drown his sorrows.

There is also for them, as a class, the same disability of enjoying social life, except in the public-house, as is noticeable in most of the hardest-working and poorest classes. I would in no way decry the excellent work done by various religious people in all parts of London. The "missions," in their way, are excellent enough for those who patronise them; but my heart goes out to the lads and girls whose only common ground of meeting is the street— whose love-making and courtship are almost inevitably connected with the public-house or gutter—people who yet have in them the making of good citizens. They need, in their leisure moments, wholesome, big-hearted friends, men and women who have had happy opportunities, grace, and education. If such men and women, and there are many such pining for some absorbing interest in life, would form guilds of comradeship with the coster and factory youths and girls, and provide them with places to meet in, and intelligent entertainment, where all sermonising or religious lessons were sternly deleted, there would be, I venture to say, an enormous betterment effected among these much tempted people.

The social side of the costers' life is against their rising in the scale of wealth; they live amongst unhealthy surroundings, they have no home life in the true sense of the word, and consequently they have little inducement to be thrifty. They look out for to-day, take little thought for the morrow, but none for the future beyond.

These are the characteristics of the coster class. They work hard and are brave in the face of hardship and privation: they drink hard, and are utterly improvident. If these evils could be educated away, we should gain a prosperous class of street traders—but the coster type would soon be extinct.

Anna Martin

WHEN SHE DIED AT AGE SEVENTY-NINE in December of 1937, Anna Martin (born in 1858) was well known in her adoptive neighborhood, the South London dockside district of Rotherhithe. An obituary notice in the *South London Press* called her "a tireless worker right up to her death" who had given "hundreds of pounds away to the poor she loved." The writer gushed, "A distressed man or woman had only to call at her door to receive help. Often, in the street, she would stop to care for anyone looking ill or hungry."[1]

Martin was not only a kindly personage, but also an active suffragist and a tax resister.[2] Further, there is some evidence that she helped to found a private birth control clinic in 1908.[3] She was also a pungent social critic who spent thirty-eight years working with the women of Rotherhithe as an associate of the Nonconformist (Methodist) Bermondsey Settlement.

Martin had led an adventurous life before arriving at the settlement. Born in Ireland and from a family of scholars, she was one of the first women students at London University, matriculating in 1880 and receiving her B.A. in 1886.[4] She spent several years in Cape Colony as vice principal of a girls' school, working with close friend Laura A. Robinson, who was the school's principal. Martin and Robinson returned to London in the late 1890s determined to "work in some part of the East End of London." In 1899 they became associated with the Bermondsey Settlement, founded in the early 1890s, which included an associated women's branch.[5]

Originally published as "The Irresponsibility of the Father," part 1, in The Nineteenth Century and After *84 (December 1918): 1091–96 and 1099–1103. Two sequels were published in the March and May 1919 issues of the same journal.*

As a settlement worker concentrating on the district's married women, Martin tried to minimize the class distance between herself and her clients. The women's settlement was situated in two ordinary houses rather than in the imposing building that housed the men, and Martin lived nearby with two friends. Martin also tried to advance Rotherhithe women's political education. She founded the Guild of Women Citizens, which offered a feminist education for the local women (important feminists like Emmeline Pethick-Lawrence, Maude Royden, and Evelyn Sharp[6] came to speak there); in turn, these women served as a constituency for the suffrage movement, attending marches and demonstrations. When an interviewer asked about these mothers' gatherings, Martin snapped, "It's not a Mothers' Meeting: I started my meeting in protest to mothers' meetings."[7]

Just about all of Martin's pamphlets and articles were written in the 1910s, a period when Labour and feminist groups were putting pressure on the national and on local governments to provide better services to children and to women, and officials themselves had taken a new interest in infant and child welfare. During World War I these discussions intensified. Martin was acutely aware of the sacrifice and ingenuity that working-class women exercised to ensure family survival. As she later put it in a letter to Emmeline Pethick-Lawrence, "I used to come in from a round of visits feeling that there were no subjects under the flag—black, yellow, or brown—who were so utterly neglected: that they were forsaken by god and Man. The wives were nothing but serfs and most social reforms took the form of giving the screw another turn!"[8] She was outraged by such proposed measures as raising the age at which children could leave school and go to work to earn money to help their mothers. Wealthy male politicians were culprits, in Martin's view, but so were official representatives of the male working class. Working-class husbands, too, took for granted the comforts and privileges their wives supplied, which gave them a standard of living that was considerably higher than their own incomes would have allowed. The women had little input into these discussions: "The remedial schemes put forward all agree in this—that they absolutely ignore the opinions and experience of the one class in the nation which has first-hand knowledge of the matter in question."[9]

Martin believed, however, that the suffragist agitation of the early twentieth century was beginning to have an impact on the domestic lives of these very poor women. As she wrote to *The Suffragette* in 1913, "Ten years ago they accepted hunger, ill-treatment, and social neglect, as a matter of course. Now, on all hands, one hears the note of rebellion. They no longer seem to themselves as 'made for men,' but are beginning to make personal claims on life."[10] The five-pound maternity benefit mentioned in the article may be a reference to a proposal by Eleanor Rathbone's Family Endowment Council to institute a generous weekly government allowance for mothers. A cash sum paid to each mother (whose husbands were insured under the National Health Insurance Act) had already been legislated in 1913, but this was only thirty shillings.

NOTES

1. Obituary in *South London Press*, December 3, 1937, 24. The obituary gives her age as seventy-nine, which indicates a birth date of 1858.
2. Women's Tax Resistance League secretary Margaret Kineton Parkes included Martin in a list of tax resisters. See Hilary Frances, "'Pay the Piper, Call the Tune!' The Women's Tax Resistance League," in *The Women's Suffrage Movement: New Feminist Perspectives*, ed. Maroula Joannou and June Purvis (Manchester: Manchester University Press, 1998), 75, n. 20.
3. Angus McLaren, *Birth Control in Nineteenth-Century England: A Social and Intellectual History* (London: Croom Helm, 1978), 211, n. 38, citing M. Greed and Edith How-Martyn, *The Birth-Control Movement in England* (1930).
4. This information is from examination cards in the University of London Archives, retrieved by archivist Nicolas Jeffs. In a lecture Martin gave in Sunderland, she described her secondary education as "from Milton Mount and Private Study."
5. Obituary by Rev. J. Scott Lidgett, Warden of Bermondsey Settlement, *The Times*, December 6, 1937; "In Memoriam," *Bermondsey Settlement Magazine*, February 1907, 17–19.
6. Letter from Martin to Elizabeth Robins, April 16, 1919, Robins Papers, Sales Library, New York University, series 2, subseries B, box 18, folder 120; My thanks to Angela John for pointing out this correspondence to me).
7. "The Problem of the Women," *Bermondsey Settlement Magazine*, April–May 1916, 21.
8. Quoted in Emmeline Pethick-Lawrence, *My Part in a Changing World* (London: Victor Gollancz, l939), 346.
9. Martin, *Married Working Woman*, 29.
10. "A Word of Sympathy," letter to the editor, *The Suffragette*, March 28, 1913, 392.

FURTHER READING

For more writing by Anna Martin, see *The Married Working Woman: A Study* (London: National Union of Women's Suffrage Societies, 1911; reprint, Westport, MA: Garland Press, 1980); and "The Mother and Social Reform," *The Nineteenth Century and After* 73 (May 1913): 1060–79, (June 1913): 1235–55. Martin's two-part article "Working-Women and Drink," *The Nineteenth Century and After* 78 (December 1915): 1378–94, and 79 (January 1916): 85–104, is a scathing attack on Home Office surveillance of soldiers' wives' drinking.

Seth Koven presents information on Martin and the Bermondsey Settlement in *Slumming: Sexual and Social Politics in Victorian London* (Princeton, NJ: Princeton University Press, 2004), 201–3. I discuss her ideas and use her as a source in my book *Love and Toil: Motherhood in Outcast London, 1870–1918* (New York: Oxford University Press,

1993) and in "Mothers and the State in Britain, 1904–1914," in *The European Experience of Declining Fertility, 1850–1970: The Quiet Revolution,* ed. John Gillis, Louise Tilly, and David Levine (Oxford: Blackwell, 1992).

‒‒‒‒‒∞∞∞‒‒‒‒‒

The Irresponsibility of the Father

It may well seem an act of temerity to introduce a note of criticism into the chorus of approval which has attended the recent campaign for the saving of child and infant life. Each new step has been welcomed alike by Socialist and by individualist; applauded by *The Herald* and by *The Times;* blessed by the Women's Co-operative Guild and by the leaders of Society and Fashion.

Nevertheless, 'Woe unto you when all men speak well of you,' is sometimes as true of movements as it is of individuals, and general approval is sometimes the result only of general misapprehension.

Dates sufficiently disprove the cynical assertion that anxiety as to child survival is mainly due to the desire of the employing classes to secure fresh supplies of raw material for the military and industrial machines, in compensation for that destroyed by the War. Sir George Newman published his book on Infant Mortality in 1906; National Conferences were held on the subject in that year and in 1908; about the same time Sir Benjamin Broadbent was making his practical experiments in Huddersfield; the Royal Commission on the Birth Rate was appointed in 1913. Furthermore, the Local Government Board between 1908 and 1914 conducted a series of careful examinations into the causes of excessive child mortality, and embodied the results in reports containing an almost bewildering mass of information on every aspect of the problem which was open to statistical treatment. Nor did the Board confine itself to collecting facts and figures. By persistent pressure it persuaded, or compelled, backward sanitary districts to improve their water supply, get rid of municipal dirt, and look to their unpaved yards, and the Central Authority is, in all probability, well justified in claiming that in these areas it was instrumental in saving in seven years nearly 200,000 infant lives.

Measures are now demanded which shall more directly deal with the individual child and its mother. These include the compulsory adoption by all local authorities of the Notification of Births Act and the general appointment of Health Visitors; the establishment of numerous infant consultation centres and of ante-natal and post-natal clinics; the notification of pregnancy and the multiplication of schools for mothers; the provision of municipal midwives; the prohibition of the sale of certain abortifacients; the development of maternity wards and hospitals; the medical supervision of all children up to the age of five; the raising of the maternity benefit to 5*l.*; the restriction of the industrial employment of women before and after the birth of their children.

Such an array of proposed legislative beneficence is well-nigh overwhelming, and the matron of the mean streets may indeed seem the spoilt child of Parliaments. When one begins, however, to consider how these schemes and projects will affect the typical Mrs. Jones or Mrs. Smith of one's intimate personal acquaintance, doubts arise. It is all to the good, of course, that Authority has at last formally recognised that 'The welfare of infants depends in very large measure on that of their mothers,' but there is no sign that any effort has been made to grasp the realities of that mother's life; and one would almost surmise a distinct reluctance to face unpleasant facts. True, every woman who faces suffering and death to give the world new life has an indisputable claim to every alleviation the community can afford her; true, the measures enumerated above may, and doubtless will, be of real service in individual cases, and as regards certain limited social strata. Moreover, these schemes may, and doubtless will, open a wide field for the altruistic instincts of many kindly people, and provide employment for an army of worthy officials. They will not, *pace* Mr. Herbert Samuel, 'fill healthy and happy homes with healthy and happy children.' The writer believes it to be demonstrable that were every town and village equipped tomorrow with the whole paraphernalia demanded by the medical profession and its following, the nation would not be perceptibly nearer its desired goal—a numerous adult population physically and mentally sound.

Broadly speaking, babies die and children pine because no one is responsible for providing them with the necessaries of life. They suffer not from their mother's lack of love and knowledge, but from her lack of pence.

Owing to the separation allowances [government payments to wives of soldiers], the condition of the women and therefore of their children sensibly improved between the outbreak of the War and the rise of prices, a fact noted in London both in the reports of the great hospitals and of the Education Department. At the time of writing the gain has been at least counterbalanced by the increased cost of living, but the demand at good wages for women's labour has introduced another factor which is helping to maintain the higher standard of comfort, though at the cost of the mother's absence from her home. No stress can, however, be laid on a purely temporary phenomenon, and, if we desire to understand the nature of the permanent influence of the economic status of the married working-woman, we must disregard the contemporary disturbance of values and prices, and concentrate our attention on her condition prior to August 1914.

It is unnecessary for the argument of these articles to dwell solely, or mainly, on the lot of the wives and mothers among those 8,000,000 persons declared by Sir Robert Giffen to be living under the conditions of a family income of a pound a week. It will suffice to consider the case of a respectable woman, living in London or in any large town, having four children and a good steady husband who regularly handed over to her a housekeeping allowance of 23s. Such a family was considered to stand well above the poverty line and as a rule to be ineligible for free meals or for gifts of boots. How far did the income of such a woman correspond to her liabilities? Investigation invariably showed that the weekly expenditure of decent households differed little from each other. After necessaries had been paid for, there was indeed no margin left for the indulgence of individual tastes and likings. If a little less was spent on coal, a little more went on gas; if aged parents or delicate children necessitated a higher insurance rate, the woman had to find cheaper, and consequently less healthy, premises. The budget given below may therefore be taken as fairly typical, though in many places rents were higher. First came the question of the husband's keep. In every working-class family this is the first charge on the income, taking precedence even of rent. The man fairly argues that if he is not fed he cannot work, and, happily both for his class and for his nation, the most unselfish husband alive refuses to live on bread and tea. Careful inquiries showed that, at pre-war prices, the cost of the food personally consumed by the male head of the household was never less than 5s. a week. This estimate allowed full value for its by-products, such as 'liquor,' or dripping which helped towards the children's dinners. Few men, however, could be henpecked into dispensing with a 'relish' at the morning and evening meals. 'If it's only a penny bloater and a bit of cheese,' groaned their spouses, 'they've got to have it.' Seeing that the cost of the dietary in English prisons worked out at about 7½d. per head per diem, the free citizen could hardly be blamed for insisting on faring better than the gaol-bird to the extent of another penny or so a day.

Next came certain fixed charges. The woman could, and did, on occasion, tide over a difficult week by letting such items as the rent or the boot-club run, but on the year as a whole she was compelled to find at least the following weekly amounts:

	s.	d.
Rent (three rooms)	6	6
Insurance	0	8
Gas (weekly average)	1	2
Coal (all the year round)	1	0
Soap, wood, and household oddments	1	0
Boots (weekly average for mother and four children)	1	3
Clothing (weekly average for mother and four children)	1	3
Total	12	10

No woman indeed ever allowed that such sums were adequate. You can't boot a child for 3s. 3d. a quarter,' they asserted, 'unless you or the father can do the mending, and unless you have the luck never to buy a bad pair. And you can't keep kids tidy on a threepenny or a fourpenny club unless you buy some secondhand things as well, and twist and turn. A shilling a week, moreover, doesn't really keep you in coal—you must get in some coke as well.'

It is important to note that if the matron of the mean streets did not wish to find herself at odds with her world, none of the above expenditure was really optional. Many a one left to her own judgment would have packed the family into a couple of rooms so as to leave more money for food, but she was barred from this expedient no less by the sanitary authorities than by her employer-husband. Comfort for him after his day's work was the understood condition of her weekly 23s., and the wife dared not risk his being driven to the public-house by lack of peace and quiet at home. Every shilling spent there would have meant at the week's end just so much out of her pocket. Had she economised in soap, soda, or hot water, and so sent uncleanly children to school, the N.S.P.C.C. [National Society for the Prevention of Cruelty to Children] might have been set to work. The teachers themselves are driven from behind. At whatever cost, they must present clean and tidy children to the inspectors, or suffer in their reports. So powerful and remorseless is the pressure they apply that even in the poorest schools only a small percentage of the scholars show serious defects of clothing or manifest failure as regards personal cleanliness. This fact is, to the superficial observer, a welcome proof of the improved social condition of the masses. The mothers only too often know better, and puzzled school doctors report that it is frequently the neglected (*sic*) children who are the best nourished and have the best teeth. The pecuniary position, then, was as follows:

After the mother of four children had received from her husband a weekly housekeeping allowance of 23*s.*, fed the man on the most meagre scale he could be expected to tolerate, and defrayed her practically compulsory weekly outgoings, she had left over the sum of 5*s.* 2*d.* With this amount in her pocket, an average of less than twopence per day per head (less than the price of a pint of milk), she was left to provide not only her own and her children's food but also for the unexpected and incidental outlays which crop up in every household, large or small. It would be interesting to learn precisely from the distinguished patrons of the much belauded Baby Week Exhibitions at Westminster in what way they expected those enterprises to promote the welfare either of such a woman's infant or of herself—or of the hundreds of thousands of women who were still worse off.

It is, unfortunately, not possible to offer any exact estimate of the proportion of married women who, before the War, were thus receiving from their husbands a maintenance far below subsistence level for themselves and their children, but it was undoubtedly very large.

Mr. Sidney Webb in his *Estimate of Wages of the Manual Working Class for 1912* calculated that out of 8,700,000 adult male workers in the country, no fewer than 4,240,000 men in situations and 700,000 casual labourers—over 56 per cent. of the total number—earned at, or under, the rate of 27*s.* 6*d.* a week. It is clear that no court in the country would have considered that even the better paid of such of these men as were married could, or should, surrender more than 23*s.* for their domestic expenses, and public opinion would have been outraged if a wife had demanded a greater proportion of her husband's wages. Out of their own 'bits' the men had to pay for their boots, clothes, clubs, trams, beer and tobacco. Sometimes, of course, the earnings of older children eased the situation, or the gifts of relations and friends, but the fact remains that in a huge section of the population, whenever the number of children rose to three or four, the latter and their mother were forced to depend for food on the precarious and ill-paid labour of the woman herself, handicapped by her domestic duties, and, only too often, by continual pregnancies, and by every form of physical suffering.

As statisticians tell us that in order to cover wastage [infant and child deaths], emigration and childless marriages, an average family of four children is necessary to keep the population at a satisfactory level, the above figures, did they stand alone, would be serious enough, but the analysis must be carried further. The case of the workers (44 per cent of the whole number) must be considered who before August 1914 earned more than 27*s. 6d.* a week, and who, therefore, might be supposed to provide more adequately for their dependents—so called. To take for granted, however, as so many airy theorists do, that the economic well-being of wife and children is assured, provided the husband be well paid, is to shut one's eyes to glaring facts. The mental attitude, indeed, has not yet entirely disappeared which, in past days, led to the murder of a wife being considered a finable offence; whereas that of a husband was petty treason, only to be expiated by death at the stake. There is still a lurking feeling that a man in his capacity of husband should be sacrosanct, and that it is indecorous, if not indecent, to call in question his conduct in that capacity.

Nevertheless, to take such a position is to declare that, alone among the institutions of the country, the home and the family must remain unreformed and unadapted to changing conditions. What surer way of signing their death warrant? . . .

The enormous expenditure on alcohol, declared by the Parliamentary War Savings Committee to have averaged before the War 6*s. 6d.* per family per week, is in itself more than enough to demonstrate that well-paid men by no means necessarily regard their earnings as a 'family' wage. It is computed by competent judges that half the families in the country spend little or nothing on alcohol, so the amount spent by those who drink must be very large. All social inquirers agree that there is little intemperance among men who earn small, regular wages. Workers of this class can only indulge to excess at the cost of entirely stripping themselves of their homes, and experience shows that few are so dominated by the passion for alcohol as to pay this price. Casual labourers drink to excess at times, but during their lean months cannot afford to indulge. Women, again, have, as a rule, too little command of money to allow of their furnishing any considerable part of the huge total expended yearly on intoxicants. The main support of the public-house is the man who can afford to drink freely and yet reserve just enough to enable his wife to struggle along and keep a roof over his head. In 1900, for instance, we are told that the expenditure upon drink in Port Glasgow averaged 30*l.* a family. Allowing for abstaining households, and for those in which the consumption of alcohol was strictly moderate, it is clear that many men must have spent 15*s.* or 20*s.* a week on self-indulgence. The wives and families of such men were manifestly no better off because of the husband's high earnings.

To the number of married women, therefore, who suffer from grievous personal poverty because of the lowness of their husbands' wages must be added the wives of those better-paid workers who either exact a high personal standard of living for themselves, or who bring a large number of children into the world, or who look upon the economic exploitation of the wife as part of the marriage bargain. Yet ladies of high degree breathe gentle aspirations that improved education in domestic life may inspire the next generation of mothers with the desire to stay at home during the infancy of their children, and medical Officers of Health plead for laws forbidding women with young children to work in factories. Other reformers lament 'the deplorable misdirection of energy' in the case of women who take in home-work, and, consequently, have neither time nor strength to care for their families. They therefore call for legislation which shall have the effect of making home-work unprofitable. It apparently occurs to no one that there is any absurdity in demanding that women should sit at home and starve.

The foregoing paragraphs may be illustrated by giving the result of an investigation made early in 1914 into the domestic budgets of twenty-two London families in which the spectacles ordered for a child by the school doctor had not been procured. In three instances it proved impracticable to obtain precise information; in four, pecuniary causes had nothing to do with the failure to provide the glasses; in fifteen, the mother and dependent children could not possibly have obtained the barest necessaries of life, let alone luxuries like spectacles, with the money supplied by the husband. The fifteen families differed a good deal as to actual income and general social standing, as particulars of the two occupying either end of the scale will show:

(a) Father, crippled, a tin labourer working by piece; occasionally earned more, but as a rule could only give wife 16s. or 17s. Daughter, aged nineteen, slept at home and paid 2s. a week for her bed. Home wretched and squalid. Children found eating dry bread for their dinner. Wife too devitalised to try to earn, and, besides, had a baby three months old. Family only kept in being by private and public charity. The baby subsequently died, but had the local School for Mothers succeeded in keeping it alive it is difficult to see what benefit would have accrued to itself, its relations, or the community.

(b) A family which in its own eyes and in that of its neighbours was extremely flourishing and respectable. 'When I tell you,' said Mrs. T., an active and intelligent woman, 'that I have five at work and handle 2*l*. 17*s*. a week; it seems absurd even to myself to say I can't find 3*s*. 6*d*. for Mary's glasses. My man earns 22*s*. and gives me 19*s*. We have three children still going to school. I reckon I get rent and coal, besides their keep, out of what the older ones contribute, and that leaves me father's money to feed him, me, and the little ones, and pay for gas, insurance, and clothes.' Further analysis showed that even in this well-to-do household the amount available for the actual food of mother and dependent children worked out at less than threepence per day per head.

In considering the economic position of the mother, it is easy to lay too much stress on the total family earnings. The pecuniary burden is doubt-less lightened when the children begin to work, but the father's contribu-tion at the same time often tends to lessen owing to his increasing age. Furthermore, though there are many beautiful exceptions, young folk of both sexes are fully conscious, nowadays, of their personal claims on life, and tend to give as little as they can towards the upkeep of the home. The mother, poor soul, does not dare to demand a larger sum, or to reduce the scale of living. Her children are her sole stake in life, and she will sacrifice everything to keep them content under her own wing. Besides, she herself is pleased to see Jane in a becoming hat, to know that John is saving money in order to join a summer camp, or that Tom is 'paying off' for a bicycle. No one realises—least of all the mother herself—that these good things are being wrung out of the woman's flesh and blood. By the time the family has grown up, moreover, she has only too often been drilled and broken into being the uncomplaining slave of the whole household. One finds elderly women suffering from ulcerated legs, varicose veins, heart complaints, chronic rheumatism, doing the entire domestic work for six or seven adults. Yet these women could on their own showing quite well afford to pay for domestic help. Any increase in the income of the family goes automatically towards augmenting its amenities—its supply of food, light, warmth and social enjoyments, and a penny is seldom appropriated by the mother for the easing of her own lot.

The normal economic condition of the wives has recently been illustrated in another way. In 1916 there suddenly opened out the possibility of their earning the lordly wage of from 25*s*. to 30*s*. a week. With dismay one heard of woman after woman whom one knew to be suffering from serious organic disorders engaging in hard muscular toil and keeping pace with men doing the same work. Moreover to the women neither meal times nor evening hours brought rest. 'I get home to breakfast from eight to nine,' said Mrs. S., who was lifting and trucking hundredweights of meal for ten hours a day, 'but I never sit down. I just eat a bit of bread and drink a cup of tea as I get the baby washed and the children off to school. After work I do the washing and clean the place.' Such women were lately working fourteen and fifteen hours a day, yet, so far from utterly breaking down, their health often sensibly improved. They themselves explained the apparent miracle by saying that they were at last able to secure sufficient food, were not 'styed up' in their little dark and damp homes, and above all, were free from the gnawing anxiety of never knowing how to satisfy the landlord or how to pay their debts. . . .

That the ill-housed, ill-clothed, ill-fed mother was, before the War, no merely local nor temporary phenomenon is clearly shown by a little book entitled *Maternity*, published in 1915 by the Women's Co-operative Guild. The volume consists of 160 letters, stated to be fair samples of the 400 received by the Central Committee. The writers, who, at some time or other, have held office in the Guild, may certainly be assumed to be better husbanded; better endowed and educated, less isolated and depressed than are the majority of the poorer married working-women in the Kingdom. Yet the letters telling of their authors' experiences during their child-bearing years paint a terrible picture of overwork, semi-starvation, heartrending physical suffering and unending mental strain and stress. How, indeed, could it be otherwise? At the end of the letters appear such statements as the following:

'Wages 2l. 2s. 0d. Eight children, one still-born, eight miscarriages'; or
'Wages 16s. to 27s. Six children, one miscarriage';
'Wages 25s. Four children, ten miscarriages.'

Yet the list of the husbands' occupations at the end of the volume shows a large proportion of skilled trades, and is sufficient proof that the men were by no means personally poverty-stricken. A man's mates, in fact, insist on his conforming to the standard of life which they consider right. He dare not, for instance, go to work in a ragged shirt or broken boots, or be without a penny in his pocket for incidental calls.

Surprisingly little bitterness is displayed even towards those husbands to whose direct voluntary action the penury of the wife is due. After one or two impotent struggles the women realise their helplessness and the futility of 'rows,' philosophically declare that 'men are naturally selfish,' and turn to their children for consolation. Each individual woman slips into her slavery gradually. At first marriage offered a welcome escape from dull and uninspiring industrial toil, and the first baby gave a glimpse of heaven. It takes some years for her position to become acute, and then, as the older matrons explain: 'She can't do nothing.' For the sake of her brood, therefore, she settles down to make the best of things. As long as they keep their self-respect, the women struggle to keep their troubles to themselves. 'I can stand going short,' said one, 'I can even stand being knocked down, but I couldn't stand the neighbours pitying me.' The men are, indeed, less to blame than one is sometimes tempted to think. It must be remembered that the Industrial Revolution has done much to weaken the tie between the male breadwinner and his home. It has broken up the old family life in which father, mother and children spent their days together, co-operatively working for their common needs. The man's daylight hours are now usually spent among strangers, and he perforce finds his friends and his interests in places and in ways with which his domestic circle has nothing to do. Unless, therefore, his family instincts are strong, he gradually comes to look upon his home as a kind of private boarding house, in which he holds the privileged position of being able to demand everything, while giving as little as he chooses.

On this disintegration of married life, there are, it is true, powerful checks, or the family as an institution would have perished long ago. In the best cases these checks render even the iniquities of the English marriage law inoperative as far as directly regards the individuals concerned, and, even in the worst, act as a restraining force. The natural attraction between the sexes, the love of offspring, the national sense of fair play, the interdependence of husband and wife, the pressure of family and of public opinion, all operate in mitigating in various degrees the condition of the wife. Nevertheless, in simple truth, there are no such pitiless sweaters in the world as working-class husbands, taken as a class, though use and wont have blinded both men and women to the fact. The servitude of the wife seems natural and inevitable because there has been no experience of any other social order, and so great is the tyranny of words over the human mind that men actually talk of 'supporting' their wives, and feel themselves in so doing to be something of philanthropists. They never realise that they are, in fact, exploiting for their own advantage the cheapest labour in the world. The Eternal Verities, however, cannot be eluded, and, as the writer hopes to show in another article, no one in the long run has paid a heavier price for the serfdom of their wives than working-men themselves.

Honnor Morten

BETHNAL GREEN AUTOBIOGRAPHER GEORGE ACORN recalled a sour note in
Honnor Morten's lecture to working-class schoolboys (probably in the mid-
1890s) on hygiene in the home. Most of the boys lived in overcrowded and
sparsely furnished quarters. They were dumbfounded when Morten advised
them, as Acorn recalled, to "let the sunshine into our homes whether the carpets suffered or not. Carpets!"[1] Morten (1861–1913), daughter of a wealthy
Richmond solicitor and niece of a well-known novelist, would learn much
more about London poverty.

In her late thirties, Morten, "the merriest of saints," as one friend
described her, was depicted by a fellow journalist as "a light, pale girl, with
dark, steady eyes, and hair as black as can be" who carried a silver cigarette
case and wore odd "barbaric" jewelry. "A happier and cheerier woman I
never met," said minor novelist William Pett Ridge, who also mentioned
her "shrewdness" and "humour."[2]

She was a leader and expert in many arenas during her truncated life. She
began nurse's training at London Hospital when she was twenty and eventually also received a midwifery diploma from the London Obstetrical
Society.[3] The selection reprinted here, from her fictionalized journal, clearly
draws on her nursing history. She was a nursing volunteer from 1885 to 1888,
and then began to demonstrate interests in public speaking, journalism, and
health policy and administration. She wrote articles for the *Hospital,* the

---

Originally published as "Eating the Apple," chap. 2 of From a Nurse's Notebook *(London:
Scientific Press, 1899), 8–12, 13–15, 16–20, 21, 22–29. Christened Violet Honnor Morten, she
always signed her work "Honnor Morten." The only mention of her full name I have found
is in a one-line death announcement in the* London Times, *July 14, 1913, 1.*

Daily News, and other periodicals; published several classic nursing manuals; and, in 1889, founded and helped run the Women Writers Club with offices in Fleet Street. In the early 1890s, she organized the Nurses' Cooperative, and in 1898, the School Nurses' Society, which offered free nurses' care for London children.[4] When she was thirty-three, in the mid-1890s, she earned a Hygiene Certificate at Bedford College for Women of the University of London.[5] About this time she began to lecture widely on infant care, first aid, family health, and women's rights. Her audiences ranged from Women's Cooperative Guild chapters, to progressive and free-thinking organizations like the South Place Chapel and the London Ethical Society, and even to women prisoners at Wormwood Scrubs—prison reform being another of her causes.[6]

In about 1896 Morten moved from her family's "splendid old mansion by the river side"[7] in Richmond, to the densely populated inner London district of Hoxton; with two college friends, she established a small settlement along "unsectarian and socialist lines" that was associated with the Hoxton Settlement.[8] The settlers, who were both male and female, lived in ordinary workers' accommodations, kept house for themselves, and lived on incomes that approached those of their clients. In her autobiographical *From a Nurse's Notebook,* Morten expressed her delight in welcoming working-class neighbors and exulted at the local curate's terror of her Chianti, cigarettes, and unorthodox religious views.[9] Fellow journalist and friend Arthur Porritt remembers the brown cloak she wore in Fleet Street, London's newspaper center, as well as in Hoxton.[10]

During these Hoxton years, in 1897, Morten successfully ran for a place on the London School Board, a powerful body that at the time was educating about 660,000 students and employed 15,000 teachers. In its existence from 1871 to 1903, only twenty-nine women (of a total of 326) had served on it. She came in first among the candidates in her district of Hackney but wisely switched to represent the City of London district when one of her constituents raised an alarm after spotting her publicly smoking in Fleet Street on a dare.[11] On the School Board, Morten campaigned for equal pay for its women employees, for ending corporal punishment in the schools, for the assignment of school nurses for the poorest pupils, and for better facilities for retarded children.[12]

In about 1905 she started a Tolstoy-inspired settlement in Rotherfield, Sussex, which was partly funded through donations from the English translators of Tolstoy's *Resurrection.* According to a friend, the house followed a rule that "insisted on silence at the breakfast table—on the principle that people are never amiable at breakfast."[13] A few years later she established a country holiday home for disabled London children.[14]

Morten's obituary in the suffrage newspaper *Votes for Women* noted that she was a nonmilitant suffragist, yet "militant in spirit."[15] She was one of the small group of feminists (which included Anna Martin and Adele Meyer) who protested against the disenfranchisement of women by refusing to pay some of their taxes, suffering instead the confiscation and public auctioning of some of their property. Morten submitted to more than one of these auctions in the months just before her death, of throat cancer.[16]

This lifetime of enormous activity in the name of prisoners, the mentally ill, and especially of poor children (who, like George Acorn, did not always appreciate her efforts) reflected Morten's commitment to avoiding the fate of "a fine lady with nothing to do but pay great attention to dress, fashion, and society, and live the humdrum life of the woman who knows and cares nothing about how the other half of the world lives."[17] Her "firm Protestant" faith also must have motivated her, though she was rather secretive about it. She began writing a life of Protestant martyr Edward Colman and published a "little devotional book" titled *The Life of an Enclosed Nun* anonymously, revealing its authorship in a later book.[18]

NOTES

1. George Acorn (pseud.), *One of the Multitude* (London: Heinemann, 1911), 68.
2. Porritt, *The Best I Remember,* 135; Friederichs, "I Was in Prison," 302; William Pett Ridge, *I Like to Remember* (London: Hodder and Stoughton, n.d.), 248.
3. "Miss Honnor Morten," *Votes for Women,* July 18, 1913, 621.
4. Rose Petty, "School Nursing," *The Nursing Times,* June 3, 1905, 80. The school nursing service provided by the London County Council was far less generous; it focused mainly on inspecting children for head lice—which made them the most hated of school personnel.
5. She was not a top student in this demanding one-year program. Her brief records are in the Archives, Royal Holloway College, University of London (BC/AR/203/1/1 and BC/AR/220/2/2). My warm thanks to the Archives staff for their help in locating these records.
6. Friederichs, "I Was in Prison," 306–7. Morten listed her lecture topics in the *Women's Industrial News* and in the National Health Society's *Annual Reports* for the late 1890s. Many thanks to Anna Davin for noting the latter.
7. Friederichs, "I Was in Prison," 304.
8. Honnor Morten, *Questions for Women* (London: Adam and Charles Black, 1899), 92; also see Alice Stronach, "Women's Work in Social Settlements," *Windsor Magazine,* no. 36, 1912, 412.
9. The settlement is discussed, along with many others, in Vicinus, *Independent Women*), chap. 6, see especially 222–23; also Stronach, "Woman's Work in Social Settlements," 412.

By 1912, the Hoxton Settlement, in Nile Street, was gone, and Morten was involved in her country home for disabled children. Nearby, however, in Shepherdess Walk, a somewhat more conventional settlement was begun by the women's branch of the Christian Social Union, affiliated with the Maurice Hostel.

10. Porritt, *The Best I Remember,* 134.
11. Her 1898 *Who's Who* entry (London: Adam and Charles Black) lists her as the board member for the City Division; in the entry for 1900, she is listed as representing the Hackney Division. Patricia Hollis, following the account of fellow board member Thomas Gautrey, reproduces the story of Morten's scandalous smoking and her need to find another district to represent (Hollis, *Ladies Elect,* 123, n. 87).
12. Annmarie Turnbull, "'So Extremely like Parliament': The Work of the Women Members of the London School Board, 1870–1904," in *The Sexual Dynamics of History,* ed. London Feminist History Group (London: Pluto Press, 1983), 132; Hollis, *Ladies Elect,* 125; Martin, "Politics of Schooling," 157–58.
13. Porritt, *The Best,* 136.
14. "Miss Honnor Morten"; also see obituary in *The Times,* July 16, 1913, 11.
15. "Miss Honnor Morten."
16. The only mention of the cause of her death at age fifty-three is the memoir of Arthur Porritt, *The Best I Remember,* 136–37. On Morten's tax resistance: "Woman Writer's Tax Resistance," *Votes for Women,* May 23, 1913, 498; "Tax Resistance Growing," *Votes for Women,* May 30, 1913, 514. A good history of this movement is Hilary Frances, "'Pay the Piper, Call the Tune!': The Women's Tax Resistance League," in Maroula Joannou and June Purvis, eds., *The Women's Suffrage Movement: New Feminist Perspectives* (Manchester: Manchester University Press, 1998): 65–88.
17. Friederichs, "I Was in Prison," 404.
18. Porritt, *The Best I Remember,* 136; "Miss Honnor Morten."

FURTHER READING

Honnor Morten's fictionalized journal, from which the selection here originates, is *From a Nurse's Notebook* (London: Scientific Press, 1899). She also wrote a collection of short stories, *Sketches of Hospital Life* (London: Low, Marston, Searle and Rivington, 1888). Her *Nurse's Dictionary of Medical Terms and Nursing Treatment* (London: The Hospital, 1891) was reprinted into the 1950s.

Several sources, some by her contemporaries, include information about Honnor Morten: Hulda Friederichs, "'I Was in Prison'—The Story of Miss Honnor Morten's Wonderful Work," *The Young Woman* 8, October 1899–September 1900, 302–7; Patricia Hollis, *Ladies Elect: Women in English Local Government 1865–1914* (Oxford: Clarendon Press, 1987). Morten is one of four middle-class women educators discussed by Jane Martin in "Gender, the City, and the Politics of Schooling: Towards a Collective Biography of Women 'Doing Good' as Public Moralists in Victorian London," *Gender and Education* 17, no. 2 (May 2005): 143–63. Arthur Porritt, a longtime journalist for the *Christian World* and other religious papers, describes Morten appreciatively in *The Best I Remember* (London: Cassell and Company, 1922). Martha Vicinus presents several detailed sections on Morten in *Independent Women: Work and Community for Single Women 1850–1920* (Chicago: University of Chicago Press, 1985).

Eating the Apple

(Being passages from Drusilla's Diary during her first stay in hospital.)
10th May.—At last I am here shut up in my little room almost like a nun in her cell: only the nun flies from the world seeking the supernatural, I fly to the world seeking the real.

That is what I want—reality at all costs; the fruit of the tree of the knowledge of good and evil, however bitter the rind, however ashen the core. Deliberately I offer up to the great God of Knowledge all that remains of my youth and innocence, asking in return only the right to face life as it is; only freedom to see and hear; only contrast to make clear the colours of the land I leave behind. And now, come weal or woe, at least I shall not die in the dark.

14th June.—They said I should tire and return home in a few days, and, in truth, it takes all my resolution to stay. A thousand times already I have thought it was more than I could bear, and have longed to leave. There are in this great building some 500 patients, all suffering and sore-stricken, and some of them are little children.

The cries of the children seem to ring in my ears all night. I did not dream of such misery as this!

I am so thirsty with the hot air and the bad smells that I suck ice all day, and my feet are sore from the constant standing.

I vowed that I would keep sketches or notes of everything I saw and heard, that I would study human nature remorselessly, and dive right down to the region of the soul. But there is much one must not even think about, far less put down in black and white. And yet the outward seeming is artistic; it is the detail that is so coarse, so undrawable.

A man died yesterday; it was typhoid fever and he was delirious. His hands waved in the air and he muttered and muttered, and sometimes called out "Alice!" quite loudly and clearly. There was no Alice there; he died alone and unclaimed, and the body was sent to the dissecting-room.

16th June.—The wards are long and bare, with light grey walls; ranged down each side are neat beds, covered with white counterpanes; the white sunlight comes streaming in through a row of high, curtainless windows. Tables and lockers, with white-tiled tops, are dotted here and there. The long lines of perspective and the effect of whiteness and peace is very beautiful, particularly if a pretty nurse in uniform is coming walking up the ward. (The breadth and simplicity of a nursing uniform are very effective.) In the whiteness and stillness comes a rush of blackness and noise, the surgeon and his students; presently comes the cry of pain, the short, sharp orders of the surgeon, the swift service of the nurse. The crowd moves away from the bed, and one sees the man's face whiter than ever against the white pillows.

17th June.—Only a week and already I begin to grow callous. Twenty was groaning while I was at tea this evening and I did not go to him. I could have done nothing, only said something sympathetic, but I have felt shamed and sorry ever since. I meant this to have been a daily record, but I have no time, and by night my mind is a complete blank. But it is good to be too busy to think, to see and know are far better. Neither life nor death, neither pain nor pleasure, shall henceforth hold a secret from me. Wisdom that wants experience is useless; far from me be the conclusions of other men, close to me the bitter teaching of this weary hospital world.

3rd July.—What a hell of pain this hospital is! I shall never sleep to-night, why should I? Will *he* sleep, with his crushed and mangled limbs? His face is before me, fierce with pain, yet unyielding; the lips closed tightly, the eyes burning and rebellious. No cry, no sound, but the bitter anger in those eyes! Strange he should take the accident in this way; others are brought in moaning or half-fainting, feeling and knowing nothing but pain. But this man is angry—is angry with God. . . .

10th July.—Strangely enough my health is perfect here, now I have got used to the continual standing. And it is a splendid thing to be strong, it is a glorious thing to be able. I am so glad my art taught me not to admire small waists and distorted feet. It saddens me often to see how women ill-treat their bodies, and so long as it is done the progress of women must be delayed. Quite a fourth of a woman's life is spent practically in agony, while the average sickness for a man is four days in a year. Doctors shrug their shoulders and say "Nature!" I don't believe it is nature, and I hope for great things when more women doctors are qualified and practising. The type of wisdom, the sphinx, had the head of a woman and the body of a lion. It is the body of the lion we need to cultivate now.

18th July.—Longfellow says of the sea—

Only those who share its peril
Comprehend its mystery,

and this is true of life also. Until I came here and risked death, I never knew the divine depths of life's mystery. Blanco White has a sonnet on how the darkness of night makes visible the stars, and the enormous extent of the universe; and Thoreau says: "The shadows of poverty and meanness gather round us, and lo! creation widens to our view". So I feel my life grows larger daily, and when this afternoon a trim visitor asked me if I did not object to dusting the tables and washing up the mugs, it was quite an effort to think of these things, and to grasp that to some these trifles are of importance, and even hide from them all the height and depth of this hospital life. Great heavens! I was given two hands and one mind; why should it be more undignified to use my hands than my mind? No, no! may no part of me "fust unused," neither body nor spirit, but all grow together that I may more fitly grasp the great mysteries which surround me. . . .

10th August. — What horrors life contains! There is a girl dying in the ward I am now in; she is only nineteen and has a most beautiful profile, and beautiful hair. She has a mania for pouring forth confessions, and they are hideous. There was a proverb I heard in Italy: "As foul as a priest's ear". I begin to understand its significance. Part of Annie's story I could guess, but one part opens up new horrors to my eyes. She said she found black-mailing paid better than being on the street. She was in league with a policeman, and she used to wait about a quiet street on his beat until she saw a well-dressed man come along; then she would throw herself down in a sham fit and ask the man to unloose her collar; if he acceded she promptly called "police!" and her accomplice came up and she charged the victim with assault. The policeman would point out to the victim that he must take him to the station, and suggest he had better square the woman with a fiver. As a rule this was done, and the accomplices shared the spoil. Nor did the plot always end there, for sometimes the victim was followed to his home and systematically black-mailed for years. On her own showing Annie has wrecked many a happy home by her infamous and unfounded charges, yet nothing can be done now to right the wrong. Oh God! what a death-bed!

21st October. — I have had scarlet fever and been away for seven weeks. It was very horrid being ill, and sometimes at the fever hospital when you wanted a drink the nurse would say coolly: "Don't be impatient, wait a bit". Well, it has taught me never to speak like that myself to a patient. It was so ugly and lonely at that fever hospital, but the fortnight at the sea afterwards was good. Only ward memories haunted me; the bitter taste of the apple was ever in my mouth. Those lines of Mrs. Browning's torment me:—

Each footstep of your treading,
    Treads out some murmur that ye heard before,
Farewell! the streams of Eden,
    Ye shall hear never more.

Well, after all, I am glad to be back in the rush of work again, and the garden of Eden is not the only beautiful place. On the top of a bus coming from the station to-day I saw a feast of colour such as neither Italy nor Greece ever offered me. We came over Waterloo Bridge, and it was nearing sunset; the sky was dusky orange, and all the distances were cloudy purple. The Thames, a shimmering, changing bronze, came thickly stealing down between the dark houses on the West and the red-glowing houses on the East, and broken here and there by a black moving barge. And the great roar of the traffic rose up all around me, like the moaning prayer of an angry giant. If man spoils the country, God glorifies the town.

24th October.—Doctors and nurses are the martyrs of modern life. I took up a nursing paper to-day and found four deaths chronicled: (1) a probationer [a nurse in training] aged twenty-seven, from typhoid contracted while on duty; (2) a probationer, aged eighteen, at a children's hospital, from pneumonia following measles; (3) a nurse, aged twenty, at a fever hospital, from heart disease following scarlet fever; (4) a district nurse from diphtheria contracted from a patient. And that is a one week's record. The dreadful thing is the quiet way in which death goes on swallowing up the young lives, and no one pays any heed. Thousands of the rank and file suffer and die in some great cause ere the hero comes along whom chance makes victor, and who takes the laurels won by all the forgotten dead.

8th November.—We get many suicides in, and I have come to scorn them. The reason is so often just pique, just a woman's flash of temper and an attempt to revenge herself: "I'll make him suffer," is her chief thought. This is not noble and not nice, and makes one distrust Epictetus' praise of the "open door". The last case we had in, however, was a man, a poet; to-day he was allowed to speak for the first time, and he eagerly asked me had the papers had any account of the affair? had any reporters been to inquire after him? I dared not give his egotism the shock of the whole truth—that no one had taken the least notice of his childish attempt—in case he should tear away the bandages and commit suicide in earnest. But how horribly petty it is! Poor Amy Levy with a little genius but less courage, trying to grasp in death the recognition refused her in life, and only becoming a nine days' wonder to a small section of society. Then Chatterton [an eighteenth-century poet who killed himself at age seventeen] is talked about but never read: that is a poor sort of fame. No, life may be bitter, but it must be lived out to the end if any true work is to be done. . . .

30th December.—The children's ward is delightful; oh, the pleasure of feeling two warm arms clasped round your neck and soft little kisses falling on your cheek! It is restful to be with innocent, trusting children, and it is nice to be able to lift and move them without effort. I am glad my present post is so pleasant, for I feel depressed at the close of the year, and the thought of the studio haunts me. I have a fear my hand has lost its cunning—the same sort of fear that sent me here. How one disappointment falls on the top of another in youth! First men kill love, then the priests kill faith, then knowledge kills hope. What is there left? Truth. Therefore faith, hope, love, these three being dead, life, properly speaking, may be said to begin. . . . Well, so far what I have found is this, that Truth is only the knowledge that nothing is true, that everything is an alloy; that every action and every motive has two springs; that every philosophy and every religion has two sides—and I would gladly barter this wisdom for the tiniest grain of faith, for the faintest gleam of love!

10th January.—There is laughter even in hospital, but there is ever a grimness about our jokes. To-day Sir John was going through St. Martin's Ward; the patient in No. 14 bed had just died; it was always a screen case, and before Sister had time to explain to Sir John he drew back the screen a bit in his brisk way and without looking round the curtain said: "How are you to-day, my man? Better? That's right, go on just the same."

14th January.—It is not always those who wear the cross who bear the cross. I have just been nursing saint and sinner side by side, and all my sympathy was with the sinner. No. 9 was a young woman of about twenty-three, arrogant, righteous overmuch, given to talking of altars and the Eucharist and to praying with a crucifix clasped in her hands. As death drew near her arrogance became fear, religion seemed to loose its consoling power, pain seemed unbearable. I had no peace with the girl; she was perpetually calling to me to do this or that, and she prayed and moaned aloud to the distress of the other patients. She was so terribly anxious about her own soul and body. No. 8 was a quiet, worn little woman of thirty—looking fifty. Her wistful eyes would follow the chaplain about the ward, but she wouldn't speak to him: "'Taint no use to worry about me; Number Nine's a-calling for you, sir". Never a grumble, never a cry, though a slow disease was eating away her life. "Thank ye, miss," came from her white lips after each service rendered, and the half-frightened eyes looked gratefully at me. I tried to tempt her to speak, but she only shook her head and muttered: "Too late," or, "I can't give away the others". But how bravely she bore suffering, how thoughtful she was for those around her. If she had sinned in the past, if old wild riots did arise in accusation against her, still she died in silence which spoke much.

5th March.—Two months since I wrote in my diary; the fact is that this life begins to interest me for itself—the science of healing begins to attract me almost more than the study of human nature displayed naked beneath my eyes. It begins to dawn on me that I am happy and content, yet I cannot quite be satisfied to forget my art. Still, art is merely the dream of action, and it is better to do than to depict. . . . But it is beautiful to dream, and to show others one's dreams. . . . If I could only get back into the children's ward again and see them answer my smile. The children have all before them; it is worth while to help them to live. But why some of the men and women want to be cured in order to go forth and perpetually toil for fourteen hours and sleep six I cannot imagine. Is it life merely to get up and work until you lie down again? They might just as well die and be done with it, for they must be weary of it all. You can see it in their eyes—they do not smile in answer to mine. Their faces reflect the things within; the faces of the children reflect the things without.

22nd March.—What a brutal thing custom is; I have fallen into the routine here till I am becoming a mere machine, and losing all perception of the spiritual. Soon my patients will be "cases" and my bookshelves will hold only huge volumes on therapeutics and surgery. I must get away from here; I must get back to the woods and fields. The wild cherries must be in flower now, and the daffodils beside the lake. Oh, how beautiful, how fresh, the home farm must be looking! And here the pale sunlight filters faintly through the smoke, and the pavement never seems to dry. Perhaps this may be because I am only out in the early morning; I am on night duty, and sleep through the middle of the day. It is strange the long night in the dim ward; the curtains of each bed are drawn, the gas turned down, there are no students or doctors about. I have a shaded lamp on my table, but I do not read much. The chant of the city fascinates me; I cannot help trying to fathom it. The rattle Westward of the busses and cabs gradually decreasing, the "shrill shopping" of the women, the return of the drunken husbands near midnight, the last jingle of the tram bells. Then the rumble of the market-carts, the rush of a fire engine, and, after such a short interval, the tram bells and the busses begin again, and then the cries of the milk and coal men, and the steady roar of the traffic once more. That is how the city talks to us all night in this unfashionable neighbourhood, telling of the toil that never ceases, the wheels that go to and fro for ever.

24*th March.*—It is no use:—

> The wild birds sing in the heart of spring,
> And the green boughs beckon me.

I have asked for a holiday and am off home for a week. Ugh! how loathsome disease is, how hateful the smell of carbolic, how sickening the sight of the surgeon's knives. But I will forget it all. I go home—home to the fields and flowers.

4*th April.*—It is so easy to write "forget," it is so difficult to do. The woods were there, the daffodils were out—but the place was joyless, the days were empty, nature had become nothing to me. If I sat and talked about daffodils my mind was all the time pondering about the tracheotomy case; my eyes looked at the country but my brain beheld the hospital wards. And when I sat at my easel and took up my brush it fell listlessly from my hand. What was the use of painting? How could I sit there and deal in dreams and forget all the sin and suffering, all the terrible realities of life? How could I be happy there when I knew there was all this misery here?

> Father, I choose; I will not take a heaven
> Haunted by shrieks of far-off misery.

Oh, Eden, Eden! I have eaten the apple, and the gates are closed behind me!

Margaret Wynne Nevinson

BORN MARGARET WYNNE JONES IN LEICESTER, Margaret Nevinson (1858–1932) was yet another clergyman's daughter. Her high church Anglican father, the Rev. Timothy Jones, was a classical scholar who taught his five sons and his only daughter Latin and Greek. He was Welsh born and Welsh speaking, his wife was half Welsh, and Margaret valued her Welsh identity throughout her life.[1] The death of her beloved father in the late 1870s led to family financial problems, and Margaret Jones looked for work. A university education was out of the question. She eventually spent time as a teacher and accompanist at a music school in Germany. Upon her return to Britain in about 1880, she taught at South Hampstead High School for Girls in London, her classical education landing her the job.[2] She later got a degree through a part-time correspondence course at the University of St. Andrews in Scotland.

Margaret Nevinson began exploring London poverty soon after her marriage in 1884 to Henry Nevinson, who later became a well-known journalist. On the couple's return from a year's residence in Germany, and encouraged by Samuel and Henrietta Barnett of nearby Toynbee Hall, they settled in newly built "workmen's flats" in Whitechapel, overlooking the famous Petticoat Lane market.[3] Whereas the working-class residents of their building lived in two or three rooms per family, however, the Nevinsons and

———————

"The Evacuation of the Workhouse" is from Nevinson's collection of some of her journalism, in Workhouse Characters and Other Sketches of the Life of the Poor *(London: George Allen and Unwin Ltd. [1918]). The sketches, all written after 1905, had been published in various daily newspapers.*

their infant daughter rented two contiguous flats, with a total of six rooms, and brought their maid with them!

Margaret got involved in East London social work right away. In the mid-1880s, she found paid employment collecting rents for Octavia Hill in the Katharine Buildings in East Smithfield and the newer Lolesworth Buildings on Commercial Street. Rent collecting, though, was mainly "an expensive hobby,"[4] because Nevinson was too softhearted toward the impecunious tenants to extract the full sums due. She was also deeply involved in the work of Toynbee Hall, teaching French classes (which she continued to do for twenty years), organizing evenings of entertainment, and for a time running one of the settlement's girls' clubs, a project she disliked. The Nevinson family moved to Hampstead in 1887, but Margaret Nevinson maintained her extensive commitments to East London.

While she was still a schoolteacher in the early 1880s, Nevinson joined other feminists in their campaign for the Married Women's Property Act, which was passed in 1882 and which gave wives control over their earnings and other property. She joined the Women's Social and Political Union in 1905, soon after its formation, but left just two years later for the breakaway Women's Freedom League. Her husband, also an active suffragist, remained much longer with the WSPU.

By the early 1900s, Margaret and Henry Nevinson had separated, though they continued to share their Hampstead house; they speak of each other in their 1920s autobiographies coolly and seldom.[5] Their 1884 wedding was probably a result of Margaret's premarital pregnancy. Henry's diaries refer to their "dismal marriage" and to his wife's tendency "to contradict me on every point & all occasions." Margaret's religious scruples prevented a divorce, but Henry Nevinson, a serious womanizer, formed a close relationship with the journalist Evelyn Sharp and married her upon his wife's death. Margaret Nevinson's fiction from the 1880s and 1890s suggests how wounding she found Henry's relationship with Sharp.[6]

For most of the rest of her life, Nevinson, who had a second child, a son (C. R. W., the well-known modernist artist), combined journalism with community service, local government office holding, and feminist political activism as a member of the Women's Freedom League. She was a poor law guardian in Hampstead continuously from 1904 to the end of 1921, an experience reflected in the selection included here, which was part of a much larger group of her workhouse sketches and stories.[7] She was also a school manager for twenty-five years, serving in east and northwest London schools.[8] In 1920, nominated by the WFL, she was appointed a justice of the peace for Hampstead, the first woman justice in London.[9] She flirted with Fabian socialism in her youth, but eventually became a staunch Liberal. She was an officer of the Women's Peace Crusade in the 1920s and, like many of her feminist peers, an active League of Nations supporter.

As a journalist, Nevinson mostly wrote nonfiction about the lives of poor women and men. She published frequently for newspapers like the *Daily Chronicle,* the *Westminster Gazette,* the *Daily News,* and the *Manchester Guardian;* major periodicals; and suffragist papers. She wrote a number of suffrage pamphlets along with a play satirizing the husband's legal right to incarcerate his wife in the workhouse. *In the Workhouse,* which was dramatized by the Pioneer Players, was a contributing factor in a change to the law.

NOTES

1. This is the point made by Angela John in "Margaret Wynne Nevinson."
2. Nevinson, *Life's Fitful Fever,* 59.
3. See Henry Nevinson, *Changes and Chances* (London: Nisbet, 1923), 79.
4. Nevinson, *Life's Fitful Fever,* 86, 90.
5. See, for example, *Changes and Chances,* 82.
6. John, "Margaret Wynne Nevinson," 5; discussed further in her biography of Henry Nevinson, *War, Journalism, and the Shaping of the Twentieth Century;* the quotations are from *Changes and Chances,* 20. See also 16–17.
7. On poor law guardians, see the glossary. Also see Jerry White, *London in the Twentieth Century* (London: Penguin Books, 2001), 357; and Patricia Hollis, *Ladies Elect: Women in English Local Government 1865–1914* (Oxford: Clarendon Press, 1987), 8–9, 208.
8. School managers (later called Care Committees) were volunteers who organized services for schoolchildren in poor districts. See the glossary. Also see M. E. Bulkley, *The Feeding of School Children* (London: G. Bell, 1914); Brian Simon, *Education and the Labour Movement 1870–1920* (London: Lawrence and Wishart, 1974); Ellen Ross, "Hungry Children: Housewives and London Charity, 1870–1918," in *The Uses of Charity: The Poor on Relief in the Nineteenth-Century Metropolis,* ed. Peter Mandler (Philadelphia: University of Pennsylvania Press, 1990); and Susan K. Pennybacker, *A Vision for London 1889–1914: Labour, Everyday Life and the LCC Experiment* (New York: Routledge, 1995), 202–10; and James Vernon, "The Ethics of Hunger and the Assembly of Society: The Techno-Politics of the School Meal in Modern Britain," *American Historical Review* 110, no. 3 (June 2005): 693–725.
9. Angela John's entry in the Oxford DNB; *Who Was Who among English and European Authors 1931–49* (Detroit: Gale Research Co., 1978).

FURTHER READING

For more writing by Margaret Nevinson, see *Fragments of Life: Tales and Sketches* (London: G. Allen and Unwin, 1922); *The Legal Wrongs of Married Women* (London: Women's Freedom League, 1923); and *Life's Fitful Fever: A Volume of Memories* (London: Adam and Charles Black, 1926).

For information about Nevinson, see the BDBF (vol. 1), the entry by Angela John in the Oxford DNB, and *The Suffrage Annual and Women's Who's Who* (London: Stanley Paul, 1913). See also Angela John's chapter "Margaret Wynne Nevinson: Gender and National Identity in the Early Twentieth Century," in *Festschrift for K. O. Morgan and R. A. Griffiths,* ed. R. R. Davies and Geraint H. Jenkins (Cardiff: University of Wales Press, 2004), and her book *War, Journalism, and the Shaping of the Twentieth Century: The Life and Times of Henry W. Nevinson* (London: I. B. Tauris, 2006). For more on the triangular marriage of the Nevinsons, see Wendell Harris, "H. W. Nevinson, Margaret Wynne Nevinson, Evelyn Sharp: Little-Known Writers and Crusaders," *English Literature in Transition* 45, no. 3 (2002).

⁓⁓⁓

The Evacuation of the Workhouse

The workhouse is being evacuated; the whole premises, infirmary and House, have been taken over by the War Office as a military hospital; after weeks of waiting final orders have come, and to-day motor-omnibuses and ambulances are carrying off the inmates to a neighbouring parish.

One feels how widespread and far-reaching are the sufferings caused by war, and spite of this bright May sunshine one realizes that the whole earth is full of darkness and cruel habitations, the white blossoms of the spring seem like funeral flowers, and the red tulips glow like a field of blood.

It never occurred to me before that any one could have any feeling, except repugnance, towards a workhouse, but some one—I think it was the prisoner of Chillon [in Byron's poem]—grew attached to his prison, and evidently it is the same with these old folk. Old faces work painfully, tears stand in bright old eyes, knotted old fingers clutch ours in farewell, and some of the old women break down utterly and sob bitterly. On the journey some of them lose all sense of control, take off their bonnets, and let down their hair, obeying a human instinct of despair which scholars will remember dates back to the siege of Troy. "It's all the home I've known for twenty years, and I be right sorry to go," says an aged man, as he shakes my hand.

Folks live long in the workhouse, and seventy and eighty years are regarded as comparative youth by the older people of ninety and upwards; to the aged any change is upheaval; they have got used to their bed, their particular chair, their daily routine, and to have to leave the accustomed looms in the light of a perilous adventure. Perhaps heaviest of all is the sense of exile; it is a long walk to the adjoining parish, and bus fares will be hard to spare with bread at ninepence a quartern. "I've been on the danger list and my son came every day to see me," says one old lady, "but he won't be able to get so far now."

Alarming rumours are being spread by a pessimist much travelled in vagrant wards, but they are speedily contradicted by an optimist, also an expert in Poor Law both in theory and practice.

We try to cheer them, but our comfort is not whole-hearted; we can guess how the chafing of the unaccustomed, the new discipline, the crowds of unfamiliar faces will jar upon the aged. We try to impress upon them the joy of self-sacrifice, the needs of our wounded soldiers, the patriotic pride in giving up something for them. Oh, yes, they know all that, the Guardians had been and talked to them "just like a meeting," they understand about the soldiers, they want to do their best for them; but it is hard. The workhouse is nothing if not military in its traditions; heroes of South Africa, of Balaclava, and the Crimea have found asylum in the white-washed wards; many of the present inmates have been soldiers, and there are few who have not some relatives—grandsons and great-grandsons—fighting in the trenches. One of the oldest of the "grannies," aged ninety-three, went off smiling, proud, as she said, "to do her bit."

The sick are being brought down now into the ambulances—the phthisical, the paralytic, the bed-ridden—blinking in the sunlight from their mattress-tomb, one poor woman stricken with blindness and deafness, who in spite of nervousness looks forward to her first motor-drive. These are less troubled; they are younger, and the sick hope ever for a quick cure, and the majority are only in for temporary illness. Then come the babies, astonishingly smart and well-dressed, including the youngest inmate, aged but eight days.

The costumes are odd and eccentric, and in spite of misery a good deal of good-tempered chaff flies round. All inmates [usually required to wear a kind of uniform] are to leave in their own clothes, and strange garments have been brought to the light of day, whilst much concern is expressed about excellent coats and skirts moth-eaten or mislaid in the course of twenty-five years. The storage of the workhouse often suffers strain, and the wholesome practice of "stoving" all clothes does not improve the colours nor contribute to the preservation of what *modistes* call *la ligne*. Fortunately, all fashions come round again, and we try to assure the women that the voluminous skirts and high collars of last century are *le dernier cri* in Bond Street, but it is difficult for one woman to deceive another over the question of fashion.

For twelve hours the 'buses and ambulances have plied backwards and forwards, and now the last load home has started, and tired nurses and harassed officials wave their last good-bye, thankful the long day has come at length to an end. In a few days other loads will arrive, all young these and all soldiers, many of them, perhaps, as the advertisements say, belonging to the nobility and gentry. The workhouse has ceased to be. From to-day it will be no longer rate-supported; the nurses and the whole staff draw rations and are in the pay and service of the War Office. As soon as possible gilt letters will announce it as a "Military Hospital."

On the table before me lies a copy of the local paper, and I read with surprise the thanks of a public body for our "offer to give up the workhouse as a military hospital, and expressing appreciation of the patriotic action of the Guardians in the matter."

In my opinion we made no offer; we merely obeyed a command, and the people who did a patriotic action were those who turned out of their home, such as it was; but in this world credit is given where it is not due, and thanks are bestowed on the wrong people. We reap where we have not sown and gather where we have not strawed.

16

Sylvia Pankhurst

IN HER LONG POLITICAL LIFE, Sylvia Pankhurst (1882–1960) was a women's suffrage crusader, socialist, pacifist, Communist, anti-Fascist activist, and friend and protector of Ethiopia. Arriving in her thirties, she lived for twelve years in the East London dock and industrial district of Bow and was a passionate defender of its women. Her life in the neighborhood is commemorated by a statue in East London's Victoria Park, the starting point of many of her suffrage processions. A House of Lords committee has been holding off a campaign led by feminist M.P.'s and others to place a life-size sculpture of Pankhurst on College Green, across from Westminster Palace in London. Though the sculpture is finished, the standoff continued as this volume went to press.[1]

Sylvia and her sister Christabel, with two other siblings, were the children of leading Manchester reformers Richard and Emmeline Pankhurst. Both parents were committed feminists and socialists, and Richard Pankhurst, twenty years older than his wife, had connections among Chartists and with philosopher John Stuart Mill. (As an M.P., Mill introduced the nation's first women's suffrage bill in 1867.) The elder Pankhursts were involved in the formation of the Independent Labour Party in the 1890s. Sylvia was especially close to her father and was devastated by his death, which occurred when she was still in her teens. In her early suffrage years with the Women's Social and Political Union (WSPU), the militant suffrage organization dom-

"The Martyrdom of a Disabled Soldier's Wife" was originally published in The Woman's Dreadnought *3, no. 23 (September 2, 1916): 540, "The East London Peace Demonstration: A Little Plain Speaking" in* The Woman's Dreadnought *4, no. 4 (April 21, 1917): 728. Reprinted with the permission of Professor Richard Pankhurst.*

inated by Sylvia's imperious mother and sister, Pankhurst was a student at the Royal College of Art. Suffrage processions, exhibitions, and other events were embellished by her work, a combination of "embryonic socialist realism" and "dilute Pre-Raphaelite allegory," as Lisa Tickner has described it.[2]

In 1912, Pankhurst and her Michigan-born friend and benefactor Zelie Anderson, who had been involved in settlements in Chicago, established an office and home on the Bow Road. There had been many years of suffrage and labor organizing in East London, with several branches of the WSPU there, dating from 1906.[3] The district got national prominence when its Labour M.P., George Lansbury, challenged Herbert Asquith, the Liberal prime minister, over the government's harsh treatment of imprisoned suffragettes. Lansbury decided to run his reelection campaign on a simple women's suffrage platform, and suffragists of all stripes descended on the area.[4] Pankhurst and Anderson's organization, the East London Federation of Suffragettes (ELFS), officially a branch of the WSPU, also supported Lansbury.

Pankhurst was, through 1917, both a political agitator and a philanthropist, raising money to help hard cases, offering cheap meals, or intervening with local authorities or landlords.[5] The ELFS offered some of the programs found at settlements and missions: socials, elocution lessons, and drill (calisthenics); classes were subject to cancelation if their instructors were imprisoned.[6] The welfare role of her organization had expanded dramatically after 1914 in response to the hardships of the war years, when local industries were devastated by the war economy, and soldiers' wives often had great difficulties getting the allowances officially granted them. The ELFS opened a clothing and boot factory, a toy factory, a child-care center ("The Mother's Arms"), a cut-rate restaurant, and a jam factory.

Her family's long history of involvement with socialist causes encouraged Sylvia to think of suffrage in terms of its support for working-class women and to work for suffrage in cooperation with socialists—including Sylvia's close friend, Labour politician Kier Hardie. WSPU headquarters had declared men in general off limits. By the last year of the war, after the Russian Revolution, Sylvia Pankhurst had come to see herself as a part of an international pro-Bolshevik movement, and by the time women over twenty-eight were granted the vote in 1918, she took only a mild interest in the fact.

The newspaper from which these two selections come, *The Woman's Dreadnought,* was a weekly, between four and eight pages long, founded in March 1914 and edited by Pankhurst. It was published for ten years.

Pankhurst always contributed an editorial, even in 1914, when she was imprisoned nine times during one six-month period. It sold for a halfpenny an issue, though it appears that most copies were given away to publicize and recruit for the ELFS. The paper, which opposed England's participation in World War I, provided suffrage news, case studies of local injustices, reports on women's work and lives outside of the district, and regular accounts of Sylvia Pankhurst's arrests and imprisonments, as well as her travels. A prominent theme was the East Londoners' struggles for survival under wartime conditions of inflation and absent or disabled wage earners—struggles ignored by callous and inefficient welfare agencies. A variety of authors contributed articles; the two that follow were signed by Sylvia Pankhurst herself. From mid-1917 on, now titled the *Workers' Dreadnought,* it carried more news about pacifism and socialism and about the Bolshevik regime in Russia. Pankhurst was imprisoned for five months for "sedition" in 1920, under conditions even harsher than those she had endured as a suffrage protester, for publishing articles on antiwar military men. She closed down the *Dreadnought* in 1924.[7]

NOTES

1. See Julie Bindel, "Raise Sylvia's Statue Now!" *The Guardian (London),* March 24, 2006, 2.
2. Lisa Tickner, *The Spectacle of Women: Imagery of the Suffrage Campaign 1907–14* (Chicago: University of Chicago Press, 1988), 28.
3. Winslow, *Sylvia Pankhurst,* 34, 32.
4. Sylvia's part in this complex story is told in Winslow, *Sylvia Pankhurst,* 36–38. Lansbury lost the election, and support from the WSPU in particular appears to have been a liability in the campaign.
5. Her East London base also enabled her independence from her mother and sister, who worked out of WSPU headquarters in Central London. Technically, Sylvia's East London Federation was a part of the WSPU until January 1914. See Andrew Rosen, *Rise Up, Women! The Militant Campaign of the Women's Social and Political Union 1903–1914* (London: Routledge, 1974), 225; and Purvis, *Emmeline Pankhurst,* 246. Purvis points out that the only report of the Paris meeting in which Christabel "expelled" her sister from the WSPU is Sylvia's, in *The Suffragette.*
6. ELFS Minute Book 206, May 1913 through July 1914, at International Institute of Social History, Amsterdam, and available on microfilm with the Sylvia Pankhurst Papers.
7. For these incidents see Winslow, *Sylvia Pankhurst,* 100–104 and chap. 5.

FURTHER READING

For more writing by Sylvia Pankhurst, see *The Suffragette: The History of the Women's Militant Suffrage Movement 1905–1910* (London: Gay and Hancock, 1911; reprint, New York: Source Book Press, 1970); *Save the Mothers* (London: Alfred A. Knopf, 1930); *The Suffragette Movement. An Intimate Account of Persons and Details* (London: Longmans,

1931); *The Home Front* (London: Hutchinson, 1932); and *The Life of Emmeline Pankhurst: The Suffragette Struggle for Women's Citizenship* (London: T. W. Laurie, 1935). There are also several anthologies of her writings.

Jane Marcus, ed., *Suffrage and the Pankhursts* (London: Routledge, 1987), includes more than fifty pages of Sylvia's articles from the *Woman's Dreadnought. Women, Suffrage, and Politics: The Papers of Sylvia Pankhurst 1882–1960 from the Internationaal Instituut voor Sociale Geschiedenis* (Amsterdam: 1991) is based on the Instituut's enormous archive of Pankhurst's papers. Katherine Dodd, ed., includes an extensive bibliography of Pankhurst's writings in *A Sylvia Pankhurst Reader* (Manchester: Manchester University Press, 1993).

The literature on the Pankhursts and the WSPU is immense. What follows is material dealing with Sylvia herself. Entries in the BDBF and the Oxford DNB (by June Hannam) contain biographical information about Pankhurst. See also Barbara Castle, *Sylvia and Christabel Pankhurst* (Harmondsworth, England: Penguin, 1987), and David Mitchell, *The Fighting Pankhursts: A Study in Tenacity* (New York: Macmillan, 1967). Richard Marsden Pankhurst, Sylvia's son, wrote *Sylvia Pankhurst: Artist and Crusader* (London: Paddington Press, 1979), and also *Sylvia Pankhurst: Counsel for Ethiopia* (London: Global Press, 2003). Information about Sylvia is included in June Purvis, *Emmeline Pankhurst* (London: Routledge, 2002). Patricia W. Romero's *E. Sylvia Pankhurst: Portrait of a Radical* (New Haven, CT: Yale University Press, 1987) is an ungenerous portrait of Pankhurst, but it contains valuable sections on Pankhurst's involvement in Ethiopia. Barbara Winslow, *Sylvia Pankhurst: Sexual Politics and Political Activism* (London: University College Press, 1996), focuses on the years Pankhurst lived in East London. Also: Mary Davis, *Sylvia Pankhurst: A Life in Radical Politics* (London: Pluto Press, 1999), and Shirley Harrison, *Sylvia Pankhurst: A Maverick Life 1882–1960* (London: Aurum Press, 2004).

<hr/>

The Martyrdom of a Disabled Soldier's Wife

"Ask the lady to come upstairs," we said. But the answer came up the one short flight to us: "Oh, no, she is not fit to walk upstairs." So we went down to where she sat panting for breath, a woman not forty years of age. A tidy woman, endowed by nature with good features, a clear skin, and bright hair, but now ashy pale and full of trouble. We partly knew her story, and she supplemented it, speaking painfully in a slow, hoarse voice.

Before the War her husband was a head scaffolder, a steady, hard-working man. There were six children: two boys aged fourteen and two years, and four girls aged seventeen, twelve and five, and a new born baby. The eldest girl had hip disease, and would never be able to earn her living.

The husband earned £2 2s. 6d. a week, and though careful housekeeping was needed, the family lived in comparative comfort.

The husband was an ex-soldier, and had fought in the Boer War. When this War broke out he re-enlisted. He was a strongly-built man, and in the whole of his married life had never had a day's illness. But when he was put to sleep under canvas on marshy ground in wet weather, and without proper protection, he was stricken with rheumatoid arthritis in the arms and legs; his hands were drawn so that he could scarcely open them, and he was discharged on December 16th, 1914. His pay ceased, his wife's separation allowance ceased, and he came home a broken man, racked with pain, and scarcely able to hobble with the aid of a stick.

The woman applied on her husband's behalf to the local office of the Soldiers' and Sailors' Families' Association, where she was granted £2, but she was told that the Association could do no more. On December 21st, she registered as an applicant for relief under the Soldiers' and Sailors' Families' Association. The clerk told her that a visitor would call on her during the week, but a fortnight passed and no visitor appeared, and later both husband and wife went round to learn why no visitor had called on them. The clerk replied that the matter had been overlooked. Still no visitor appeared, and in response to a third application the clerk said that the case had not "gone through," but that he would see that it was attended to immediately, but nothing happened. During this time the family had no money to depend on but the earnings of the eldest little lad, aged fourteen.

The family's unhappy plight came to the knowledge of one of the Workers' Suffrage Federation nurses, and we approached the Soldiers' and Sailors' Families' Association, as the Mayor's Committee in this borough did not deal with military and naval cases. The S.S.F.A. then made a grant of 17s. 6d. a week.

We wrote to the War Office urging that this grant was too small, and Keir Hardie, who learnt of the case from us, also wrote to the Financial Secretary in regard to it on February 11th, 1915, but without result.

On March 22nd, we wrote to the War Office, Chelsea Hospital and to Mr. Herbert Samuel, Chairman of the Prince of Wales's Fund, pointing out that even under the Prince of Wales's Fund regulations a family in distress through the War was entitled to £1 a week, and urging that an adequate pension should be given. Meanwhile the home had been dismantled and everything possible had been pawned to buy food.

On March 27th, the man was examined by Chelsea Hospital, and on April 5th the Secretary wrote to say that "the Lords and other Commissioners of the Hospital" had "been pleased to award him a pension of eighteenpence a day for twelve months conditional, with effect from

December 17th, 1914." The S.S.F.A. grant now ceased, but the family were for the moment overjoyed, because, owing to the accumulation of arrears, they were able to satisfy their chronic hunger and to get a number of necessaries out of pawn.

But the future had to be considered, and we wrote to Chelsea Hospital on April 24th, explaining that the ex-soldier was still quite unable to work, and claiming 25s. a week on his behalf and 2s. 6d. for each of his five dependent children on the strength of the recommendation of the Select Committee. On April 29th, Chelsea Hospital replied that the Select Committee's recommendations had not yet received official sanction, and therefore could not be acted upon. Under existing regulations, no more than eighteenpence a day could be granted.

In May, 1915, the ex-soldier managed for three weeks to do a little work, but had to stop as a result of acute pain and illness.

In May and also on June 11th, new regulations having been issued, we again applied for an increased pension, and having learnt from our doctor that treatment by radiant heat and massage were necessary to secure the ex-soldier's recovery, we urged that he should be treated at a military hospital. The latter request was ignored, but on July 15th Chelsea Hospital replied that the pension had been increased to 18s. 9d. per week for the man and 10s. a week for his five children. We again asked for 25s. for the man and 2s. 6d. for each child, and on September 11th, 1915, nine months after the man's discharge, Chelsea Hospital at last wrote conceding this demand for six months conditional. The 37s. 6d. then promised did not long continue. It was soon reduced to 28s. 9d. without our knowledge, for the man and wife were tired of complaining.

On April 15th, 1916, the ex-soldier secured a labourer's job, which, with periods of illness in between, he kept till July 26th, being then absolutely obliged to stop working. Since his discharge he has never known what it is to be out of pain. His knee gives way unexpectedly, and he has had several nasty falls through it. This period and the three weeks in May, 1915, are the only times at which he has been able to work since his discharge. When he appeared before the Medical Board for his half-yearly examination on June 19th, 1916, the man was closely questioned on this matter, and also in regard to his pre-War work and earnings. Whoever took down the particulars made a ghastly mistake, for the pre-War earnings were substituted for the after-War earnings, and a note was made that he was earning at the time of examination 42s. 6d. a week, and that he had earned this amount regularly for the past twelve months. Therefore, without any reason being given to him, his pension was reduced to fifteenpence a day, and his children's pensions were stopped.

The weekly income of the family now consisted of 8s. 9d. pension, which the local Pensions' Committee makes up to £1; 10s. earned by the eldest boy; 6s. earned by the second girl, who went into a biscuit factory in July, as soon as she reached the age of fourteen, making £1 16s. 9d. in all, instead of the £2 2s. 6d. that the man earned before the War. In the meantime, the children have grown older and cost more to clothe and feed than they did in 1914; two of them are wage-earners, and at least a part of their earnings must be devoted to their individual expenses for fares and food out of the home; the cost of living has risen enormously, and the husband has become an ailing man, always in pain and needing extra nourishment and care, which he cannot get. The baby girl, born bonny and healthy on June 1st, 1914, failed as she grew older, especially after being weaned, for very often there was neither food nor money in the house, and her poor mother could not buy the milk that was necessary for her. In September, 1915, the child became seriously ill, and on November 18th, she died in the sick asylum. The youngest boy and another little girl are both poorly. The mother's health has gone, too; she is suffering from heart-strain, and she is expecting another little one next month.

Before the War her husband gave her 35s. a week for housekeeping, and beside that kept the family in boots, clothed the youngest boy, and bought many other extras, including eggs for the children's breakfast. The pre-War and present housekeeping budgets differ very greatly. Every item in the present budget is qualified by the proviso "if I can get it":—

Pre-War Budget.

	s.	d.
Gas, 10s. 9d. a month	2	8½
Rent	8	0
Tea, 1 lb.	1	4
Sugar, 6 lbs. at 1¾d.	0	10½
Cocoa, 1 lb.	1	4
Butter, 3½ lbs. at 1s. 2d.	4	1
Dripping, 1 lb	0	6
Flour, 1 peck at 6d. a quartern	1	10
Meat, 4 lbs. at 7d.	2	4
Potatoes, 6 lbs. a day—3d.	1	9
Greens, 2d. a day	1	2
Coals, ¾ cwt. [hundredweight] at 1s. 6d. (summer)	1	1½
2 cwts. at 1s. 6d. (winter), 3s.		

	s.	d.
"Turtle" Soap, 1 lb.	0	3
Soda, 2 lbs. for ½d.	0	0½
Bleacher [bleach]	0	1
Blue	0	0½
White Starch, ½lb.	0	1½
Matches, 1 dozen	0	1
Rice, 1 lb.	0	2
Currants, 1 lb.	0	4
Barley, ½ pt. at 5d.	0	2½
Macaroni, 2 lbs. at 2½d.	0	5
Milk, 7 quarts at 4d.	2	4
Eggs	1	6
Bread, 2½ quarters [four-pound loaves] a day at 4½d.	6	6¾
Insurance	2	0
Boot Club	0	3
£2	1	5

When the husband worked overtime, as he often did, he gave his wife more money; she also got $1 a month from her sister in Canada, who cannot now afford it as her sons are at the Front.

Now.

	s.	d.
Gas, 4s. 2d. a month	1	0½
Rent (13s. back rent owing)	8	0
Tea, ½ lb.	1	1
Sugar, 3 lbs. at 5d.	1	3
Cocoa, ¼ lb. at 2s.	0	6
Margarine, 2d. a day	1	2
Dripping, ½ lb. at 10d.	0	5
Flour, 1¼ quarters at 8½d.	0	10¾
Meat, 3 lbs. at 1s.	3	0
Potatoes, 4 lbs. a day at 2d.	4	8
Greens, 3d. worth 3 times a week	0	9
Coals, 14 lbs. at 3d.	0	3
Coke 4d., Wood 3½d.	0	7½
"Turtle" Soap, 1 lb.	0	4¾
Soda, 2 lbs. at 1d.	0	2
Bleacher	0	1
Blue, ½d. worth fortnightly	0	0½
White Starch (none)		

Matches, 1 box (6½d., doz., little shops won't sell doz.)	0	1
Rice, 1 lb.	0	2½
Currants, ½ lb. at 5d.	0	2½
Barley (none)		
Macaroni (none)		
Milk, 1d. a day	0	7
Bread, 9 quarterns at 9d.	6	9
Eggs (none)		
Insurance	2	0
Boot Club	0	3
Herrings and Bloaters, 1½d. each, Kippers, 2d. per pair, Skate clippings, 5d., average a week	1	9
£1	16	2

They are all going short of food, the mother is worn out with anxiety, she has grown weak with denying herself food in order to leave more for her husband and children. Unconsciously our eyes rest on her broken boots. She draws her feet back embarrassed and explains that she has had to pawn her other boots, and then covering her left hand, that she has pawned her wedding ring.

The East London Peace Demonstration:
A Little Plain Speaking

Good fathers and mothers all, teach these things to your children:—

> Do not push and strike people because you think they are going to say something which someone has said you will not agree with.
>
> Do not hit those who are smaller and weaker than yourselves because you know they have not the strength to retaliate.
>
> Do not go in gangs to attack one or two people.
>
> Do not choose to blacken the eyes or make bleed the nose of the strangers in your midst because you think that they will not be able to find you again and hand you over to the police of whom you are afraid.
>
> Do not slink away when those who fight for you are assaulted, nor pass on the other side of the way when rude people call them names.

Do not bite the hand that fed you because its owner is with what may be the minority; do not publicly spurn and revile those who have comforted you, whom you respect and to whom you will turn again in time of anxiety and trouble, merely because you do not wish to be unpopular with the horde that kicks and swears and destroys other people's goods.

Do not allow yourselves to be bribed to attack those with whom you have no quarrel.

Good fathers and mothers, teach your children to avoid these faults, for as the twig is bent so shall the tree grow; those who grow up in the spirit which prompts these actions will always be oppressed, and they will not become brave and happy and well beloved.

. . . . .

The sun shone joyously on the peace procession last Sunday. "Spring and Peace must come together" said the first banner. And the others followed: "In this War there is a nation without frontiers united in anguish: it is the Nation of Mothers", "The Children of All Nations Want their Fathers Home", "Half the World is Drenched in Blood." At the rear was a black banner with a skull which said, "5,000,000 killed: How many More?" "All are Comrades," said the white banner of the Forest Gate N.-C.F. [Non-Conscription Fellowship, a draft resistance organization]. The red flag of the Walthamstow B.S.P. [British Socialist Party], the red and the purple, white and green of the Workers' Suffrage Federation, the children riding in decorated carts, the Islington Young Citizen Scouts beating their drums and bearing their banner, "Feed My Lambs," made a brave show. Fully a thousand people marched in the procession, and, as we always do in East London, masses of us preferred to swarm along in the gutter and on the pavements beside the procession proper, so that two larger processions walked on either side of those who were marshalled behind the banners. Near the head of the procession marched a young officer, and close by a soldier discharged without pension. Another ex-soldier, who was going to hospital next day, wore his trade union regalia and was busy selling miniature red flags. On every step of the four miles from Beckton Road corner to the Park, sympathetic crowds greeted us, clapping and waving hands. At Poplar Hospital nurses and wounded soldiers cheered us. At Bow obelisk all the world was out to see. Poor mothers with clothes too shabby and boots too old to walk far, and overwhelmed with household cares, smiled and sent their dear hopes with us. Friends came running to join us, gaily, because they had come to bear their witness for the cause of peace. Gallant Mrs. Despard [founder of the suffrage organization Women's Freedom League; she was a pacifist in the First World War], sister of General French and of Mrs. Harvey, who was killed at her hospital post in Serbia, met us in the Roman Road to walk the last part of the way with us.

The mounted police rode ahead, and there were some four or five constables on foot: all was in order: there was nothing for them to do. Many members of the Criminal Investigation Department of Scotland Yard began to appear as we reached our destination. We knew them well from pre-War days. Why had they come? We have never found them affording protection to pacifists or calling to account those who despitefully use them.

As we marched over the bridge at the end of Grove Road, facing the Park, hostility began to show itself for the first time. There were masses of people around the gates, and the Park itself seemed to be tightly packed with people. Friends in front made a narrow passage-way, and we entered amid cheers of welcome and some hostile shouts. The friends seemed to be in a great majority. Then a crowd of men and lads came running towards us and began tearing at the banners. The struggle for them continued for a long time. The little Citizen Scouts were roughly handled.

The first flag was soon torn from its bamboo pole, and the pole itself was twisted, but Councillor Ben Gardner bore it on, and we followed it to the meeting ground. There in the press of people we saw that the carts brought there to serve as platforms were crowded with jingoes who had no intention of making way for the authorised speakers. Two Hackney Councillors were recognised as being amongst those who were making noisy incitements to disorder. The platforms had been captured by the rowdies, the speakers were lost in the skirmish, so with two or three friends beside us we set our back against the wall of the tea house and began to speak. We found then that the majority of those around us were prepared at least to listen, and many were anxious to give active help. A knot of opponents to the right of us pushed and shouted, but a stalwart sailor who knew the art of standing very firm kept them back, though they cried to him, "Jack, you aren't on their side, are you?"

Presently the Park-keepers came running up to tell us that we must not speak in that place. We agreed to move, and very obligingly they tried to push a way for us into the centre of the meeting ground. "Will you stop here?" they said when we got there; but the opponents had formed up behind them and behind the opponents were masses of people pressing forward to see what was the matter; whilst friends anxious to get us out of harm's way came hurrying from either side. What might have been a meeting had become a stampede. It was useless to argue: we were hurried on to the gates. On our way we saw surprising numbers of people whom we knew, amongst them Mr. A. W. Carter, of the N.U.R., who formed a very effective barricade against any attempt at violence.

In another part of the park Mrs. Despard had mounted the railings to address the crowd. "We don't want the German terms: we want our terms!" the Jingoes yelled at her. The aged lady answered: "You will have neither the German terms nor your own terms; you will have God's terms." They were nonplussed for a moment, then shouted to her to go before she was hurt. "I am not afraid of Englishmen," she answered. "None of you will hurt me." Nor did they; her fearlessness overawed them. Mrs. Bouvier also addressed the crowd for a time, but one cannot long keep a meeting going when one is uncomfortably perched upon the railings.

The Rev. Herbert Dunnico, who was to have spoken at the meeting, estimates that there were 50,000 people in the park, and that the entire disturbance was created by 500 people. We do not know whether his estimate is correct, but the attacking party certainly had a great advantage because many of them did not scruple to kick and thump and push, and some of them used sticks, whereas the demonstrators preferred not to hit back. We do not wish to strike our brothers and sisters; we went to the park on Sunday, as we shall go again, not to fight them, but to reason with them. We wish to win them to our cause, not to put them to flight. Blows cannot alter convictions and ideas; our opponents cannot change our view by their violence; but by our arguments we shall in time convert them.

We asked a neighbour with whom our relations have long been on terms of neighbourly friendship to do us a little service, but he shut his door in our face, and when later on we went to him and protested against his lack of courtesy and kindness, our neighbour told us that he had treated us so for the sake of his home. Alas! too many people think more of the furniture in their houses than of their souls, and we find that sometimes the poor, as well as the rich, think more of their property than of other people's lives! The capitalist system has set its mark upon the workers, as well as upon their masters, and the legal code which places more value upon property than upon human life has its influence on the minds of many men.

Perhaps the most regrettable part of the business was that the organisers of the disturbance had bribed children to take part in it. One little boy went to the tea-house in the park and asked for some biscuits. The lady behind the counter said, "Do you want a pennyworth?" He answered excitedly: "Oh, no; I want much more than that. I have had 6d. given me to smash up the suffragettes' meeting!" The lady behind the counter therefore refused to serve him. It is terribly injurious to the children to exploit them in this way. When we complain that some of the children and some of the girls and lads appear to enjoy rushing in hordes to bate those whom they think unable to retaliate, we must remember that life is very dull and drab in the mean streets of little houses, for which the landlords charge such heavy rents, and that the beauty and colour and vivid variety for which the young growing soul craves is not easily found in East London.

On the canal bridge in Old Ford Road Edward Fuller, who was with his wife, was attacked by a little mob of tall youths. They seized him by the back of the collar and beat him about the head, and yelling: "Throw him in the Cut!" tried to drag him to the wall. In the midst of the struggle he fainted, and his wife prevented him from falling. Two of us ran to their aid. We heard a woman we did not recognise, crying: "Don't hit him when he's' fainting: wait till he's better." We threw our arms about the two who seemed to be the ringleaders and clung to them, arguing about the War, and in the heat of the discussion they forgot their prey.

"He's no right to talk about Peace," they shouted. "We shall have to go to the front soon, and perhaps lose our lives!" "We want to save you," we said. They fell back on the usual argument: "If we don't crush the Germans now they will make war on us again in a few years." They did not appear to know that the last big war Britain fought was against Russia, and that in that war Russia was so far from being crushed that the nations fighting against her had in the end to accept the terms which they had refused a year before. Yet Russia did not rise again in a few years to fight us. The Crimean War was not a fight to a finish. The Franco-German War, though France was not utterly crushed, as some say they would crush the Germans, may more truthfully be called a fight to a finish. France was humiliated, robbed of two of her provinces, and made to pay a heavy indemnity. But France quickly rose again, entered into an alliance with Russia and Britain, and is to-day fighting with them against Germany. Of what use is it, then, to pretend that to fight to a finish will prevent a future war?

On Sunday it was sad to find gangs of men and women so cowardly as to set upon one or two individuals, chivvying them from point to point and beating them with fists or sticks. In the park a lady and her daughters put protecting arms around a youth who was attacked; whereupon the mob of rowdies turned on them. One of the daughters fainted and was carried away by W.S.F. members; the other lost her hat and had her face and head bruised. Mrs. Hasler and Miss Beamish, who went out to look for absent friends, came back with faces bruised and bleeding.

At the Women's Hall Nurse Hebbes and the other helpers had many severe cuts and bruises to attend to, but as far as we know there were no really serious injuries. Mrs. Hasler had a ring wrenched from her finger, Mrs. Cole lost a cameo brooch and a scarf, and she and several others lost their hats. Ever since, telephone messages and letters of inquiry, encouragement and congratulation have poured in upon us at Old Ford Road. Everyone who saw the procession is agreed that it was a triumph, and that its reception in Canning Town and Bow clearly indicates the growth of Peace feeling. Those who passed quietly amongst the people in the park, talking to them and hearing what they had to say, tell us that the larger part of the crowd had come to listen to the speakers and was displeased that others had broken up the meeting. One of our friends who was returning home on a 47 'bus from Liverpool Street suddenly heard a soldier talking about the affair. He said that he had been wounded three times and had a wife and four children, and that now he was about to be sent back to the front. He had been to the Peace meeting in Victoria Park, and declared that if there had been more men there who had been in the trenches and had suffered as he had, the people who had attacked the Peacemakers would not have come out alive! This is a strange world, but certainly it seemed to us that the soldiers had little to do with last Sunday's disturbance.

The meeting is over, but the agitation continues. We shall be in the Park next Sunday.

17

Florence Petty

FLORENCE PETTY (1870–1930s or 1940s) was associated with the St. Pancras School for Mothers, founded in 1907 primarily as a clinic and school of "mothercraft" for the very poor population in Somers Town, the overcrowded district just west of Euston Station.[1] Petty defined herself as a "Lecturer and Demonstrator in Health Foods." She was one of a small group of nutrition experts who criticized the way cooking was taught in schools on the grounds that the appliances and recipes used were completely inappropriate for working-class wives. Instructors needed to learn how people actually cooked and ate.[2] Thus Petty stepped into actual kitchens. She befriended women attending classes at the School for Mothers and offered to give them lessons in their own homes using the fuel, pots, and ingredients that they normally used. Her "case papers" describing these visits, complete with recipes, make up a large section of *The Pudding Lady.*

A World War I edition of this book stressed recipes for cheap and nutritious meals that could be made given the limited ingredients and high prices of the later war years. Petty wrote or compiled other cookbooks for wartime as well, one on making and using a "fuelless cooker," the other, *Practical Hints,* featuring recipes for three hundred dishes. Petty had by this time become qualified as a sanitary inspector.[3]

Case papers from Miss Bibby, Miss Colles, Miss Petty, and Dr. Sykes, The Pudding Lady: A New Departure in Social Work *(London: Stead's Publishing House, for the St. Pancras School for Mothers [1910]), 36–39, 74–75, and 88–89.*

NOTES

1. *Who Was Who among English and European Authors 1931–49* (Detroit: Gale Research Co., 1978). No date of death is included, though Petty must have died sometime during the interval covered by this volume of *Who Was Who.* The West London Mission was active in welfare in Somers Town.

2. Mary Davies, "The Teaching of Cookery," *Contemporary Review* 73 (January 1898): 106–14.

3. Based on reviews and announcements in the National Union of Women Workers of Great Britain and Ireland, *Occasional Papers,* no. 70, March 1916, 52; and no. 74, April 1917, 37.

—⊗⊗⊗—

Case Papers

1.

Name.—A.

Family.—Father and mother and six children.

Occupations.—Father: Out of work; has been to Hollesley Bay [a "training colony" for unemployed men in rural Suffolk]; previously a currier, before that twelve years in the Army.

Mother: Home duties; before marriage was an attendant at an asylum.

Children: At school, 2; under school age, 4.

Dwelling.—Two ground floor rooms; rent, 6s. 6d. a week.

Health.—Mother not strong; two children ricketty.

Cleanliness.—Clean when husband in work, but physical and moral courage rather in abeyance now.

Washing Facilities.—Wash-house in yard.

Bathing Facilities.—One zinc bath and one basin.

Sanitary Conditions.—House not very clean; water fetched in from yard.

Cooking Apparatus.—Small open fire; no oven.

Cooking Utensils, Etc.—Two saucepans and frying pan; very little crockery and knives and forks. Two cupboards (one large).

Source of Education.—Father: Country school (*Ely*); newspapers; books.

Mother: Country school (Devonshire); reading and classes at the Welcome.

Cooking lessons were given during the husband's work at Hollesley Bay. At my first visit (after preliminary), on October 14th, I found that Mrs. A. had brought in ½ qrtn. flour, ¼ lb. suet, 1d. baking powder, and 1d. raisins. The suet was ready chopped and the raisins stoned. She made three puddings, one with raisins, two plain, and was so excited when they were successful that she sent the raisin one to the "Sister" and the "cooking lady" at the Welcome, "to show."

The cost of the three puddings was 3¾d.; we used part of the suet and a very little butter to grease the cups and paper for the top. The three youngest children had nearly half a pudding each, and the remaining piece was divided between the two big girls, the mother (who dines at the Welcome) keeping a tiny mouthful, just to taste it. The two big girls have dinner at school. The children had a teaspoonful of golden syrup each with their pudding, and seemed to enjoy it very much.

At the second lesson Mrs. A. had brought in 1½d. tomatoes, 1d. pot-herbs, 1d. packet desiccated soup, and flour. The baby was asleep, and the three children and a neighbour's child, all rather dirty, were round the table most of the time. The mother seemed helpless amongst them sometimes. I got her to grate and chop the vegetables, which we then put on to boil with the tomatoes and half the packet of soup. Then she made the suet mixture, making twelve little balls, and as soon as the stew was boiling they were put in. I had seen that a good kettleful of water was heating at the same time. We then started to wash the three children. The boy of three is very strong-willed, and the mother says she finds it very difficult at times to wash him, particularly his neck, as he says she tickles him, and he screams. It was rather a business, but they all got clean, and the mother did their hair, so that they all looked fresh and nice. The cost of the stew was 5½d., and it did for two days for the three children.

Mrs. A. was telling some of the mothers at the Welcome about this stew, and they said, "That is what we want, miss; somebody to show us how to make nourishing meals for the children out of the little money we have." Mrs. A. also says she has learnt from the lectures at the Welcome how she went wrong in the feeding of the two children who have rickets so badly. "Too much starch and not enough fat," she said. Both the father and mother seem to come from good yeoman stock, and to be the poorest of all their families on both sides. The father seems to have a strong character, and is afraid of his wife sinking to the level of the other Somers Town women. The influence of the Welcome is certainly helping her in every way to get a new grip of the powers and faculties she was losing.

Third lesson. The mother wanted to make ginger pudding. We used her materials, except the suet, which I had with me, and we made the pudding, the children having golden syrup with it. We also had a consultation over cutting up garments and making them into clothes for the little one.

Fourth lesson. We made macaroni and tomato stew, thickened with oatmeal (fine). Cost 5½d., enough for five children, and a small share for mother. The mother is fond of reading; they prefer "Lloyd's" as a weekly, because husband says "it's more edifying, and does not give so many ghastly details as some of the others."

Fifth lesson. We made lentil stew with rice—cost 3¼d.—with an additional piece of bread for each. The mother has improved much, but still needs pulling up. She has been giving the children a good deal of tea, and I talked strongly on this point to her.

Sixth lesson. The husband had come back from Hollesley Bay, and she was anxious to show him how she could make a pudding, so we made a date one. . . .

xx.

Name.—T.

Family.—Father, mother, two children.

Occupations.—Father: £1 a week when in work at eating-house.

Mother: 12s. to 18s. a week as laundress. Father has no work when wife is earning well.

Dwelling.—One room first floor; rent, 3s. 6d. per week.

Health.—Not good. Mother weak chest. Father seems mentally deficient.

Cleanliness.—Not good, but mother has been ill since birth of baby.

Washing Facilities.—One basin; wash-house in yard. Goes to public baths when money runs to it.

Bathing Facilities.—One basin (the above one, used for everything; pudding was mixed in it); no bath.

Sanitary Conditions.—Staircases and passages not clean; windows shut at both visits (assured that they were only just shut!). Two windows to living-room.

Cooking Apparatus.—Open fire, no oven.

Cooking Utensils.—Small saucepan; very few spoons, etc., only odd cups and saucers.

Two small cupboards in room.

Source of Education.—Father: Board School very occasionally.

Mother: Board School and Welcome.

Remarks.—The husband got work just after my second visit, but evidently owing to bad temper cannot keep a situation long. The wife proudly told me that when he had a fit on he would not think twice of lifting the bed and throwing it out of the window! They have not been so badly off before. This time the mother had been ill for some time, and the husband could hear of no work. Her baby is small, and evidently has not sufficient nourishment. The midwife had said it ought to have milk, but at present it was rather impossible to pay for milk. The two-year-old looks clean and well cared-for. The room has practically no furniture except the bed. There is an old box which does duty for a table. At the first visit I got the husband to bustle round, get 1d. coal, make up the fire, and wash the basin for mixing the pudding in. (It was the basin they washed in). They were also astonished at how easily a pudding could be made, had never thought a suet pudding could be so light, had never heard of baking powder being used.

The mother stores milk in a jam jar on the outside window ledge, with a piece of glass on top. The drinking water was fetched up from the yard in a kettle.

At later visits I found that the mother had got stronger, and had again started laundry work; so things were better. . . .

One Family, One Cupboard.

The contents of one cupboard in the home of a poor, but tidy, family have been noted down as follows:—

Lowest Compartment.—Coals, splintered wood, old newspapers, boots, potatoes, onions, a stray carrot or so, one or two cabbage leaves.

1st Shelf from the Bottom.—A frying pan (back to the wall), odd pickle or jam jars, and empty tins and bottles, a paper of tin-tacks, a penny bottle of ink (no cork), a penny tin of vaseline (no lid), a piece of soap, an old hair brush and comb, bits of string, a few bent hairpins, screw-driver and other tools, an odd book or two, a magazine, and "Comic Cuts."

2nd Shelf from the Bottom.—A plate, with meat bones and a few cold potatoes and bacon rinds, a bottle of vinegar, a screw of pepper in a bit of paper, a gorgeous biscuit tin, with the King in scarlet uniform, a paper of tea inside, a blue glass sugar basin, with brown sugar, condensed milk in an opened tin, brown teapot, and white and gold cups and saucers (incomplete), a few odd jugs, a yellow basin, lots of odd saucers, several spoons, forks, and knives in various stages of use, round tin trays, some loose jam in a pie dish, some pickled red cabbage, a reel of thread, with a needle stuck in it, a battered thimble, a box of baby's powder with puff in it, a bit of soap, a few safety-pins, a paper of flower seeds, and a little blue-bag.

Top Shelf.—A bundle of old papers, some more tins, bottles, pickle jars and jam pots, an old black shawl rolled up, an old black sailor hat standing on its side, with hat-pins in it, old boots, a broken birdcage, a saucepan with a hole in it, etc., stuffed out of the way.

Ellen Henrietta Ranyard

BORN TO A NONCONFORMIST FAMILY in the poor south London waterside district of Nine Elms, Ellen Henrietta Ranyard, née White (1810–1879), moved to exurban Kent with her family during her teens. She began doing missionary work as a teenager, but explained her lifelong commitment to the church with a story of a close friend's death. At age sixteen, she and her friend together visited a household where there was "fever." Both girls became ill. Ellen survived, but her friend died and was deeply mourned.[1]

Her exposition of the Bible for children, *The Book and Its Story: A Narrative for the Young*, published in 1852, was phenomenally successful, going through many editions. This convinced Ellen, who had married Benjamin Ranyard in 1839, to move back to London to establish a Bible society there. In 1857 the Ranyards settled in Bloomsbury. Struck by the deep poverty of the overcrowded Central London district of St. Giles, Ellen Ranyard decided on a special mission to women, which she named the Bible and Domestic Female Mission. Competent, pious neighborhood women of any Protestant denomination were recruited and paid modest salaries to sell installment plan Bibles door to door in their own neighborhoods. Meeting the weekly payments would serve as a future convert's gesture of commitment, and weekly visits to collect payments would be natural occasions for conversation.[2] The working-class Bible women reported to middle-class Dis-

---

"Dinner for the Bread-Winner" and "Report of the Deptford Bible-Nurse" were originally published in The Missing Link Magazine, *the Ranyard Mission's monthly newsletter, vol. 14, no. 2 (February 1, 1878): 43–46 and 46–47; "A Scalded Child and Our Holloway Nurse" appeared in the same periodical, vol. 14, no. 12 (December 2, 1878): 387–89.*

trict "Superintendents," often wives of local clergymen; it was these Superintendents who sent on to the monthly newsletter the stories of suffering, courage, and conversion collected by their Bible women. The selections from the *Missing Link Magazine* reprinted here show the hand of Ranyard, the Superintendents, and the Bible women as well.

The Bible sellers were remarkably successful, Ranyard's fund-raising equally so, and the organization expanded rapidly. Ranyard's workers combined the roles of missionary, social worker, and nurse. From the beginning, they freely offered practical domestic advice, and in 1868 Ranyard organized nurses' training at Guy's Hospital for some Bible women.[3] The nurses had access to food, blankets, and other necessities for their clients through their Lady Superintendents, who donated them or subsidized them with funds supplied by their friends. In the mission's early years it even ran dormitories for girls working in the garment trades.[4] The Ranyard organization did not disband until 1965.

Ranyard's effort demonstrates the close links between domestic and foreign missionary activity. The all-male London City Mission (LCM), active since the 1830s, provided one exemplar for Ranyard's organization. But the British and Foreign Bible Society (BFBS) is arguably more important to the history of Ranyard's movement. Ranyard had spent years canvassing for the Society, which promoted Bible reading worldwide and published its own cheap editions for sale; the BFBS helped Ranyard by supplying her with free Bibles. Ranyard followed the BFBS policy of selling Bibles "without note or comment" to avoid doctrinal controversies.[5] Ranyard's approach, in turn, influenced the foreign missionary Hudson Taylor, who, like Ranyard, staffed his missions to China with laypeople rather than clergymen, and even included women among his missionaries.[6]

The Ranyards' son, Arthur Cowper Ranyard (1845–1894), became an important astronomer and served on the London County Council in the 1890s.[7]

NOTES

1. See the Ranyard entry in the DNB.
2. Donald Lewis, *Lighten Their Darkness: The Evangelical Mission to Working-Class London, 1828–1860* (Westport, CT: Greenwood Press, 1986), 221–22. The Society of Parochial Mission Women, founded in 1860, also used local women as Bible sellers and was modeled on Ranyard's organization, though the Parochial Mission women reported to the local clergyman. Ranyard was too anticlerical for such a plan. See Maud Hamilton, "Mission Women," *The Nineteenth Century* 16 (December 1884): 984–90.

3. Prochaska, "Body and Soul," 339–43.
4. Kathleen Heasman, *Evangelicals in Action: An Appraisal of Their Social Work in the Victorian Era* (London: Geoffrey Bles, 1962), 119.
5. Leslie Howson, *Cheap Bibles: Nineteenth-Century Publishing and the British and Foreign Bible Society* (Cambridge: Cambridge University Press, 1991), 6–7.
6. DNB, 47; also Lewis, *Lighten Their Darkness*, 221–22; Peter Williams, "'The Missing Link': The Recruitment of Women Missionaries in Some English Evangelical Missionary Societies in the Nineteenth Century," in *Women and Missions: Past and Present,* ed. Fiona Bowie, Deborah Kirkwood, and Shirley Ardener (Oxford: Berg Publishers, 1993), 47–48.
7. Arthur Cowper Ranyard, DNB.

FURTHER READING

Under the initials L. N. R., Ellen Henrietta Ranyard published *The Book and Its Story: A Narrative for the Young on the Occasion of the Jubilee of the British and Foreign Bible Society* (London: Kent and Co., 1856). In her own name, Ranyard published *The Missing Link; or, Bible-women in the Homes of the London Poor* (London: James Nisbet, 1859), which was reissued in many editions, and *Nurses for the Needy; or, Bible Women Nurses in the Homes of the London Poor* (London: Nisbet, 1875). *The Missing Link Magazine,* a monthly newsletter edited by Ranyard, was published under that title from 1864 to 1884; the name changed to *Bible Women and Nurses* in 1884 and was published under that title until 1916; the name changed several more times through 1965.

For information about Ellen Ranyard and the Domestic Female Mission, see the DNB, vol. 16, and the Oxford DNB entry by Lori Williamson. See also Elspeth Platt, *The Story of the Ranyard Mission, 1837–1937* (London: Hodder and Stoughton, 1937); Mary Poovey, *Making a Social Body: British Cultural Formation, 1830–1864* (Chicago: University of Chicago Press, 1995), 42–52; and F. K. Prochaska, "Body and Soul: Bible Nurses and the Poor in Victorian London," *Historical Research* 60 (1987): 336–48.

Dinner for the Bread-Winner

In this age of many charities, each striving to cast light upon the lot of our poorer neighbours, and find the most excellent way of rendering them help, we often hear the question, "Why do the poor continue so poor, notwithstanding all we give them?"

Those who know most of the backways of our great cities can only answer that the demon *drink* is the main cause—this drink to which many a man is driven by his wretched home and by the thriftless wife, who knows so little of wifely duties and simple management, that were the wages doubled starvation would still seem to stare the family in the face. No comfort and no food to be had at home, naturally sends the husband to the warmth and light of the gin-palace, where he can smoke his pipe in peace, and stay his hunger on false stimulants.

But can we not do something more to help the poor to help themselves, keeping alive an honest self-respect instead of sinking into mere recipients of charity.

Listen to the story of a loving Bible-woman who has thus helped many helpless ones.

In a busy corner of this great London, where factory skirts factory, and houses swarming with workers lie closely packed together, a north-country Bible-woman was planted. For three years she seemed to see no fruit of her labours, the people were hard to reach, but by-and-bye, by slow degrees, she became known and trusted by many poor mothers; the children loved her too, and would run after her, crying, "Acky, Acky, won't you come and see my mother?"

She visited one home, if home it could be called, for it was always dirty, an untidy hearth, and much litter and confusion everywhere—empty beer-cans, a dip stuck in a gingerbeer bottle, a red herring, rags, broken crockery strewed the place. One day she called and found the man at home, and he begged her to get them a grocery ticket from some lady, as he and the rest of them had nothing; *and yet* he was in work, and it was only Tuesday. There were three sickly children, and it was always the same tale. The husband was cross and out of patience, declaring that he would stand it no longer, but would go right away and leave them all.

"No, no," said Mrs. A——, "you must not do that." And then she quietly added that she thought there must be some mismanagement for them to be always so poor.

"I don't know," answered he. "I get a bit of meat on Sundays, but nought all the week besides. I earn 23*s*. a week. Could you do better?"

"Yes; I could give you meat every day for that," she answered.

Nothing more was said at the time; but calling again shortly, she found the man at home with rheumatism, and he told her "how they had been thinking over what she had said, and would she show them how to manage differently." So it was agreed, with full concurrence of both husband and wife, that she should have the money and lay it out for them. The man begged hard to have 3*s*. for his beer, but she persuaded him to try hot coffee or cocoa. On Friday night Mrs. A—— and the wife went to market together. They bought some leg of beef, and taking 6 or 7 lbs. they got it cheaper.

Next day she showed them how to cook it; and put on 3lbs. of the best part of the beef, with an onion, carrot, turnip, piece of parsley, and some barley. This stewed gently for some hours, but before the meat was done to rags it was removed. The soup when finished filled a two gallon stone jar, which the Bible-woman lent them. The other half of the beef was salted. The meat that was taken out of the pot served for the husband and wife, and the children had the soup, which lasted till Wednesday. Then they stewed the salted meat with 6lbs. of potatoes, which saved bread. This dined them until Friday came round again. She bought a quarter of a pound of tea-dust and some coffee for breakfast; the man had hot soup for supper instead of beer.

The next week Mrs. A. baked the same joint of meat for a change, and the third week they had an ox-cheek. This was bought in pieces, as it cost less than a whole one, and she could choose the parts wanted. Every Friday she wrote on a card an account of the week's expenditure, for the husband to see. She did not meet him again till three weeks had expired, when he exclaimed, "Well, I have had jolly dinners every day: never fared like it all my life before."

And so it went on for seven months, Mrs. A—— doing all the shopping at first, and then the wife doing it under her direction until "she could run alone."

This was how a week's money was spent:—

Lodging	0	3	6	Carried forward	0	15	7
Bread	0	3	9	Flour	0	0	7
Meat	0	3	7	Children's school			
Tea, coffee, sugar	0	1	3	and Bible	0	0	6
Oil, matches	0	0	4½	Burial club	0	0	4
Coal coke,				Man's club for			
and wood	0	1	2	clothes	0	1	0
Rice, barley, peas	0	0	6	Woman's club	0	1	0
Vegetables	0	1	0	Doctor*	0	2	0
Treacle	0	0	1½	Shoe club for all	0	1	0
Starch, soap, soda,				Cotton, tape,			
blue, pepper, salt	0	0	4	buttons	0	0	2
	0	15	7		1	2	2

*They owed a doctor 2l. 10s., for which he summoned them, and Mrs. A—— agreed to pay off the debt 2s. a week.

At the end of six weeks when the husband could be trusted not to spend the surplus tenpence in drink, it was handed over to him to place in the bank.

Mrs. A—— persuaded the wife to buy soap and soda; before this time the children were rarely washed, and when they were, a flower pot with a cork stuck in the hole at the bottom served as a bath.

The whole family have now emigrated with a good stock of clothes and tools, and the Bible-woman has taught eight other households to manage carefully, and to pay their way.

E. C. L.

N.B. (By the Editor.)—The one thing which may be observed as missing in the dietary is MILK, and the spare tenpence might perhaps have been well spent on Swiss milk for the children, the tin of which costs 7½d., and will keep good for a week. At the present price of milk, the poor, in general, cannot buy it.

In trying by every means to help our poor neighbours to cast out the "demon drink," this getting them to think how to lay out their money in nourishing food has perhaps not been half enough considered. We are most thankful for a sketch of a practical attempt at such help, given by a good Bible-woman with tact and prudence, and aided, as she was, by conference with and consent of her kind Superintending Lady. It may give a hint for confidential interviews with many a poor mother to learn what she provides for her family, and in what ways she might do still better.

Report of the Deptford Bible-Nurse

At the end of a second year's work in Deptford, we are glad to be able to give a still more satisfactory report of Nurse H——'s work. She is becoming well known, and is the valued friend of many mothers. She possesses much tact, and considerable power of influencing her patients in a quiet way. I do not know what some of them would do without her.

There is one home that she visits early every morning, and is the daily comfort of a poor paralysed widow, who must lie in bed until her nurse appears. She has been helpless for seven years; is a respectable person, speaking with the thin voice of an habitual invalid. Her husband was a seaman, and subscribed to the Odd Fellows Club, from which she has hitherto received a pension of 2*s*. 6*d*. a week; this, with 2*s*. 6*d*. from the parish, and 2*s*. 6*d*. earned by her eldest girl, have been their only means of support. Alice, aged fourteen, has a little place a mile and a half off, to which she goes from eight till four; and, on her return, the child has to do all the work of her poor home.

Three months ago the pension unexpectedly ceased. It is a serious matter when any income is suddenly decreased one-third, and it has been a sore trial to helpless Mrs. P——, who told me how she lies and thinks till her head aches, how and where she can save a penny. She has had another great trouble lately in the very serious illness of the youngest child, Maggie. For five weeks she lingered between life and death, only soothed by the unwearying attention of the Nurse; only induced to take food or medicine by the magic of "the lady's" name. It was a terrible time for them in the one room, with the one bed and the lessened income, but no murmur ever escaped the poor mother.

Last May Nurse attended a man who had met with an accident at his work. He had great faith in her powers, and was truly grateful for the kind care and soothing lotion that soon healed his arm. Like so many others, he spent most of his earnings at the public-house, and ill-treated his wife at home. Nurse had often seen her distress, having been her adviser in many little illnesses, and she used this opportunity to speak to the husband of his evil habit, saying that "this was his sowing time, and as he sowed so he would reap."

He always listened attentively, and we are thankful to learn that ever since this accident he has left off drink and become a teetotaler, a kind husband, a loving father. The wages are brought home regularly, and with overtime money he has bought books for his children. He does not say much, but is a changed man in all his actions.

We have another instance of a "hard drinker" forsaking the publican and leading an altered life. K—— used to get drunk every Saturday night, on receiving his wages, at the gin-palace, and cared nothing for his motherless children. But some months since he also hurt his leg, and Nurse was able to speak the kindly grave word of warning, which has again borne almost unhoped-for fruit. . . .

We add a few of our Nurse Reports to show the nature of the agency:—

A Scalded Child and Our Holloway Nurse.

John G—— was dreadfully scalded from the upsetting of a coffee-pot. He was a child of five years old, and as he was sitting down the boiling coffee flowed round him, so that many parts of his body were injured. His mother ran off with him to the hospital, but they had not a spare bed; and after having his wounds dressed, she had to bring him home again. Her husband had left her some time previously, with five boys to provide for; and she had just now succeeded in getting three weeks' charing at Major B——'s, but how could she leave this poor suffering child?

"The landlady happened to know me," says Nurse——, "and came and asked me if I would look in and see if I could do anything for them." I went and unbandaged the wounds, and said, "Well, I think I can attend to him as well as if he went to the hospital; or, if you like it better, I will take him there every day for you, so that you may go to your work." The woman was most thankful, and said, "I'll leave it all in your hands—do as you think best."

I went twice every day to dress his wounds with linseed oil and carbolic lotion, and gave him a little magnesia to cool him; kept him in bed, and made paddings to relieve the pressure on the worst parts; and in a fortnight he was able to be carried out of doors for a little air, and in another fortnight I hope he will be running about again. All this time the mother has not attended to him once, nor have I seen her since the first day, as she goes to work early in the morning and returns late in the evenings. She has left the child entirely to me.

A Croup Case.

"Last Sunday evening I was called to another poor child, three years old, who was seized with croup. The doctor had given her emetics, but they were of no use, and when he was fetched again, he said. 'The child will die; there is just one chance if you will allow me to do it, by opening the windpipe.' The parents gave consent, and he and his assistant performed the operation, and inserted a tube into the opening, which would want cleansing with a feather every ten minutes, and taking out and replacing once in two hours. The mother said she could not do it, and the neighbours would not touch it, so the doctor thought it had better not have been done; but knowing me, he told them to go and fetch me, and mention his name, and he knew I would come; so although it is against our rule to sit up at night, I could not refuse. I felt very nervous when I found what was required, as I had never had such a case before, but I did it first while the doctor was there, under his direction, and he kindly said he could not have done it better. The poor child is going on satisfactorily, and the parents are so thankful. They say the doctor and I together have saved their child's life. The tube will not be removed permanently for a fortnight, but the danger seems now to be past."

Nurse M——'s Case.

"I visited," says Nurse M——, "Mrs. P——, a widow of 78 or more. Found her quite helpless from dirt and disease. The Bible-woman and I had both tried to get in many times, but could not gain admittance; but one morning, finding the door a little open, I pushed it farther and went in. When I saw the state she was in, I said, 'I should like to cleanse you and make you comfortable.' To this she strongly objected, and said she wanted nothing done for her; but I answered, 'Well, then, I must go to the relieving officer and have you removed, as I cannot allow you to remain in this dirty state.'

"She then consented to my washing her, which I did. While doing so her daughter, who lives across the street, and two other women came to look on, but I told them they had better go home and make their own homes tidy than stand looking at me. The people about there are the dirtiest I ever met with. They are principally costermongers, sweeps, dustmen, &c., and all seem dirty and drunken together. After I had washed her I said, 'I think I must attend to your head.' It was in a sad state; it seemed as though no brush or comb had touched it for twenty years. I cut as much of her hair off as possible, which I need not say was swarming with vermin, and the back of the head eaten into holes by them. I then fetched a box of ointment and rubbed into it, and poulticed the wounds to draw the vermin out. Her finger-nails were half-an-inch long, and grimed with dirt; I cut them, and well washed her hands. And when it was all done she was very thankful. 'God bless you,' she said, 'a thousand times, for coming to me!' Her daughter stood looking at me, so I told her she must clean the room, which she did after that. This case receives 3s. from the parish, but pays 2s. 6d. for her room. How she is supported I cannot tell, unless by some visitors from the church occasionally looking in and helping her, and the neighbours sometimes take her a little. I made her a cup of cocoa, which warmed her beautifully, she said."

From the same Nurse:—

"Mrs. P.'s is a dreadful cancer case, but very different from the last, for she is very clean in herself and her little room. A married daughter lives with her, and is very kind to her, and keeps her very clean. She suffers most severely. I often find her deluged in blood, which bursts from the wound at different times. She is so thankful for the lotion and wadding and the attention that I can give her. Her husband is much afflicted, and can do but little work. They are very poor; 2s. 6d. was given to-day for this case."

Nurse T——'s Case — Mr. B——.

"This poor man has abscesses all over his back and hips and is in a sad state. He cannot lie excepting on his face, therefore cannot read as he used to do. It is such a comfort to him for me or the Bible-woman to read to him. He wants a great deal of attention, for the discharge pours away continually, and the only wonder is that he is still alive. He cannot take anything solid, but beef-tea and an egg beaten up with milk occasionally is all the nourishment he can take. He often says, 'I cannot read, but I have been talking with Jesus and He talks to me.' He is a dear Christian man, most willing to go, but says he trys [sic] from his heart to say, 'Not my will but thine be done.' He is waiting patiently, and knows Jesus will take him when he is ready. This case had 2s. 6d. relief this morning."

Maud Pember Reeves

THE NARRATOR OF THIS RESPECTFUL AND GRAPHIC ACCOUNT of working-
class life in the London district of North Lambeth (just south of the Thames)
is Maud Pember Reeves (1865–1953), describing a project carried out by the
Fabian Women's Group (FWG). Founded in 1908 by Pember Reeves and
the anarchist Charlotte Wilson, the FWG intended both to give women
more prominence in the Fabian Society and "to study women's economic
independence in relation to socialism." In 1910 the group had more than
two hundred members. They included Beatrice Webb; the historian Alice
Clark; the popular children's author Edith Nesbit; LCC member Susan
Lawrence; and the labor activists and future politicians Margaret Bondfield
and Marion Phillips. The FWG members produced a large and sophisticated body of writings.[1]

Initiated by Pember Reeves, in 1909 the FWG's Motherhood Special
Fund Committee began a study of the domestic lives of forty-two families
with new babies living on a subsistence wage of about a pound a week. The
FWG had raised money and was able to give each mother extra cash for her
children's food for their first year of life. The Fabians expected that the extra
money would improve infant health and survival statistics for the sample
group, which it definitely did—demonstrating that high child death rates
in slum areas were caused by poverty and not maternal ignorance or neg-
ligence.[2] Their conclusions, first published in 1912 as a Fabian Tract, soon
appeared as *Round about a Pound a Week*. The book was a defense of the

"The District," "Thrift," and "The Poor and Marriage," originally published as chapters 1,
5, and 11, respectively, in Round about a Pound a Week (1913; reprint, London: Virago, 1979),
1–7, 66–74, and 146–58.

intelligence and industry of working-class women so often maligned by infant welfare officials. It also argued for the state to aid families through affordable housing, a minimum wage, midwives' training, and public feeding of infants. And like so many other discussions of poverty in this era, it incorporated several detailed family budgets.

A New Zealander since age two, Pember Reeves (her full name was Magdalene Stuart) had led a successful drive for female suffrage in her native country, which in 1893 became the first nation in the world where women could vote. Maud was one of ten children born to a bank manager and his well-read and well-traveled wife. An eager student, Maud Stuart attended a newly founded girls' high school in Christchurch, and continued her education later at Canterbury College. After her 1885 marriage to William Pember Reeves, a reforming politician, and while raising their children, she helped her husband to edit his weekly newspaper alongside her college courses and energetic suffrage agitation.

She did not move to London until 1896, when her husband, who had been Minister of Labour in New Zealand, became Agent-General in London for the New Zealand government. Maud Pember Reeves immediately became politically active in British suffrage and labor organizations, and after 1907 was on the executive committee of the Fabian Society. The FWG was formed in her Kensington drawing room, and she was clearly central in carrying out the research for *Round about a Pound a Week*. During the First World War she was director of the Education and Propaganda Department in the Ministry of Food. Her daughter Amber, when a student at Cambridge, had a notorious affair with H. G. Wells, a close friend of her mother's. After the death of the Reeves's son Fabian in the war, Maud was somewhat less politically active.

NOTES

1. See Alexander, *Women's Fabian Tracts,* introduction.
2. Pember Reeves, *Round about a Pound,* 194.

FURTHER READING

For more writing by Maud Pember Reeves, see *Family Life on a Pound a Week* (Fabian Tract no. 162, 1912); reprint ed., *Round about a Pound a Week,* introduction by Sally Alexander (London: Virago, 1979). Pember Reeves contributed to the pamphlet *The Needs of Little Children: Report of a Conference on the Care of Babies and Young Children* (London: Women's Labour League, 1912) and wrote "Colonial Developments in Factory Legislation," in *The Case for the Factory Acts,* ed. Beatrice Webb (London: G. Richards, 1901).

For information about Pember Reeves, see the BDBF, vol. 2, and the Oxford DNB entry by Sally Alexander, who interviewed Pember Reeves's daughter Amber in 1978. My thanks to Dr. Alexander for sending me her entry before its publication. See also Alexander's introduction to a collection titled *Women's Fabian Tracts* (London: Routledge, 1988, new ed. 2001) and R. Fry, *Maud and Amber: A New Zealand Mother and Daughter and the Women's Cause, 1865–1981* (Christchurch, NZ: Canterbury University Press, 1992).

∞∞∞

The District

Take a tram from Victoria to Vauxhall Station. Get out under the railway arch which faces Vauxhall Bridge, and there you will find Kennington Lane. The railway arch roofs in a din which reduces the roar of trains continually passing overhead to a vibrating, muffled rumble. From either end of the arch comes a close procession of trams, motor-buses, brewers' drays, coal-lorries, carts filled with unspeakable material for glue factory and tannery, motor-cars, coster-barrows, and people. It is a stopping-place for tramcars and motor-buses; therefore little knots of agitated persons continually collect on both pathways, and dive between the vehicles and descending passengers in order to board the particular bus or tram they desire. At rhythmic intervals all traffic through the arch is suspended to allow a flood of trams, buses, drays, and vans, to surge and rattle and bang across the opening of the archway which faces the river.

At the opposite end there is no cross-current. The trams slide away to the right towards the Oval. In front is Kennington Lane, and to the left, at right angles, a narrow street connects with Vauxhall Walk, leading farther on into Lambeth Walk, both locally better known as The Walk. Such is the western gateway to the district stretching north to Lambeth Road, south to Lansdowne Road, and east to Walworth Road, where live the people whose lives form the subject of this book.

They are not the poorest people of the district. Far from it! They are, putting aside the tradesmen whose shops line the big thoroughfares such as Kennington Road or Kennington Park Road, some of the more enviable and settled inhabitants of this part of the world. The poorest people—the river-side casual, the workhouse in-and-out, the bar-room loafer—are anxiously ignored by these respectable persons whose work is permanent, as permanency goes in Lambeth, and whose wages range from 18s. to 30s. a week.

They generally are somebody's labourer, mate, or handyman. Painters' labourers, plumbers' labourers, builders' handymen, dustmen's mates, print-ers' labourers, potters' labourers, trouncers for carmen, are common amongst them. Or they may be fish-fryers, tailors' pressers, feather-cleaners' assis-tants, railway-carriage washers, employees of dust contractors, carmen for Borough Council contractors, or packers of various descriptions. They are respectable men in full work, at a more or less top wage, young, with fam-ilies still increasing, and they will be lucky if they are never worse off than they now are. Their wives are quiet, decent, "keep themselves-to-themselves" kind of women, and the children are the most punctual and regular schol-ars, the most clean-headed children of the poorer schools in Kennington and Lambeth.

The streets they live in are monotonously and drearily decent, lying back from the main arteries, and with little traffic other than a stray barrel-organ, a coal-lorry selling by the hundredweight sack, or a taxi-cab going to or from its driver's dinner at home. At certain hours in the day—before morning school, at midday, and after four o'clock—these narrow streets become full of screaming, running, shouting children. Early in the morning men come from every door and pass out of sight. At different times during the evening the same men straggle home again. At all other hours the street is quiet and desperately dull. Less ultra-respectable neighbourhoods may have a certain picturesqueness, or give a sense of community of interest or of careless com-radeship, with their untidy women chatting in the doorways and their unoccupied men lounging at the street corners; but in these superior streets a kind of dull aloofness seems to be the order of the day.

The inhabitants keep themselves to themselves, and watch the doings of the other people from behind window curtains, knowing perfectly that every incoming and outgoing of their own is also jealously recorded by crit-ical eyes up and down the street. A sympathetic stranger walking the length of one of these thoroughfares feels the atmosphere of criticism. The rent-collector, the insurance agent, the coal-man, may pass the time of day with worn women in the doorways, but a friendly smile from the stranger receives no response. A weekly caller becomes the abashed object of intense interest on the part of everybody in the street, from the curious glances of the green-grocer's lady at the corner to the appraising stare of the fat little baker who always manages to be on his doorstep across the road. And every-where along the street is the visitor conscious of eyes which disappear from behind veiled windows. This consciousness accentuates the dispiriting outlook.

The houses are outwardly decent—two stories of grimy brick. The roadway is narrow, but on the whole well kept, and on the pavement outside many doors there is to be noticed, in a greater or less condition of freshness, a semicircle of hearth-stone, which has for its radius the length of the housewife's arm as she kneels on the step. In some streets little paved alley-ways lead behind the front row of houses, and twist and turn among still smaller dwellings at the back—dwellings where the front door leads downwards into a room instead of upwards into a passage. Districts of this kind cover dreary acres—the same little two-story house, with or without an inconceivably drearier basement, with the same kind of baker's shop at the corner faced by the same kind of greengrocer's shop opposite. The ugly, constantly-recurring school buildings are a relief to the spirit oppressed by the awful monotony.

The people who live in these places are not really more like one another than the people who live in Belgrave Square or South Kensington. But there is no mixture of rich and poor, no startling contrast, no crossing-sweeper and no super-taxpayer, and the first impression is that of uniformity. As a matter of fact, the characteristics of Mrs. Smith of Kennington and the characteristics of Mrs. Brown who lives next door are more easily to be differentiated by a stranger in the street than are the characteristics of Mrs. Smythe of Bayswater from those of Mrs. Browne who occupies the house next to her.

Mrs. Smith and Mrs. Brown, though they may never be seen by the passer-by, are able to imprint their personality on the street because their ways are open, and meant to be open, to all whom it may concern. Mrs. Smith likes red ochre at her door, in spite of the children's boots messing it all over the floor. Moreover, she likes to cover the big flagstone in front of the door, and two lesser stones, one on each side; she makes the edges coincide with the cracks, and produces a two-winged effect of deep importance. It is likely that Mrs. Smith's mother lived in a village where not to do your doorstep thus was a social sin, where perhaps there was but one flagstone, and Mrs. Smith in her childhood was accustomed to square edges.

Mrs. Brown "can't abide that nasty stuff," and uses good hearthstone, as her mother taught her to do. Mrs. Brown prefers also the semicircular sweep of the arm which secures the rounded edge and curved effect which satisfy her sense of propriety and usualness.

Mrs. Smith has a geranium in a pot in her front window, and the lace curtains which shield her privacy behind it are starched and blued according to some severe precedent ignored by the other ladies of the neighbourhood.

Mrs. Brown goes in for a scheme of window decoration which shows the dirt less. She has a row of red and yellow cocoa tins to make a bright effect.

The merest outsider calling for the first time on Mrs. Smith knows her beforehand for the decent, cleanly soul she is, and only wonders whether the struggle of life has worn her temper to fiddle-strings or whether some optimistic strain in her nature still allows her to hope on. The same outsider looking at Mrs. Brown's front door and window would realize her to be one who puts a good face on things, and, if it happened to be the right time of a day which was not washing-day, probably would expect, after the proper ceremonial had been gone through, to be asked in to sit behind the cocoa tins.

Who could tell anything half so interesting from the front doors of Mrs. Smythe and Mrs. Browne of Bayswater? Who could tell, on meeting each of these ladies face to face, more than her official age and the probable state of her husband's purse?

The children of the street are equally different from one another both in character and appearance, and are often startlingly good-looking. They have shrill voices, clumsy clothes, the look of being small for their age, and they are liable to be comfortably dirty, but there the characteristics they have in common cease. They may be wonderfully fair, with delicate skins and pale hair; they may have red hair, with snub-nosed, freckled faces; or they may be dark and intense, with long, thick eyelashes and slender, lithe bodies. Some are apathetic, some are restless. They are often intelligent; but while some are able to bring their intelligence to bear on their daily life, others seem quite unable to do so. They are abnormally noisy. Had they been well housed, well fed, well clothed, and well tended, from birth, what kind of raw material would they have shown themselves to be?

Thrift

It is just that a short chapter should be devoted to the thrift of such a class of wage-earners and their wives as are described here. It is a common idea that there is no thrift among them. It would be better for their children if this were true. As a matter of fact, sums varying from 6d. a week to 1s. 6d., 1s. 8d., or even 2s., go out from incomes which are so small that these sums represent, perhaps, from 2½ to 10 per cent. of the whole household allowance. The object of this thrift is, unfortunately, not of the slightest benefit to the children of the families concerned. The money is spent or saved or invested, whichever is the proper term, on burial insurance. No living child is better fed or better clothed because its parents, decent folk, scrape up a penny a week to pay the insurance collector on its account. Rather is it less well fed and less well clothed to the extent of 1d. a week—an appreciable amount when it is, perhaps, one of eight persons living on £1 a week.

One of the criticisms levelled at these respectable, hard-working, independent people is that they do like to squander money on funerals. It is a view held by everyone who does not know the real circumstances. It is also held by many who do know them, but who confuse the fact that poor people show a great interest in one another's funerals with the erroneous idea that they could bury their dead for half the amount if they liked. Sometimes, in the case of adult men, this may be so. When alive, the man, perhaps, was a member of a society for burial benefit, and at his death the club or society bury him with much pomp and ceremony. In the case of the young children of people living on from 18s. to 30s. a week, the parents do not squander money on funerals which might be undertaken for half the price.

A working man and his wife who have a family are confronted with the problem of burial at once. They are likely to lose one or more of their children. The poorer they are, the more likely are they to lose them. Shall they run the risk of burial by the parish, or shall they take Time by the forelock and insure each child as it is born, at the rate of a penny a week? If they decide not to insure, and they lose a child, the question resolves itself into one of borrowing the sum necessary to pay the funeral expenses, or of undergoing the disgrace of a pauper funeral. The pauper funeral carries with it the pauperization of the father of the child—a humiliation which adds disgrace to the natural grief of the parents. More than that, they declare that the pauper funeral is wanting in dignity and in respect to their dead. One woman expressed the feeling of many more when she said she would as soon have the dust-cart call for the body of her child as that "there Black Mariar." This may be sheer prejudice on the part of poor parents, but it is a prejudice which richer parents—even the most educated and highly born of them—if confronted with the same problem when burying their own children, would fully share. Refusing, then, if uninsured, to accept the pauper burial, with its consequent political and social degradation of a perfectly respectable family, the parents try to borrow the money needed. Up and down the street sums are collected in pence and six-pences until the price of a child's funeral on the cheapest scale is secured. Funerals are not run on credit; but the neighbours, who may be absolute strangers, will contribute rather than suffer the degradation to pauperism of one of themselves. For months afterwards the mother and remaining children will eat less in order to pay back the money borrowed. The father of the family cannot eat less. He is already eating as little as will enable him to earn the family wage. To starve him would be bad economy. He must fare as usual. The rest of the family can eat less without bothering anybody—and do.

What is the sum necessary to stand between a working man and pauperdom should he suffer the loss of a child? Inquiry among undertakers in Lambeth and Kennington resulted in the discovery that a very young baby could be buried by one undertaker for 18s., and by a dozen others for 20s. To this must be added the fee of 10s. to the cemetery paid by the undertaker, which brought his charges up to 28s. or 30s. No firm could be discovered who would do it for less. When a child's body is too long to go under the box-seat of the driver, the price of the funeral goes up. A sort of age scale is roughly in action, which makes a funeral of a child of three more expensive than that of a child of six months Thirty shillings, then, is the lowest sum to be faced by the grieving parents. But how is a man whose whole weekly income may be but two-thirds of that amount to produce at sight 30s. or more? Of course he cannot. Sheer dread of the horrible problem drives his wife to pay out 10d., 11d., or 1s., a week year after year—money which, as far as the welfare of the children themselves go, might as well be thrown into the sea.

A penny a week paid from birth just barely pays the funeral expenses as the child grows older. It does not completely pay them in early infancy. Thirteen weekly pennies must be paid before any benefit is due, and the first sum due is not sufficient; but it is a help. As each child must be insured separately, the money paid for the child who does not die is no relief when a death occurs. Insurance, whether State or other insurance, is always a gamble, and people on £1 a week cannot afford a gamble. A peculiar hardship attaches to burial insurance. A man may have paid regularly for years, may fall out of work through illness or other misfortune, and may lose all benefit. When out of work his children are more likely to die, and he may have to suffer the disgrace of a pauper funeral after five years or more of regular payment for burial insurance.

Great numbers of premature confinements occur among women who live the lives these wives and mothers do. A premature confinement, if the child breathes, means an uninsured funeral. True, an undertaker will sometimes provide a coffin which he slips into another funeral, evade the cemetery fee, and only charge 10s.; but even 10s. is a terrible sum to produce at the moment. Great is the anxiety on the part of the mother to be able to prove that her child was stillborn.

The three-year-old daughter of a carter out of work died of tuberculosis. The father, whose policies had lapsed, borrowed the sum of £2 5s. necessary to bury the child. The mother was four months paying the debt off by reducing the food of herself and of the five other children. The funeral cortège consisted of one vehicle, in which the little coffin went under the driver's seat. The parents and a neighbour sat in the back part of the vehicle. They saw the child buried in a common grave with twelve other coffins of all sizes. "We 'ad to keep a sharp eye out for Edie," they said; "she were so little she were almost 'id."

The following is an account kept of the funeral of a child of six months who died of infantile cholera in the deadly month of August, 1911. The parents had insured her for 2d. a week, being unusually careful people. The sum received was £2.

	£	s.	d.
Funeral	1	12	0
Death certificate	0	1	3
Gravediggers	0	2	0
Hearse attendants	0	2	0
Woman to lay her out	0	2	0
Insurance agent	0	1	0
Flowers	0	0	6
Black tie for father	0	1	0
	2	1	9

The child was buried in a common grave with three others. There is no display and no extravagance in this list. The tips to the gravediggers, hearse attendants, and insurance agent, were all urgently applied for, though not in every case by the person who received the money. The cost of the child's illness had amounted to 10s., chiefly spent on special food. The survivors lived on reduced rations for two weeks in order to get square again. The father's wage was 24s., every penny of which he always handed over to his wife.

The usual amount paid for burial insurance is 1d. a week for each child, 2d. for the mother, and 3d. for the father, making 11d. a week for a family with six children, though some overcautious women make the sum more.

Another form of thrift is some sort of paying-out club. Usually payments of this kind come out of the father's pocket-money, but a few instances where the women made them came within the experience of the investigators. One club was named a "didly club." Its method seemed to consist in each member paying a certain woman ¼d. the first week, ½d. the next week, ¾d. the next week, and so on, always adding ¼d. to the previous payment. The money was to be divided at Christmas. It was a mere way of saving, as no interest of any kind was to be paid. Needless to relate, about October the woman to whom the money had been paid disappeared. Stocking clubs, crockery clubs, and Christmas dinner clubs, make short appearances in the budgets. They usually entail a weekly payment of 3d. or 4d., and when the object—the children's winter stockings, the new plates, or the Christmas dinner—has been attained, the payments cease.

One form of money transaction which is hardly regarded as justifiable when poor people resort to it, but which at the same time is the ordinary, laudable, business custom of rich men—namely, borrowing—is carried on by the poor under very distressing conditions. When no friend or friends can be found to help at a crisis, many a woman has been driven—perhaps to pay the rent—to go to what she calls a lender. A few shillings are borrowed—perhaps five or six. The terms are a penny a week on every shilling borrowed, with, it may be a kind of tip of half a crown at the end when all the principle and interest has been paid off. A woman borrowing 6s. pays 6d. a week in sheer interest—that is, £1 6s. a year—without reducing her debt a penny. She is paying 433 per cent. on her loan. She does not know the law, and she could not afford to invoke its aid if she did know it. She goes on being bled because it is the local accepted rate of a "lender." Only one of the women whose budgets appear in these pages has had recourse to this kind of borrowing, but the custom is well known by them all.

Such is the passion for weekly regular payments among these women that, had the Post Office initiated regular collection of pennies instead of the industrial insurance companies doing so, either the Post Office would now be in possession of the enormous accumulated capital of these companies, or the people on 20s. a week would have been much better off. The great bulk of the pennies so urgently needed for other purposes, and paid for burial insurance, is never returned in any form whatsoever to the people who pay them. The small proportion which does come to them is swallowed up in a burial, and no one but the undertaker is the better for it. As a form of thrift which shall help the future, or be a standby if misfortune should befall, burial insurance is a calamitous blunder. Yet the respectable poor man is forced to resort to it unless he is to run the risk of being made a pauper by any bereavement which may happen to him. It is a terrible object lesson in how not to manage. If the sum of £11,000,000 a year stated to be paid in weekly pennies by the poor to the industrial burial insurance companies were to be spent on better house room and better food—if in fact, the one great universal thrift of the poor were not for death, but were for life—we should have a stronger nation. The only real solution of this horrible problem would seem to be the making of decent burial a free and honourable public service.

The Poor and Marriage

So many strictures are made on the improvident marriages of the poor that it is necessary to look at the matter from the point of view of the poor themselves.

If the poor were not improvident, they would hardly dare to live their lives at all. There is no security for them. Any work which they do may stop at a week's notice. Much work may be, and is, stopped with no notice of any kind. The man is paid daily, and one evening he is paid as usual, but told that he will not be needed again. Such a system breeds improvidence; and if casual labour and daily paid labour are necessary to society, then society must excuse the faults which are the obvious outcome of such a system.

In the case of marriage, as things now are, the moment a man's money approaches a figure which seems to him a possible one he marries. For the first year or even two years he may have less ready money but more comfort. The wife keeps their one room clean and pleasant, and cooks, none too well perhaps, but possibly with more attention to his special needs than his former landlady did, or than his mother did, who had her own husband as well as her other children to cater for. The wage may be £1 a week. He gives the wife 18s. and retains 2s. for himself. The result of her management may closely approach the following budget of two actual young people who came within the investigation.

Mr. W., aged twenty, a toy-packer in City warehouse—wages 20s.; allows 18s. He has been married eighteen months, and when this budget was drawn up a baby was expected any day. His wages were raised from 18s. a year ago. His wife before marriage was a machinist on piece-work, and could earn 10s. a week. She worked for six months after marriage, and paid for most of the furniture in their one room; also she provided the coming baby's clothes. She is clean and thrifty, writes a good hand, and keeps excellent accounts. She is nineteen.

Out of the 2s. retained by the husband, he pays 6d. a week into a clothing club, and of course his 4d. is deducted for State Insurance. With the rest "he does what he likes." Sometimes he likes to give the wife an extra penny for her housekeeping. The menu, from the list of food purchases given on next page, appears to consist of a sufficiency of bread, of meat, of potatoes, and perhaps of greens, as the husband's dinners eaten away from home probably include greens for him. Some cold meat, with bread and butter and tea, would be provided for the evening meal; bread, butter, and tea would be the invariable breakfast.

Date of budget, January 16, 1913:

	s.	d.
Rent (one good room upstairs; two windows)	5	0
Burial insurance	0	3
Boot club	0	6
Coal (1 cwt. [hundredweight] stove coal for foreign stove, which stands out into the room, and will be very dangerous when the baby begins to crawl)	1	3
Gas	0	8
Soap	0	3
Oil	0	2
Matches	0	1½
	8	2½

Left for food   9s.   9½d.

	s.	d.
Six loaves	1	4½
Husband's dinners (he is given 6d. daily by his wife for his dinner, which he eats away from home)	3	0
Meat	3	2½
½ lb. butter	0	6
1 lb. flour	0	1½
1 tin of milk	0	4
4 ozs. tea	0	4
1 lb. moist sugar	0	2
½ lb. dripping	0	3
8 lbs. potatoes	0	4
4 lbs. greens	0	2
	9	9½

An average per head of 4s. 10¾d. a week for food.

If the wages never rise, and if the family grows larger, the amounts spent on burial insurance, soap, coal, gas, and, later on, rent will increase, leaving less and less for food, with more people to feed on the less amount. Extra bedding will eventually have to be bought, though the parents will naturally put off that moment as long as possible. Should the wage rise gradually to 24s., or even 25s., it would not all go upon the general living. The man would naturally take a larger amount of pocket-money, and out of the extra sum which he might allow the wife, he would certainly expect better living. A "relish to his tea," costing 2d. a day, mounts up to 1s. a week, and a "rasher to his breakfast" costs the same. So an increase of 2s. might be completely swallowed up in extra food for the worker. And it would be really needed by him, as his proportion of the money spent would tend to diminish with more mouths to fill.

Another instance of a young couple starting on £1 a week is that of Mr. H., who is twenty-two, and works in a brewery. Every third week he has night work. He allows his wife his whole wage. There is one child of six months. The wife is twenty. She worked in a polish factory until marriage, when she was dismissed, with a small bonus, as the firm does not employ married women. With the bonus she helped to furnish. She is an excellent housewife, and keeps her room comfortable.

Date of budget, January 16, 1913.

	s.	d.
Rent (one room, small; one window, upstairs)	3	6
Husband's fares	1	0
Husband's pocket-money	1	0
State sickness insurance	0	4
Four weeks' burial insurance (Mr. H. had been ill on half pay, and burial insurance had stood over)	1	0
Soap, soda	0	3½
1 cwt. coal	1	6
Gas	0	6
Wood	0	2
Newspaper	0	1
Boracic powder	0	1
Cotton	0	2
Needles	0	0½
Buttons	0	1
Paid off loan (5s. borrowed from a brother during husband's illness)	1	0
	10	9

This leaves for food, 9s. 3d. between three people, or an average of 3s. 1d. a head.

	s.	d.
9 loaves	1	10½
8 ozs. tea	0	8
2 lbs. moist sugar	0	4
1 tin of milk (a smaller tin than Mrs. W.'s)	0	3½
½ lb. butter (slightly better than Mrs. W.'s)	0	7
2 lbs. flour	0	3
8 lbs. potatoes	0	4
Vegetables	0	7
Salt, mustard, sauce	0	2½
Fruit	0	6
Fish	1	0
Bacon	0	4½
Mineral water (recommended by doctor for Mr. H. during his illness)	0	3
Meat	2	0
	9	3

Owing to Mr. H. getting home to his meals, there is more elasticity in this menu. Much less meat is eaten, and fish and bacon appear instead. More bread, more tea, more vegetables are eaten, and fruit is added. The usual breakfast is bread, butter, and tea; the dinner a small amount of meat, with potatoes and vegetables; the evening meal, fish or bacon, with potatoes, as well as the eternal bread, butter, and tea. All these four young people are steady and intelligent. They have enough to eat, but they are put to it for proper clothing already. The H.'s will have to move sooner than the W.'s if their family increases, as their room, though a pleasant one, is not above half the size of the other.

It is obvious that with both these young men marriage is, so far, both pleasant and successful. It is worth the sacrifice in pocket-money which it must entail upon them. Their working life is much the same as it was during their bachelorhood, while their free time is more comfortable and more interesting. Should they have waited to marry until later in life, they would probably have lived no cheaper as bachelors, though the money would have been spent differently, and they would have been less wholesomely comfortable.

The young women's lives are far more changed. They tell you that, though they are a bit lonely at times, and miss the companionship of the factory life and the money of their own to spend, and are rather frightened at the swift approach of motherhood, "You get accustomed to it," and "It won't be so lonely when the baby comes," and "He's very handy when he's at home." The first baby is a source of great interest and pleasure to both parents, especially if it is well managed and does not cry at night, though one young father who was accustomed to a restless baby said he "missed it ter'ble at night" when it was away in hospital. It is different when the children multiply and the room becomes crowded and food is less plentiful. Then the case of the man is hard and unattractive; the amount of self-sacrifice demanded of him, if he be at all tender-hearted towards his family, is outrageous. He must never smoke, he must never take a glass of ale; he must walk to and from his work in all weathers; he must have no recreations but the continual mending of his children's boots; he must neither read nor go to picture palaces nor take holidays, if he is to do all that social reformers expect of him when they theoretically parcel out his tiny income. Needless to say, the poorly paid man is not so immeasurably superior to the middle-class man in the matter of self-denial and self-control as he seems expected to be. He does smoke, he does sometimes take a glass of ale; he does, in fact, appropriate a proportion of the money he earns to his own pleasure. It is not a large proportion as a rule, but it upsets the nice calculations which are based upon the supposition that a man earning 25s. a week spends every penny of it in the support of his family. He is, most probably, a hard-working, steady, sober man; but he may spend perhaps 2d. a day on beer, 1d. a day on tobacco, and 2d. a day on tram fares, and that without being a monster of selfishness, or wishing to deprive his children of their food. In most budgets he keeps from 2s. to 2s. 6d. for himself, in some 5s. or 6s., and in some nothing. He varies as his brethren vary in other classes. Sometimes he walks to and from work; sometimes he pays his fares out of the money he keeps; and sometimes he gets them paid out of the money with which he supplies his wife.

Though fond of the children when they are there, this life of stress and strain makes the women dread nothing so much as the conviction that there is to be still another baby with its inevitable consequences—more crowding, more illness, more worry, more work, and less food, less strength, less time to manage with.

There are people who argue that marriage should be put off by the poor until they have saved up enough to secure their economic independence, and that it would not hurt young men on £1 a week to put off marriage till they are thirty, they, meantime, saving hard during those ten years. Should the poorly paid workman overcome his young impulse to marry the moment his wage reaches £1 a week, and should he remain a bachelor until thirty, it is quite certain that he would not marry at all. This may be a good thing or a bad thing, but it would be so. A man who for ten years had had the spending of 20s. a week—and it is a sum which is soon spent without providing luxuries—would not, at thirty, when perhaps cold reason would direct his impulse, feel inclined to share his £1 a week with an uncertain number of other people. His present bent is towards married life. It provides him for the first year or two with attention to his comfort and with privacy and freedom for his personality, as well as satisfying his natural craving for sex-relationship. Should he thwart that impulse, he, being an average, normal man, will have to find other ways of dealing with these desires of his. He is not likely to starve every instinct for ten years in order, perhaps, to save a sum which might bring in an income of a couple of shillings a week to add to his weekly wage. He would know, by the time he was thirty, that even 22s. a week does not guarantee a family against misery and want. The self-sacrifice demanded of the father of even a small family on such an income would appal him.

The young couple who marry and live contentedly on 20s. a week are usually members of families of at least four or five persons, and have struggled through their childhood on their share of an income which may have been anything from 20s. to 25s. or 26s. a week. Their standard of comfort is disastrously low, and they do not for the first year or two realise that even two or three children will develop into a burden which is too great for their strength. It is not the greater number of children alone: it is the greater cost of accommodating, feeding, and clothing boys and girls as they get older which increases the strain. Moreover, the separation of interests soon begins to show itself. The husband goes to the same work—hard, long, and monotonous—but at least a change from the growing discomfort of the home. He gets accustomed to seeing his wife slave, and she gets accustomed to seeing him appear and disappear on his daily round of work, which gradually appeals less and less to her imagination, till, at thirty, she hardly knows what his duties are—so overwhelmed is she in the flood of her own most absorbing duties and economies. Her economies interfere with his comfort, and are irksome to him; so he gets out of touch with her point of view. He cannot see why the cooking should be less satisfactory than it used to be, and says so. She knows she needs a new saucepan, but cannot possibly afford to buy one, and says so. He makes his wife the same allowance, and expects the same amount of food. She has more mouths to fill, and grows impatient because he does not understand that, though their first baby did not seem to make much difference, a boy of three, plus a baby, makes the old problem into quite a new one.

One of her questions is the balance between rent and food, which is of enormous importance. Yet she never can feel certain that she has found the right solution. Shall they all live in one room? Or shall they take two basement rooms at an equally low rent, but spend more on gas and coal, and suffer more from damp and cold? Or shall they take two rooms above stairs and take the extra rent out of the food? Her own appetite may not be very large, so she decides perhaps on the two better rooms upstairs. She may decide wisely, as we think, but the sacrifice in food is not to be ignored in its results on the health of the children.

Another of her problems is, How is she to keep her husband, the bread-winner, in full efficiency out of the few shillings she can spend on food, and at the same time satisfy the appetites of the children? She decides to feed him sufficiently and to make what is over do for herself and the children. This is not considered and thought-out self-sacrifice on her part. It is the pressure of circumstances. The wage-earner must be fed. The arrangement made between husband and wife in cases where the man's work is at a distance—that 6d. a day, or 3s. a week, should be allowed by her for his dinners—may have begun, as in the case already quoted, before any children had appeared, and may continue when there are six children. Even if the wage has increased, and if, instead of 20s., the worker is getting 23s. or 24s., he probably keeps an extra shilling for himself. Instead of allowing his wife 18s. a week, he allows her 20s. or 21s. If she has several children, the father's weekly 3s. for dinner is far harder to compass than when she managed for two only on 18s. Rent, instead of being from 3s. 6d. to 5s. for one "good" upstairs room, amounts to from 6s. to 7s. for two upstairs rooms, or, if house-room be sacrificed to food, rent may be 5s. 6d. for two deadly basement rooms. Insurance has mounted from 3d. a week to 9d. a week. Gas which was 6d. is now 1s., on account of the extra cooking. Soap and other cleaning materials have increased in quantity, and therefore in expense from 2d. to 5½d. Clothing is a problem for which very few weekly figures are available. It must be covered by payments to clothing and boot clubs, or each article must be bought when needed. In any case the expense is greater and the amount of money available for food grows less. The unvarying amount paid for the bread-winner's necessary daily food becomes a greater proportion of the food bill, and leaves all the increasing deficit to be met out of the food of the mother and children. It is unavoidable that it should be so; nobody wastes time thinking about it; but the fact that it is so forces the mother to take a different point of view from that of the father. So each of them gradually grows to understand the other less.

Both parents are probably devoted to the children. The husband, who is sick of his wife's complaints, and can't be bothered with her story of how she has no boots to wear, listens with sympathy and understanding to her tale of woe about Tommy having no boots to his feet. The boy who cannot speak at three years of age, or the girl who is deficient in weight, in height, and in wits, often is the father's special pet, for whom he will sacrifice both food and sleep, while the mother's whole life is spent in a dreary effort to do her best for them all round.

Much has been said and written, and much more will be said and written, on the question of the poor and large families. We wrangle as to whether their numerous children are an improvidence and an insult to the community, or whether, on the contrary, the poorest class is the only class which, in that respect, does its duty to the nation. One thing is quite certain, and it is that it would be as unthinkable as impossible to bring compulsion to bear on the poor because they are poor. For those who deplore large families in the case of poor people, it must be a comfort to remember a fact which experience shews us, that as poverty decreases, and as the standard of comfort rises, so does the size of the family diminish. Should we be able to conquer the problem of poverty, we should automatically solve the problem of the excessively large family.

Maude Alethea Stanley

MAUDE ALETHEA STANLEY (1833–1915) was one of nine siblings (two others died in infancy) who grew up in a remarkable family: ancient, wealthy, multiply titled, Liberal, and eccentric.[1] Alderley Park, the house in Cheshire to which the Stanley family moved in 1850, had about forty bedrooms (not counting servants' rooms), six large reception rooms, and three hundred acres of parkland.[2] Maude's sharp-tongued and no-nonsense mother, Henrietta Maria, Lady Stanley of Alderley, was a founder of Girton College.[3] She steadfastly vetoed the building of a college chapel, but willingly donated Girton's first chemical laboratory and library.[4] Maude's younger sister Kate, along with her young husband, John Russell, Viscount Amberley, were women's suffragists and birth control advocates. Kate was also devoted to women's education and had worked with her mother to found Girton.[5] The youngest of the Stanley sisters, Rosalind, who became Countess of Carlisle, was a Liberal Party activist, advocate of trade unions for women, and also a suffragist. Brother Algernon's conversion to Roman Catholicism and his position as "Domestic Prelate of the Pope" was most unusual in an aristocratic English family, and certainly so was the eldest son Henry's becoming a Muslim.

Of the five Stanley sisters who survived into adulthood, Maude was the only one to remain single. She was obviously what I would call the family's "designated spinster." Letters she wrote to her sister Kate in the 1860s, when Maude was in her thirties, reveal her depression at being the only child left at home. Kate reassuringly called her the "favourite sister" and

---

Originally published as chapter 3, "Drunkenness," in Work about the Five Dials *(London: Macmillan, 1878).*

Figure 7. Maude Alethea Stanley. This portrait was taken by Camille Silvy, a well-known photographer, in 1861—years before Stanley began her London parish visiting. Here, at age twenty-nine, she is one of the ladies of Alderley, a palatial country estate in Cheshire said to have at least forty bedrooms. Reprinted with the permission of the National Portrait Gallery, London.

pointed out that the parents and her brothers needed her: "What would they do without a sister at home[?]"[6]

In 1869 the Stanley family was in crisis. Edward John, the second baron Stanley, died that year and Henry, the Muslim convert and eldest son, inherited his title as third baron. The Baron's widow, and most of the Stanley offspring, apparently unperturbed about the heir's religious proclivities, were deeply distraught at Henry's announcement that he had secretly married an unknown Spanish woman in 1862. The house would now belong to Henry. Maude talked at this time of going out to nurse the wounded in the Franco-Prussian war, but seems to have settled for a long trip abroad. On her return, when she and Henrietta moved into their London residence, she began her urban explorations.[7]

Maude Stanley began door-to-door visiting in the Five Dials district of St. Anne's, the very poor—but formerly aristocratic—Soho parish where one of her brothers, she says, was a curate.[8] Conventional parish "visiting" is an odd choice for a Stanley woman, and she in fact concedes that being a "district visitor under the sanction of the clergyman of the parish" is indeed "an old-fashioned way." Maude's lifelong low church piety makes sense of this choice, however, along with her pragmatic sense that a Church of England district visitor, more than most others, "can penetrate into houses where none other could enter." Indeed she believed that as a parish visitor "I knew every house."[9]

Stanley was indefatigable: she started evening classes, Sunday schools, country outings, and many other activities for the Five Dials district. Stanley's approach eventually became more secular and social-work oriented. In 1880 she founded what she called the first Club for Working Girls, at 59 Greek Street, Soho, and the welfare of working teenaged girls became her life passion. In the early 1880s she helped to organize the Girls' Club Union, a London umbrella organization that eventually was embraced by more activist women such as those of the Women's Industrial Council. In the early 1900s, she founded a second club in Walworth, in South London. One journalist termed her "Mother of Girls' Clubs," and today she is thought of as an important pioneer in work with youth.[10]

Like so many other genteel slum residents, she became involved in local government and in social policy. Early in the 1870s she began serving as a manager of the Charing Cross Road School, and continued in this role for the next thirty years or more.[11] She was a poor law guardian for St. Anne's Soho; a member of the Metropolitan Asylums Board from 1884 on, and a governor of the Borough Polytechnic after 1892. She also testified before the 1904 Interdepartmental Committee on Physical Deterioration.[12]

When in London, Maude lived with her mother at 40 Dover Street, then at 32 Smith Square, Westminster, near the Houses of Parliament. After her mother's death in 1895, Maude Stanley continued to live on a "comparatively small income," as a friend put it,[13] at the family house—which was being increasingly encroached upon by office buildings. Later in her life, Maude Stanley was a "severe-looking elderly lady" who was known as an unflagging and welcoming hostess and conversationalist, whose guests often included people who "had a share in social movements." She was a devoted aunt to dozens of nieces and nephews.[14]

When Charles Booth's researchers interviewed Stanley in the late 1890s, she was in her mid-fifties and had been at work in Soho for about twenty years. His notes suggest that Stanley doubted that her interviewer—who indeed appears skeptical of philanthropists like her—understood either the district or her work there.[15] The younger male interviewer found her opinionated and domineering. His notes also reveal a telling example of her use of her aristocratic privilege in her social work. When Stanley's sharp dispute with a local Roman Catholic priest angered the latter so much that he threatened to excommunicate any Catholic girl who set foot in Stanley's club, she used family contacts to go over the priest's head: "Miss S. saw the Cardinal," the interview notes read, "and a kind of armed neutrality seems to have prevailed ever since." In this interview Stanley also deplored the "tremendous influx of Jews into Soho" by the late 1890s; their work in the garment trades "makes it harder for the Christian girls to get a living."[16]

Maude Stanley embodies many of the paradoxes of aristocratic slum philanthropists: they were service-givers with claims to expertise and authority based on their social knowledge, both friends and disciplinary agents of their working-class clients, and frequenters of slums—but with contacts in high places. As a club leader, Stanley stressed keeping order and civilizing the uncouth. Yet she traveled abroad with groups of club girls, took pride in showing local mothers the pleasures of a "holiday," and, as long-time acquaintance William Pett Ridge remembered, she repeatedly "took considerable trouble over some friendless girl."[17]

Other than prison terms for their drunken or violent partners, working-class wives and husbands had no way to handle them. The Matrimonial Causes Act of 1878, passed the year Stanley's book was published, permitted magistrates to grant separations to wives with violent husbands, but was not a real solution to the problems Maude Stanley describes in this chapter.

NOTES

1. Sources for this sketch are *The Autobiography of Bertrand Russell 1872–1914* (Boston: Little, Brown, and Company, 1967); Ronald W. Clar, *The Life of Bertrand Russell* (London: Jonathan Cape and Weidenfield and Nicolson, 1975); Philippa Levine, *Feminist Lives in Victorian England: Private Roles and Public Commitment* (Oxford: Basil Blackwell, 1990); Nancy Mitford, *The Stanleys of Alderley, Their Letters between the Years 1851–1865* (London: Chapman and Hall, 1939); *Who Was Who 1897–1916: Lodge's Peerage, Baronetage and Knightage* (London: Kelly's Directories Ltd., 1912); *Debrett's Peerage, Baronetage, Knightage, and Companionage* (London: Dean and Son, Ltd., 1905); Lionel M. Angus-Butterworth, *Old Cheshire Families and Their Seats* (Manchester: Sherratt and Hughes, 1932); Valerie Bonham's entry in the Oxford DNB; and the Stanley genealogy at the front of the Stanley family archive (DSA section) at the Cheshire and Chester Archives and Local Studies Library.
2. Peter de Figueiredo and Julian Freuherz, *Cheshire County Houses* (Chicester, England: Phillimore and Co., 1988), 20; Virginia Surtees, *The Artist and the Aristocrat: George and Rosalind Howard: Earl and Countess of Carlisle* (Salisbury, England: Michael Russell Publishing, 1988), 29.
3. Dillon was her surname. The Stanley women have confused a number of historians. Ray Strachey, in *The Cause,* reprint ed. (Port Washington, NY: Kennikat Press, 1969), 148, calls Maude's mother Augusta; Patricia Hollis lists Maude as Lyulph Stanley's aunt rather than his sister (*Ladies Elect: Women in English Local Government, 1865–1914* [Oxford: Clarendon Press, 1987], 231); Philippa Levine, in *Feminist Lives,* has mother and daughter conflated (25).
4. References to Lady Henrietta Stanley's "sharp tongue" and her insisting on "no formality of any kind" were made by coworkers at Girton, which she helped administer for a time in 1872. See Barbara Stephen, *Emily Davies and Girton College* (London: Constable, 1927), 269. Construction on the chapel began the day of her death. For Henrietta M. Stanley's views on Girton, see her article, "Personal Recollections of Women's Education," in *The Nineteenth Century* 6 (1879): 308–21. On Henrietta's other contributions to Girton, see Barbara Stephen, *Girton College 1869–1932* (Cambridge: Cambridge University Press, 1933). None of Lady Stanley's daughters attended Girton College.
5. Kate Amberley, who, with her husband, died very young, was ten years Maude's junior. Kate was Bertrand Russell's mother. In his autobiography he remembers his Aunt Maude as a stern and gloomy individual (*Autobiography of Bertrand Russell,* 32).
6. Mitford, *Stanleys of Alderley,* 353–54; Letter from Kate Amberley to Maude Stanley, November 24, 1864, in Cheshire and Chester Archives and Local Studies Library, DSA 175/1 (1860–65).
7. This family crisis is partially revealed in a group of letters to Maude Stanley from her mother in 1869–70 (DSA 173). Henrietta was "so shattered" by news of the marriage; "my heart has nearly stopped," she wrote to Maude (August 18, 1869). Henrietta was glad that her husband had died without learning of his son's dishonorable marriage (August 19). She and Maude discuss cutting their expenses and Henrietta writes (November 6, 1869) bitterly of all of the "estates" that "will come into Henry's hands."
8. Her parish work began in the early 1870s, according to her testimony before the Inter-

departmental Committee on Physical Deterioration, *Parliamentary Papers* 1904, vol. 32, Cmd. 2175, Qq. 13367–68. Also see [Maude A. Stanley], *Work about the Five Dials* (London: Macmillan, 1878), 3, 5. Five Dials, near the better known Seven Dials, would soon be obliterated by new road construction in Soho.

9. *Work about the Five Dials,* 3, 5; Interdepartmental Committee on Physical Deterioration, Q. 13368. See also her letter to the *Charity Organisation Review* no. 83 (November 1891), 408.

10. Mrs. Hirst Alexander, "Working Girls' Clubs in London," *The Temple Magazine* 4, no. 1 (October 1896–September 1897), 1056; "Maude Stanley."

11. Interdepartmental Committee on Physical Deterioration, Q. 11394.

12. Ibid., 11367–86.

13. Her wealth at her death was more than thirty-five thousand pounds, according to Valerie Bonham's entry in the Oxford DNB, so it was probably her own choice to live modestly.

14. But she insisted on their arriving punctually. William Pett Ridge, *I Like to Remember* (London: Hodder and Stoughton, n.d.), 18, 250–51; Mrs. Belloc Lowndes, *The Merry Wives of Westminster* (London: Macmillan, 1946), 38–39.

15. After reading all of the Booth secretaries' Soho interviews, Judith Walkowitz concluded that they were quite skeptical in general about people like Stanley (personal communication, January 20, 2003).

16. For the Religious Influences series, Charles Booth's staff, according to Rosemary O'Day, consisted of Ernest Aves, George Arkell, George Duckworth, Jesse Argyll, and Arthur Baxter. See her "Interviews and Investigations: Charles Booth and the Making of the Religious Influences Survey," in *Retrieved Riches: Social Investigation in Britain 1840–1914,* ed. David Englander and Rosemary O'Day (Aldershot, England: Ashgate, 1998), 143–59. The interview with Stanley is not signed. Interview with honorable Maude A. Stanley, Smith Square, Westminster, July 12, [1898], Charles Booth Papers microfilms B240, reel 67, 122–35. Thanks to Judy Walkowitz for pointing out this interview.

17. Booth Papers interview; Pett Ridge, *I Like to Remember,* 251.

FURTHER READING

For more writing by Maude Alethea Stanley, see "West-End Improvements," *The Nineteenth Century* 9 (May 1881): 849–55, and *Clubs for Working Girls* (London: Macmillan, 1890; rev. ed., London: G. Richards, 1904). There were several more editions of the latter book; more recently it was reprinted in *Studies in Social Education* vol. 1, *1860–1890,* ed. Frank Booton (Hove, England: Benfield Press, 1985). Substantial excerpts from both of Stanley's books may be found online at the Informal Education Archives, www.infed.org.archives/etexts/stanley.

Note 1 in this chapter lists additional references on Maude, Henrietta, Maria, and the other Stanleys. See also Brian Heeney, *The Women's Movement in the Church of England 1850–1930* (Oxford: The Clarendon Press, 1988); William McGregor, *Making Men: The History of Boys' Clubs and Related Movements in Great Britain* (London: University of London Press, 1953), esp. 66–68 and 348–50; Mark K. Smith, *Developing Youth Work* (Milton Keynes, England: Open University Press, 1988); and Smith's entry "Maude Stanley" online at the Informal Education Archives, www.infed.org/thinkers/stanley.htm.

Drunkenness

All who visit the poor will know how many of their misfortunes are caused by drunkenness. Most of the cases brought before the magistrate arise from this vice, and much of the sickness of the children is caused by the intemperance of the parents. A great deal is being done to counteract this evil, and when we see coffee-houses rivalling the attraction of the public-houses there will be some chance of increased sobriety. There are already established in the neighbourhood of the Five Dials many coffee and eating-houses, one or two in most streets; but they are small houses, having perhaps their regular customers, but not showing a brilliant front like the Rose and the Crown which has been lately established in Knightsbridge, and which gives a feeling of brightness and conviviality inside, a worthy rival of the gin-palace. When coffee-palaces and taverns, not coffee-houses, are widely established, the working man will greatly make use of them, and there will be fewer saddened homes.

Although but few drunken persons are met with in the street, there is a vast amount of drinking and crime following close upon it. But as I have come home after ten o'clock in the evening from the night school, I have rarely met a drunken man or woman. There will be occasional outbursts of drunkenness in the houses, when the quarrelling will awake and disturb all the neighbours. In one house where I visit, a drunken man threw his wife out of the second floor window, an incident which seems merely sensational when introduced into Mr. Jenkins's book on drunkenness, *The Devil's Chain,* but which is nevertheless strictly true. Therefore, though the passer-by may meet but few drunkards, the district visitor will know numerous cases where, the father or the mother being given over to this habit, are bringing about such misery as is painful to dwell upon. In a few cases I have been able to rescue a boy or a girl from the wickedness entailed on them by their parents.

In general, the most desperate outbreaks will be after the Bank Holidays, when large numbers of respectable working people go with their children to spend the day in the country, the lowest taking their enjoyment in the public house. But I am glad to say that the police tell us that there has been less drinking this Christmas than in former years. Let us hope this is the beginning of better times. In three homes that I have visited I have often found the father in the middle of the day lying drunk in bed; yet out of each of these homes has a girl been rescued from almost certain ruin.

One was in such a deplorable state that she was taken to the police court as homeless and destitute, and committed to a certified Industrial School.

When she appeared before the magistrate she was in rags, without shoes or stockings; unable to read or write, her time had been spent literally in the gutter, playing and quarrelling all day, and her only knowledge was that of vice. Libbie is now a tall, nice-looking, bright girl, ready to go to service, having learned all that is needed to make her a good servant; and during the years she has been in the school, she has shown herself uniformly good and tractable.

Once she was allowed, in consequence of an oft-repeated request, to spend a few hours at her home: she had a yearning to see her mother and little brothers and sisters; but the disappointment of that visit was very bitter. Her mother was told the day she was to expect her, and when Libbie came, seemed glad to see her and proud of her improved appearance; but the child's feeling of horror at the filth and misery she saw was great. When she was called for by the friend who took charge of her for this visit, she was found standing alone in the street. Her mother had wearied of the two hours her child had had to stop with her, and was gone away to some friend or public-house, leaving Libbie in the house, which was such a mass of dirt that she feared to sit down. Her little brother and sister were playing barefooted in the gutter, and when she came away with her friend, the poor child burst into tears at the thought of such misery.

In this case, as in the next two, the only chance of saving the girl was a complete separation from such homes. The second was taken from almost as bad a home. Mary Lamb was fifteen, and seemed anxious to do well; so by providing her with clothes, the cost of which she repaid, a small place was got for her with a good mistress. This she kept for two years, leaving it for the foolish reason servants often give of wanting a change. However, I got her another one at Stepney, where she is still living, coming up on the August Bank Holiday to a party I have in the country on that day.

Finding a good place for a girl is the best thing a district visitor can do for her. It involves little expense, as the clothes needed by her can, with advantage to herself, be easily repaid out of her wages. It will cost the visitor trouble and time, but it is worth it, and can be done by answering advertisements or by inquiring at registry offices. The interest shown by a lady in a girl will sometimes induce a good mistress to engage her.

Almost all the young women who may be found in the lying-in wards of workhouses are servant-girls, and from them you can learn the danger of service under a bad or indifferent mistress. Jenny Ash had suffered more from the drunkenness of her father than the two last-mentioned girls, and it was months and years before she could be said to be safely landed in a respectable life. The first time I saw her was in her father's room. The mother, whom I had called on, was out, and the girl, who was in service at a public-house close by, had run across, as she often did, to see her mother. I knew she had had a child a few months back that had died. I spoke to her of herself, and she soon began to tell me how miserable she was, and how she longed to get right away, saying she knew she could never keep straight among all her bad companions. I promised to help her, and appointed to meet her there the next day. I came, but Jenny never appeared; and I heard after from the mother that her wages had been raised when her mistress heard she would leave, and Jenny had not had the courage to meet me again.

The cause of Jenny's first trouble was the drunken habits of her father. He could as a coach-builder earn £2 or more a week; but on Saturday he would generally, on leaving work, go to the public-house, drinking away a large part of his wages, till he was turned out; then he would stagger home and become violent; and often has Jenny been turned into the street by her brutal father, not knowing where to spend the night.

I often thought of her after this unsuccessful attempt to save Jenny, but saw nothing of her till, some months after, the mother met me in the street, and asked me to find her poor girl and rescue her from the misery she was in. I went back with Mrs. Ash and heard her story, which was, that Jenny had left her place and had come home; but her father would not allow her to remain, because he said she had misconducted herself, and the poor girl for weeks had slept on staircases or elsewhere. The mother said she had been able sometimes secretly to give her food, and she would show me where I might find her. I followed Mrs. Ash, who pointed out to me a small sweet-shop. I may say, by the way, that this sweet shop is kept by a poor Irish widow, who informed her visitor one day that she had five sisters, all married in Ireland to the nobility. This poor widow had shown much kindness to Jenny during the past weeks.

I went into her shop and said, "I think Jenny Ash is here: will you tell her I should like to see her?" The widow dived into a very dark back room, and after a few minutes Jenny emerged. I told her I had heard of the trouble she was in, and had come to repeat my offer to take her to another home, where she could begin a new life. After a little persuasion she said she would come with me; and would I wait till she had "tidied" herself. She could only improve her appearance by soap and water, for her clothes were worn and scanty. I came back in ten minutes, and bade her follow me. We soon got into a cab and drove to Lambeth. There I took her to a Home, where Mrs. Williams, the matron, is a loving, motherly woman.

I took the girl in with me, and said, "I have brought you Jenny, Mrs. Williams, whom we have been so long looking for; you will be glad to see her." Mrs. Williams took her by the hand and said, "My dear child, I am so glad you have come to me; I will take you downstairs to the others, and you shall help to get the dinner ready."

I need not say that Mrs. Williams won Jenny's heart, and put into her an ardent desire to become good. She stayed here some weeks, and then went to a Home at Streatham. I often had letters from Jenny, telling me how she was learning to wash, trying to correct her bad temper, and how much she longed to see me. After she had been there a year I went down to see her, and found her looking pretty well, and happy. But somehow my visit seemed to have unsettled her. Why I cannot tell, except that perhaps the fact of her being visited by a lady had caused the others to be jealous, and unkind to her. Anyhow, a month or two later I heard she had left, and the next news I had of her was that she was in a situation, unfortunately not a good one.

I saw her once or twice by sending word by her mother, where she should meet me; but I feared for the future, and indeed after a while her mother told me she had left her place, and was living with the father of her first child, and was expecting another. I then sent for Jenny again, and when she came, I almost persuaded her to leave the young man she was with if he would not marry her, and promised that I would then see to her. She said she must think about it, and would bring me her answer in a week. When she did come they were no longer living together, for he was in prison. There had been a "fight" in the street, he had rushed into the fray, she said, to save a woman. The police had come, and he was locked up.

Now the complication was great. I knew that if Jenny was not married before her child was born, she would probably never be married, and have nothing but a downward course of ruin. So I proposed to her to get the banns published and that she should tell him of it when she went to meet him, as he had asked her to do, when his sentence would be finished. She had shown me a letter from him from prison, calling her his wife, and using many tender expressions of love for her, and anxiety as to how she would get on without him. The banns were published, and she was soon at the prison door. She was married the following Sunday just in time, and never let her husband know what part I had had in giving her this advice, or in furnishing her with money for the marriage fees. I have seen her since, and she is making a good wife, and keeps a tidy home.

Sometimes the law will step in and rescue the wife from the ill-treatment she has often to endure from her lord and master. But it does not make the home a very cheerful one, when the husband returns from his imprisonment to the wife, who has been the cause of it. A woman was telling me last summer how she dreaded the return of her husband at Christmas, who had been shut up for brutally ill-using her, and how much better she could get on without him. Another woman I knew whose husband was sentenced for three months on her account. Having probably felt remorse for the punishment she had got for him, she celebrated his return by a good drink at the public-house; but on getting home they fell to fighting, and the husband inflicted injuries on his wife of so severe a nature, that he was now sentenced to the longest term of imprisonment possible, ten years. Fortunately she is now dead [Stanley means here that she is now free of such misery], so that the next return will not be commemorated in like fashion.

Some women bear with much ill-treatment without any complaint, and for the sake of their children will endure a great deal. Mrs. Dunn was a small, delicate woman with four children. I had known her for two or three years, and she had often told me her troubles, more inclined to do so from the great influence a few kind words had had upon her, words that were spoken to her by a lady when she was a girl. She had a stepmother who was very unkind to her, and she went early to service. In one place where she was the scrub of a lodging-house, one of the lodgers, a lady, used to notice her, and now and again say a kind word to her, and tell her to be a good girl. Sarah left this place, but never forgot the words of kindness. They were the only ones she had ever heard. She was once in great extremity, and these words were as a talisman protecting her from evil.

She had been living at home at the time she was sixteen. Her father was lately dead. The stepmother took some pretext to quarrel with her, turned her into the street, and said she might find her own home. It was late in the evening, too late Sarah felt, to seek her friend whom she was sure would help her. So utterly disconsolate she wandered about the streets till she met a girl whom she knew. On hearing her story, the girl begged Sarah to come and live with her, and offered her amusements and pleasures without end. Sarah, with no prospect of any rest for the night, but remembering the friend she would seek in the morning, fled from her temptress. An inspiration led her to a workhouse, and knocking at those forbidding doors, they were opened to her, and there she found a safe refuge.

Much courage it must have needed for one so young who had never been inside that house, so dreaded by the respectable poor, or known any one else who had done so, yet to seek admittance there for herself. The next morning she left the workhouse, saw the lady, who believed her story, and found her a place which she kept till her marriage. This, and much besides of her life, she told me after the event I am going to speak of.

I was at home one afternoon when Mrs. Dunn was announced. She said, "I hope you will forgive my coming, but I want very particularly to speak to you." Her husband, she told me, had come home that afternoon, had accused her of misconduct, and had beaten and kicked her, and finally driven her out of the house. She had made no noise for the sake of her children, and came to me, as years before she had sought her other friend.

I felt sure the husband's jealousy was the result of his own imagination, caused partly, as I afterwards found, by a touch of madness. I took Mrs. Dunn first to the clergyman of the parish to ask his advice, and we got her taken into that kind shelter, the House of Charity, and we bade her stay there till her husband would have her back. Both the clergyman and I went next day to the husband, told him where his wife was, what we had done for her, and begged him to fetch her back, which after three days he did. The part that both the clergyman and myself took in the business was evidently pleasing to Dunn by the presents he gave us. To me he sent by his wife a box with my initials carved upon it, with a message, saying that he sent it as a remembrance of the way in which I had befriended his wife.

The instances I have hitherto given have reference to the drunkenness of men only; there are also many, though not so many, drunken women. Some I have helped for a long time, not knowing that they were given to drink; but once I have found out by some outbreak that this was an old established vice, though perhaps only of occasional occurrence, I have ceased to help them; for unless there are means of removing such women to quite a new neighbourhood, there is no chance of reformation.

The most desperate and hopeless case of a drunken woman that I have come in contact with was that of Mrs. Joiner. I have never seen her, but some months back I got a letter saying that the writer knew I was always ready to help any girls, and so he wrote to ask me to come and see after his Mary, and that if I asked Mr. Otter, he would know all about the undersigned, "Joiner." There was no address in the letter.

It was a fortnight after I got this letter, being in the country at the time, before I could call on Mr. Otter, a seller of cat's meat whom I knew. He said, Yes, he knew Joiner, a steady, hard-working man, with a desperate wife, always drunk, and now in prison. They had lived in his street; but where he now was Otter could not say; however, Joiner's boy often came for cat's meat, and if I waited I might see him.

I waited a while, and the boy came; and I made him lead me to his home. In a third-floor back room, in a wretched house, I found a girl of seventeen sitting by the fire in ragged clothes, and a young woman with two children. I learned that this was the home of Joiner's son, and that these were his children. He and his father were wood-carvers, and worked together in Wardour Street.

The brother had taken into his room his two sisters and his little brother, whilst the mother was for the eighth time sent to prison, coming out, as the young woman told me, each time worse and more depraved. The longest stay she had made there was eight months, after having in semi-drunkenness held her child to the fire till its toes were roasted off. The poor child is now dead; but there are three children still left—a very pretty girl of twelve, one of seventeen, and a boy. The girl, whom I found in wretched clothing, told me that the good clothes she had on coming home from service had been taken from her by her mother, who had sold them for drink, and now the want of clothes kept her at home.

I left word that he, Joiner, should come and speak to me the next evening at the night-school. He then told me that, having received no answer for so many days to the letter he had sent to me, his brother-in-law, who was in a good position on the railway, had undertaken to send the girl of twelve years old to Suffolk, to a relation, as he was anxious that she should have left London before her mother came out of prison at Christmas. I said to him, "How kind your son's wife has been in taking in your children." "Ah," he said, "she is kind, but they are not married." When I asked him if he had never tried to persuade his son to marry, he said, "Yes, a time or two I have told him of it before the other workmen, but he has taken no notice." On further conversation on this subject I found he would be glad if they were married, so I promised to try what I could do. I found that the chief reason of their not being married was the expense of the marriage fees. Young Joiner was willing enough, but they could not get together the necessary ten shillings. I made the circumstances known to the clergyman of the parish, and they are now married. Joiner seemed, as one may imagine, bewildered by the certain prospect of misery before him, his one wish being to get his children away in safe hands, as whenever his wife is out of prison he must have her to live with him. It may well be said that drunkenness is the chief cause of the misery of the poor. This vice is produced by many evils, and of these overcrowding and want of education are the chief; but of them we will speak in another chapter.

Dorothy Tennant (Lady Stanley)

DOROTHY TENNANT (LADY STANLEY; 1855–1926) was a successful print-maker and portrait and genre painter. She specialized in sympathetically depicting children, especially poor and ragged ones, but her portrait of French President Leon Gambetta was bought by U.S. newspaper magnate Joseph Pulitzer for his own collection. She studied art in the 1870s with Edward Poynter at the Slade School, and with other renowned artists in London and in Paris. Her work was exhibited at the Grosvenor Gallery in London, the Walker Art Gallery in Liverpool, the Manchester City Art Gallery, the Royal Academy, and the Salon de Paris, among other galleries. Tennant was one of just a few controversial women art school graduates to paint nudes and exhibit them in prominent galleries. In the early 1880s, as Tennant later told an interviewer, she felt "great pride" in being able to enlarge her art studio "entirely with my own earnings," though she claimed that she still could not afford to heat it.[1]

She was the daughter of wealthy Glamorganshire landowner and some-time M.P. Charles Tennant, and of Gertrude Tennant, a prominent London hostess famous for the lavish scale of her entertaining and her friendships with prominent artists. Until Dorothy married, when she was in her mid-thirties, she shared a room with her mother in their opulent family home in Whitehall—to which ragged children were occasionally brought by her

---

Text originally published as the introduction to London Street Arabs *(London: Cassell and Company [now a division of The Orion Publishing Group], 1890), 5–12. The illustrations are also from* London Street Arabs, *where Tennant gathered pictures she had published earlier in various periodicals. All attempts to trace the copyright holder of* London Street Arabs *were unsuccessful.*

Figure 8. Ragged street boys, from Dorothy Tennant, *London Street Arabs*. The boy posing as the hungry street musician in the image on the right is also the model for the figure in Tennant's striking oil painting *His First Offense*. The vaguely menacing figure behind him is not a gentleman, to judge by his posture and rumpled jacket.

servants to sit as models. Her enormous privilege and apparently somewhat coy manner notwithstanding, Tennant felt sympathy and affection toward the street children she drew. If she had been able to run for Parliament, she said, she would have been "Procurator of the Poor." Yet she often seems oblivious of their actual poverty and objectifies them, referring, in the present selection, to her raggedy subject as "a very fine specimen."[2]

In 1885, at one of her mother's dinners, she met the American-born journalist Henry Morton Stanley, the African explorer now notorious for the ruthlessness and cruelty with which he treated his African staff during his Congo explorations, as well as for the part he played in the creation of the still more infamous Congo Free State. The two became better acquainted while Tennant painted Stanley's portrait. Stanley, not surprisingly, disliked Dorothy's "enthusiasm for the proletariat." In 1890 they married in a lavish Westminster Abbey wedding, with large crowds of spectators outside.

Figure 9. Children and a hurdy-gurdy, from Dorothy Tennant, *London Street Arabs*. Children dancing to street musicians was a popular subject of literature, art, and photography. Renowned French graphic artist Gustave Doré depicted a similar scene in *London: A Pilgrimage* (London: Grant and Co., 1872). It would have been familiar to Tennant. The latter's children are livelier than Doré's prototype, where the girls, carrying their baby siblings, are hampered in their movements. The exotic-looking musician, and the children's shabby finery and lively movement, give this image an air of carnival.

Figure 10. From *London Street Arabs*. Renderings of homeless adults or children huddled against a wall for shelter were conventional. The pathos of this image is intensified by the children's beauty and the boy's protective wakefulness as the girl, presumably his sister, sleeps. In general, illustrations in wide-circulation periodicals where Tennant's sketches were originally published were more sentimental than works of high art for cognoscenti. Child-rescue organizations drew heavily on images like this one.

The wedding guests included many London schoolchildren and child street sellers.[3] Dorothy continued to work, however, under her professional name. Henry died in 1904, after only thirteen years of married life; Dorothy married Dr. Henry Curtis in 1907.

Seven Dials, near Covent Garden market, a notorious slum in Dorothy Tennant's time, is now a popular shopping area.

NOTES

1. Lawrence, "Artist-Laureate of the Street Arab," 263; Alison Smith, "The 'British Matron' and the Body Beautiful: The Nude Debate of 1885," in *After the Pre-Raphaelites: Art and Aestheticism in Victorian England,* ed. Elizabeth Prettjohn (New Brunswick, NJ: Rutgers University Press, 1999), 225.

2. On her sympathy toward her subjects, see McLynn, *Stanley,* 24; and Lawrence, "Artist Street-Laureate of the Street Arab," 264. Lawrence, writing in the 1890s, assured his readers that this interest was not a matter of fashionable "slumming."

3. The information on Tennant's wedding and married life is from Hird, *H. M. Stanley*, 278–85. Hird, the biographer authorized by Dorothy, dedicated the book to her and quotes her extensively. The detailed account of the wedding in *The Times* (July 14, 1890, 6), does not mention street children among the spectators. It does list heads of state and aristocrats as well as gifts of royal caliber.

FURTHER READING

In addition to *London Street Arabs* (London: Cassell Company, 1890), Dorothy Tennant published *Miss Pim's Camouflage* (Boston and New York: Houghton Mifflin, 1918) and *Ragamuffins: Twenty-four Drawings and Verses* (Boston: Houghton Mifflin), 1929. She also edited *The Autobiography of Sir Henry Morton Stanley* (Boston and New York: Houghton Mifflin, 1909).

There is some information about Tennant in biographies of her husband. See John Bierman, *Dark Safari: The Life behind the Legend of Henry Morton Stanley* (London: Hodder and Stoughton, 1990); Frank Hird, *H. M. Stanley: The Authorized Life* (London: Stanley Paul and Co., 1935); and Frank McLynn, *Stanley: Sorcerer's Apprentice* (London: Hodder and Stoughton, 1990). Also A. H. Lawrence, "The Artist-Laureate of the Street Arab: Miss Dorothy Tennant (Mrs. H. M. Stanley) and her Work," *The Temple Magazine* 2 (October 1897–September 1898): 262–66; Grant M. Waters, *Dictionary of British Artists Working 1900–1950.* (Eastbourne, England: Eastbourne Fine Art, 1975).

∾∾∾

By Way of Introduction

I cannot remember my first ragamuffin drawing. There has always been a strange affinity between me and the London "gamin." Born in London, fond of walking through its streets, parks, and squares, the first interesting object I must have seen was doubtless some dear little child in tatters; and as I loved drawing even more than I loved the ragamuffin, it was quite natural for me to try and "make a picture of him."

My first serious essay was a set of "Scenes in Seven Dials." In my childish imagination Seven Dials meant the home of the ragamuffin, and I entreated in vain to be taken there for my morning walk. I next remember illustrating [the 1839 novel] "Passages from the Life of Jack Sheppard," and resolving in my own mind that when I grew up I should be the champion painter of the poor, and, of course, a very great artist indeed.

Most of the pictures I had seen of ragged life appeared to me false and made up. They were all so deplorably piteous—pale, whining children with sunken eyes, holding up bunches of violets to heedless passers-by; dying match-girls, sorrowful water-cress girls, emaciated mothers clasping weeping babes. How was it, I asked myself, that the other side is so seldom

Figure 11. A trade in progress between a ragged and a well-dressed boy, from *London Street Arabs*. In reality, the poor child would have been much smaller than his well-bred friend.

represented? The merry, reckless, happy-go-lucky urchin; the tom-boy girl; the plump, untidy mother dancing and tossing her ragged baby; who had given this side of London life? Murillo's "Beggar Boys" most nearly approached my ideal—but *where* was the modern Murillo? Surely there is material for the painter in our parks, our streets, our Embankment by the banks of the Thames. Oh! the pictures on Bank Holiday in Battersea Park, or in St. James's Park! The pretty scenes of courting and playing, the girls lying on the grass, the babies tumbling over them, mop-headed boys playing at cricket, the groups at the fountains—every day, every hour, there are pictures worth painting to be seen in or about London. Why go to Venice when we have such pictures at home? Stand in Endell Street and watch the

Figure 12. Children playing blind man's bluff, from Dorothy Tennant, *London Street Arabs*. Without a distracting city street background, the children's graceful and flirtatious movements charm the viewer. Artists from a sixteenth-century French miniaturist to Bruegel, Goya, and Fragonard have depicted this ancient European game.

little fountain not far from the Baths and Workhouse—just too high for the baby; who is just too heavy for the little brother or sister to lift. What an upheaving and struggling before the water trickles over the lips and down the neck—down, over the ragged frock, into the very boots which gape so wide at the ankle! How I wish I could draw them as I see them, as I feel them—but there is such a wide chasm between conceiving and carrying out. No ragamuffin is ever vulgar or common. If the pictures render him so, it is the artist's fault, since he always puts himself into his work. All his vulgarity and affectations go into the drawing, just as simplicity, dignity, and love of truth are to be found in the work if found in the artist.

What everlasting laurels a really great artist might win for himself, merely by painting London! Hogarth loved the ragamuffin and the Londoner, and has told us the story of his day better than any book can tell it. It is not so very difficult, if you are gifted to start with, and are *meant* to be a painter. You must first walk about little back streets and alleys towards sunset; stroll round the lake in St. James's Park, or along the Embankment by the steps leading down to the water. Saturday is the best day, of course. Then look, and look without worrying your mind to remember; take it all in—the movements, the groups, the attitudes—without troubling yourself much as to detail.

Of an evening, sit at a table with a good lamp, pencil and paper, and let your pencil do what it likes. After a while something will take shape, probably a vague recollection of your walks—just like the incoherent jumble of a dream. Then you wake up and begin to compose with a little more method. The boy carries a baby on his back, and stops to talk with a girl driving a heavily-laden old perambulator. A row of urchins sit along the kerb, their feet in the gutter, enjoying the cool mud, so soft and grateful after the hot asphalte pavements.

Picture after picture comes of itself, and if one of the sketches particularly takes your fancy, you rise the next morning with a glowing determination to "set to work" without loss of time. Perhaps the necessary ingredients of your picture are a red-headed boy, and a fair curly-headed boy, a small girl and a big baby, and an old hamper. All these have to be found and brought home. One must not be too exacting about the colour and style of hair and dress, etc. The best thing is to keep your properties in the studio. A good supply of rags is essential (carefully fumigated, camphored, and peppered), and you can then dress up your too respectable ragamuffin till he looks as disreputable as you can wish.

If you have no rags to start with, and shrink from keeping them *by* you, the best way is to find an average boy, win his confidence, give him sixpence, and promise him another sixpence if he will bring you a boy more ragged than himself. This second boy must be invited to do the same, and urged to bring one yet more "raggety." You can in this way get down to a very fine specimen, but the drawback is the loss of time caused by the cajoling, the difficulty of explaining what you want and why you want it, and the great probability of failure after all your expenditure of time, eloquence, and sixpences. It *is* disheartening to find Joey Brown who promises to bring Tommy Gedge—describing him as "raggety all over:" a boy "wot never washes hisself,"—after two hours' waiting, arrive triumphant, dragging reluctant Tommy, shy and overcome by his own magnificence and cleanliness, in a 3s. 6d. suit, stiff sailor hat, face shining with soap and cocoanut oil which drips from his smoothed hair. Joey walks round his friend in the deepest admiration, trying to soothe his envy by remarking that "them sort of boots don't wear," and that "the buttons look well enough at first, but the tops drop off that there kind, only leaving the shanks." Here, if you have by you a good supply of old "cords" (corduroy trousers) and a very ragged shirt, a length of worn or "chewed" string for braces, and an old boot, Tommy can be made to look himself again; he will probably weep, but that helps to make his face dirty, and is therefore to be

Figure 13. Street seller with her children, from Dorothy Tennant, *London Street Arabs*. Tennant's sentimental rendering here is of another standard London street figure and conventional artist's subject: the girl or woman flower seller. Tennant's young woman looks sorrowful and imploring as pedestrians hustle past her on a rainy and chilly day. Her two toddlers—one of them barefooted— are cute, but they are clutching her aggressively, and she appears to be expecting another child.

slightly encouraged. The hair is the chief drawback, but it *can* be worried up into a mop again if vigorously shampooed by his friend. And *there* you have your model quite ready!

But you must remember that Tommy will never reappear after that first sitting unless you can manage not only to soothe his wounded vanity, but also to keep him well amused and to excite pleasurable expectation for the next sitting. On the first day, therefore, very little work is done. You must make Tommy's acquaintance, study "his lines," and "take him in" as well as you can. He will probably fall into attitudes which will serve for future sketches, and which probably will come out in the evening scribbles. The time therefore is not altogether lost, though very little actual work is done. . . .

I could quote many instances of ragamuffin goodwill and ingenuity, but this is not an article or essay I am writing, it is merely an introduction—a "few words"—to accompany these little ragamuffin drawings, so that long anecdotes would be quite out of place. I will say good-bye to the ragamuffin by quoting a few of his definitions, as they give some insight into the mind of the little animal, and show how difficult it is for us to understand them or be understood by them.

I asked a little girl how she would define *love*. Unhesitatingly she replied, "It's going errands."

I asked a boy the meaning of the word *guilt*. "It means telling on another boy."

I asked Harry Sullivan to define a *gentleman*. He replied, not without some fervour, "Oh! a fellow who has a watch and chain."

I suppose he read disapprobation in my face, for he hastily added, "And loves Jesus."

This same boy had a very hazy idea of Old Testament history. He had heard of Adam and Eve—"They stole apples and were turned out of the *gardin,* and then they had to work for their living till the sweat poured down."

A girl of eleven told me how she wished to live in the country, "because then I shouldn't see a lot of people having a lot of things I can't have." . . .

A dear little boy of six told me he loved Christmas Day because on Christmas Eve he hung up his stocking, and the next morning he found a present inside. "What did you find last Christmas?" I inquired. "A half-penny," he said, smiling with pleasure at the recollection, "but," he added truthfully, "I put it in myself over-night." . . .

And now I *will* end, because there seems no reason why I *should* end. The little ragamuffins of my acquaintance have told me many and many a quaint or droll story, but they somehow lose their fun when they are put down in print, just as the grace and charm of the children's attitude are partly lost in the drawings. The pictures that have been gathered together in this volume are illustrations done at different times for different stories which have appeared in *Little Folks, The Quiver,* etc. . . .

Ethel Brilliana
(Mrs. Alec) Tweedie

THE QUEEN WAS A TOP-NOTCH PERIODICAL that published serious articles on literary and social subjects along with accounts of the doings of royalty, the latest fashions, and advertisements for elegant merchandise. Tweedie's piece on the Petticoat Lane Sunday outdoor market is notable both for its somewhat friendly depiction of Jews in the district, many of them Yiddish speakers with whom she communicated easily in German, and for its dense collection of stereotypes. However, it is mainly the story of a shopping outing that celebrates London's movement, excitement, and diversity as the narrator moves about in semidisguise. The market was (and is) in Whitechapel, a district that had recently, in the 1880s and 1890s, been populated by Jews escaping violence and hardship in eastern Europe. Petticoat Lane was famous for its food stalls, its old-clothes sellers, and the fast patter of its vendors.

Tweedie (c. 1862–1940) was the daughter of a prominent London physician, George Harley. Tweedie's mother's inherited wealth allowed the family to live in "luxury." Traveling was a vocation she began in her twenties with a tour of Iceland by steamer and on horseback. Her future husband courted her by following her there unannounced. They married and had two children. But after Alec Tweedie's premature death in 1896, Ethel's writing, formerly a hobby, became her livelihood.

She wrote hundreds of articles for newspapers and magazines, as well as a total of twenty-six books—in addition to editing three more. She was a passionate supporter of women's rights, including the right to ride horses "man-

Originally published as "Petticoat-Lane" in The Queen, The Lady's Newspaper and Court Chronicle *97, April 20, 1895, 674, under the byline Mrs. Alec Tweedie.*

fashion," a point emphasized by the pictures of women riding astride on the frontispiece of her Iceland book. Her many travel books encompassed Scandinavia, Mexico, the United States, Russia, and China. In these accounts Tweedie was prone to denigrate whole peoples whom she encountered, such as southern Italians, Mexican peasants, and the entire population of India—yet she was a critic of some aspects of British imperialism. She appears relatively well informed, if politically conventional.

Tweedie also, as her *Who Was Who* entry relates, was active in "many philanthropic and charitable committees," served on the board of directors of two London hospitals, and received official recognition from the Italian government for the help she offered to victims of the Sicilian earthquake of 1912. She was also a fellow of several learned societies.

Though her work was generally well received, critics commented unfavorably on Tweedie's chatty and flippant style; more recent readers find some of her books "melodramatic" and smacking of "bathos." Her life had its share of sorrow. Her husband lost his fortune and died young; a close friend died at about the same time; one of her sons died in the First World War, and the other a few years later in a plane crash—yet she wrote in the same light-hearted style throughout her career.

NOTES

This account is based on the biographical pieces in the DLB, the Oxford DNB, and *Who Was Who 1929–1940*, as well as on Robinson, *Wayward Women*.

FURTHER READING

For more writing by Ethel Brilliana (Mrs. Alec) Tweedie, see *George Harley, F. R. S., or The Life of a London Physician* (London: Scientific Press, 1899). Her travel writing includes *A Girl's Ride in Iceland* and *The Oberammergau Passion Play* (both 1890), *A Winter Jaunt to Norway* (1894), *Through Finland in Carts* (1897), and *America as I Saw It* (1913). Her autobiographical books include *Thirteen Years of a Busy Woman's Life* (1912), *My Tablecloths: A Few Reminiscences* (1916), *Tight Corners of My Adventurous Life* (1923 and 1933), and *Me and Mine: A Medley of Thoughts and Memories* (1932).

For information about Tweedie, see the entry in the DLB, vol. 174, by Josephine McQuail; Elizabeth Baigent's entry in the Oxford DNB; and *Who Was Who 1929–1940* (London: Adam and Charles Black, 1941). See also Dorothy Middleton, *Victorian Lady Travelers* (1965; reprint, Chicago: Academy Publishers, 1993); Jane Robinson, *Wayward Women: A Guide to Women Travelers* (Oxford: Oxford University Press, 1990), which includes a tart appraisal of Tweedie's work; and Jane Robinson, *Unsuitable for Ladies: An Anthology of Women Travellers* (Oxford: Oxford University Press, 1994).

Petticoat-Lane

There are many strange sights in London little dreamed of by the fashionable world. London is so huge, and its inhabitants so varied, that everything, from filth to spotlessness, from starvation to millionairedom, from imbecility to genius, can be found within its magic circle. One of the strangest sights to a person interested in all sides of life is the Sunday market in Petticoat-lane; it is, indeed, remarkable. Petticoat-lane, it must be remembered, is the haunt of the Jew, and not of the aristocratic member of that persuasion, with his silk hat and well-shaved chin, but his more needy brother, and that funny street luxuriating in the name of Petticoat-lane is one of his greatest haunts. The title is misplaced, for "Trouser-walk" would be much more appropriate. There are but few petticoats to be sold, but there are hundreds of trousers, of every shape, size, and colour, at 3s. 6d. a pair, and less! Garments which originally came from some swell tailor's find their way at last to the Jew's barrow in Petticoat-lane.

Taking a train from Baker-street one Sunday morning about half-past nine, dressed in our oldest and least noticeable black clothes, we went to Aldgate Station, from which point a few minutes' walk brought us to the street whither we were bound. It was still early, for the chief sales take place between eleven and one, so we had time to walk leisurely through the street of barrows, on which every conceivable article was for sale. They contained a wonderful collection; in one was an elaborate oil painting, in a golden frame, depicting a man in the smartest of clothes holding his head in his hand, beneath which was written, "Moses, the head of the tailors." On his barrow were stacks of trousers, frock coats, round coats, corduroy breeches, &c., and at the moment we passed he was busy completing a bargain with a woman for a pair of really nice looking shooting knickerbockers for 8d.

"How on earth do they get hold of such good clothes as that and sell them so cheaply?" we asked a friend.

"In this way," he replied. "When I was a young man studying at a crammer's [school] an old Jew, commonly known as 'Old Clo',' used to come round once a month and persuade us youngsters to sell our worn-out clothes. I am sorry to say," he added with a laugh, "when we were hard up, a good many clothes were parted with that our fond Mammas would hardly have called 'worn out;' but into 'Old Clo's' blue bag they were bun-

Figure 14. Middlesex Street (Petticoat Lane), c. 1900. The photo was probably taken on a Sunday morning, when most of the women in the district were preparing the Sunday dinner. Thus the market is packed with men. The Jewish merchants and street sellers of Whitechapel, where the market is located, were quite willing to work on Sundays. Reprinted with the permission of the City of London, London Metropolitan Archives.

dled, and a shilling or two from his grimy fingers found their way into our pockets."

Here was a revelation, but it accounted for many of the articles which we saw exposed in Petticoat-lane. New boots fetched about 2s. 6d. a pair, but old ones, at 4d. or 6d., seemed to find more ready purchasers. Another stall was devoted to eatables. Enormous gherkins, in tubs of salt and water, were apparently tempting morsels; a little girl bought one for 1d., and proceeded down the street munching the luscious morsel. Dutch herrings in tubs were in demand, while French almonds, "twenty-five a penny," sold well. The people purchased pounds of "bits of apple"—that is to say, apples from which the bad pieces had been cut away; Jewish cakes, including the thin Passover cake; enormous brown or white loaves of bread attracted crowds, while the refreshment stalls themselves were quite a feature. A penny seemed the current coin, and little plates of whelks or mussels were sold for 1d., or, again, a large onion standing in vinegar, or a hot dish of dried peas and cabbage, or stewed eels in jelly. A cup of coffee and a piece of cake were also 1d.; indeed, it was quite remarkable the large amount that copper coin would procure. The "very best medicine" was sold for 1d. a glass. One large placard contained the following: "Genuine Dutch drops. Cures every known disease. Penny a glass." Immediately under which followed a list of all the most horrible diseases for which it was efficacious. "J. Elboz" adorned another barrow, his chief ware being "Quinine nerve tonic, a most invigorating beverage. One penny a glass."

Everybody, to our surprise, seemed to be talking German, and, accosting a friendly faced old man in that language, we asked him if he came from "der Vaterland?" "No," he replied in German, but with a curious accent; "I am talking the Jewish language, Jeddish or Kosher; but it is so like German we can understand, or be understood by, people from the Fatherland." And he was right. Although many of his words were different, and his pronunciation was hardly "hoch Deutsch," it was quite easy to converse with the gentleman.

As we passed down Middlesex-street and along Wentworth-street, or into the intricacies of Bell-lane, we found to our delight we could converse freely with the ladies and gentlemen of the Hebrew persuasion, although we could not read the inscriptions over the doors of many of the houses, the names being written in Hebrew. On several of the stalls Hebrew books were for sale, chiefly relating to the Passover. Another very Jewish custom was retailed at the butcher's, where the meat, it was notified, "was killed according to Jewish rites." Numbers of the women of course wore wigs, for these, like the strict Jewish women in Morocco, shave their heads when they get married and don a perruque. Those wigs were wonderful; always black or brown, parted down the middle, and well plastered down on each side in a manner which, to say the least, was not becoming. The unmarried girls, as if to show their independence, had cut their hair into deep fringes [bangs], which they either wore in paper or else standing straight up on end! Corsets were a very favourite article for sale, and yet, judging by the figures of the Jewesses about, none of them indulged in their kindly support.

It was very strange to note the craving for Oriental splendour in the bright colours displayed. Besides the gaudy flowers, which were being manufactured into bonnets by the women of the millinery stall between the visits of her customers, bright woollen shawls, in red or yellow, green or blue, abounded, while Turkey red and gorgeous chintz of vivid hues were everywhere noticeable. Not only in the display of bright colours was this Oriental trait visible, but in the people themselves. There was hardly a face among that vast crowd that looked English; black eyes, and blacker hair, olive skins, and generally Southern colouring, vouched for their ancient origin. Some of the younger women were strikingly handsome, more especially the children, but the fatness and coarseness of the older dames was appalling; while the enormous noses and cunning look of many of the men left no doubt as to their religious belief. They were in many cases the poorest of the poor, yet they were orderly and even deferential as we passed, answering our questions politely, and rather pleased than otherwise, at our interest in their wares. No one was drunk or rude and we only saw one fight between an awful woman and a still more awful man, the subject of discussion apparently being a halfpenny. We made several purchases. Yes, kind reader, you may stare, but there are many nice things to be bought in Petticoat-lane, and bought for very little because—softly be it spoken—they are probably stolen goods. Rows and rows of opera glasses were for sale, beautiful opera glasses in handsome cases. How did they come there, unless brought by some light fingered gentleman from a race meeting?

Our attention was suddenly attracted by a tremendous noise, and, turning to see from whence it emanated, we discovered the auctions had begun. There on the step of a barrow, in a dress profusely covered in big check, a red woollen shawl bound across her chest, and a wondrous bonnet of flowers and feathers, stood a stout Jewess; in her hand was a large pudding basin, which she was banging with a stick to show it was not cracked, and in Jeddish she was inviting bids and extolling the virtues of her wares, and ultimately sold her basin for that magic penny. Jugs, mugs, pots, and pans were quickly got rid of by this enthusiastic lady, whose shrill voice and general deportment were quite worth a visit to the East-end to see. Next door to her, as if trying to outvie the noise she was making, a young man, in cockney English, was disposing of bars of soap; white soap, yellow soap, and very dark brown soap were all going from 1d. to 1½d. a pound.

Beyond him was a sweetmeat man, whom we heard for at least an hour calling out "Four ounces a penny! four ounces a penny," only pausing to pack the selected cherry drops or brandy balls into a yellow paper parcel for the purchaser.

Yes, Petticoat-lane on Sunday morning is intensely interesting. It is a peep into another phase of life. Cunning and craft are visible side by side with kind-hearted charity; vice elbows virtue; hideousness hustles beauty; but so it is through life. Middlesex-street is but a peep into a phase of existence the ordinary well-to-do person of the West-end dreams not of; and yet these people, with their own tongue, their own religion, their own manners, and their own customs, are a living, breathing part of this great metropolis. The old houses are rapidly tumbling down or being pulled down; more sanitary and less picturesque buildings are taking their place; each year finds the inhabitants more civilised, according to what polite society calls civilisation, but yet much of the ancient Jew and the Jewish ways remains amongst us in the little frequented districts.

23

Kate Warburton

BORN KATHERINE ANNE EGERTON WARBURTON, "Mother Kate" (1840–1923), as she was known for her entire adult life, became an Anglican nun in her teens.[1] She was a Church of England priest's daughter from "an ancient Cheshire family."[2] Like many clerical children, Kate spent a lot of time outdoors with her horses and dogs so that the house would be quiet for her father's work.[3] Her father, who died when she was nine, was keenly interested in the Oxford movement and brought his children up with "high church views," including reverence for religious orders—viewed with far less sympathy by other branches of Protestantism. Kate Warburton and her brothers were also fascinated by reports of the work of missionaries in the London dock area, who seemed like "medieval saints."[4]

Warburton was only eighteen when she was received as a novice by the Sisters of St. Margaret's, East Grinstead (1858), and soon began her career as a nun.[5] The East Grinstead order was an active one that focused its work on the poor, orphans, and the sick. The first neighborhood to which Warburton was sent was the London parish of Saint Mary's, Crown Street, in the poverty-stricken Five Dials district of Soho, which Maude Stanley describes in this volume (chapter 20). In 1865 she was transferred to Haggerston, in East London, where she joined a small group of nuns attached to Saint Augustine's Church who carried out a wide range of social and religious services in the area. They ran an orphanage, nursed the sick (the 1866 cholera epidemic helped them to earn credibility in the district), and offered children's after-school classes. The services they offered helped overcome the

"An Epiphany Pilgrimage: The Story of a Boys' Tea at S. Saviour's Walthamstow" originally *appeared in* Old Soho Days and Other Memories *(London: A. R. Mowbray, 1906), 116–22.*

local population's distrust of their elaborate and very nun-like habit.[6] In the 1870s there were twenty-two sisters living in four ordinary buildings in the area, though eventually a priory was erected. Mother Kate, who remained in Haggerston for the rest of her life, was deeply involved in the material struggles of the parish and in Haggerston community life, serving for many years as a school manager.

Warburton enjoyed depicting "her" poor children and adults, mainly in religious publications, and she also wrote about church affairs and festivals. She also published two books of memoirs, one of which is the origin of the selection included here.

Epiphany, or Three Kings' Day, January 6, is the last of the traditional twelve days of Christmas. It is sometimes celebrated with a feast. Walthamstow, where the "feast" in this account took place, was a new industrial suburb on London's eastern edge.

NOTES

1. The biographical details on Warburton are based mainly on her *Memories of a Sister of S. Saviour's Priory,* 1, 2, 27, and from newspaper clippings filed under Warburton's name at the Hackney Archives Department, particularly "A Visit to St. Saviour's Priory," *The Monthly Placket* 18 (1875), 568–70; and Rev. Sydney W. Hart, "Mother Kate," *Hackney Gazette* (n.d.).
2. Quoting Peter G. Cobb's entry in the Oxford DNB.
3. Children of clergymen often developed outdoor skills for this reason. Midori Yamaguchi, "'Unselfish' Desires: Daughters of the Anglican Clergy, 1830–1914." Ph.D. diss., Department of Sociology, University of Essex, 2001, 58.
4. *Memories of a Sister,* 7.
5. More than ten thousand women, mainly daughters of clergy or wealthy gentry, had tried the life of a Church of England nun by the end of the nineteenth century. Just about all of them offered service to the poor rather than joining the contemplative orders. See Susan Mumm, ed., *All Saints Sisters of the Poor: An Anglican Sisterhood in the Nineteenth Century* (Woodbridge, England: Boydell Press, Church of England Record Society, 2001), xii.
6. "A Visit to St. Saviour's Priory," 568.

FURTHER READING

For more writing by Kate Warburton, see *Old Soho Days and Other Memories* (London: Mowbray and Co., 1906) and *Memories of a Sister of S. Saviour's Priory* (London: Mowbray and Co., 1903).

Entries on Warburton and St. Saviour's are in Charles Booth's *Life and Labour of the People in London,* 3rd series, vol. 2 89–92 (1902). See also Susan Munn, *Stolen Daughters, Virgin Mothers: Anglican Sisterhoods in Victorian Britain* (London: Leicester University Press, 1985); Martha Vicinus, *Independent Women: Work and Community for Single Women 1850–1920* (Chicago: University of Chicago Press, 1985), esp. chap. 2, on sisterhoods and deaconesses.

An Epiphany Pilgrimage

An Epiphany pilgrimage, from Haggerston to Walthamstow! On a dark, cold night, on the 7th of January, 1896, my friend and I hurried across London Fields to the G.E. Railway Station, whose crimson, green, and yellow lights flashed out in the distance against the black, opaque foreground. "Train just due—hurry up!" said the ticket clerk, and we rushed along miles of passage and staircase, to find ourselves hot and breathless on the dimly-lighted platform, while at least four trains passed before ours puffed slowly up, chock-full of passengers from the city. Room for two was found, where we wedged ourselves in, and a boy who followed us leant against the steaming window. Not a long journey—Hackney Downs, Clapton, and then S. James Street. One of the Sisters met us and piloted us along flaring, noisy, busy S. James Street, then suddenly turned up sundry dark, narrow lanes and backways, which, she said, led to S. Alban's Hall, but in which—if by good luck we had ever found them—we should have been most certainly lost but for her kind guidance. "What a place to get your throat cut on a dark night!" said one of us. "Yes, is it not?" she said. "I was here one night when I found two women fighting, and tried to stop them, and the husbands came up, and each, of course, accused the other's wife of being the cause of the quarrel; but here we are," as we emerged from the dark lane into a wider space, where a large building confronted us. She knocked with her knuckles, and we knocked with sticks and umbrellas, and a few boys listening outside tendered sundry information and advice, and at last the door opened, and we were ushered upon a scene of great festivity, the din of which had fairly drowned our piteous appeals for admission.

The room was large and square and bright, and highly decorated with festoons and wreaths of green, and hung with bright pictures of Scotsmen in philibegs [kilts], which much pleased my friend, who is a Highlander. The company assembled at tea was the most lovely assemblage of roughs you can imagine. Lads of all ages, from twelve or fourteen up to two or three and twenty—for the most part costers, or bricklayers and labourers, apparently—in mud-encrusted hobnails, striped jerseys, and rough brown working clothes. A large proportion had their heads polled [shorn], except for a thick forelock which hung over the forehead, which style of headdress, I believe, is very suitable for boxing. These guests were seated at large tables, very cheery, very comfortable, and very gracious, being waited upon by the Rev. C. Maitland, at that time Vicar of S. Saviour's, and his wife, assisted by two other clergy, the two Sisters, and some of the Church workers. Mr. Ware, one of the Priory "old boys," who lived at Walthamstow, acted as generalissimo of the forces, and marched up and down and round about, very stalwart, very strong and determined, much respected, and somewhat feared. What the Sisters would do without his kindly aid every night in the management of these boys we do not really know. Mrs. Ware, also a native of Haggerston and a member of the Guild of S. Michael and All Angels, was assisting with all her might to dispense the food. They all looked comfortable and well filled, and indeed we do not wonder, for we heard they had been busy the last three-quarters of an hour steadily working their way through sausage rolls, bread and butter, cake, and other delicacies up to the present point, when nature, sorely against the masculine will, obliged them to say, "Can't eat no more!" "I'm only filling their cups half up now," said the Vicar's wife; "I really believe they have had about ten each!" and so I should think they had. "I ain't eat so much I don't know when!" was the remark one heard from various quarters.

A due period being allowed for stowing away cups and coffee urns, during which young Walthamstow leant their elbows on the tables and surveyed each other and the world in general with the smiling benignity consequent on having eaten as much as they could, discussion arose as to which entertainment was to be next on the board—singing or boxing; and finally the authorities decided on the former. Vigorous, active, ubiquitous Mr. Ware had the boards removed and leant against the wall, and the trestles packed away somewhere, and the chairs ranged in a gigantic circle facing the platform, on which one of the clergy mounted and presided at the piano. "Now then, which of you fellows will give us a song?" A small, rather pretty-looking boy, slightly better dressed than some, got up, and with a remarkably good voice sang something tuneful and sentimental, with a chorus, in which approving young Walthamstow joined, leaning well back in their chairs, with legs wide apart, hands in trousers pockets, and a "fag" in their mouths. Fags were scarce articles among them, as their money did not always rise to the price, and I noticed that when one, with a sort of monarchal air, flung a half-smoked one into the middle of the circle, a gaunt-looking youth sprang forward, snatched it up alight, and put it between his lips with evident relish. "That little 'un," said a lad sitting near me, "as is a-singing now, 'e's a *pro,* 'e sings at the music-halls!" Other songs succeeded this little *pro's* performance, and a nice-looking, costermongery sort of a fellow sang a fascinating song we had heard last year from the girls of the Good Shepherd, called "They led him to the hillside." We could not catch all the words on either occasion, and a printed copy seemed unprocurable, but it sounded like a song of '98, about suffering and dying in the cause of the freedom of Ireland.

Due space having been allowed for song-singing, Mr. Ware's tall gray figure appeared to the fore, saying, "Now, my lads, widen out a bit, and we'll have a turn with the gloves." These gloves, we remembered, were the kind gift of some gentleman who had heard of the lads' needs through the *Orient Magazine*. And now there was a great upheaval among the crowd. Stalwart shoulders and cropped heads of lads, who had been sitting in the background, rose up and commenced "peeling," thereby revealing very unwashed, ragged shirts, or apologies for shirts, and general defects altogether in the garments. A big heavy-weight and a lighter-built fellow put on the gloves and stepped forward first. "See him?" said young Music Hall, who sat near, "that's (some pugilistic celebrity—I could not catch the name) and the little 'un he's a-bringing out." Great expectation and keen interest were evinced as the two combatants playfully dabbed each other about in the ring, the big one ducking and the little one sparring up, with no end of talent evinced, till a hoarse voice, which sounded as if it was used to holloa "greens," came from a knot of big lads, and shouted, "*Time!*" and the panting combatants retreated to their corners, where their friends flicked a silk handkerchief in their faces and wiped them round the ears to cool them. "Have a blow, gents?" ejaculated young Music Hall. "Time's up," cried the hoarse costery voice, and they advanced, stepped round, and recommenced the exhibition, sparring till time was cried again, the chair-taking and flicking operation repeated; and then the hoarse voice proclaimed, "Third and final round, gents!" and the boxing recommenced till the time-keeper pronounced it over. Two little lads went in next, with more zeal than skill, and less command of their temper, and then a big couple came forward, donned the gloves, shook hands, and began a sort of kindly, smiling cat's-play, though it was curious to notice the keen, quick look of their eyes as they watched each other. "See them? you'll see some sport now," breathlessly ejaculated my little Music Hall neighbour; "them's amateurs, and they're real good 'uns." They certainly seemed better tempered, more nimble on their feet, and lighter with their blows than their predecessors.

My friend, who was sitting on the edge of the platform talking to a big fellow, told me afterwards that one of the two combatants, who looked no more than a big lad, was a married man with a family! What amused us was that outside the ring sundry of the little ones had assumed gloves, and were boxing in a wild and daring fashion, gyrating all over the place, once even getting into the ring among the heroes, and thereby becoming all four involved in a hopeless tangle, all being mixed up, striking out desperately anywhere, looking like a muddled up Manx Arms—legs kicking everywhere—white gloves hitting out nowhere! They elicited peals of laughter from the jolly audience. Rounds of oranges succeeded the rounds of the champions, and then the singing was resumed, and at this point my friend and I left to catch the ten o'clock train.

Our impression of this entertainment was that it was a most wholesome and hearty one. The object was to keep these rough, uncouth lads out of harm's way, and the public-houses; to let them amuse themselves in their own fashion, and to let them see they *could* do so, and have perfect enjoyment, without drinking and swearing and bad company. They were a rough lot; they worked at bricklaying, costering, odd jobs, or nothing at all; but the Sisters had got them to come under the shadow of S. Alban's warm, well-lighted hall, and were doing what they could for them, humanizing them, getting them to receive what Christianity they could, albeit in homeopathic doses. The friendly, kindly Vicar and his wife and the other clergy threw themselves into it all so heartily, that one's impression was that wherever these lads in after days might go—and they are a very wandering, nomadic race—they would always carry away with them pleasant memories of Church teaching and Church people, of the gentle, white-capped Sister, and the kindly-spoken clergy, and the strong sympathetic young Churchman who presided over these amusements: and so the meetings in S. Alban's Hall will have been to many of these wandering Gentiles a true Epiphany, the Star which shall shine to guide them through the dark and forsaken roads along which most of their lives lie.

Beatrice (Potter) Webb

THIS ARTICLE FROM A WELL-KNOWN PERIODICAL originated during Beatrice Potter's period as a London slum explorer and philanthropist, from about 1883 to 1888 or 1889. In 1883, encouraged by two of her sisters already at work there, Beatrice Potter (1867–1954), one of nine daughters born to a wealthy Gloucestershire businessman and his Lancashire-born wife, got involved with the Charity Organisation Society (COS). Her first assignment was as a house-to-house "visitor" investigating Soho applicants. As she wrote in her diary, she took this post not in the "spirit of charity" but in the conviction that the problem of poverty was a central political question of the day.[1] Beatrice Potter had had an unusual education that emphasized philosophy and social thought. Her interest in poverty was from the beginning quite clinical; the prospect of COS work she thought would "work in well with my 'human' studies. One learns very little about human nature from [high] society. It is too much clothed with the 'conventionalities and seemings'."[2]

Next, Potter worked in the Katharine Buildings, workers' housing at the western edge of London's dock district. Here her job was, along with colleague Ella Pycroft, collecting rents weekly from the building's tenants. Finally, in 1885 she began to investigate conditions among dockers and in the garment industry as a part of her cousin Charles Booth's massive study of London life. As an element of this work, she lodged in East London and

Originally published as "Pages from a Work-Girl's Diary" in The Nineteenth Century *139 (September 1888): 301–14; later titled "The Diary of an Investigator," it was published in* Problems of Modern Industry, *ed. Sidney and Beatrice Webb (London: Longman, Green, 1898). Reprinted with the permission of the London School of Economics.*

took a number of tailoring jobs incognito to get firsthand knowledge of the structure of the tailoring trades.[3] Her first public appearance as an expert on poverty and industrial conditions was in 1888 and 1889, when she testified at the House of Lords Committee on the Sweating System.

"Pages from a Work-Girl's Diary" was in press at the time of the committee hearings. This piece is closely based on her detailed diary entries, which include word-for-word reports of conversations with employers and workers in the industry and make a very interesting companion piece to the published version. For her "Work-Girl's" article, Potter added new deprecating remarks about Jews and deleted comments that would have been read as indecent: the fact, for example, that Potter was told that one of the girls "has had three babies by her father, and another has had one by her brother."[4] The tailoring study and a separate entry on the Jewish community in London were also published in Booth's London survey, their original destination.

Potter eventually turned her back on the female slum explorers like Pycroft, declaring that these "unknown saints" were "exceedingly pathetic." She rejected most opportunities to write about "women's" topics such as female labor (as both Booth and the economist Alfred Marshall had urged her to do), cast off the face-to-face method of social observation so effective in the article that follows, and was rather wary in her friendships with women. She only belatedly supported the women's suffrage campaign.[5] Her rent collecting and COS "visiting" years ultimately paid off, however. When, years later, her husband Sidney Webb was an M.P. representing the mining borough of Seaham, she proved an extremely effective constituency worker and organizer.

In the late 1880s, Potter was beginning to elaborate the professional and political identity that would define her life. She discovered the Fabian Society and met the leaders of the 1889 East London dockers' strike. Early in 1890 her cousin Margaret Harkness introduced her to Sidney Webb. Two years later Beatrice Potter married Webb. (She deeply resented "parting with my *name*.")[6] Her first post-Booth project, which she began in 1889, involved document-based research, much more commonly done by her male peers;[7] this was a history of the cooperative movement, an exemplar of working-class intelligence and self-help. The Webbs, working together over many years, carried out detailed studies of other institutions they thought represented the future for English workers: trades unions, local government, and socialism.

The Webbs have often been treated as a single unit. They were given a joint entry in the DLB, for example, as well as in the DNB. Sidney is the more significant partner in the traditional sense since he was active in local and national politics for over half a century. He served in Parliament and on the LCC, was chairman of the Labour Party, and Colonial Secretary. In recent decades, however, scholars have found Beatrice the more interesting partner in large part because of her detailed and self-aware diaries, kept from before the age of fifteen until just eleven days before her death, and which she began to edit and organize for publication as an autobiography in 1922. The diaries cover everything in her life from her worries about a wayward younger sister, to her painful decision not to marry suitor Joseph Chamberlain, to her hopes for the Bolshevik regime in Russia. Her husband, she says, was uneasy about this form of personal writing, saying it was "far too subjective"; some sections seemed to him "the sentimental scribbling of a woman." But Beatrice deeply enjoyed working on *My Apprenticeship,* the first volume of which was completed in the fall of 1925. The book was an immediate critical success. She viewed it as a piece of creative writing and in any case consoled herself that no matter what, it would "have some *value* [emphasis hers] as a description of 'Victorianism.'"[8]

Beatrice Webb was a skilled administrator and forceful exponent of her causes. She masterminded the influential Minority Report of the (1905–1909) Royal Commission on the Poor Laws; Helen Bosanquet was part of the far larger majority. Both Webbs crowed triumphantly when, in 1929, the Conservative Minister of Health Neville Chamberlain accepted one of their central 1909 recommendations, the abolition of poor law boards of guardians.[9] Despite her deep depression about World War I, she served on several important wartime government boards, including one whose mandate was a reorganization of the structure of the central government, with its departments and ministries. She was the only woman to serve on the committee that formulated rules governing wartime production, when hundreds of thousands of union men were replaced by women, girls, and boys. Here Webb proved herself a staunch defender of the rights of women workers.

NOTES

1. Webb, *My Apprenticeship,* 257–59; Nord, *Apprenticeship of Beatrice Webb,* 123.
2. MacKenzie and MacKenzie, *Diaries of Beatrice Webb,* 1: 83.
3. Webb, *My Apprenticeship,* 311. Also see Rosemary O'Day, "Before the Webbs: Beatrice Potter's Early Investigations for Charles Booth's Inquiry," *History* 78 (February 1993): 218–42.
4. Ms. Diary, Passfield Papers, vol. 12, April 11, 1888, 40.

5. Webb, *My Apprenticeship,* 275; Nord, *Apprenticeship of Beatrice Webb,* 148–49.
6. MacKenzie and MacKenzie, *Diaries of Beatrice Webb,* 1: 371. On the morning of her marriage she wrote in her diary, "Exit Beatrice Potter. Enter Beatrice Webb, or rather (Mrs) Sidney Webb for I lose alas! Both names" (July 23, 1892, entry).
7. Lewis, *Women and Social Action,* 84–85.
8. These quotations are from MacKenzie and MacKenzie, *Diaries of Beatrice Webb,* 4: 49 (March 19, 1925, entry).
9. McBrier, *An Edwardian Mixed Doubles,* 366–67. Beatrice's metaphor: the Webbs were "chuckling over their chickens!"

FURTHER READING

The Webb collection (Passfield Papers) in the British Library of Political and Economic Science, Archives Department, maintains a bibliography of all of Beatrice (and Sidney) Webb's enormous body of writings. Beatrice's manuscript and typescript diaries are also housed there. A bibliography of Beatrice Webb's published work is found in Deborah Epstein Nord, *The Apprenticeship of Beatrice Webb* (Amherst: University of Massachusetts Press, 1985), 283–85.

Webb contributed articles on the docks, the East London Jewish community, and the tailoring trade to Charles Booth's massive *Life and Labour of the People in London.* The following piece was in its earliest volume: *East London* (London: Williams and Norgate, 1889), which, with its companion volume, was later included in the full seventeen-volume work. See also "The Dock Life of East London," *The Nineteenth Century* 22 (October 1887): 483–99; "East London Labour," *The Nineteenth Century* 24 (August 1888): 161–83; and *The Consumers' Cooperative Movement in Great Britain* (London: Longmans, 1921), coauthored with Sidney James Webb, Baron Passfield.

More recent publications of her work are *My Apprenticeship* (reprint, Cambridge: Cambridge University Press, 1979); Norman MacKenzie, ed., *The Letters of Sidney and Beatrice Webb,* 3 vols. (Cambridge: Cambridge University Press, 1978); and Norman MacKenzie and Jeanne MacKenzie, eds., *The Diaries of Beatrice Webb,* 4 vols. (Cambridge, MA: Harvard University Press, 1982–85; abridged ed., 2 vols. London: Virago, 2001).

For biographical information about Beatrice Webb, see the entry by John Davis in the Oxford DNB and the entry by Margaret Cole in the DLB. See also Barbara Caine's superb *Destined to Be Wives: The Sisters of Beatrice Webb* (Oxford: Clarendon Press, 1986); Jane Lewis, *Women and Social Action in Victorian and Edwardian England* (Palo Alto, CA: Stanford University Press, 1991), 83–145; A. M. McBriar, *An Edwardian Mixed Doubles. The Bosanquets versus the Webbs: A Study in British Social Policy, 1890–1929* (Oxford: Clarendon Press, 1987); Deborah Epstein Nord, *The Apprenticeship of Beatrice Webb* (Amherst: University of Massachusetts Press, 1985); Lisanne Radice, *Beatrice and Sidney Webb: Fabian Socialists* (London: Macmillan, 1984); and Carole Seymour-Jones, *Beatrice Webb: Woman of Conflict* (New York: HarperCollins, 1993).

Pages from a Work-Girl's Diary

It is midday. The sun's rays beat fiercely on the crowded alleys of the Jewish settlement: the air is moist from the heavy rains. An unsavoury steam rises from the down-trodden slime of the East End streets and mixes with the stronger odours of the fried fish, the decomposing vegetables, and the second-hand meat which assert their presence to the eyes and nostrils of the passers-by.

For a brief interval the 'whirr' of the sewing-machines and the muffled sound of the presser's iron have ceased. Machinists and pressers, well-clothed and decorated with heavy watch-chains; Jewish girls with flashy hats, full figures, and large bustles; furtive-eyed Polish immigrants with their pallid faces and crouching forms; and here and there poverty-stricken Christian women—all alike hurry to and from the midday meal: while the labour-masters, with their wives and daughters, sit or lounge round about the house-door, and exchange notes on the incompetency of 'season hands,' the low price of work, the blackmail of shop foremen, or discuss the more agreeable topic of the last 'deal' in Petticoat Lane and the last venture on race-horses.

Jostled on and off the pavement, I wander on and on, seeking work. Hour after hour I have paced the highways and byways of the London Ghetto. No bills up except for a 'good tailoress,' and at these places I dare not apply, for I feel myself an impostor, and as yet my conscience and my fingers are equally unhardened. Each step I take I am more faint-hearted and more weary in body and limb. At last, in sheer despair, I summon up my courage. In a window the usual bill, but seated on the doorstep a fat cheerful-looking daughter of Israel, who seems to invite application.

'Do you want a plain 'and?' say I, aping ineffectually a work-woman's manner and accent, and attaining only supreme awkwardness.

The Jewess glances quickly, first at my buttonless boots, then at my short but already bedraggled skirt, upwards along the straight line of my ill-fitting coat, to the tumbled black bonnet which sits ill at ease over an unkempt twist of hair.

'No,' is the curt reply.

'I can do all except buttonholes,' I insist in a more natural tone.

She looks at my face and hesitates. 'Where have you worked?'

'In the country,' I answer vaguely.

She turns her head slowly towards the passage of the house. 'Rebecca, do you want a hand?'

'Suited an hour ago,' shouts back Rebecca.

'There, there, you see,' remarks the Jewess in a deprecating and kindly voice as her head sinks into the circles of fat surrounding it. 'You will find plenty of bills in the next street; no fear of a decent young person, as knows her work, staying out o' door this time of year;' and then, turning to the woman by her side: 'It's rare tho' to find one as does. In these last three days, if we've sat down one, we've sat a dozen to the table, and not a woman amongst them as knows how to baste out a coat fit for the machine.'

Encouraged by these last words I turn round and trudge on. I ask at every house with a bill up, but always the same scrutinising glance at my clothes and the fatal words, 'We are suited!'

Is it because it is the middle of the week, or because they think I'm not genuine? think I. And at the next shop window I look nervously at my reflection, and am startled at my utterly forlorn appearance—destitute enough to be 'sweated' by any master.

'Sure, there's not much on 'er back to take to the h'old uncle,' remarks an Irish servant to her mistress, as I turn away from the last house advertising for a 'good tailoress.'

I feel horribly sick and ill; and I am so painfully conscious of my old clothes that I dare not ask for refreshment at an eating-house or even at a public. Any way I will have air, so I drag one foot after another into the Hackney thoroughfare. Straight in front of me, in a retail slop-shop of the lowest description, I see a large placard: 'Trouser and Vest Hands Wanted Immediately.' In another moment I am within a large workroom crowded with women and girls as ill-clothed as myself. At the head of a long table, examining finished garments, stands a hard-featured, shrewd-looking Jewess, in a stamped cotton velvet and with a gold-rimmed eyeglass.

'Do you want trouser hands?'

'Yes we do—indoor.'

'I'm a trouser finisher.'

The Jewess examines me from head to foot. My standard of dress suits her. 'Call at eight o'clock to-morrow morning.' And she turns from me to look over a pair of trousers handed up the table.

'What price do you pay?' say I with firmness.

'Why, according to the work done, to be sure. All prices,' she answers laconically.

'Then to-morrow at eight.' And I leave the shop hurriedly to escape that hard gaze of my future mistress. Again in the open street: the dazed-headiness, the dragging back-ache, and the sore feet—all the physical ills and moral depressions of the out o' work—seem suddenly swept away. At length, after this weary pilgrimage, I have secured work. The cool evening breeze, the picturesque life and stirring activity of the broad highway, even the sounds and sights of East London, add to my feeling of intense exhilaration. Only one drawback to perfect content: *Can* I 'finish' trousers?

At a few minutes past eight the following morning I am standing in front of 'MOSES AND SON. CHEAP CLOTHING.' In the window two shop-boys are arranging the show garments: coats and vests (sold together) 17s. to 22s.; trousers from 4s. 6d. up to 11s. 6d.

'Coats evidently made out: I wonder where and at what price?' ponders the investigator as the work-girl loiters at the door.

'You'd better come in,' says the friendly voice of a fellow worker as she brushes past me. 'You're a new-comer; the missus will expect you to be there sharp.'

I follow her into the retail shop and thence through a roughly made wooden door. The workroom is long and irregularly shaped, somewhat low and dark near the entrance, but expanding into a lofty skylight at the further end. The walls are lined with match-boarding; in a prominent place, framed and under glass, hang the *Factory and Workshop Regulations*. Close by the door, and well within reach of the gas-stove (used for heating irons), two small but high tables serve the pressers: a long low plank table, furnished with a wooden rail for the feet, forms on either side of it, chairs top and bottom, runs lengthways for the trouser finishers; a high table for the basters; and, directly, under the skylight, two other tables for machinists and vest hands complete the furniture of the room. Through an open door, at the extreme end of the workshop, you can see the private kitchen of the Moses family, and beyond, in a very limited backyard, an outhouse, and, near to it, a tap and sink for the use of all the inmates of the establishment.

Some thirty women and girls are crowding in. The first arrivals hang bonnets and shawls on the scanty supply of nails jotted here and there along the wooden partition separating the front shop from the workroom; the later comers shed their outdoor garments in various corners. There is a general Babel of voices as each 'hand' settles down in front of the bundle of work and the old tobacco or candle box that holds the cottons, twist, gimp, needles, thimble, and scissors belonging to her. They are all English or Irish women, with the exception of some half-dozen well-dressed 'young ladies' (daughters of the house), one of whom acts as forewoman, while the others are already at work on the vests. The 'missus' is still at breakfast. A few minutes after the half-hour the two pressers (English lads are the only men employed) saunter lazily into the room, light up the gas jet, and prepare the irons.

The forewoman calls for a pair of trousers, already machined, and hands them to me. I turn them over and over, puzzled to know where to begin. The work is quite different from that of the *bespoke* shop, at which I was trained—much coarser and not so well arranged. Besides, I have no cotton, thread, twist, or gimp. The woman next me explains: 'You'll 'ave to bring trimmings; we h'ain't supplied with them things y'ere; but I'll lend you some, jist to set off with.'

'What ought I to buy?' I ask, feeling rather helpless.

At this moment the 'missus' sweeps into the room. She is a big woman, enormously developed in the hips and thighs; she has strongly marked Jewish features, and, I see now, she is blind of one eye. The sardonic and enigmatical expression of her countenance puzzles me with its far-off associations, until I remember the caricatures, sold in City shops for portraits, of the great Disraeli. Her hair is crisp and oily—once jet black, now, in places, gray—it twists itself in scanty locks over her forehead. The same stamped cotton velvet, of a large flowery pattern, that she wore yesterday; a heavy watch-chain, plentiful supply of rings, and a spotlessly clean apron.

'Good-morning to you,' she says graciously to the whole assembly as she walks round our table towards my seat. 'Sarah, have you given this young person some work?'

'Yes,' replies Sarah; 'fourpence halfpenny's.'

'I have not got any trimmings. I did not know that I had to supply them. Where I worked before they were given,' I ejaculate humbly.

'That's easily managed; the shop's just round the corner—Or, Sarah,' she calls across the table, 'you're going out—just get the young person her trimmings. The lady next you will tell you what you want,' she adds in a lower tone, bending over between us.

The 'lady' next me is already my friend. She is a neat and respectable married woman with a look of conscious superiority to her surroundings. Like all the trouser hands she is paid by the piece; but in spite of this she is ready to give me up time in explaining how I am to set about my work.

'You'll feel a bit strange the first day. 'Ave you been long out o' work?'

'Yes,' I answer abruptly.

'Ah! that accounts for you're being a bit awkward-like. One's fingers feel like so many thumbs after a slack time.'

And certainly mine do. I feel nervous, and very much on trial. The growing heat of the room, the form so crowded that one must sit sideways to secure even a limited freedom for one's elbows; the general strangeness of my position—all these circumstances unite to incapacitate a true hater of needlework for even the roughest of sewing. However, happily for me no one pays me much attention. As the morning wears on, the noise increases. The two pressers have worked up their spirits, and a lively exchange of chaff and bad language is thrown from the two lads at the pressing (immediately behind us) to the girls round our table. Offers of kisses, sharp despatches to the devil and his abode, a constant and meaningless use of the inevitable adjective, form the staple of the conversation between the pressers and the younger hands; while the elder women whisper scandal and news in each other's ears. From the further end of the room catches of music-hall songs break into the monotonous whirr of the sewing-machine. The somewhat crude and unrhythmical chorus—

Why should not the girls have freedom now and then?
And if a girl likes a man, why should she not propose?
Why should the little girls always be led by the nose?

seems the favourite refrain, and, judging from the gusto with which it is repeated, expresses the dominant sentiment of the work-girls. Now and again the mistress shouts out, 'Sing in time, girls; I don't mind your singing, but sing in time.' There is a free giving and taking of each other's trimmings, a kindly and general supervision of each other's work—altogether a hearty geniality of a rough sort. The enigmatical and sardonic-looking Jewess sits at the upper end of our table, scans the finished garment through her gold-rimmed eyeglass, encourages or scolds as befits the case; or, screwing up her blind eye, joins in the chatter and broad-witted talk of the work-women immediately surrounding her.

'The missus 'as sixteen children,' remarks my friend Mrs. Long confidentially—'h'eight by Mr. Moses, and h'eight by the master she buried years ago. All them girls at the bottom table ar' 'er daughters.'

'They are a nice-looking set,' say I, in a complimentary tone.

'Yes, it's a pity some of the girls in the shop h'ain't like them,' mutters my respectable friend. 'They're an awful bad lot, some of them. Why, bless you, that young person as is laughing and joking with the pressers jist be'ind us—

and here follow horrible details of the domestic vice and unnatural crime which disgrace the so-called 'Christian' life of East London.

'Eh, eh!' joins in the woman next her, with a satisfied sniff at the scandal (a regular woman of the slums, with nose and skin patched by drink), 'it's h'ill thinking of what you may'ave to touch in these sort of places.'

'Well to be sure,' rejoins Mrs. Long, nettled both by the tone of superiority and by the unwarranted interruption of her disreputable neighbour. 'I've worked at this same place for h'eight years and never yet 'ave I 'ad words with anyone. There's reg'ler work the week round, and reg'ler pay on a Saturday; and y're money kept for you, if you 'appen to be a-cleaning. There's no need to mix y'rself up with them whose look you don't like,' she adds, with just a perceptible edging away from the slum woman, as if to emphasise her words—'there's some of all sorts y'ere.'

'H'I'm one of that sort,' blusters the woman of the slums, 'that h'answers a person back when they call me bl—y names. H'I'll give the last word to no one.'

'I don't choose to 'old conversation wi' the like of they,' says Mrs. Long, pursing up her thin lips as if to end this undesired intercourse: 'it h'ain't as if *I* 'ad to work for my living. My 'usband's in reg'ler work; it's only for the hextras like that I work, and jist for them times, per'aps a month the 'ole year through, that the building trade's slack.'

This effectually silences the woman of the slums. Her husband, alas! comes home drunk every night and spends the irregularly earned pence lounging about the publics (so I am afterwards informed by Mrs. Long). She has an ill-favoured daughter by her side, with a black eye and a swollen face, with whom she exchanges work and bad language and shares greasy victuals.

'One o'clock,' shouts a shrill boy's voice.

'Stop work,' orders the mistress.

'I wish I might finish this bit,' I say pathetically to my friend, painfully conscious of the shortcoming in the quantity if not in the quality of my work.

'You mustn't; it's the dinner hour.'

The pressers are already off, the mistress and her daughters retire into the kitchen: the greater number of women and girls turn out into the street, while one or two pull baskets from under the table, spread out before them, on dirty newspapers, cracked mugs, bits of bread and butter, cold sausage or salt fish; and lift, from off the gas-stove, the tin teapot wherein their drink has been stewing since the early morning. Heartily thankful for a breath of fresh air and a change from my cramped posture, I wander up and down the open street, and end my 'dinner hour' by turning into a clean shop for a bun and a fresh cup of tea. Back again at two.

'You must work sharper than this,' remarks the mistress, who is inspecting my work. I colour up and tremble perceptibly as I meet the scrutinising gaze of the hard-featured Jewess. She looks into my eyes with a comically puzzled expression, and adds in a gentler voice: 'You must work a little quicker for your own sake. We've had worse buttonholes than these, but it don't look as if you'd been 'customed to much work.'

But now the drama of the day begins. The two pressers saunter in ten minutes after the hour. This brings down upon them the ire of the Jewess. They, however, seem masters of the situation, for they answer her back in far choicer language than that in which they were addressed—language which I fear (even in a private diary) I could hardly reproduce; they assert their right to come when they choose; they declare that if they want a day off they 'will see her to the devil and take it;' and lastly, as a climax to all insults, they threaten her with the 'factory man,' and taunt her with gambling away on racehorses the money she 'sweats' out of them.

At these last words the enigmatical and sardonic expression of the Jewess changes into one of out-bursting rage. All resemblance to the City caricatures of that great passionless spirit vanishes. The deep furrows extending from just above the nostril to the corner of the mouth—lines which must surely express some race experience of the children of Israel—open out into one universal bubble of human fury. A perfect volley of oaths fly in quick succession between the principal combatants; while woman after woman joins in the fray, taking the missus's side against the pressers. The woman of the slums actually rises in her seat and prepares to use her fists; while her daughter seizes the opportunity to empty the small bottle of brandy hidden under her mother's trimmings. Mrs. Long purses up her thin lips still more tightly, and looks down steadily at her work. At this critical point—enter the master.

Mr. Moses is a corpulent, well-dressed English Jew. His face is heavy and sensual, his eyes sheepish, his reputation among his wife's 'hands' none of the best. At this moment, his one desire is to keep the Queen's peace in his establishment. I suspect, also, from the sleepy viciousness of his expression, that he himself suffers occasionally from the missus's forcible tongue; and with this bevy of women shouting on all sides he feels the masculine side of the question. Any way, he is inclined to take a strictly impartial view of the row. 'Sit down, Mrs. Jones,' he shouts to the woman of the slums—'sit you down, or you and that —— daughter of yours leave the shop this very instant. Now, lads, just you be quiet; go on with your work and don't speak to my wife.' And then, turning to his wife, in a lower tone—'Why won't you leave them alone and not answer them?' and the rest of his speech we cannot hear; but, judging from the tone and the look, it takes the form of deprecating expostulation. I catch the words 'push of work' and 'season hands.'

'Why, if you were only a bit of a man,' cries the mistress, raising her voice so that all may hear, 'you'd throw those two bl—y rascals out. I'd throw them out at any price, if I were a woman's husband. The idea of saying how I spend my money—what's that to him? And that Jo says he'll call the factory man in. He may call the devil in (and he's welcome)—the only person as he'll notice will be himself. The idea of him saying that I spend my money on horses; as if I couldn't spend money on anything I like. As if you wouldn't give me money as I earn, when I asks you, Mr. Moses,' gasps the Jewess, as she looks threateningly at her partner, 'and never ask where it goes to.' The betting on horses is evidently a sore point.

'It isn't their business what you do with your money,' rejoins the master soothingly. 'But just let them alone, and tell those girls to be quiet. It's more than half the girls' fault—they're always at the fellows,' he adds, anxious to shift the blame into a safe quarter.

The storm lulls, and Mr. Moses returns into the front shop. But the anger of the Jewess is not yet exhausted. A stray word, and the quick firing of abusive language between the mistress and the pressers begins afresh; though this time the women, awed by the master's interference, are silent. The tall weak-looking young man, Jo by name, shouts the longest and loudest; but, as Mrs. Long whispers to me without raising her eyes from her work, 'It's 'Arry as makes the bullets—jist listen to 'im—but it's Jo as fires 'em!'

At last it subsides. Women (outdoor hands [who carry pieces out to sew at home]) troop in with bundles of finished trousers. The bubbling rage of the injured woman yields to the keen-eyed supervision of the profit-making Jewess. 'I'd have nothing but indoor hands, if I knew where to find them and had a room to put them into,' she mutters to Esther as she turns over garment after garment. 'Just look at this work, it's all soap! Call again on Monday morning, Mrs. Smith. But mind it *is* Monday and not Tuesday morning. You understand English, don't you?—Monday morning.'

A small boy creeps into the shop laden with unfinished work. 'What d'you say to this, Sarah? Mrs. Hall sends word she was washing on Monday, cleaning on Tuesday, and I suppose playing the devil on Wednesday, for here's Thursday, with shop day to-morrow, and the work's untouched. Now, girls, be quick with your work,' continues the mistress as she throws the bundle on to our table—'all this to be done extra before Friday. Perkins won't wait for no one!'

'The name of a wholesale shipping firm; so she works for export as well as for retail and pays same price for both,' inwardly notes the investigator as she glances at the shoddy garments. (The work-girl meanwhile pushes her needle into her thumb-nail, and in her agony digs her elbow into her neighbour's half-turned back, which causes a cannonade all round the table.)

'Law! how awkward she still be,' growls the woman of the slums, anxious to pick a quarrel and vent her unspent wrath.

At length teatime breaks the working-day. Pence have already been collected for the common can of milk; innumerable teapots are lifted off the gas-stove, small parcels of bread and butter, with a relish or a sweet, are everywhere unrolled. My neighbours, on either side, offer me tea, which I resolutely refuse. The mistress sips her cup at the head of the table. The obnoxious pressers have left for the half-hour. Her feelings break out—

'Pay them 5s. a day to abuse you! As if I couldn't spend my money on what I like; and as if Mr. Moses would ever ask—I'd like to see him ask me—how the money'd gone!'

All the women sympathise with her and vie with each other in abusing the absent pressers.

'It's h'awful, their language,' cries the slum woman; 'if I were the missus, I'd give the bl—y scoundrels tit for tat. Whativer's the use of bein' a missus if you've got to 'old in y're tongue?'

'As for the factory man,' continues the irate Jewess, turning to the other sore point, 'just fancy threatening me with him! Why they ar'n't fit to work in a respectable shop; they're d—d spies. I'd throw them out, if it cost me 100l. And if Mr. Moses were half a man, he'd do it too.'

At the word spy, I feel rather hot; but conscious of the innocence of my object, I remark, 'You have nothing to fear from the factory inspector; you keep the regulations exactly.'

'I don't deny,' she answers quite frankly, 'that if we're pressed for work I turn the girls upstairs; but it isn't once in three months I do it; and it all tells for their good.'

Two hours afterwards, and I have finished my second pair. 'This won't do,' she says as she looks over both pairs together. 'Here, take and undo the band of that one; I'll set this one to rights. Better have respectable persons who know little to work here than blaguards who know a lot—and a deal too much,' she mutters, smarting over the taunts of the 'factory man' and the money laid on horses.

'Eight o'clock by the Brewery clock,' cries the shrill voice.

'Ten minutes to,' shouts the missus, looking at her watch. 'However, it ain't worth while breaking the law for a few minutes. Stop work.'

This is most welcome to me. The heat since the gas has been lit is terrific, my fingers are horribly sore, and my back aches as if it would break. The women bundle up their work; one or two take it home. Everyone leaves her trimmings on the table, with scissors and thimble. Outside, the freshness of the evening air, the sensation of free movement, and rest to the weary eyes and fingers constitute the keenest physical enjoyment I have ever yet experienced.

Friday morning, and I am hopelessly tired. Jammed between my two neighbours, with the garment of hard shoddy stuff on my knee, and with the whole day's work before me, I feel on the brink of deep disgrace as a work-girl. I am 'shaky like all over,' my fingers, worn in places into holes, refuse to push the thick needle through the objectionable substance; damp hands (the more I rub them in my apron the damper they become) stretch the thin linings out of place; my whole energy is riveted on my work, with the discouraging result that it becomes worse and worse. Mrs. Long works silently by my side at high pressure to bring a pair of 'ordered' trousers in to time. And she begins to scent dismissal.

'I keeps myself to myself,' she told me yesterday. 'Down y're they're all a-going down 'ill; except them Jews as is going hup.' And to-day she applies her theory strictly, and is unwilling to 'mix herself up' with even a respectable failure. So I bungle on without help until I have finished after a fashion.

'This will never do,' angrily remarks the mistress. And then, perceiving the culprit by her side, she adds sternly: 'This won't do—this work won't suit me; you want to go and learn somewhere first. This will never do—this won't suit me,' she repeats slowly as she pulls the work to pieces. She dismisses me from her side with a wave of her eyeglass, as if to say, 'It's no good answering me back again.'

Without a word I arrange my trimmings ready to depart if the missus persists.

Is it over-fatigue, or is it the perfect realisation of my position as a disgraced work-girl? An ominous lump rises in my throat, and my eyes fill with tears. There is a dead silence. The younger hands look up from their work sympathetically; Mrs. Long, with her head down, stitches on steadily;

the woman of the slums gazes on me with bleared expression of mingled stupor and pity; fumbles underneath her work on the table and pushes something towards me. I hear the rattle of the brandy-bottle against the scissors as I see the old tobacco-box that holds her trimmings advancing towards me. Meanwhile the Jewess has screwed up her left eye and is looking at me through her eyeglass. The deep furrows of inherited experience again relax in favour of personal feeling. But this time it is human kindness instead of human fury. She beckons to me. In a second I am by her side.

'I'll see what I can do with you. If you like to stay and work on threepence-halfpennies, the same as I give to outdoor hands, you can take better work when you're fit for it. I'm sure I don't want to be hard on any decent young person as is trying to earn her living in a respectable way. There ain't so many respectable persons in the world that we can afford to starve 'em,' the Jewess adds, casting an angry glance at the pressers. 'Sarah, give her a pair of threepence-halfpennies. I'll alter these for you. You sit between those two young ladies and they'll show you. You must help one another,' she says to the girls as they make room for me; 'tho' of course they all come here to make their own living; you can't expect them to teach you for ever.'

The girl who takes me under her especial charge is a respectably dressed and delicate-looking young woman, with none of the rowdy slovenliness or tarnished finery of the typical Gentile girl of East London. Slightly made, with a pale, weary face, she looks at least thirty (she tells me she is only just nineteen); she stitches silently, and seems hardly conscious of the boisterous life of her fellow-workers; but instead of Mrs. Long's air of ever-present superiority, her form, face, manner, denote physical depression, lit up now and again by the dreamy consciousness of another world beyond the East End workroom.

'You'll soon learn,' she says kindly; 'you must watch me fix this, and then you can do the next yourself.'

Directed and encouraged by her kindness, I work on, in a calmer frame of mind, listening to the conversation of my neighbours. Among the younger hands who sit at this end of the table it chiefly concerns the attraction of the rival music-halls, or the still more important question of the presents and attentions of their different 'blokes.' For monotonous work and bad food have not depressed the physical energies of these young women. With warm hearts, with overflowing good nature, with intellects keenly alive to the varied sights of East London, these genuine daughters of the people brim over with the frank enjoyment of low life. During the day their fingers and eyes are fully occupied; in the evenings, on holidays, in the slack season, their thoughts rush out and gather in the multitudinous excitements of the East End streets; while their feelings unburden themselves in the pleasure of promiscuous lovemaking. You cannot accuse them of immorality, for they have no consciousness of sin. The veneer of morality, the hidden but secretly self-conscious vice of that little set that styles itself 'London society' (in the city of millions!) are unknown to them. They live in the Garden of Eden of uncivilised life; as yet they have not tasted the forbidden fruit of the Tree of the Knowledge of Good and Evil, and the heaven and hell of an awakened conscience are alike undreamt of. There is only one Fall possible to them—drink, leading slowly but inevitably to the drunkard's death.

'I say, Milly,' shouts one to the other, 'you tell that bl—y brother of yours that I waits 'alf an 'our for 'im houtside the Paragon last night. I'll be blessed before I serves as 'is Round the Corner [East London slang for "date"] ag'in. 'Owever, at last, I says to myself, "a watched kittle niver biles," so I walks in by myself. The dressin' there is grand,' she adds enthusiastically.

'Eh! but you sh'd see the piece they're running at the Standard!' rejoins Milly. 'Jim's promised to take me up to one of them grand places up West next Saturday. Will you come along? I'll git Tom to come. You'll want to be a making of it up by that time. Tom's in reg'lar work and a rare catch h'as a sweet'eart,' laughs the sister of the faithless swain.

'It's too much trouble to go up West,' answers the girl, anxious to prove her indifference to Tom's attentions. 'I don't care to turn h'out 'fore 'alf-past nine. It takes a full hour to clean up and git a bit of supper, and that leaves three hours for our houting like; for mother don't hexpect us back 'fore 'alf-past twelve. But I don't say I wouldn't come, as it's the 'alf day, if Tom's very pressin',' she continues. 'I've 'eard it said them grand ladies as sits in the boxes and the stalls 'as low dresses on, like so many h'actrices, and h'it's as good h'as a play jist to look on 'em. So 'Arry told me, and 'e's a rare 'un for liking the look of them lords and ladies as lives up there.'

The pale, weary girl stitches silently by my side. She works harder than the others—finished four pair yesterday and hopes to finish the same to-day. 'Are you chapel?' she asks presently.

'Yes,' I reply, attending more to the spirit than to the letter of her question.

'Do you belong to the Army?' she says inquiringly, glancing at my plain grey dress, and no doubt remembering my close black bonnet.

'No,' I answer, 'do you?'

She shakes her head: 'They've tried to get me to join since I've been in London. But we're a quieter set than they. Mother and I have only been in London these two years since father's death,' she adds in an explanatory tone. 'Mother's a skilled vest hand; not this sort of work—she wouldn't look at this. She can make 2*l.* a week in good times; but now her eyesight's going fast. And it isn't much as I earn. I was brought up to teaching.'

'And why did you not go on with it?'

'I failed in the first examination. Then father died, and mother heard there were skilled hands wanted in London, so we left our home. But I've found a Bible class in our street and I teaches there twice a week. That and the chapel on a Sunday is like a bit of the old home.' The work-girl sighs, and the far-off look of 'another world' gleams in the clear depths of her grey eyes. 'If you're going out for the dinner-hour, I might show you the chapel and the classroom,' she adds with hesitating gentleness; 'are you going home for dinner?'

'No, I shall get a cup of tea at Lockhart's, and a bun.'

'Why, you're niver a-goin' to dine off that!' cries the girl on my other side. And there is a whispering all round the table. Only a cup of tea and a bun means great poverty.

'You 'ad no tea last evening,' continues the same girl; 'now you must take a cup o' mine this afternoon.'

The hours of the day pass away quietly in work. There are no words between the mistress and the pressers, and the workshop life becomes monotonous. During the interval between dinner and tea a golden-haired young lady (married daughter of the Jewess), beautifully gloved and bonneted, covered with jewels, but with a somewhat unseasonable tippet of sable-tails, enters the workroom. She seats herself by her mother at the head of the table and chats confidentially. I hear the names of various racehorses and of forthcoming races. Apparently her husband belongs to the genus of 'betting men,' and, judging from her dress, he is a successful one. The mistress is in high good humor. At teatime she turns to me:

'Now, I'm very much interested in you; there is something in your face that's uncommon, and your voice too, that's odd—no word higher than another. The woman here will tell you, if I hadn't taken a fancy to your face and your voice I should have bundled you out long ago. Now what have you been?' she continues with gracious inquisitiveness.

'I hadn't to work when my father was in work,' I answer with literal truthfulness.

'A tidy-looking young person like you ought to get some respectable man to marry her—like my daughter here; you're more fit for that than to be making your own living in this sort of place. But, since you have come, I'll see what I can do with you. Come, you're getting on nicely,' she says encouragingly, as she looks over my work.

I am drinking the cup of tea forced on me by my neighbour. The pale, weary girl is munching her bread and butter.

'Won't you have some?' she says, as she pushes the paper towards me.

'No, thank you,' I answer.

'Sure?' and without more to do she lays a thick slice in my lap and turns away to avoid my thanks. A little bit of human kindness that goes to the heart and brings tears into the eyes of the investigator.

Work begins again. My friend has finished her third piece and is waiting for the fourth. She covers her head with her hands as she bends backward to rest the strained figure. In her grey eyes there is a look of intense weariness—weariness of body and mind. Another pair is handed to her and she begins again. She is a quick worker; but, work us hard as she may, she cannot clear much over 1s. a day after she has paid for trimmings. (A shilling a day is about the price of unskilled woman's labour.)

Another two hours and I say good-night.

'I'll be married in a week' are the last words I hear passing from Jo to Harry, 'and then my wife shall keep me.'

'I'll go to the bl—y workhouse,' jokes Harry, 'if I don't get a gal to keep me. I won't sweat here any longer for 5s. a day.'

THE GEOGRAPHY OF
LONDON WEALTH AND POVERTY

THE TEXTS COLLECTED IN *SLUM TRAVELERS* all pertain to London, an enormous city both in population and in sheer area. During the period covered by this study, people were being drawn to the metropolis by its wealth and glamour. London was the arts and culture center of the Anglophone world, with a large population of intellectuals, artists, civil servants, and professionals. Parliament met there, and it was the main residence of the royal family. Fortunes made in agriculture, industry, finance, commerce, and administration were translated into fine living in Mayfair or Belgravia—at least during the "Season" in the spring and early summer. And, as Jonathan Schneer has emphasized, London was the administrative heart of an enormous empire, an imperial capital with no rival in the world.[1]

But the metropolis also had a more workaday side as a manufacturing and trading center. In or very near London were such major industries as brewing, armaments, vehicle building, rubber, engineering, and chemicals. The Port of London was the world's busiest seaport in 1901, partly because it was a center for colonial trade in goods like spices, coffee, tea, lumber, fur, and jute. Thousands of small firms produced clothing, footwear, and furniture, among hundreds of other products. Garment manufacturing was, however, the single largest London industry at the turn of the twentieth century, employing—mainly in small workshops or in individual homes—almost a third of the city's manufacturing workers. Many London trades—such as unloading ships at the docks—were seasonal or precarious, so the male workforce had high rates of unemployment and of casual (part-time) work.[2]

Before World War I, London was the world's largest city. The area governed by the London County Council (LCC) had a population of 4.5 million in 1901, plus another 2 million in the "outer ring" suburbs beyond the county of London boundaries. By 1911, a metropolitan population of over 7 million accounted for nearly a quarter of the whole population of Britain.

Yet despite its size and importance, the metropolis was (and still is) not a single self-governing entity. Authority over London belongs to Parliament rather than to the Londoners, and its governance has been restructured many times. In the nineteenth century, a congeries of separate governing bodies had jurisdiction over such vital functions as water supply, sanitation, poor relief, public education, and the control of contagious diseases. Election to some of these agencies provided ways for women philanthropists and reformers to participate in policy making. The size, structure, and responsibilities of these governing bodies changed several times during the years covered by this study. The 118-member London County Council (LCC) was established in 1889, when two women were elected only to have their status overturned. The LCC replaced the older Metropolitan Board of Works as the main authority over the county of London, but continued to share power with other entities such as the School Board for London (1870–1902), the Metropolitan Asylums Board (established in 1867), poor law administrative districts (unions), and local vestries (districts for the supervision of health or sanitation, replaced in 1900 by twenty-eight boroughs, each with mayors, aldermen, and representative councils).[3]

How to govern this enormous city is a problem that has not yet been solved. Even since the 1970s, London has had *three* entirely different forms of government. The Greater London Council (GLC), established in 1965, was abolished twenty-one years later by Parliament's Conservatives, who were both enraged by its extensive cultural programs, aid to ethnic communities, and huge subsidies for public transportation, and scandalized by the provocative behavior of its chief executive, "Red" Ken Livingstone. In place of the GLC, the Conservatives offered Londoners a system in which local government power was split among nearly a *hundred* different bodies! In 1998, Tony Blair's New Labour established a less bizarre governing assembly, the Greater London Authority, approved by referendum.[4] In May of 2000, Londoners elected their twenty-five-member assembly and chose, as their first mayor, none other than Ken Livingstone.

Unlike Paris, New York, or Vienna, which in Victorian and Edwardian times had districts of tall tenements and apartment buildings, London's characteristic dwelling was an attached house of three or four stories. Especially in the nineteenth century, these structures proliferated rapidly, creating a sprawling built-up area. Many two- or three-story houses were subdivided into separate dwellings of one or two rooms—the most common living situations of the poor and near poor in London. Large apartment buildings, beloved of housing reformers and philanthropists in Britain because of their economies of scale, but disliked by most Londoners, were concentrated in the poorest districts and usually housed the poorest tenants. The construction of the suburban railroad network enlarged the built-up area even further beyond its 1889 boundaries. By 1914, there were houses stretching continuously from Ealing in the west to East Ham in the east (to take just one of the city's measurements), a distance of about eighteen miles; ribbons of suburban villas as well as scattered outlying pockets of poverty stretched still further out into the countryside.

London's population included a high proportion of children; poor districts had more of them, and they figure in many of the texts in this volume. As a well-born little girl, London artist Dorothy Tennant was fascinated by the clutches of "ragamuffins" she always saw on her morning walks with her nanny.[5] Working-class streets and courtyards swarmed winter and summer with children of all ages whose shouts could be heard until well after dark. In 1871, 43 percent of the city's population was fifteen or under, compared with 20 percent at the end of the twentieth century. In 1901, London's population was still nearly a third children, despite a birthrate that had been declining for four decades and the continuing in-migration of single adults. Poorer districts had extra high proportions of children in 1901: populations in the East London boroughs of Shoreditch, Bethnal Green, or Finsbury, for instance, were well over a third children, while in well-off Hampstead or Stoke Newington, children comprised only about a quarter of the whole.[6]

Nineteenth- and early twentieth-century London, to a twentieth-century American, or perhaps even to a Londoner today, exhibited only limited racial and ethnic diversity. Its citizens were nearly all white and of European origin. A small Chinese population dwelled along the West India Dock Road in Limehouse. African, Indian, or Arab sailors—who made up at least 10 percent of British merchant crews in this period—could be found in London waiting for return ship, or having jumped ship to escape extremely harsh conditions. They sometimes settled and married in the dockland districts of East London. Indian and West Indian servants and nannies were often marooned in London, no longer wanted by employers who had brought them all the way to England.[7] The largest group of non-English Londoners, however, comprised the children and grandchildren of the 107,000 Irish men and women who had settled there by 1861; they numbered about 435,000 in 1901. While especially concentrated in Seven Dials and Drury Lane in Central London, as well as in Whitechapel and South-wark, they could be found in every London borough, including many populated by clerks and skilled workers. Their Irishness and Catholicism were, a generation later, becoming a little less distinct. Small Czech, German, and Italian communities also flourished—about twelve thousand of the latter in 1911—centered in Westminster, St. Pancras, Holborn, and Finsbury. Women of Italian ancestry often worked in garment shops; men worked as organ grinders, artisans, and increasingly as waiters, cooks, and bakers as the restaurant trade in Central London took off. London was also very important as a center for political exiles from France, Italy, Germany, and Russia—the fallout from a century of continental revolution and repression.[8]

It was Jews who were the exotic others to late nineteenth-century Londoners. As Jerry White points out, the census listed Germans—a high percentage of them Jewish—as the largest foreign-born group in London before the 1890s, with about thirty-one thousand. By the 1890s, a much larger Jewish community had formed in eastern Whitechapel, as sixty thousand refugees from eastern Europe joined the small and well-assimilated community descending from earlier Dutch or Spanish Sephardic immigrants. The census counted 135,000 Jewish Londoners in 1901. But as early as 1910, the Jews had begun to disperse into nearby and better-off boroughs like Dalston and Stamford Hill; after World War I, the "north-west passage" brought many to Golders Green or Finchley in northwest London.[9]

Urban explorers were particularly concerned with the truly poor of the metropolis, who made up a sizeable minority of the whole population. According to Charles Booth's monumental description and classification, in the late 1880s and 1890s, during a period of economic depression, over a third of the population of East London and Hackney lived in various degrees of "poverty," and East London's figures did not differ significantly from those of London as a whole. The most fortunate of the four groups whom Booth classed as poor had household incomes of only eighteen to twenty-one shillings (about a pound) a week, just "barely sufficient for decent independent life," as Booth termed it. Another large proportion of the metropolitan population, about 40 percent, were only slightly more comfortable, but could easily fall into poverty due to a wage earner's illness or unemployment.[10]

As the nineteenth century progressed, those with the resources to do so began to leave such inner-city districts as the City, Shoreditch, Whitechapel, Rotherhithe, or the Borough. Inner London lost population, and

with that, its attraction for social explorers. Few visitors and only a few philanthropies documented the lives of the families who moved into the new
communities being built on the edges of London. Enthusiasm for urban
exploration faded after the First World War, as formerly teeming, animated
neighborhoods lost population to offices, warehouses, and more recently,
luxury flats and global chain boutiques.

NOTES

This appendix includes some material borrowed from my book *Love and Toil: Motherhood
in Outcast London 1870–1918* (New York: Oxford University Press, 1993), 11–15.

1. Jonathan Schneer, *London 1900: The Imperial Metropolis* (New Haven, CT: Yale University Press, 1999), 6–7.
2. On London (and suburban) industries see Raphael Samuel, "The Workshop of the World: Steam Power and Hand Technology in Mid-Victorian Britain," *History Workshop Journal* 3 (spring 1977): 6–72, and Gareth Stedman Jones, *Outcast London: A Study in the Relationship between Classes in Victorian Society* (Harmondsworth, England: Penguin Books, 1976), chap. 1.
3. This paragraph is based on the introduction to Paul Thompson's *Socialists, Liberals and Labour: The Struggle for London 1885–1914* (London: Routledge, 1967), which lucidly explains the dizzying number of administrative bodies that made up the urban entity called London. See also David Owen et al., *The Government of Victorian London, 1855–1899: The Metropolitan Board of Works, the Vestries and the City Corporation* (Cambridge, MA: Harvard University Press, 1982), and Ken Young and Patricia L. Garside, *Metropolitan London: Politics and Urban Change, 1837–1901* (London: Holmes and Meier, 1982). On the urban development of London, for some of the paragraphs that follow, I used Asa Briggs, *Victorian Cities* (Harmondsworth, England: Penguin Books, 1968), 311–19; Stedman Jones, *Outcast London,* chaps. 1, 6, and 11; and Donald J. Olsen, *The City as a Work of Art: London, Paris, Vienna* (New Haven, CT: Yale University Press, 1986), 132–37, 159–65, 183–85.
4. A brief, lively survey can be found in Peter Ackroyd's *London: The Biography* (London: Chatto and Windus, 2000).
5. Dorothy Tennant, *London Street Arabs* (London: Cassell and Company, 1890), 5.
6. Calculations made from 1871 Census, *Parliamentary Papers* 1873, vol. 71, pt. 1, table 1, 3; Census of London, 1901, LCC, *London Statistics,* 1903, 12–13. The 1901 figures for proportions of the population fifteen and under are as follows: Shoreditch 36 percent, Bethnal Green 38 percent, Finsbury 35 percent; Hampstead 24 percent, and Stoke Newington 27 percent. The later figures (1981) are based on the following: Office of Population Censuses and Surveys, Census of 1981 Key Statistics for Local Authorities Great Britain (London: HMSO, 1984). All figures are for children fifteen and under.
7. Rosina Visram, *Ayahs, Lascars and Princes: Indians in Britain 1700–1947* (London: Pluto Press, 1986), chaps 2, 3, 4. Henry Nevinson's remarkable short story, "Sissero's Return," about a marriage between a black sailor and a red-headed docker's daughter is reprinted in *Working-Class Stories of the 1890s,* ed. P. J. Keating (London: Routledge, 1975).
8. On the Italians, see [Maude A. Stanley], *Work about the Five Dials* (London: Macmillan,

1878), and the annual reports of the City of Westminster Health Society (founded in 1904), whose target population included Soho, with its many Italian needlewomen. Very valuable are Lucio Sponsa, *Italian Immigrants in Nineteenth-Century Britain: Realities and Images* (Leicester: Leicester University Press, 1988), 14, 19–23). My remarks on the Irish are based on Lynn Hollen Lees, *Exiles of Erin: Irish Migrants in Victorian London* (Manchester: Manchester University Press, 1979); Hugh McLeod, *Class and Religion in the Late Victorian City* (London: Croom Helm, 1974), 40, n. 35, and pp. 72–80; K. S. Inglis, *Churches and the Working Classes in Victorian England* (London: Routledge, 1963), chap. 3; Colin G. Pooley, "Segregation or Integration? The Residential Experience of the Irish in Mid-Victorian Britain," in *The Irish in Britain 1815–1939* (Savage, MD: Barnes and Noble, 1989); Chaim Bermant, *London's East End: Point of Arrival* (New York: Macmillan, 1975), chap. 6; and Graham Davis, *The Irish in Britain 1815–1914* (Dublin: Gill and Macmillan, 1991). See also Schneer, *London 1900,* 7.

9. Statistics on German nationals from Jerry White, *London in the Twentieth Century: A City and Its People* (London: Viking, 2001), 106–7. On the Jews in London, ibid., 107–13; also David Feldman, "The Importance of Being English: Jewish Immigration and the Decay of Liberal England," in *Metropolis/London,* esp. 56. Schneer, *London 1900,* includes a good short survey of London's nationalities (7–9).

10. Charles Booth, *Life and Labour of the People in London, First Series: Poverty,* 5 vols. (London: Macmillan and Company, 1902), vol. 1, table 1, 35. See also vol. 2, 21, for his London-wide poverty figures.

THE TEXTS ARRANGED THEMATICALLY

THE CHRISTIAN IMPULSE: CONVERSION AND SERVICE

Ellen Henrietta Ranyard, *The Missing Link Magazine,* short selections, 1878

Maude Alethea Stanley, chapter 3, "Drunkenness," from *Work about the Five Dials,* 1878

Kate Warburton, "An Epiphany Pilgrimage: The Story of a Boys' Tea at S. Saviour's Walthamstow," from *Old Soho Days and Other Memories,* 1906

WORKHOUSE ACCOUNTS

Mary (Kingsland) Higgs, "In a London Tramp Ward," from *Glimpses into the Abyss,* 1906

Margaret Wynne Nevinson, "The Evacuation of the Workhouse," from *Workhouse Characters,* 1918

SICKNESS AND HEALTH

Ellen Henrietta Ranyard, *The Missing Link Magazine,* short selections, 1878

Honnor Morten, "Eating the Apple," chap. 2 of *From a Nurse's Notebook,* 1899

Maud Pember Reeves, "Thrift," from *Round about a Pound a Week,* 1913

THE LADY INCOGNITO

Beatrice (Potter) Webb, "Pages from a Work-Girl's Diary," *The Nineteenth Century,* 1888

Olive Christian Malvery, "Gilding the Gutter: An Account of the Lives of the Costermongers," from *Pearson's Magazine,* 1905

Mary (Kingsland) Higgs, "In a London Tramp Ward," from *Glimpses into the Abyss,* 1906

CHILDREN

Dorothy Tennant (Lady Stanley), *London Street Arabs,* 1890

Kate Warburton, "An Epiphany Pilgrimage: The Story of a Boys' Tea at S. Saviour's Walthamstow," from *Old Soho Days and Other Memories,* 1906

Clara Ellen Grant, "A School Settlement," from *The School Child,* 1911

Margaret McMillan, "A Slum Mother," from *The Woman Worker,* 1908; and "Guy and the Stars," from *The Nursery School,* 1919

IN THE HOMES OF THE POOR

"A Lady Resident," "Sketch of Life in Buildings," from Booth's *Life and Labour of the People in London,* 1889

Helen (Dendy) Bosanquet, "Marriage in East London," from *Aspects of the Social Problem,* 1895

Florence Petty, Case papers from *The Pudding Lady: A New Departure in Social Work,* 1910

Maud Pember Reeves, "The District," from *Round about a Pound a Week,* 1913

Anna Martin, "The Irresponsibility of the Father," *The Nineteenth Century and After,* 1918

Margaret McMillan, "A Slum Mother," from *The Woman Worker,* 1908; and "Guy and the Stars," from *The Nursery School,* 1919

NEIGHBORHOODS AND STREETS

Amy Levy, "A London Plane-Tree," "London in July," "Ballade of an Omnibus," "Ballade of a Special Edition," and "The Piano-Organ," from *A London-Plane Tree, and Other Verse,* 1889

Dorothy Tennant (Lady Stanley), *London Street Arabs,* 1890

Helen (Dendy) Bosanquet, "Marriage in East London," from *Aspects of the Social Problem,* 1895

Ethel Brilliana (Mrs. Alec) Tweedie, "Petticoat-Lane," from *The Queen, The Lady's Newspaper,* 1895

Olive Christian Malvery, "Gilding the Gutter: An Account of the Lives of the Costermongers," from *Pearson's Magazine,* 1905

Maud Pember Reeves, "The District" and "Thrift," from *Round about a Pound a Week,* 1913

WIVES AND HUSBANDS

Maude Alethea Stanley, "Drunkenness," from *Work about the Five Dials,* 1878

Helen (Dendy) Bosanquet, "Marriage in East London," from *Aspects of the Social Problem,* 1895

Maud Pember Reeves, "The Poor and Marriage," from *Round about a Pound a Week,* 1913

Anna Martin, "The Irresponsibility of the Father," *The Nineteenth Century and After,* 1918

WORK AND WAGES FOR WOMEN

Annie (Wood) Besant, "White Slavery in London," from *The Link,* 1888

Beatrice (Potter) Webb, "Pages from a Work-Girl's Diary," *The Nineteenth Century,* 1888

Margaret Harkness, "Barmaids," from *Toilers in London,* 1889

Edith (Mrs. F. G.) Hogg, "The Fur-Pullers of South London," *The Nineteenth Century,* 1897

Clementina Black and Adele (Lady Carl) Meyer, from *Makers of Our Clothes,* 1909

Agnes Kate Foxwell, chapter 4 from *Munition Lasses: Six Months as Principal Overlooker in Danger Buildings,* 1917

JEWISH LONDON

Beatrice (Potter) Webb, "Pages from a Work-Girl's Diary," *The Nineteenth Century,* 1888

Amy Levy, five poems from *A London Plane-Tree, and Other Verse,* 1889

Ethel Brilliana (Mrs. Alec) Tweedie, "Petticoat-Lane," *The Queen, The Lady's Newspaper,* 1895

FEMINISTS AND SUFFRAGE ACTIVISTS VIEW LONDON POVERTY

Annie (Wood) Besant, "White Slavery in London," from *The Link,* 1888

Edith (Mrs. F. G.) Hogg, "The Fur-Pullers of South London," *The Nineteenth Century,* 1897

Honnor Morten, "Eating the Apple," from *From a Nurse's Notebook,* 1899

Mary (Kingsland) Higgs, "In a London Tramp Ward," from *Glimpses into the Abyss,* 1906

Clementina Black and Adele (Lady Carl) Meyer, from *Makers of Our Clothes,* 1909

Maud Pember Reeves, "The District" and "Thrift," from *Round about a Pound a Week,* 1913

Margaret Wynne Nevinson, "The Evacuation of the Workhouse," 1918

Sylvia Pankhurst, articles from *The Woman's Dreadnought,* 1916 and 1917

Anna Martin, "The Irresponsibility of the Father," *The Nineteenth Century and After,* 1918

LONDON DURING WORLD WAR I

Margaret Wynne Nevinson, "The Evacuation of the Workhouse," 1918

Sylvia Pankhurst, articles from *The Woman's Dreadnought,* 1916 and 1917

Agnes Kate Foxwell, chapter 4 of *Munition Lasses: Six Months as Principal Overlooker in Danger Buildings,* 1917

Anna Martin, "The Irresponsibility of the Father," *The Nineteenth Century and After,* 1918

GENRES OTHER THAN NONFICTION

Poetry

Amy Levy, five poems on London from *A London Plane-Tree, and Other Verse,* 1889

Short Fiction

Honnor Morten, "Eating the Apple," chapter 2 of *From a Nurse's Notebook,* 1899

Margaret Wynne Nevinson, "The Evacuation of the Workhouse," 1918

Margaret McMillan, "A Slum Mother," from *The Woman Worker,* 1908, and "Guy and the Stars," from *The Nursery School,* 1919

Visual Art

Dorothy Tennant (Lady Stanley), *London Street Arabs,* 1890

GLOSSARY OF TERMS, INSTITUTIONS, AND ORGANIZATIONS

Brief, accurate identifications of items not included in this glossary may be found on the Internet at www.spartacus.schoolnet.co/uk.

ANGLICAN CHURCH. In 1534 Henry VIII separated the Church of England from the Roman Catholic Church. The monarch became "supreme head" of the new Protestant church; its spiritual and administrative leader was, and is, the Archbishop of Canterbury. The Anglican Church, as it was called, remains the established (official) Church of England; it was disestablished in Wales, however, in 1918. Until 1828 only Church of England members could attend universities or hold government offices or military commissions. The Anglican Church includes adherents who favor formal worship with incense and clerical vestments as well as those who prefer simpler services closer to the reformed Protestant tradition. Anglican clergymen are referred to as priests rather than ministers, and monastic orders are permitted. The church's foundation documents are the Thirty-Nine Articles of Faith and the Book of Common Prayer. See also NONCONFORMISTS.

BLOATERS AND KIPPERS. Part of Britain's culinary heritage, these different forms of salted and smoked herring appear in a number of the family budgets reproduced in these readings. Kippered herrings, developed in Northumbria, were introduced in London in the 1840s. They became a popular protein in London working-class households, especially for Sunday meals, and appeared in middle-class menus as well. Herring may be heavily or lightly preserved by a combination of salting and smoking. Kippers are herrings split in half; bloaters are kept whole for the preserving process.

BOARD SCHOOLS; SCHOOL BOARD FOR LONDON (SBL). The Education Act of 1870 created 2,500 elected boards throughout the country to administer a new compulsory educational system. Initially, the boards were to offer education for children from ages five to ten. London's School Board was responsible for providing elementary education as well as some adult education programs. The SBL consisted of fifty-five members, elected by male and female taxpayers. Women were also eligible for positions on school boards themselves. London was divided into eleven divisions, each of which could elect from four to seven members, based on population.

CARE COMMITTEES. See SCHOOL MANAGERS.

CASUAL WARD. See WORKHOUSES.

CHARITY ORGANISATION SOCIETY (COS). The COS was founded in 1869 with the aim of standardizing the granting of charitable aid and of making it harder for the beneficiaries to cheat by applying to multiple organizations. The storefront neighborhood COS offices were popular sites for young women volunteers, and some branch workers were salaried. The COS, despite its name, was wary of charity: receiving relief undermined thrift, hard work, and sobriety. The COS emphasis on careful casework and a thorough knowledge of social conditions gave it a major role in the professionalization of social work and the promotion of social research.

CONSTITUTIONAL SUFFRAGISTS. The constitutional suffragists, the majority in the women's suffrage movement, focused on increasing parliamentary support for women's suffrage through meetings, demonstrations, and petitions. This is the older branch of the suffrage movement, originating in the 1860s. In 1897, the several societies working for suffrage formed the National Union of Women's Suffrage Societies (NUWSS). They concentrated on getting pro-suffrage candidates elected to Parliament and on encouraging M.P.'s to introduce suffrage bills ("private-member bills," as opposed to those introduced by the prime minister or his cabinet). See also MILITANT SUFFRAGISTS.

DOCK STRIKE OF 1889. London was a major international port city before 1914, its many large docks and warehouses humming with workers of many different trades. In the late 1880s several unions of a new kind had been forming, departing from traditional craft unions to incorporate the unskilled; the match workers' union, which Annie Besant helped organize, was one of these "new unions." The dockers' strike broke out suddenly in mid-August 1889 with a dispute over bonuses that led workers at one of the docks to walk off the job site. Other dockers followed suit, and many of the strikers formed a new union, the Dock, Wharf, and Riverside Labourers, headed by Ben Tillett. It soon claimed 24,000 London members. The strikers' demands included a pay rate of 6d (a "tanner") per hour and a daily minimum of four hours' continuous work. The strike continued for five weeks while the union survived on donations from supporters all over Britain and from unions abroad. The striking dockers' enormous, dignified, and well-staged processions through central London created good will among the propertied classes. The strike dragged on, though, until a settlement was reached as the result of the efforts of Cardinal Manning, the Catholic Archbishop of Westminster, who served as the chief mediator in the dispute. One result of the settlement was that many men who had eked out a living through occasional part-time jobs at the docks would no longer be hired under a new system that gave smaller groups of workers more regular work. But the dockers' strike was followed in the 1890s with the formation of several other "new unions."

EVANGELICAL MOVEMENT. The term *Evangelical* applies, on the one hand, to the movements and denominations that grew out of the eighteenth-century Methodist religious revival. The term also denotes a strand within the Church of England itself. Evangelicals believed in the personal experience of religion and its potential for spiritual transformation of the individual. They focused on believers' recognition of their sinfulness, the need for conversion, and the grace conferred by Christ's sacrifice. Evangelicals often worked together across denominations in philanthropies and political campaigns.

FABIAN SOCIETY. The Fabian Society was founded in London in 1883 and became one of Britain's most influential socialist organizations. The name refers to a Roman general, Fabius Cunctator, who was skilled at avoiding pitched battles, thus wearing out his opponents and eventually achieving victory. The Fabians were, not surprisingly, advocates of gradual rather than revolutionary social changes. They believed that experts, well trained and working efficiently, could best institute needed reforms, and they placed their hopes not only in national legislation but also in local government. To promote the general welfare, the state could appropriate private property in land or capital, as these were social in origin. The Fabians held the interesting position that the "special skills" of professionals were also social in origin and thus could be commanded by the state. Members at various points included Annie Besant, H. G. Wells, George Bernard Shaw, Maud Pember Reeves, Clementina Black, and Sidney and Beatrice Webb. The Fabians helped to form the Labour Party in 1900 and affiliated with it. The society still exists today and has many chapters throughout the United Kingdom.

FIRST CLASS DEGREE. At Oxford, Cambridge, and many other universities in Britain, students take a series of exams at the end of their three or four years of study. The "class" of their degree is based on the results of these exams. A first designates major distinction; a second is good; a third is somewhat below average. For an unfortunate few, there is also a fourth, or pass. At Cambridge University only, scoring in the highest ranks in mathematics makes the student a Wrangler; the very top math student is the Senior Wrangler. Helen Bosanquet's moral sciences degree at Newnham College was a first; Mary Higgs's, in natural sciences at Girton College, was a second.

GIRLS' CLUBS. Girls' (or boys') clubs, usually aimed at teenagers, were sponsored by settlement houses, missions, and other organizations or individuals. They met in the evening so that those who were full-time workers—most of the boys and a large proportion of the girls in poor districts—could participate. Their purpose varied according to the sponsor, and the clubs had different degrees of self-government. All clubs had in common the goal of continuing the young people's education and offering wholesome amusements such as singing, French, needlework, gymnastics, and games; many also had libraries and speakers on current events. Many a middle-class woman in charge of such a club had a story to tell of mayhem and humiliation by club girls who rejected her authority or found her curriculum ridiculous. Yet the clubs were popular and had an impact on many children. By early in the twentieth century there were London-wide and national federations of girls' clubs, which met for performances and competitions. Mark Smith, of the Informal Education Archives, an organization and Web site dedicated to promoting lifelong learning, sees these clubs and their leaders as precursors of today's youth workers. See the Web site maintained by Smith (http://www.infed.org/archives/).

GIRTON COLLEGE. Efforts to establish an institution of higher education for women began in the mid-1860s, led by Emily Davies. In 1873, after several years in temporary quarters, Girton moved to its current site two miles north of Cambridge—a site chosen to protect the young women from presumed wild and marauding male undergraduates. The other pioneering women's college at Cambridge was Newnham College. It was founded in 1871 by philosopher Henry Sidgwick, who had already begun offering lectures to women. Students who had attended Newnham and Girton did not receive official Cambridge University degrees until 1948.

HIGH CHURCH. The term *high church* refers to Catholic-sympathizing members of the Anglican Church; high church adherents opposed the rational and undogmatic bent of many eighteenth- and early-nineteenth-century church leaders. John Henry Newman (1801–1890) is one of the best-known high churchmen. The Oxford movement formed around him in the 1830s. This important group would have been considerably larger if so many of its adherents had not actually converted to Catholicism! High church Anglicans were also called "ritualists" because they stressed the importance of church ritual: elaborate vestments for clergymen, the use of incense and candles in churches, and a focus on the Mass.

HOME RULE. Home Rule refers to (limited) autonomy and self-government for England's harshly ruled nearby colony, Ireland. The Act of Union in 1800 dissolved the Irish Parliament. Irish representatives, instead, sat in the British Parliament in London, and through the 1880s, this bloc played a significant role in parliamentary politics. Politicians in England feared that Home Rule would threaten the enormous English property holdings on Irish soil as well as Northern Ireland's large Protestant population. As prime minister, William Gladstone introduced Home Rule bills twice, though both were defeated. In general, Liberals came to support Home Rule, while the Conservatives espoused "unionism," that is, the union of England and Ireland, sweetened with land reforms for the Irish peasantry. In 1912 the Liberals succeeded in passing the Government of Ireland Act (it did not include Northern Ireland), but it was on hold until after World War I. By then, Irish activists were demanding complete independence rather than Home Rule.

HUNDREDWEIGHT (CWT.). This traditional measure of weight was the equivalent of 112 pounds.

INDEPENDENT LABOUR PARTY (ILP). Founded in 1893 under the leadership of Keir Hardie, the ILP's aim was to help members of the working class get elected to Parliament. In 1900, the ILP joined with a number of labor unions and other organizations to form a separate labor-oriented parliamentary party, originally called the Labour Representation Committee. Its named was changed to Labour Party after the general election of 1906. Labour participated, for the first time, in a coalition government in 1915.

LABOUR PARTY. See INDEPENDENT LABOUR PARTY.

LADY. It is nearly impossible to define the term *lady.* In her 1910 study, *The Lady: Studies of Certain Significant Phases of Her History* (1910; reprint, Chicago: University of Chicago Press, 1970), Emily James Putnam offered an approximate meaning: "the female of the favoured social class." This would locate ladies as the daughters or wives of the approximately 10 percent of Britain's population who were upper middle class or upper class, their wealth acquired through businesses, land, and the professions. But being a lady was not simply a function of household wealth. Many subtle and unspoken elements intermixed in a figure who would be perceived by peers as a lady: accent, voice, education, choice of vocabulary, hairstyle, and habits of dress—such as the wearing of gloves of the right color and length. A true lady would not raise her voice or show uninhibited emotion outside of her own household. *Genteel* is a close synonym. Nearly all of the twenty-four women whose writings are collected here, plus most of those discussed in the introduction, were ladies, but not all were rich. Some who were born into genteel middle-class homes had little money themselves in adulthood and had to earn their own livings. Yet their manners and speech would have signaled their origins. Beatrice Potter calls attention to these signs in her description of her experiences as a seamstress in a Jewish-owned East London workshop (see chapter 24). Potter was in quite elaborate disguise, yet the proprietor of the shop treats her with indulgence, saying, "There is something in your face that's uncommon, and your voice too, that's odd—no word higher than another."

LADY MARGARET HALL. See SOMERVILLE COLLEGE.

LADY RENT COLLECTORS/HOUSING MANAGERS. In 1865, Octavia Hill completed the purchase of three houses in a court called Paradise Place near Baker Street, not far from Hill's own home. Each Paradise Place room housed an entire family, a pattern common throughout London's slums. The project was funded in part by essayist and social reformer John Ruskin, Hill's friend and employer at that time. It was Hill's idea to persuade inner-city landlords to use well-educated women as managers of their properties; these women would demonstrate to the nation that decent housing could be provided to poor tenants at low rents while still offering a profit for the landlords. At the same time, the tenants would benefit from their interaction with their refined and knowledgeable rent collectors. By the time she died in 1912, Octavia Hill controlled fifteen hundred different properties. Other rent collectors mentioned or reprinted in these selections are Emma Cons, Margaret Harkness, Margaret Nevinson, Ella Pycroft, Henrietta Rowland (Barnett), Kate Potter, and Beatrice Potter.

LONDON COUNTY COUNCIL. The ultimate authority to govern London belonged to Parliament rather than to its inhabitants, and over the years Parliament has contrived many different schemes for London. The London County Council was established under the 1888 Local Government Act, which went into effect the next year. The Council itself had 118 members. The electorate for these councilors was based on a property but not a gender qualification, so out of a total population of over 5 million in 1901, about 600,000 voted, including 100,000 women. Many older jurisdictions continued to exist after 1889, and the LCC did not at first have control over such basic functions as policing and education. It did have jurisdiction over parks, streets, bridges and tunnels, fire safety, sewers, street improvements, and new housing programs.

LOW CHURCH. The term *low church* refers to the Evangelical movement within the Anglican Church. The Clapham sect (whose most prominent member was the antislavery leader William Wilberforce) early in the nineteenth century and Charles Simeon at Cambridge University were centers of low church belief and activity. Later in the century, the philanthropist Anthony Ashley Cooper, Seventh Earl of Shaftesbury, was probably the best known. Maude Stanley, in this collection, was a lifelong low church Anglican. See also EVANGELICAL MOVEMENT.

MAGISTRATES. Magistrates are minor judicial officials appointed by the Lord Chancellor, with jurisdiction over such common crimes as theft and assault. There are several hundred magistrates' courts in Britain today; each is presided over by at least two lay (volunteer and unpaid) magistrates. Magistrates also decide which crimes are serious enough to be prosecuted in higher courts. In 1920 Margaret Nevinson was appointed the first woman magistrate in London and served in that position for decades.

MARRIED WOMEN'S PROPERTY ACTS. Married Women's Property Acts were passed in 1870 and again in 1882 in response to a campaign (1868 to 1882) led by Elizabeth Wolstoneholme Elmy and Ursula Mellor Bright. Under common law, when women married, their husbands received all of their property except land—though husbands were also entitled to the rents and income from their wives' land. Wives could not sue or be sued, sign contracts, or even make a will on their own. Under the 1870 act, wives could control their wages, savings, and some investment and inheritances. The 1882 act granted married women all the property they held before and after their marriages. Thus wives had many of the rights of single women.

MILITANT SUFFRAGISTS. Militant suffragists were convinced not only of the urgency of the suffrage cause but also of the need for dramatic measures to achieve it. The Women's Social and Political Union (WSPU), founded in 1903, led by Emmeline Pankhurst, her daughter Christabel, and, until 1913, her other daughter, Sylvia, is the best known of the militant organizations. Members of other groups, however, often joined them in their actions, which ranged from processions and demonstrations to civil disobedience, attacks on police, the breaking of the plate-glass windows of fancy shops to invite arrest by the police, and the burning of golf links and other places dear to members of the government. Many of the women arrested went on hunger strikes, and were brutally force-fed. WSPU techniques generated a great deal of press attention and increased public support for the cause.

MODEL DWELLINGS. The term *model dwellings* refers to apartment-style buildings constructed by philanthropic organizations. They were intended to supply economical and sanitary apartments for workers at fair rents and with reasonable profits to their owners. The Peabody Trust was one of the earliest of such companies. The East London Dwellings Company, formed in 1884 at the urging of Samuel Barnett (see SETTLEMENTS, SETTLEMENT MOVEMENT), constructed several model dwellings within a few years of its formation. Octavia Hill was asked to manage some of them. Among the company's properties were the Katharine Buildings, near Tower Bridge (see chapters 7, 15, and 24). Model dwellings were not ideal homes. To save construction costs, the individual apartments often did not have running water, which had to be fetched on a landing. The flats usually did not have their own toilets. The rooms were small; the rents were often higher than those in surrounding slums;

and tenants had to abide by regulations on the number of inhabitants per room, punctuality of rent payments, cleanliness, and so on. Furthermore, the inhabitants of some buildings may have resented the weekly visits from their "lady rent collectors."

NATIONAL UNION OF WOMEN'S SUFFRAGE SOCIETIES (NUWSS). See CONSTITUTIONAL SUFFRAGISTS.

NEWNHAM COLLEGE. See GIRTON COLLEGE.

NONCONFORMISTS. Nonconformists were members of Protestant denominations that did not accept the Church of England's Thirty-Nine Articles of Faith (see ANGLICAN CHURCH). Technically this term also applies to Catholics, but is not usually used in that way. Nonconformism encompasses such "Old Dissent" pre–Civil War sects as Presbyterians, Baptists, and Congregationalists. "New Dissent" sects formed in the eighteenth century and later—such as Methodists, Plymouth Brethren, Unitarians, and the Salvation Army—are also Nonconformists. Nonconformist church attendance was about equal to that of the Church of England. Nonconformists were central in Victorian political life. In the earlier decades of the nineteenth century they provided ardent support for the abolition of slavery and the slave trade. Later they spearheaded temperance, championed housing reform and aid to the urban poor, opposed the Contagious Diseases Acts, and advocated voting rights for women.

ORDER OF THE BRITISH EMPIRE (OBE). The Order of the British Empire (OBE) is one of several "orders of chivalry" conferred by the monarch. The OBE was created in 1917 to demonstrate the monarchy's recognition of the war efforts of individuals throughout the empire and was the first order of chivalry that women could receive. After World War I the OBE was redefined to honor contributions to the arts and to charitable and welfare organizations. There are currently one hundred thousand people throughout the world who are members of this order. Clara Grant and Mary Higgs, among the authors included in this book, received this award.

POOR LAW GUARDIANS. Under the 1834 Poor Law, poor law guardians were locally elected officials who set policy and oversaw the administration of aid to the poor. The harsh 1834 law prohibited "outdoor relief"—cash or food that recipients could use at home. Those who were destitute would have to go to workhouses (see WORKHOUSES), designed to offer inmates the barest minimum of comforts. By the late nineteenth century, children, the ill, and often the elderly were cared for in specialized branches. There were thirty-one boards of guardians in the county of London in 1900, with a total of 814 members. Elaborate property qualifications determined who could vote for local guardians and who could serve in that capacity. Women were allowed to vote and to serve, but there were very few before the passage of the Parish and District Councils Act of 1894. This law dramatically lowered the property qualification and thus facilitated the election of women as well as working-class men. Nearly nine hundred women were serving as guardians in the country as a whole in 1895.

POOR LAW UNIONS. Officials formed these administrative units in response to the Poor Law Amendment Act of 1834. Before that year the parish, an ancient church-centered unit, was responsible for caring for its poor. Policy for the newly established unions was made by boards of guardians, who after 1894 were elected fairly democratically, with women property holders able to vote and hold office. Workhouses were the unions' responsibility. The poor-relief policies of the unions varied widely. In those with active Labour or socialist parties (after 1894), the guardians were especially generous—to the great annoyance of the national government, which abolished them in 1930.

SCHOOL MANAGERS. School managers were school-based volunteers in London and other large towns who organized services for pupils in poor districts such as free or cheap meals, clothing, boots, country holidays, and medical care. They were renamed Care Committees under the 1906 Education (Provision of Meals) Act and were assigned the job of organizing dinners for schoolchildren and investigating families' ability to pay for them. Members were mainly well-off ladies and gentlemen, but also included clergymen, wives of clergymen, teachers, and local settlement house residents. By 1914 there were at least eight thousand Care Committee volunteers in London, as well as a handful of paid supervisors.

SETTLEMENTS, SETTLEMENT MOVEMENT. In the early 1880s socialist ideas were spreading along with pressure to extend the vote to new groups of working-class men. Several dramatic exposés of slum horrors—incest, disease, violence—were also published. In this context a number of socially concerned intellectuals began to suggest that privileged young people go beyond occasional acts of charity and instead actually inhabit slum districts. Living among the people, they could offer help more easily while learning about poverty conditions in order to improve them. Settling privileged individuals in the slums could—it was thought—re-create some of the now lost intimacy between country squires and their tenants in earlier centuries. The first formal "settlement," Toynbee Hall, was founded in 1884, soon after Samuel Barnett, socially activist vicar of a small parish in Whitechapel, gave an inspiring lecture at Oxford University titled "Settlements of University Men in Great Towns." The settlement opened near Barnett's church. It was named after political economist Arnold Toynbee (uncle of the historian), who died in 1883 at age thirty. University-educated men began flocking to Toynbee Hall, which offered evening classes from philosophy to shorthand, activities for children, cultural events, and speakers. Many got involved in local government or labor affairs. Overseen by Barnett's energetic wife Henrietta, many child-oriented philanthropies also used the settlement as a base. The success and visibility of Toynbee Hall led to the formation of several dozen other settlements in London and other large cities. Toynbee Hall is still in operation, despite bomb damage during World War II.

SLUM. The word *slum* may have originated in Britain in the 1810s as a slang word for "slumber"; it came to designate an unsavory back room or a remote isolated back alley. A little later, the term *back slum* was being used, and from the middle of the nineteenth century, it was abbreviated to *slum*. Older terms like *rookery* and *den* were synonyms. Some would have defined nearly all of South and East London as slums by the 1880s; others pointed out the hundreds of quiet and respectable streets in these areas. By the 1880s or so, the word *slumming* was used, often with irony, to denote wealthy visitors coming to observe the inhabitants of slums for their own interest and amusement.

SOCIAL DEMOCRATIC FEDERATION (SDF). Founded in 1881 as a Marxist action group with numerous branches in London and the rest of the country, the SDF was led by H. M. Hyndman (1842–1921). The SDF was especially active in 1886 and 1887, defending the right to hold outdoor meetings; this organization was energetic in municipal politics as well. The SDF's specialty, however, was probably agitation on behalf of the unemployed, an area neglected by most other left-leaning organizations. The SDF was one of the organizations involved in founding the Labour Party (Labour Representation Committee was its original name), but withdrew from the coalition in 1901. A great many Labour leaders passed through the SDF at some point in their careers: John Burns, Tom Mann, and Ben Tillett, among others. Annie Besant, Charlotte Despard, and Margaret McMillan were also members for a time.

SOMERVILLE COLLEGE. At Oxford University, Somerville College (opened 1879 and nondenominational) and Lady Margaret Hall (Church of England affiliated) were the first women's colleges. Initially the colleges were not formally affiliated with the university, and were just places where women lived while they attended lectures open to the public. Somerville and Lady Margaret Hall administrators hired tutors by private arrangement with moonlighting faculty. Students eventually could take Oxford examinations, but until 1920, when the women's colleges were recognized as part of the university, would not get an Oxford degree.

TOYNBEE HALL. See SETTLEMENTS, SETTLEMENT MOVEMENT.

THE WOMEN'S FREEDOM LEAGUE (WFL). The Women's Freedom League was founded in 1907 by seventy breakaway members of the Pankhurst-dominated WSPU who sought a more democratic suffrage organization. Margaret Nevinson and Charlotte Despard were among them. WFL members were willing to be arrested to dramatize their cause, and some also refused to pay taxes to protest their lack of national vote, but they opposed the violent methods (such as arson) of the WSPU. The organization eventually had about four thousand members in sixty branches. The London branch also operated a small settlement house, headed by Charlotte Despard. The WFL put out an informative and well-written newspaper, *The Vote*. Unlike many of the suffrage organizations, the WFL continued its suffrage agitation during World War I, and many of its members were pacifists.

WOMEN'S INDUSTRIAL COUNCIL (WIC). An outgrowth of the Women's Trade Union Association, the Women's Industrial Council was founded in 1894 and existed for about twenty-five years. Both organizations saw themselves as groups of "women of leisure and ability" who would help working women, with the WIC's emphasis being the collection and dissemination of information. The membership included a number of male labor leaders and politicians, and women with a variety of political positions from socialist to liberal. See chapters 3, 6, and 9.

WOMEN'S SOCIAL AND POLITICAL UNION (WSPU). See MILITANT SUFFRAGISTS.

WOMEN'S UNIVERSITY SETTLEMENT. The Women's University Settlement (WUS), the first women's settlement, was launched in 1887 with the formation of a committee representing most of the women's colleges and aiming to form a "Women's University Association for Work in the

Poorer Districts of London." The members were encouraged by Henrietta Barnett and housing reformer Octavia Hill, among others, and chose as their home a stern but serviceable building at Nelson Square, Blackfriars Road, Southwark. Within a few years there were about thirty women working regularly in the district, though there was only room for five of them in Nelson Square. The settlers sponsored art exhibits, concerts, clubs, and parties for children, but are particularly notable for their dedication to such existing philanthropies as the Children's Country Holiday Fund, the Metropolitan Association for Befriending Young Servants, the Invalid Children's Aid Association, and housing management for Octavia Hill (see LADY RENT COLLECTORS/HOUSING MANAGERS). The WUS leaders placed themselves firmly within the world of social work and aimed to train future members of this newly forming profession. They sponsored lectures on such welfare topics as the poor law, local government, and sanitation, a program that was eventually absorbed by the London School of Economics. See also SETTLEMENTS, SETTLEMENT MOVEMENT.

WORKHOUSES. Workhouses were institutions, usually sponsored by groups of poor law guardians (unions of local welfare boards), to which destitute people could resort for shelter. According to the 1834 Poor Law, still officially in effect in the late nineteenth century, workhouses were intended to be so harsh that they would attract only the really desperate. Men and women, even married couples, were separated, as well as parents and children; meaningless and exhausting work was often required; food, heat, and medical care were distributed very meagerly. In the 1880s, when a few social reformers began to appear among the guardians setting local poor-law policy, some London unions modified or rejected this model; they began to offer aid to the poor without making them go to workhouses. In any case workhouses could not accommodate the massive requests for relief that characterized periods of economic recession. Casual wards in many workhouses provided a night's lodging and a few meals for the homeless, at an even lower standard than that of the regular workhouses. See also POOR LAW GUARDIANS.

INDEX

Italicized page numbers indicate illustrations.

Aberdeen, Ishbel, Countess of, 105n1
Acorn, George, 161, 163
Adams, Henry, 53
Adderley, James, 3
Adler, Nettie, 106n4
alcohol, 93. *See also* barmaids; drinking and drunkenness
Alderley Park (Cheshire), 226
Anderson, Zelie, 179
Anti-Sweating League: investigation by, 56–63; participants in, 53–54
Asquith, Herbert, 179
Astor, Nancy, 124, 125
aurality. *See* listening
Aveling, Edward, 46, 91n4

Baby Week Exhibitions, 155
Balfour, Arthur, 83
Barker, Lilian, 72, 74n3
barmaids, 92–96
Barnes, Earl, 83
Barnett, Henrietta, 16, 172
Barnett, Samuel, 15, 20, 86, 172
Barrows, Herbert, 48
Battersea Park, 244–45
Bedford College: social work training program of, 65; students of, 72, 73, 162
Behlmer, George, 30–31n10
Belgrave Square, 212
Belgravia, 281

benefits: burial, 214, 216–17; maternity, 150, 152
Bermondsey Settlement, 16, 148–49
Besant, Annie (née Wood): background of, 45–46; diverse activities of, 46–47; friendships of, 89; writing of, 11–12; works: "White Slavery in London," 48–51
Besant, Frank, 45–46
Bethnal Green: housing in, 24; population of, 283; women's settlement in, 20
Bible and Domestic Female Mission (Central London): activities of, 198–99
Bibles: door-to-door sales of, 198–99, 200–207
birth control, 46, 148
Black, Clementina: background of, 52–53; on Bryant and May, 47; on founding of WIC, 105n1; friendships of, 118; further reading on, 56; on listening, 15; on minimum-wage laws, 54; writing of, 56; works: *Makers of Our Clothes,* 56–63
Black, Constance. *See* Garnett, Constance (née Black)
Black, David, 52
Black, Emma, 52
Black, Grace, 52
Blair, Tony, 282
Blavatsky, Helena P., 47
Bloody Sunday (1887), 46, 91

Bloomsbury: Harkness in, 90; Passmore Edwards settlement in, 23, 25; Ranyards in, 198; working girls' hostel in, 125
Boer War, 27, 181–86
Bolshevik Revolution, 179, 264
Bondfield, Margaret, 54, 208
Booth, Charles: on fur pullers, 107; social survey and investigators of, 6, 15, 16, 229, 262, 284; works: *Life and Labour,* 40, 263
Booth, Mary, 16
Borough Polytechnic, 229
Bosanquet, Bernard, 6, 16, 65
Bosanquet, Helen (née Dendy): background of, 64–65; on chronicling poverty, 13; further reading on, 66; marriage of, 16; recovering writings of, 6; Royal Commission on Poor Laws and, 264; works: "Marriage in East London," 66–71
Bow Common: Fern Street settlement in, 82, 85, 126; peace demonstration in, 187–88, 191; residents of, 81–82, 178
box making, 50, 108
Bradford (Yorkshire): McMillan in, 125, 126
Bradlaugh, Charles, 46
British and Foreign Bible Society (BFBS), 199
British Weekly: on barmaids, 92–96; *Toilers* series in, 90n
Broadbent, Benjamin, 151
Browning, Elizabeth Barrett, 168
Browning, Robert, 105
brush drawing: fur pulling and, 108
Bryant, Theodore, 48–51
Bryant and May (match manufacturers), 47, 48–51
buildings (working-class apartments): caretakers of, 42; characteristics of, 283; Columbia Square, 24; daily life in, 41–44; East London Dwellings, 40, 90; Katharine Buildings as exemplar of, 40, 90, 172, 262; terms for, 40
Burdett-Coutts, Angela, 10, 24
Buzard, James, 26
Byron, George Gordon, Lord, 175

cab drivers, 24
Caine, Barbara, 22

"Called to the Bar" (Beale), 92
Cambridge natural science tripos, 98
canary girls, 73
Canning Town: peace demonstration in, 191; settlement and hospital, 27
Canterbury College, 209
cap shops, Woolwich Arsenal, 73, 76. See *also* munitions work
Care Committees (school managers): activities of, 3–4; Guild of, 54; and McMillan, 30n8, 125; Nevinson's work on, 173; school settlements and, 85–88; Stanley's work on, 228
casual wards. *See* workhouses
Catholic Church: laywomen and, 3; Stanley and, 226, 229
Central London: population of, 283–85; Ranyard's mission in, 198–99
Certeau, Michel de, 29n2
Chamberlain, Joseph, 264
Chamberlain, Neville, 264
Champion, H. H., 48
Charing Cross Road School, 228
charity: of munitions workers, 77; public welfare vs., 65; Soho house of, 237; as woman's sphere, 19
Charity Organisation Society (COS), 3, 13, 16, 64, 262
Chartist movement, 7, 178
Chase, Ellen, 15
Chatterton, Thomas, 169
Chaucer, Geoffrey, 105
Chelsea Hospital, 182–83
Cheltenham College, 20
Cheshire, 226
Chesteron, Ada, 6
child labor investigations, 104–5
children: 1917 peace demonstration and, 186–87, 189–90; bathing of, 194; Bible edition for, 198; charm of, 213; devaluing of female, 71; drunken parents' abuse of, 232–33, 234–35, 238; as economic burden, 69, 70, 223–25; free meals for, *82;* funerals for, 214–18; games of, *245;* health care for, 85, 125–26, 151–52; holiday home for disabled, 163; hospital ward for, 169; illustrations of, *2, 240, 241, 242, 244, 245, 247;* infant-welfare work expanded for,

4; joyful reception of first, 159, 222; labors of, 111, 184; legislation, 151–60; London's population of, 283; milk for, 203; nurses' home visits and reports on, 204–6; premature births of, 215–16; spectacles for, 157–58. *See also* Care Committees; education; infant mortality; schools; street arabs; working girls

Child Study movement, 83

China: missionaries in, 27, 199

Christian Socialism, 20–21

Christian Social Union, 163–64n9

churches and parishes (local): assisting abused wives, 237; neighborhood role of, 59; Stanley's parish visits and, 228; weddings at, 66–67; women as parish visitors, 15–16. *See also* clergymen

Church of England: Epiphany celebration in, 257; Evangelical movement in, 20–21; nuns of, 256–57; parish visits of, 6–7, 228; women's roles in, 15–16, 19. *See also* clergymen

cigarette smoking, 161, 162, 259

civil servants: women as, 89

Clark, Alice, 208

class: attempts to overcome barriers of, 149; buildings reflective of inhabitants', 41; effects on schoolchildren, 126; privileges of upper, 229, 239–40; visibility of, 16, 17

clergymen: concern with poverty of, 20–21; as contacts in investigations, 57–59; dependence on women of, 16; households of, 4, 256

clothing and fashion: schoolchildren's, 154–55; moral implications of, 17–18; of nurses, 166; refashioning of, 195; Sunday markets and, 251–52; Tennant's sketches and, 244–48; visibility of class in, 16, 17; for weddings, 67; of workhouse inmates, 99, 102, 176

clubs: Jewish Working Girls, *9*, 105n1, 140, 228, 229; Odd Fellows, 203–4; for saving, 86, 216–17; Women Writers, 162

Collet, Clara, 10

Colman, Edward, 163

Common Cause (NUWSS journal), 53

Congo Free State, 28, 240

Cons, Emma, 5, 13, 34n48

Contagious Diseases Acts (1860s), 14

cookbooks, 192–97

cooperatives: attitudes toward, 68; housekeeping, 53; of nurses, 162; research on, 263; Women's Cooperative Guild, 162

Copelman, Dina, xiv

COS (Charity Organisation Society), 3, 13, 16, 64, 262

costermongers, account of life among, 139–47

Courtney, Leonard, 16

courtship, 67–68

Covent Garden, 140–47

Crackanthorpe, Blanche Alethea, 36n75

Craik, Dinah Mulock, 21

Creighton (Mrs. Louise), 116

Crimean War, 190

Curtis, Henry, 242

daily life: of Beatrice Potter as a working girl, 266–79; in model dwellings, 42–44

Daily News, 54, 56, 161–62

Dalston, 284

Dame Colet House (Stepney), 20

"dangerous trades," 106–16. *See also* munitions work

Davidoff, Leonore, 21

Delafield, E. M., 13

Dendy, Helen. *See* Bosanquet, Helen (née Dendy)

Dendy, Mary, 65

Deptford: Bible-women in, 200–207; Ellen Chase in, 15; McMillan's health clinic of, 126; schools of, 125

Despard (Mrs. Charlotte), 188, 189

Devil's Chain, The (Jenkins), 232

Dickens, Charles, 10, 12, 23, 24, 25

disabled people: family budget of soldier, 181–86; holiday home for young, 163; nurses' home visits and reports on, 203–4, 206–7

district visiting societies: establishment of, 6–7; women in, 15–16, 23

Dixon, Joy, 47

Dobson, Austin, 118n2

dock workers' strike (1889), 5, 90, 263

domestic service: dislike of, 92; placement

domestic service *(continued):*
in, 233–35, 236–37; unwed mothers in, 233–34, 235

Doré, Gustave, *241*

dressmakers. *See* garment workers

drinking and drunkenness: assistance in overcoming, 201–3, 204; of barmaids, 94–95; of costermongers, 141, 145, 147; effects of, 134–35; impact on family and budget, 153, 154, 156, 200–201; Stanley on problems of, 229, 232–38

Dublin University Magazine, 119

Duckworth, Julia, 33n38

Duckworth, Stella, 11, 22–23

Dunnico, Herbert, 189

East Grinstead, 256

East London: 1917 peace demonstration in, 186–91; Anglican nuns in Haggerston, 256–57, 258–61; Bryant and May in, 47; dock workers' strike in, 5, 90, 263; garment work in, 262–63, 266–79; marriages of poor in, 66–71; population of, 283; poverty in, 284; settlements in, 16, 86, 172, 173; suffrage organizing in, 178, 179; teachers in, 81; wartime conditions in, 179, 180; women's explorations of, 5, 89–90; workers' housing in, 40, 41–44, 90, 172, 262

East London Dwellings Company, 40, 90

East London Federation of Suffragettes (ELFS), 9, 179, 180

East Smithfield: workers' housing in, 40, 90, 172, 173, 262

Eder, David, 126

education: of Anglicans, 4; compulsory, 3, 8, *82;* early childhood, 82–83, 124, 125–26; reform efforts in, 19, 24, 47, 162; women's, 19–20. *See also* schools

Education Act (1870), 8

Education and Propaganda Department (Ministry of Food), 209

ELFS (East London Federation of Suffragettes), 9, 179, 180

Elliott, Dorice Williams, 36n75

employers: investigators' experiences with, 58; room and board for barmaids pro-

vided by, 93–94, 95. *See also* factories; home work

Employment of Children Act (1903), 105

Engels, Friedrich, 5

Ethiopia, 178

ethnicity, 283–84. *See also* Irish population; Jewish people

Fabian Society: executive committee of, 209; labor practices discussed, 48–51; members of, 47, 208, 263

Fabian Women's Group (FWG): North Lambeth project of, 208, 210–25

factories: diversity of, 281; fur pulling in, 107, 113–14; munitions work in, 74–80; regulations on, 115–16, 268, 274–75; wartime production, 264; Webb's work in, 266–79; work in Bryant and May as "white slavery," 47–51

family budgets: of disabled soldier, 181–86; Fabians' study of, 209, 216, 219, 220–21; men's wages and, 153–60; Ranyard's management tips, 201–3; rent and food balance in, 224

Family Endowment Council, 150

family life: Fabians' study of, 208, 210–25; overcrowding's effect on, 70–71; Petty's nutritional advice for, 192–97. *See also* family budgets; men and fathers; mothers and motherhood

Fels, Joseph, 126

feminism: female concern with poverty linked to, 8–10; property rights and, 173; working-class women changed by, 149–50. *See also individual feminists;* suffragettes and suffrage

Fern Street Settlement, 82, 85–88

fiction: cultural work of, 36n75; on interracial marriage, 285n7; of London poverty, 90, 91; nonfiction juxtaposed to, 10–12; references to, 105; slum reportage linked to, 33n31; slum travelers depicted in, 25–26

filling shops, 75–79. *See also* munitions work

Finchley, 284

Finsbury, 283, 284

firing: of barmaids, 94; of married working women, 220

flower seller, *247*

food: budgets for, 201–3, 219, 221, 224–25; cost of, 153; free meals, monitoring of recipients, 3–4; nutritious recipes for, 192–97; Sunday markets and, 252–53, 254; workplace lunches, 93, 114, 271–72

Foster, Shirley, 12

Foxwell, Agnes Kate: background of, 72–73; further reading on, 74; works: *Munition Lasses,* 74–80

Franco-Prussian War, 190, 228

Freeman, Mark, 33n31

French Revolution, 6

Fry, Elizabeth, 19

Frye, Northrop, 14

funerals, 214–18

fur pullers: account of, 104, 106–16; factory work conditions of, 107, 113–14; home work conditions of, 108–9, 110–13; hours of, 110–11; safety measures for, 114–15; as slaves, 106–7; tasks of, 109, 113

FWG. *See* Fabian Women's Group (FWG)

Gambetta, Leon, 239

Gandhi, Mohandas, 47

Garden Suburb (Oldham), 98

Gardner, Ben, 188

garment workers: conditions and wages of, 56–63, 262–63, 268–70; dinner break for, 271–72; factory regulations and, 268, 274–75; fatigue of, 275–76; good nature and hopes of, 276–79; home work of, 56–63, 273–74; looking for position as, 266–68; size of industry, 281

Garnett, Constance (née Black), 40, 52, 118n4

Garnett, David, 40–41n3

Garnett, Edward, 118n4

Garnett, Richard, 118

Gaskell, Elizabeth, 11, 25

Gautrey, Thomas, 164n11

gender: in church and social work, 15–18; in crime definitions, 156; of resident settlement workers, 86–87; Victorian ideology and, 18–20. *See also* men and

fathers; mothers and motherhood; women

gentleman: definition of, 248

Giffen, Robert, 153

Girls' Club Union, 228

Girton College, Cambridge, 98, 226, 230n4

Gissing, George, 10, 17, 118

Gladstone, Margaret. *See* MacDonald, Margaret (née Gladstone)

Gladstone, William, 50

Golders Green, 284

Grant, Clara Ellen: background of, 81; destination of, 26; on early childhood education, 82–83; further reading on, 84; health center at settlement of, 85, 126; works: "School Settlement, A," 85–88

Great Britain: Board of Education of, 125; monetary system of, xiii–xiv; surveillance and spectatorship in, 3–4, 14, 154–55

Greater London Authority, 282

Greater London Council (GLC), 282

Green, T. H., 65

Greenwich Observatory, 133

Greenwood, James, 12

Guest, Lady Charlotte, 24

Guild of Women Citizens (founded by Anna Martin), 149

Guy's Hospital, 89, 199

Hackney, 284

Haggerston, 256–57, 258–61

Hampstead, 172, 173, 283

Hardie, Kier, 179, 182

Harkness, Margaret: background of, 89–90; friendships of, 117, 263; further reading on, 91; mentioned, 40; writing of, 10, 11, 13; works: "Barmaids," 92–96; *Toilers,* 90n

Harley, George, 249

Harrow, 72

health. *See* health care; illnesses

health care: centers for, 53, 83, 85, 126; for elderly, 158; nutritional aspects of, 192; for poor schoolchildren, 85, 125–26; proposed measures on women's and children's, 151–52. *See also* hospitals; illnesses health registers, 115

Higgs, Mary (née Kingsland): background of, 97–98; further reading on, 98–99; writing of, 6, 13–14; works: "In a London Tramp Ward," 99–103

Hill, Octavia, 11, 15, 19, 20, 22, 173

Hills, Jack, 23

Hills, Stella Duckworth, 11, 22–23

Hilton, Marie, 1, 13

Hochschild, Adam, 38–39n106

Hodson, Alice, 13, 17

Hogarth, William, 245

Hogg, Edith (Mrs. F. G.): background of, 104–5; further reading on, 106; writing of, 12; works: "Fur-Pullers of South London, The," 104, 106–16

Holborn, 284

holidays: for disabled children, 163; drunkenness linked to bank holidays, 232; Stanley's country, for mothers, 229; Tennant's sketches and, 244–45; as wage loss, 51; for a working girl, 233

Hollesley Bay (Suffolk), 193, 195

Hollis, Patricia, 164n11

homeless people: illustration of, 242; incognito investigations of, 97, 99–103, 136; shelters for, 97, 136; social theory on, 97–98

home work: fur pulling as, 108–9, 110–13; garment making as, 56–63, 273–74; Hogg's recommendations on, 115–16, 157; investigations of conditions and wages in, 56–63, 104; WIC conference on, 116

horseback riding, 249–50

Hospital (periodical), 161–62

hospitals: disabled soldier's case and, 182–83; nurse's fictionalized account of, 165–71; workhouse infirmary, 175–76. See also health care; illnesses

House of Charity, 237

housing: Burdett'Couts's in Bethnal Green, 24; of costermongers, 141–42, 143–45; differences among, 212–13; examples of, 211–12, 282–83; household budgets and, 70, 153–60; Somers Town case details on, 193–97. See also buildings (working-class apartments); family budgets; settlement houses

Hoxton Settlement, 162, 163–64n9

Hughes, Hugh Price, 20

Hughes, Katherine Price, 18, 20

husbands. See marriage and marital relations

illnesses: case notes on, 194, 195, 196; of disabled soldier and his family, 181–84; of elderly women, 158; of eyes, 78; of fur pullers, 110, 111, 114; in hospitals, 165–71; housing issues and, 141; jaundice as, 73; of munitions workers, 73; nurses' home visits and reports on, 203–7; of women at workhouse, 99–103. See also disabled people; health care; hospitals

Independent Labour Party (ILP), 125, 126, 178

India: 1857 mutiny in, 7; Besant's support for independence of, 47; Malvery's birth in, 136; travel books on, 91; Tweedie's denigration of, 250; women philanthropists' interests in, 26–27

India rubber and gas workers, 5

infant mortality: causes of, 208–9; example of, 184; funeral costs and, 214–18; statistics on, 127, 151–52, 155–56

insurance: burial, 214–18; National Health, 150

Interdepartmental Committee on Physical Deterioration, 229, 230–31n8

Irish population, 3, 283–84

Islington Young Citizen Scouts, 187, 188

James, Henry, 53

James, William, 97

Jewish people: assistance for refugees, 3; in garment work, 266–79; Levy's depictions of, 118; Malvery's series on, 138; as others, 284; portraits of, 53, 55n7; Potter's view of, 263; residence patterns of, 229, 284; Tweedie's depiction of, 249, 251–55

Jewish Working Girls' Club, 9

Jones, Margaret Wynne. See Nevinson, Margaret Wynne (née Jones)

Jones, Timothy, 172

journalism: "new," 12, 14–15; social realism in, 138

Justice (weekly), 83
justices of the peace: first woman, 173–74

Katharine Buildings (East Smithfield), 40, 90, 172, 262
Kennington, 208, 210–13
Kent County Council, 125
Kingsland, Caroline, 98
Kingsland, Mary. *See* Higgs, Mary (née Kingsland)
Kingsland, William, 98
Kingsley, Mary, 13
Koven, Seth, 3, 11, 36n67

labor: "dangerous" trades of, 114; growth of movement, 7; strikes of, 5, 12, 47, *49*, 90, 263. *See also* unemployment; *type of work*
Labour party, 26, 29, 47, 83, 105n1, 264
ladies: use of term, 29n1
ladies bountiful, 23, 72, 74n3
ladies incognito: as costermongers, 137–38, 139–47; as garment workers, 262–63, 266–79; as homeless women, 97, 99–103, 136
lady rent collectors, 11, 15, 20, 22, 40, 90, 172, 173, 262
Lansbury, George, 179
Law and Liberty League, 46
Lawrence, Frederick (later Patrick-Lawrence), 16
Lawrence, Susan, 29, 208
LCC (London County Council), 110, 163n4, 281–82
LCM (London City Mission), 7, 199
Levy, Amy: background of, 117–18; friendships of, 53, 89; further reading on, 119; Morten on, 169; poems: "Ballade of an Omnibus," 120–21; "Ballade of a Special Edition," 121–22; "London in July, 120; "London Plane-Tree, A," 119–20; "London Poets," 123; "Out of Town," 122; "Piano-Organ, The," 122–23
Lewis, Jane, 64
Lidgett, J. Scott, 20
Limehouse, 283
Linnell, Alfred, 46
listening, 14–15, 60

literature. *See* fiction; newspapers and periodicals; poetry
Livingstone, David, 28
Livingstone, "Red" Ken, 282
loans, 145, 217
Lolesworth Buildings (East Smithfield), 173
London: Bloody Sunday in, 46, 91; female literary-philanthropy milieu in, 89–90, 117–18; map of, *xxiii;* poetry on, 119–23; political and social changes in, 6–8; poverty and wealth in, 281–86; sounds of, 171; Sunday outdoor market in, 249, 251–55; transportation expansion in, 8, 22–23, 283; women's influence on, 23–24
London, Jack, 6, 138
London City Mission (LCM), 7, 199
London County Council (LCC), 110, 163n4, 281–82
London dock strike (1889), 5, 90, 263
London Ethical Society, 65, 162
London Hospital, 161
London Missionary Society, 7
London Obstetrical Society, 161
London School Board. *See* School Board for London
London School of Economics, 65
London University, 72, 148. *See also* Bedford College
Longfellow, Henry Wadsworth, 166–67
Lugard, Frederick J. D., 27
Lytton, Constance, 9

MacDonald, Margaret (née Gladstone), 54, 104, 105n1
MacDonald, Ramsay, 54, 105n1
Mackirdy, Archibald, 136
Malvery, Olive Christian: background of, 136–38; further reading on, 138; photograph of, *137;* works: "Gilding the Gutter," 139–47
Mansfield House (settlement), 16
Marcella (Ward), 25–26
"Marcella crop": use of term, 25
Marcus, Jane, 37n83
markets, 24, 142, 143, 146, 249, 251–55, *252*
marriage and marital relations: courtship and, 67–68; of disabled soldier and his wife, 181–86; disintegration of, due to

marriage and marital relations *(continued)*: industrialization, 160; as escape from overcrowded homes, 70–71, 159; Married Women's Property Act, 173; poverty and, 67–70, 218–25; pros/cons of, 62; quarrels and abuse in, 43–44, 229, 232–38; question of postponement of, 222–23; short story on interracial, 285n7; as slavery for women, 149–50; Stanley's interest in, 235, 238; wedding traditions, 66–67; working women fired after, 220. *See also* men and fathers; family life; mothers and motherhood

Married Women's Property Act (1882), 173

Marryat, Ellen, 45

Marshall, Alfred, 263

Martin, Anna: background of, 148–49; further reading on, 150–51; as tax resister, 150n2, 163; on women's and children's welfare, 149–50; works: "Irresponsibility of the Father, The," 148, 151–60

Marx, Eleanor: background of, 5; friendships of, 53, 89–90, 117; goals of, 1, 37–38n90; as supporter of East London strikers, 1–3, 5; translations by, 118

Marx, Karl, 1, 5

Matchmakers' Union, 12, 47, *49*

match making, 12, *49, 50*

Maternity (Women's Co-operative Guild), 159

Matrimonial Causes Act (1878), 229

Maurice Hostel, 163–64n9

Mayfair, 281

Mayfield House (Bethnal Green), 20

Mayhew, Henry, 12, 29n2

Mayor, Alice, 21

Mayor, Flora, 21

McKibbin, Ross, 64

McMillan, Margaret: background of, 124–25; Care Committee work of, 30n8; further reading on, 127; health care activism of, 83, 125–26; writing of, 11, 12; works: "Guy and the Stars," 130–35; "Slum Mother, A," 127–29

McMillan, Rachel, 124–25

Meade, L. T., 11

Mearns, Andrew, 20

men and fathers: as bar hangers-on, 93;

dock strike of, 5, 90, 263; family budgets and cost of feeding, 151–60, 215, 223–25

Methodism, 20–21. *See also* Bermondsey Settlement; Nonconformists; West London Mission (Soho)

Metropolitan Asylums Board, 228, 282

Metropolitan Board of Works, 282

Metropolitan Railway bars, 92–93, 94, 95

Meux, Valerie Susan Langdon (brewing heiress), 125

Meyer, Adele (Lady Carl; née Levis): background of, 5, 53–54; further reading on, 55–56; on listening, 15; as tax resister, 163; works: *Makers of Our Clothes*, 56–63

Meyer, Carl, 53, 55n3

Middlesex Street: Sunday outdoor market of, 249, 251–55

midwifery training, 161

Mill, John Stuart, 178

minimum-wage laws: Black's support for, 54; investigation as precursor to, 56–63

Missing Link Magazine, The: on breadwinner's dinner, 200–203; Deptford Bible-nurse, 203–4; on nursing cases, 204–7

missionaries: destinations of, 26–27; door-to-door Bible sales and, 198–99; London City Mission, 7, 199; native agency principle of, 27; plans of, 81; reports and lectures of, 12

missions, foreign, 27, 199

model dwellings, 24, 25, 33n38, 40

Money, Chiozza, xiv

money-lenders, 145, 217

Montagu, Lily, *9*, 54, 105n1

Morant, Robert, 125–26

Morten, Honnor: background of, 161–63; further reading on, 164; writing of, 10, 11; works: "Eating the Apple," 165–71

Motherhood Special Fund Committee (Fabian), 208–9

mothers and motherhood: case studies on, 193–97; depiction of, 127–29; holidays for, 229; joy at becoming, 159; maternity benefit for, 150, 152; nervousness about becoming, 222; pre-WWI conditions of, 159; proposals for welfare of, 151–60; St.

Pancras school and health center for, 53, 55, 192

munitions work, 72–73, 74–80; day-to-day routines of, 74–76; general observations of, 76–78; women supervisors in, 72, 74n3

murder, of wife as "finable" offense, 156, 232

muscular Christianity, 20–22

My District Visitors (anon.), 23

National Health Insurance Act, 150

National Secular Society, 46

National Society for the Prevention of Cruelty to Children (NSPCC), 154

National Union of Women's Suffrage Societies (NUWSS), 53

National Union of Women Workers, 26–27

native agency principle, 27

Nehru, Jawaharlal, 47

neighborhoods: Black and Meyer's study of, 60–61; church and parish role in, 59; inner city losing population, 284–85; North Lambeth and Kennington, 210–13; population decline in, 284–85

neighborliness, 42

Nesbit, Edith, 208

Nevinson, C. R. W., 173

Nevinson, Henry, 40, 172, 173, 285n7

Nevinson, Margaret Wynne (née Jones): activism of, 54, 172–74; background of, 172; further reading on, 174–75; as rent collector, 40, 90; writing of, 10, 11; works: "Evacuation of the Workhouse, The," 175–77; *In the Workhouse,* 174

new journalism, 12, 14–15

Newman, George, 151

Newnham College, Cambridge, 52, 65, 119

Newport (Essex), 53

newspapers and periodicals: Levy's poem about special edition of, 121–22; photographic innovations of, 136–38; slum travelers caricatured in, 13–14. *See also* journalism; new journalism; *specific publications*

New Woman: concept of, 8; fictional depictions of, 25–26

Nightingale, Florence, 21

Nineteenth Century (periodical): on fathers' irresponsibility, 148, 151–60; on fur pullers, 104, 106–16; on women as civil servants, 89; on women's higher education, 230n4; on women's rights, 36n75; on working-girl's diary, 266–79

Nonconformists, 3, 5, 16, 20–21, 65, 198. *See also* Bermondsey Settlement; West London Mission

Non-Conscription Fellowship, 187

Nord, Deborah, 25

Norman, Helen (from Gissing's *Workers in the Dawn*), 17

Notification of Births Act, 151–52

NSPCC (National Society for the Prevention of Cruelty to Children), 154

nurses: associations of district, 3, 162; fictionalized diary of, 165–71; home visits and reports of, 203–7; illnesses and death of, 167–68; at school settlement, 85; training of, 89, 161, 199; uniform of, 17

Nurses' Cooperative, 162

nutrition experts, 192

NUWSS (National Union of Women's Suffrage Societies), 53

OBE, 83, 98

O'Day, Rosemary, 40

Odd Fellows Club, 203–4

Oldham, 97, 98

Old Vic Theater, 34n48

organizations. *See* clubs; *specific organizations*

Orient Magazine, 260

Pankhurst, Christabel, 178, 180n5

Pankhurst, Emmeline, 178, 180n5

Pankhurst, Richard, 178

Pankhurst, Sylvia: background of, 178; further reading on, 180–81; labor and suffrage organizing of, 9, 179–80; works: "East London Peace Demonstration, The," 186–91; "Martyrdom of a Disabled Soldier's Wife, The," 181–86

paper-bag making, 112

Parkes, Margaret Kineton, 150n2

Parliament: first women elected to, 29; London governance by, 282; minimum-

Parliament *(continued):*
wage law discussed in, 56; municipal school boards dismantled by, 125; Potter's testimony for, 263; woman and child welfare recommendations and, 151–60

parliamentary acts (statutes): Aliens, 138; Contagious Diseases, 14; Education, 8; Employment of Children, 105; Married Women's Property, 173; Matrimonial Causes, 229; on medical exams of schoolchildren, 125–26; National Health Insurance, 150; on poor relief, 65, 112, 173, 264; Trade Boards, 54. *See also* regulatory measures

Passmore Edwards (settlement, Bloomsbury), 23, 25

pathos, 14, 15, *242*

pawnbrokers, pawning, 68, 182, 183, 186

peace demonstration, 186–91

"peaching" (by barmaids), 93

Pearse, Mark Guy, 15

Pearson's Magazine: on costermongers, 139–47; photographic innovations of, 136–38

pedlars, 139

Pember Reeves, Amber, 209

Pember Reeves, Fabian, 209

Pember Reeves, Maud (née Stuart): background of, 208–9; further reading on, 209–10; on monetary system, xiv; writing of, 10, 11, 12; works: "District, The," 210–13; "Poor and Marriage, The," 218–25; "Thrift," 213–18

Pember Reeves, William, 209

pensions, 84n7, 182–84, 187, 204

Pethick-Lawrence, Emmeline, 16, 149

Petticoat Lane market, 249, 251–55, *252*

Petty, Florence: background of, 192; case papers gathered by, 193–97

philanthropy: "woman element" in, 15–18; in women's history, 30n4. *See also* slum philanthropy

Phillips, Marion, 208

photographic innovations in journalism, 136–38

Plato, 97

poetry: urban discourse in Levy's, 119–23

poor and working-class people: areas of residence in London, 284–85; defense of, 4, 208–9, 210–25; differences among, 139, 210–11, 212–13; expanded voting rights of, 7; gospel of service to, 20–22; investigators' experiences with, 60; listening to, 14–15, 60; recommendations on state aid for, 209; restaurant food available for, 59–60, 93; selling Bibles to, 198–99. *See also* poverty

poor laws: fur-pullers' wages and, 112; local guardians of, 173, 228, 264; Royal Commission on, 65, 264

Poovey, Mary, 11, 14

Poplar Trades and Labour Representation Committee, 83

population: of London, 281–82, 283–85; maintaining level of, 155–56

Porritt, Arthur, 162

Potter, Beatrice. *See* Webb, Beatrice (née Potter)

Potter, Kate, 16, 22

Pottle, Mark, 138n3

poverty: clinical approach to, 262; degrees of, 210–11; extent and awareness of, 6–8; feminist concerns with, 8–9; fictional and nonfictcional accounts of, 10–12; household budget and, 153–60; large families linked to, 225; London geography of, 281–86; marriage in context of, 67–71, 218–25; Mearns's pamphlet on, 20–21; as moral weakness, 64–65. *See also* poor and working-class people; poor laws; wages

Poynter, Edward, 239

Prince of Wales's Fund, 182–83

prisons: drunken women sent to, 238; Elizabeth Fry's efforts for, 19; food expenses in, 153; husbands released from, 235, 236, 237; Morten's lectures for, 162; suffragettes in, 179, 180. *See also* workhouses

Protestantism: Bible selling of, 198–99; gospel of service in, 20–22. *See also* Church of England; missionaries; Nonconformists

Pulitzer, Joseph, 239

Purvis, June, 180n5
Pycroft, Ella, 40, 262, 263

Quakers, 98. *See also* Nonconformists
Queen, The (periodical): description of, 249; on Sunday outdoor market, 251–55
Queen Mary College (earlier, Queen Mary's Hostel for Women), 54

race, 283–84
racial prejudice, 41
ragamuffins. *See* street arabs
ragged school movement, 24
Ranyard, Arthur Cowper, 199
Ranyard, Benjamin, 198
Ranyard, Ellen Henrietta (née White): background of, 198–99; further reading on, 200; missionary techniques of, 27; pathos of, 14; works: "Dinner for the Bread-Winner," 200–203; "Report of the Deptford Bible-Nurse," 203–4; "Scalded Child and Our Holloway Nurse, A," 204–7
Rathbone, Eleanor, 29, 150
readers: Bibles for, 198–99; engaging emotions of, 11; working class as, 195
regulatory measures: ignored, 114–15; for poor families, 30–31n10; for workshops and factories, 115–16, 268, 274–75
religion: gospel of service in, 20–22. *See also* Catholic Church; Church of England; Protestantism
Ridge, William Pett, 161, 229
Robinson, Laura A., 148
Rotherhithe: dockside residents of, 148–49; population of, 284–85
Round about a Pound a Week (Fabian tract): basis for, 208–9; chapters: "District, The," 210–13; "Poor and Marriage, The," 218–25; "Thrift," 213–18
Royal College of Art, 179
Royal Commission on the Birth Rate, 151
Royal Commission on the Poor Laws, 65, 264
Royden, Maude, 149
Rubinstein, David, 47

Ruskin, John, 36n67
Russell, Bertrand, 230n5
Russell, John, 226

Said, Edward, 28
sailors, 283
Saint Augustine's Church, 256
St. James's Park, 244–45
St. Pancras, 284
St. Pancras School for Mothers (Somers Town): case papers from, 193–97; goals of, 53, 55, 192
St. Stephen's Church (Westminster), 24
Salisbury (teacher) Training College, 81
Salvation Army, 90, 91
Samuel, Herbert, 152, 182
sanitary authorities: inspectors of, 125, 192; overcrowding and, 154
Sargent, John Singer, 53, 55n7
savings (monetary), 68
Schneer, Jonathan, 281
School Board for London, 47, 162
School Child (journal), 83, 85
School Nurses' Society, 162
schools: age for admission to, 82–83; children inspected at, 154; municipal boards dismantled, 125; nurses in, 162, 163n4; social work based in, 3. *See also* Care Committees; education
school settlements: resident workers for, 85–86; size of, 86–87; teacher's role at, 87–88
Schreiner, Olive, 89, 117–18
scientific observation (of society), 97–98, 170
Scotland Yard, 188
Scudder, Vida, 26
secularism, 46
separate spheres: activist female reformers in context of, 18–20; effects on poor families, 160
settlement houses: administration of, 23; coed activities of, 16; educational classes of, 20, 87–88; establishment of, 25, 82, 162; health care of, 27, 85, 126; resident workers of, 85–88; Tolstoy-inspired, 162–63. *See also* school settlements

Seven Dials district, 230–31n8, 242, 243, 283–84; Tennant's sketches and, 242, 243–48

Sharp, Evelyn, 149, 173

Shaw, Flora, 27

Shaw, George Bernard, 46

shelters: for barmaids, 95–96; for cab drivers, 24; for homeless women, 97, 136

Sheppard, Jack, 243

shifting house, Woolwich Arsenal, 73, 74–76, 80

Shoreditch: daily life in, 64; population of, 283, 284–85

Sicily, 1912 earthquake in, 250

Silvertown, 5

Silvy, Camille, *227*

Simmel, George, 14

Sims, George, 12

Sisters of the People, 17–18, *18,* 20

Slade School of Art, 239

slavery: factory work as, 48–51; fur pulling as, 106–7; woman's marriage as, 149–50

slum philanthropy: gospel of service in, 20–21; recruitment for, 19–20; surveillance issues and, 3–4, 14, 154–55; women's importance in, 1, 3

slums: camping out in Deptford, 130–35; characterization of, 20; definition of, 1. *See also* housing; poverty; wages

slum travelers: aristocratic privilege of, 229, 239–40; backgrounds of, 4–6; as Bible-women, 198–99, 200–207; declining number of, 285; expanding number of, 3; feminism and, 8–10; fictional depictions of, 25–26; international destinations and connections of, 26–28; motivations of, 1, 3, 20–22, 262; photographic innovations and, 136–38; Potter's denigration of, 263; poverty chronicled by, 12–15; scientific observations by, 97–98; separate spheres issues and, 18–20; stereotypes and caricatures of, 13–14, 23–24; urban context of, 6–8; women as, 15–18

Social Democratic Federation, 90

socialists and socialism: in peace demonstration, 187; as slum travelers, 4–5; suffrage linked to, 179. *See also* Christian Socialism; Fabian Society; Independent Labour Party (ILP); *individual socialists*

social reform: examples of church-based, 32n22; feminism linked to, 8–10; secularization of, 7

social theory: "the subject" in, 31n16; on unemployment and homelessness, 97–98

social work: in munitions manufacturers, 72; school-based, 3; training for, 65; wages for professional, 86

Society of Friends, 98

Society of Parochial Mission Women, 199n2

Soho: Anglican nuns in, 256; destruction of, 230–31n8; Stanley's observations of drunkenness in, 232–38; Stanley's political and social activism in, 228–29; West London Mission in, 15, 16, 17–18, *18*

soldiers: disabled, 181–86

Soldiers' and Sailors Families' Association (SSFA), 182–83

Somers Town. *See* St. Pancras School for Mothers

Somerville College, Oxford University, 19

songs and music, 76–77, *241, 259–60,* 270

South Hampstead High School for Girls, 172

South Kensington, 212

South London: Bermondsey settlement in, 16, 148–49; dockside district residents of (Rotherhithe), 148–49; fur pullers of, 104, 106–16; girls' club in, 228; investigators' experiences in, 57–60, 210–11

South Place Chapel, 162

Southwark: fur pullers of, 104, 106–16; population of, 284

SSFA (Soldiers' and Sailors Families' Association), 182–83

Stamford Hill, 284

Stanley, Algernon, 226

Stanley, Edward John, third baron, 228

Stanley, Henrietta Maria, 226, 228, 229, 230n4

Stanley, Henry, 226, 228

Stanley, Henry Morton, 28, 240, 242

Stanley, Kate, 22, 226, 230n5

Stanley, Lady (Henry Morton's wife). *See* Tennant, Dorothy (Lady Stanley)

Stanley, Maude Alethea: background of, 21–22, 226, 228; further reading on, 231; girls' club of, *9;* photograph of, *227;* political and social activism of, 228–29; works: "Drunkenness," 232–38

Stanley, Rosalind, 226

statistics: authority of, 11; development of, 8; on population maintenance, 155–56. *See also* infant mortality

Stead, William T., 46

Steedman, Carolyn, 37–38n90, 124, 126

Steele, Valerie, 17

Steer, Mary, 27

Stephen, Caroline, 33n38, 37n83

Stepney, 20

Stoke Newington, 283

Stowe, Harriet Beecher, 14

Strand Magazine, 137

street arabs: commentary on, 243–48; illustrations of, *2, 240, 241, 242, 244, 245, 247;* use of term, 67

streets: 1917 demonstration in, 187–88; Amy Levy on, 120; children's games in, *245;* costermongers and, 139–47; hurdy-gurdy music of, *241;* of North Lambeth, 211–13; outdoor market in, 249, 251–55

strikes: of dock workers, 5, 90, 263; of gas workers, 47; of matchmakers, 12, *49*

Stuart, Maud. *See* Pember Reeves, Maud (née Stuart)

"subject, the" (concept), 31n16

Suffragette, The (periodical), 149–50

suffragettes and suffrage: demonstrations of, 178–79; efforts working-class outreach of, 9–10, 149, 182–84, 187–91; imprisonment of, 179, 180; men's expanded rights of, 7; militancy of, 54; in New Zealand, 209; NUWSS, 53; Potter's view of, 263; tax resistance of, 54, 150n2, 163; as woman's sphere or not, 19

suicides, 117, 168–69

Summers, Anne, 16, 19

surveillance society: concept of, 3–4, 14; pros/cons of, 154–55

Sussex county, 162–63

sweated labor: exhibition on, 54, 56; investigations of conditions and wages of, 56–63, 262–63; *Toilers* series on, 90n

tailors: Sunday markets and, 251–52, 253–54; Webb's investigations of conditions and wages of, 56–63, 262–63. *See also* garment workers

taxes and taxation: on employer for sub-contracting work, 116; suffragists' refusal to pay, 54, 150n2, 163

Taylor, Husdon, 27, 199

teachers: role of, 81, 87–88, 173; training for, 125, 126

Tennant, Charles, 239

Tennant, Dorothy (Lady Stanley): background of, 27–28, 239–40, 283; further reading on, 243; marriage of, 28, 240, 242; works: *London Street Arabs, 2, 240, 241, 242,* 243–48

Tennant, Gertrude, 239

Theosophy, 45, 47

Thoreau, Henry David, 167

thrift: burial insurance and, 214–18; clubs for, 86

Tickner, Lisa, 179

tips: for barmaids, 95

Tolstoy, Leo, 162–63

Toynbee Hall (Whitechapel), 16, 86, 172, 173

trade boards, 56–63

Trade Boards Act (1909), 54

Trafalgar Square, 46, 91

tramps. *See* homeless people

transportation: expansion of, 8, 22–23, 283; poem about, 120–21

travelers vs. excursionists, 26. *See also* slum travelers

travel writing, 250

Tribe, Reginald, 126

Tweedie, Alec, 249

Tweedie, Ethel Brilliana (Mrs. Alec): background of, 249–50; further reading on, 250; works: "Petticoat-Lane," 251–55

Uncle Tom's Cabin (Stowe), 14

underclothing makers. *See* garment workers

unemployment: barmaids' fear of, 94; campaign against (1905), 83; Higgs's theory of, 97–98; infant mortality and, 215–16; sudden, 94, 218; workers subject to, 281

Unitarians. *See* Nonconformists

University of London, 72, 148. *See also* Bedford College

University of St. Andrews (Scotland), 172

Upper Clapton, 59

urban areas: elite fears of expanding, 6–7; overcrowding in, 70; surveillance and spectatorship in, 3–4, 14, 154–55, 211

Vicinus, Martha, 26

Victoria Park, 186–91

visual art: galleries of, 239; references to, 105; students of, 179. *See also* Tennant, Dorothy (Lady Stanley)

Vote, The (newspaper), 10

Votes for Women (newspaper), 163

wages: of barmaids, 92–93; of brewery worker, 220–21; of Bryant and May employees, 48–51; of coach-builder, 234; of costermongers, 142, 143, 146; of fur pullers, 110, 111, 112; of garment workers, 58n, 61–62; laws on minimum, 54, 56–63; of machinists, 218–19; monetary system and, xiii–xiv; of sweated labor, 54, 56–63; of toy-packer, 218–19; of well-paid working men, 153–60, 155

Walker, Frederick, 105, 111

Walkowitz, Judith, 138nn1–2, 231n15

Walthamstow: Epiphany feast in, 257, 258–61

Warburton, Katherine Anne Egerton ("Mother Kate"): background of, 256–57; further reading on, 257; works: "Epiphany Pilgrimage, An," 258–61

Ward, Dorothy (Mary's daughter), 23

Ward, Gertrude (Mary's sister-in-law), 11, 25

Ward, Mary (Mrs. Humphry Ward): on nurse's dress, 17; Passmore Edwards settlement, 23; on slum travelers, 25–26; Somerville College and, 19; sources used, 10–11; on woman's sphere, 19

War Office, 175–77, 182

wars: Boer, 27, 181–86; Crimean, 190; Franco-Prussian, 190, 228. *See also* World War I

Webb, Beatrice (née Potter): background of, 4–5, 262; on Besant, 46; on Bosanquet, 64, 65; friendships of, 118; further reading on, 265; on Harkness, 89, 90; investigations by, 40, 262–63; at Katharine Buildings, 40, 90, 262; marriage of, 16, 263–64; organizational activities of, 105n1, 208, 263; on social reform, 7; on women philanthropists, 15; on women's assigned roles, 21; on women's writing, 13; works: *My Apprenticeship,* 264; "Pages from a Work-Girl's Diary," 266–79

Webb, Sidney, 16, 155, 263–64

Wells, H. G., 25, 209

West London Mission (Soho), 15, 16, 17–18, *18*. *See also* Sisters of the People

Westminster, City of: Baby Week Exhibitions in, 155; center and assistance for barmaids in, 95–96; hospital of, 89; population of, 284; St. Stephen's Church in, 24; Stanley's home in, 229

Westminster Hospital, 89

White, Blanco, 167

White, Ellen Henrietta. *See* Ranyard, Ellen Henrietta (née White)

White, Jerry, 284

Whitechapel: Petticoat Lane market in, 249, 251–55; population of, 284–85; workmen's flats in, 172–73. *See also* garment workers; Toynbee Hall

Whitefield's Tabernacle, 20

Whitehall, 239–40

WIC. *See* Women's Industrial Council (WIC)

Wilde, Oscar, 119

Wilson, Charlotte, 208

wives. *See* marriage and marital relations

WLL. *See* Women's Labour League (WLL)

Woman's Dreadnought, The (periodical): description of, 179–80; on disabled soldier and his family, 181–86; on peace demonstration, 186–91

Woman's World (periodical), 118n1

Woman Worker (periodical): McMillan's

story in, 130–35; publication of, 124n; on slum mothers, 127–29

women: as chroniclers of poverty, 12–15; defense of working-class, 208–9, 210–25; double day of, 159; as factory workers, 47, 48–51; family's expectations of, 21–22; generational differences in needs of, 62; health of elderly, 158; homeless, 97, 99–103, 136; rights of, 7, 36n75, 173; writing of, 6, 11–15, 162. *See also* mothers and motherhood; suffragettes and suffrage; working girls; *specific types of work*

Women's Co-operative Guild, 57, 151, 159, 162

Women's Freedom League, 9, 10, 173–74, 188

Women's Industrial Council (WIC): girls' clubs and, 228; goals of, 105n1; homework conference of, 116; investigations by, 54, 56–63; participants in, 53, 104, 105, 106; unemployment issues and, 83

Women's Labour League (WLL): investigations by, 54, 56–63; participants in, 53

Women's Peace Crusade, 174

Women's Protective and Provident League, 118

Women's Social and Political Union (WSPU), 32n29, 173, 178–79

Women's Tax Resistance League (WTRL), 54

Women's Trade Union Association, 53, 105n1. *See also* Women's Industrial Council (WIC)

Women's University Settlement, 65

Women Writers Club, 162

Woolf, Virginia, 11, 23

Woolwich Arsenal: day-to-day routines of, 74–76; general observations of, 76–78; terminology at, 73; women supervisors at, 72, 74n3

Wordsworth, William, 105

work conditions: barmaids, 92–96; fur pullers, 108–9, 110–14; garment workers, 56–63, 268–70; hours and, 49, 50, 110–11; munitions workers, 73, 75–80; women factory workers, 49, 50. *See also* illnesses; unemployment

Workers' Suffrage Federation: disabled soldier's case and, 182–84; in peace demonstration, 187–91

workhouses: casual (short-term) wards of, 98, 99–103; committee visits to, 97; detailed accounts of, 13–14; evacuation of, in WWI, 175–77; poor people's resistance to, 61, 62; as refuge, 236–37

working girls: canary girls (term), 73; clothing of, 17–18; clubs for, *9,* 105n1, 140, 228, 229; holidays for, 233; hostel for, 125; at Malvery's wedding, 136; strikes of, 12, *49;* at Tennant's wedding, 242; Webb's "diary" of, 266–79

World War I: economic effects of, 179; education and propaganda in, 209; factory production in, 264; munitions work in, 74–80; peace demonstration against, 186–91; separation allowances in, 152; unemployment in, 98; women's and children's welfare in, 149; workhouse used as military hospital in, 175–77

Wormwood Scrubs, 162

writers: women as, 6, 11–15, 162

WSPU (Women's Social and Political Union), 32n29, 173, 178–79

WTRL (Women's Tax Resistance League), 54

Wyatt, Thomas, 72

Yamaguchi, Midori, 4

Young Women's Christian Association (YWCA), 95–96

Text:	11.25/13.5 Adobe Garamond
Display:	Perpetua, Adobe Garamond
Compositor:	BookMatters, Berkeley
Cartographer:	Bill Nelson
Printer and binder:	Maple-Vail Manufacturing Group
Indexer:	Margie Towery